THE LIVES OF THE POPES
VOL. XIV.

PORTRAIT OF INNOCENT IV.
From the mosaic in St. Paul's outside-the-walls.

LEADEN BULLA OF INNOCENT IV.

[Frontispiece.

THE
LIVES OF THE POPES
IN THE MIDDLE AGES

BY THE

RT. REV. MONSIGNOR HORACE K. MANN, D.D.

" De gente Anglorum, qui maxime familiares Apostolicæ Sedis semper
existunt " (*Gesta Abb. Fontanel., A.D.* 747–752, ap. M.G. SS. II. 289).

RECTOR OF THE COLLEGIO BEDA, ROME ; CORRESPONDING MEMBER OF THE ROYAL ACADEMY OF
HISTORY OF SPAIN ; MEMBER OF THE ACCADEMIA D'ARCADIA AND OF THE R. SOCIETÀ ROMANA
DI STORIA PATRIA.

THE POPES AT THE HEIGHT OF THEIR TEMPORAL INFLUENCE

INNOCENT II. TO BLESSED BENEDICT XI.
1130–1305

(A) THE POPES AND THE HOHENSTAUFEN, 1130–1271

VOL. XIV
INNOCENT IV., THE MAGNIFICENT, 1243–1254

LONDON :
KEGAN PAUL, TRENCH, TRUBNER & CO., LTD.
ST. LOUIS, MO.: B. HERDER BOOK CO.
1928

1887

PRINTED IN GREAT BRITAIN BY
STEPHEN AUSTIN AND SONS, LTD., HERTFORD

A LIST OF THE PRINCIPAL ABBREVIATIONS
USED IN THIS VOLUME.

Potthast . . . = *Regesta Pontificum Romanorum*, ed.
A. Potthast, 2 vols., Berlin, 1874.

Reg. . . . . = One of the volumes of the *Registres des Papes* in course of publication by the French Schools of Athens and of Rome, ed. Fontemoing, Paris.

L. P. . . . . = *Liber Pontificalis*, 2 vols., ed. L. Duchesne, Paris, 1886.

M. G. H. or Pertz . . = *Monumenta Germaniæ Historica*, either *Scriptores* (M. G. SS.), or *Epistolæ* (M. G. Epp.) or *Poetæ* (M. G. PP.).

P. G. . . . . = *Patrologia Græca*, ed. Migne, Paris.

P. L. . . . . = *Patrologia Latina*, ed. Migne, Paris.

R. I. SS. . . . = *Rerum Italicarum Scriptores*, ed. Muratori, Milan, 1723 ff., or the new ed. in course of publication.

R. F. SS. . . . = *Recueil des Historiens des Gaules*, ed. Bouquet and others, Paris, 1738 ff.

R. S., following an edition of a book = The edition of the Chronicles, etc., of Great Britain and Ireland, published under the direction of the Master of the Rolls.

Rymer or Foedera . . = *Foedera, Literæ, etc., ab anno* 1101 *ad nostra usque tempora*, accurante T. Rymer. Unless the contrary is stated we quote from the original ed., London, 1704 ff.

v

Other abbreviations will be readily understood by reference to the *Sources* prefixed to each biography.

The sign † placed before a date indicates that the date in question is the year of the death of the person after whose name the sign and date are placed. The sign * placed before the title of a book indicates that the author of these volumes has seen the book in question well spoken of, but has not examined it himself.

TABLE OF CONTENTS

LIST OF ILLUSTRATIONS

INNOCENT IV.

A.D. 1243–1254.

Sources.—The most important source for the life of Innocent IV is his *Regesta*,[1] which has been edited by E. Berger, *Les Registres d'Innocent IV.* (*Reg.*), 3 vols., Paris, 1884–97. As a sign of the leisurely way in which the French School of Athens and Rome is doing its work of printing the Papal Registers, it may be noted that the first attempt at producing an Index to Innocent's most important Register was not made till 1911, when the first half of it was printed. The second half did not appear till some years later. On Innocent's *Register* it is worth while to extract a few notes from Berger's excellent *Introduction*. Since the beginning of the thirteenth century, various improvements were effected in connexion with the pontifical *Registers*, and so we find that the volumes of Innocent IV.'s *Register* are more elegant in appearance, and more convenient to use than those of his immediate predecessors. There may be observed in them a tendency to group together documents on cognate subjects, and to separate the more important documents from those which were drawn up according to a stereotyped form, to separate the *litteræ curiales* from the *litteræ communes*.[2]

The *Registers* of Innocent IV. have come down to us almost in their entirety, though that of his sixth year, June 1248 to June 1249, is incomplete, and that of his seventh year is lost. As we have them to-day, they are splendid monuments of thirteenth century penmanship, and reflect great credit on the Roman chancellary. It is unfortunately true of the *Register* of Innocent IV., as of other Papal *Registers*, that not all the letters issued by him were inserted in it.[3]

---

[1] We have evidence that his successor, Alexander IV., transcribed documents from this Register, Potthast, No. 16209.

[2] Berger supposes that the practical custom of grouping important letters was due to Marinus, who became vice-chancellor in 1244.

[3] Those who would know more of the *Register* of Innocent IV. must consult Berger's *Introduction*.

As with other *Registers* of the Popes, published by the French
School of Rome, that of Innocent IV. only gives an analysis of
most of its documents. But C. Rodenberg, in his *Epistolæ Sæc.
XIII e Regestis Pontificum Romanorum* (Rod.), has printed in
full such documents as refer to the Holy Roman Empire. The
whole of vol. ii (Berlin, 1887) and part of vol. iii are taken up
with letters of Innocent. M. B. Hauréau (Haur.) has also printed
at length a number of his letters that relate to France : *Quelques
lettres d'Innocent IV.*, Paris, 1874 (extrait du Tome XXIV, *Des
notices des Manuscrits de la Bibliothèque Nationale*). Huillard-
Bréholles (H.-B.) likewise prints in full those letters that concern
the emperor Frederick II. *Hist. diplomat. Fred. II., Tomi VI.*,
Paris, 1860. K. Hampe has found and published nearly one
hundred documents from the missing parts of Innocent's *Register* ;
ap. *Mittheilungen des Instituts für Oesterreichische Geschichts-
forschung*, xxiii Band., Musbruck, 1902, p. 545 ff. ; xxiv B.,
p. 198 ff.[1] Some letters of Innocent are also to be found in a
formulary of the papal chancery of this century, of which C.
Hoskins has given an account in his " Two Roman formularies in
Philadelphia," published in *Miscellanea F. Ehrle*, vol. iv, p. 275 ff.,
Rome, 1924.

Innocent's bulls display the motto : " Notas fac mihi Domine
vias vitæ." [2]

There is extant a contemporary biography of Innocent, written
by one of his chaplains, Nicholas de Carbio [3] or da Calvi, a
Franciscan, who afterwards (1247) became bishop of Assisi
(†probably in 1273). The Franciscan chatty chronicler, Salimbene,
cites Nicholas as one of his friends. Carbio's *life* gives a well-
arranged, well-written, accurate statement of the facts of
Innocent's career. His work is nearly always chronologically
exact, and serves to correct the many mistakes of Matthew
Paris.[4] Though a great admirer of Innocent, he does not, as
a rule, indulge in violent language when speaking of his great

---

[1] P. Sabatier discovered and printed ap. *Revue des Quest. Hist.*,
Apr. 1906, p. 634, a letter relative to the East.

[2] See Ciaconius, *Vitæ R.R. P.P.*, ii, p. 114, ed. 1677. *Cf.* " Die
unterschriften der Päpste und Kardinale in dem Bullae majores ", by
B. Katterbach, in *Miscellanea F. Ehrle*, vol. iv, p. 177 ff.

[3] Nicholas was born at Calvi or Carbio (not Curbio) near Narni.

[4] Pagnotti says, p. 44 n., " Ho indicato, nelle note al testo, non
pochi passi ne' quali Matteo di Parigi incorre in errori di cronologia."

opponent Frederick II., though it has been pointed out that he occasionally makes statements regarding him which are contrary to fact, and, on the other hand, omits facts which tell in his favour.[1] The work has been published by Muratori ap. *R. I. SS.*, t. iii, pt. i, p. 589 ff., but more accurately by Pagnotti, ap. *Archivio della R. Società Romana di Storia Patria*, vol. xxi, 1898, p. 1 ff.[2]

Consult also G. Levi's edition of the *Registro del card. Ottaviano degli Ubaldini*, 1252, Rome, 1890 ; and Höfler's *Albert von Behaim*.[3]

Most of the principal chroniclers that are concerned with the times of Innocent IV. have already been treated of. Mention, however, may be made here of one or two more who treat of the affairs of South Italy. The Roman, Saba Malaspina, a member of the papal court (scriptor Papæ) wrote his *Rerum Sicularum historia* (ap. *R. I. SS.*, viii) in 1284-5, and dedicated it to " the officials " of Martin IV. Naturally, Guelf in tone, his work, which runs from 1250-85, is generally regarded as of the first importance. The *Historia Sicula* of the Ghibelline lawyer of Messina, Bartholomew of Neocastro, covers a rather longer period (1250-93, ap. *R. I. SS.*, xiii), but was not written till 1293, and though of great value for the last ten years, is not so reliable for the earlier period. He was concerned with the " Sicilian Vespers ".

Works.—There does not appear to be in any language a modern work which treats at length of the *Life* of Innocent IV. Passing over a number of biographies of him written in the seventeenth and eighteenth centuries,[4] we may draw attention to the well-arranged little work (pp. 64) of P. Deslandres, *Innocent IV. et la Chute des Hohenstaufen*, Paris, 1907. But if there is not a full modern biography of Innocent, several authors have written excellent monographs on special episodes of his history. Berger, for instance, has prefixed to the second volume of his edition of Innocent's *Register*, an admirably impartial account of the relations between that Pontiff and France: *Saint Louis et Innocent*

---

[1] Though Gregorovius, *Rome*, v, pt. ii, p. 623, regards Carbio's book as " merely a panegyric ", he speaks of it as " one of the most attractive works of its kind ".

[2] *Cf. ib.*, vol. xvii, 1984, p. 253. We have used Pagnotti's edition.

[3] On him *vide supra*, vol. xi, p. 211 n.

[4] E.g., *Vita del gran Pontefice Innocenzio Quarto*, by the Genoese, P. Pansa, Naples, 1601.

IV. Another editor of Innocent's letters, K. Rodenberg, has
written well on his connexion with the kingdom of Sicily. *Innocenz
IV. und das Königreich Sicilien*, Halle a S., 1892. One of the
most recent writers on this particular point is E. Jordan, who has
written at great length on *Les Origines de la domination Angevine
en Italie*, Paris, 1909. But he would appear to have lost himself
in the crowd of details with which he has dealt, and he gives the
impression of guiding them, rather than of being guided by them.
G. Wesener (*De actionibus inter Inn. IV. et Fridericum II. a.
1243-4, et concilio Lugdunensi*, Bonn, 1870), and A. Theiner
(*I due concilii generali di Lione de 1245, e di Costanza del 1414*,
Rome, 1861) have both dealt with the Council of Lyons. So also
has Mr. W. E. Lunt, in an excellent article " The Sources for the
first Council of Lyons " (1245) in the *English Historical Review*,
1918, p. 72 ff. G. Roux has eleven pages in the *Revue d'hist. de
Lyon*, Lyons, 1910, on the residence of Innocent at Lyons,
practically all, however, taken from Berger. G. Cozza-Luzi has
left us a study on *Un autografo di Innocenzo IV. e Memorie di S.
Chiara di Assisi* (an extract without date or place of publication,
189?), and F. Savini a very short one on *La comunità di S. Flaviano
e la dominazione d'Innocenzo IV. in Abruzzo nel* 1254, Teramo, 1894.
A. L. Smith, *Church and State in the Middle Ages*, Oxford, 1913,
is mostly concerned with Innocent IV., and is well worth reading.
We must refer the reader to previous bibliographies for the works
of Balzani, Cherrier, Kington, Marchetti-Longhi, etc., and we
may note here that Jannelli's *Pietro della Vigna* is a long drawn
out unsatisfactory controversial work, mostly about Pietro's
birthplace.

CONTEMPORARY SOVEREIGNS.

EMPEROR AND KINGS OF THE ROMANS.	EASTERN EMPERORS.	KING OF ENGLAND.	KING OF FRANCE.
Frederick II., 1212–50. (Rival Kings : i. Henry Raspe, 1246–7. ii. William of Holland, 1247–56). Conrad IV., 1250–4.	Latin Emperor, Baldwin II, 1228–61. Emperor of Nicæa, John III. (Ducas Vatatzes), 1222–55.	Henry III., 1216–72.	St. Louis IX., 1226–70.

CHAPTER I.

ON the very day of the sudden death of Celestine IV., The long
five out of the eight cardinals who were then in Rome, vacancy,
fled from the City and betook themselves to Anagni 1241–3.
or to fortresses in the Campagna. Of the remaining
three, John of Colonna, as an " out and out " partisan
of the Emperor, was seized and imprisoned by the Senator,
and the other two remained in the City undisturbed.[1]

Accordingly on the day following the burial of
Celestine IV., which took place on Monday, November 11,
the cardinals left in Rome sent a circular note calling
on all their brethren to come to the City without delay
in order to elect a Pope. " You will have learnt," ran
the circular, " that the lord Pope died last Sunday
evening (November 10), and that he was buried on the
following day. Accordingly, since dire necessity calls
upon you to provide for the widowed Church, we beg,
we implore, and, by Christ's precious Blood, earnestly
beseech you, and indeed peremptorily summon you
to come to the City by next Friday (November 15),
in order that, after due discussion, we may, with you,
provide the Church with a pastor. You should also

---

[1] *Chron. de rebus in Ital. gest.* (also called *Annales Placentini*; see
supra, ix, p. 308 n.), ed. H.-B., p. 187; Carbio, c. 6; Ric. of S. Germ.,
an. 1241; Mat. Par., iv, 194; *Cron. S. Petri Erford. Mod.*, an. 1241.

5

know that our venerable brother John (of Colonna), when summoned by us, replied that, as he was in prison, he could not express his mind freely, nor could he be induced to make known to us what was his real mind." Given on the Tuesday after the feast of Blessed Martin (Nov. 11).[1]

To this summons the cardinals at Anagni replied that, after the unspeakable miseries they had endured in the election of Celestine,[2]—miseries which had already resulted in the death of two of their number,[3] and in reducing the others to death's door [4]—they could not recognize any canons giving those in Rome the right to summon them to a place where the treatment meted out to cardinal John of Colonna proved that there would be no freedom of choice.   Then imitating, in conclusion, the earnestness of their brethren in Rome, they adjured them to come to some agreement, so that all of them might meet together in a safe place, and elect a chief Pastor in a proper manner.   In any case, those in Rome must not venture to act without them ; and so, to prevent them, they appealed " to the Church at large, or to a General Council ".[5]

Action of the Emperor. Such was the beginning of months of dissension and intrigue among the cardinals, of which, according to the general opinion, the chief author was the Emperor Frederick.   The cardinals continued to summon each

---

[1] Ap. Hampe, *Bericht über das Konklave*, p. 26 f.

[2] They speak of : " passiones multiplices, fetores, calores continuos, et prolixos, arti carceris miserias, opprobria, improperia, fames, inedias et dolores, etc." *Ib.*, p. 27.

[3] The English cardinal Sumercote and Celestine IV.

[4] " Residui in febrium extrema deducti vix mortis imperium evaserunt, propter febrium reliquias multis ipsorum in palloribus preparatis, responsum mortis in se ipsis habentes, etc." *Ib.*

[5] " Et ne contra prohibitionem et interdictum nostrum attemptetur aliquod, quod non credimus, in hoc facto, ad generalem ecclesiam seu generale concilium appellamus." *Ib.*, p. 31.

other to meet together, and Frederick left no stone
unturned to get partisans.[1] He succeeded with some ;
but others, becoming more and more embittered against
the disturber of the Church, not content with reminding
him of his excommunication, openly called him a heretic.[2]
It would seem that the Emperor's first idea was to
prevent any election until he could get possession of
Rome and the States of the Church. His envoys were
ceaselessly endeavouring to curry favour with the
cardinals,[3] while he endeavoured to cut off communication
between them and the outside world,[4] and to seize Rome.[5]
He also contrived to delay the election of a new Pope
by pretending to give a favourable hearing to the
cardinals' request for the release of their two imprisoned
brethren, Otho and James, and by carefully refraining
from opening their prison doors.[6] As early as March,

[1] " Unde contigit, ut se invicem frequentius vocarent (the cardinals)
ad electionem, . . ." *Ann. Stadenses*, ann. 1242–3, ap. *M. G. SS.*,
xvi, p. 368.

[2] *Ib.*

[3] That he was constantly sending messengers to the cardinals,
Frederick tells us himself ; though he states that it was from his wish
to end the dissensions : " Ut per frequentes et prestantes et insignes
apocrisiarios et legatos nostre serenitatis ad cardinales egerimus
propterea ut de hujusmodi magni sacerdotis electione diligentissime
cogitarent." Ep. of June, 1243 ap. H.-B., vi, p. 90.

[4] Salimbene, *Chron.*, p. 174. " Fridericus vias clauserat usque
adeo ut multi caperentur. Timebat enim ne aliquis transiret qui
papa fieret." Salimbene says that he was often captured. *Cf. Ann.
of Tewkesbury*, an. 1241 ap. *Ann. Monast.*, i, 121, *R. S. Cf.* F.
Biondi (†1463), who cites a contemporary Parmesan writer, and who
adds that the delay in the election was caused by the cardinals agreeing
not to elect a Pope whilst their brethren were kept in prison,and hence
by Frederick in keeping them there. Ap. Pagi, *Brev. Gest. Pont.
Rom.*, vol. iii, p. 245.

[5] Cf. the words of that careful historian the Abbot Menko, *Chron.*,
ap. *M. G. SS.*, xxiii, p. 536. " Frederico . . . electionem tam occulte
quam manifeste impediente, et maxime per quosdam cardinales quos
in captivitate detinuit, sine quibus electio non poterat celebrari."

[6] Ep. Fred., ap. H.-B., vi, 35.

1242, he assured the cardinals that he was prepared to release their two brethren in order that they might take part in the election, seeing that "as Roman Cesar and Catholic sovereign (princeps) he was desirous of providing for the good of the universal Church ".[1] But, as he had no intention of releasing them except on his own terms,[2] month after month passed by, and they were still kept in confinement.

Public opinion in England, etc. Meanwhile, however, as the Emperor's intrigues to get a Pope after his own heart [3] or to block the election of one during his own time,[4] became more generally known, public feeling began to be aroused against him. In England, the archbishop of York, and that earnest bishop, Grosseteste of Lincoln, with several other bishops, met together to consider the state of the Church. They ordered fasts to be observed throughout the whole country, and prayers to be offered to God to implore Him to lift up and restore the Church of Rome, now without its bishop or Pope.[5] They also unanimously decided to send envoys to the Emperor to urge him to lay aside the tyrant, and not to hinder, but rather to

---

[1] *Ib. Cf.* ep. May 3, 1242, ap. *ib.*, p. 39., where he says that his duty as "Advocate" of the Church compels him to strive to work for the election of a Pope "well disposed to us ", and necessary to the Christian world if the Tartars are to be withstood. "Ex advocatie debito promotioni et honori Ecclesie vacare tenemur."

[2] Cf. Ric. of S. Germ., an. 1242, p. 154, ed. Gaudenzi.

[3] See the pamphlet against him which was perhaps the work of Albert von Behaim (n. 4, June, 1245, p. 61 of Albert's letters), where the author speaks of his "immissiones per angelos malos, bispilionum susurria . . . ut in sanctuarium Domini posset irrepere ad summum pontificem procreandum ". Cf. Bartholomew, who wrote the *Genoese Annals*, from 1225–48, ap. *R. I. SS.*, v, p. 501. He says Frederick wanted a Pope "ad voluntatem suam ".

[4] "Ecclesia Romana diu ab ipso imperatore oppressa pastore vacavit." *Contin. Chron. ex Pantheo excerpti*, ap. *M. G. SS.*, xxvi, p. 373.

[5] Mat. Par., iv, 173. "Pastorali et papali regimine destitutam."

advance, the good of the Roman Church. For the dangerous work of delivering this message to the Emperor, and of stirring up the bishops of other countries to act in like manner, our prelates chose some Dominicans and Franciscans. According, however, to Matthew Paris, on whom we are relying, their mission came to nothing, as Frederick simply said it was " the haughtiness and insatiable cupidity of the Roman Church herself " that was to blame and not himself.[1] Whether or not he ever uttered the words put into his mouth by Paris, it is certain that he publicly by letter attributed the blame to the cardinals themselves.[2] He also wrote that the bark of Peter, on fire with avarice, is by the fault of its sailors being overwhelmed with the swelling waves. Our Mother the Church, founded on Peter the rock, is now a widow. " Christ is without His vicar, Peter without his successor, and the Lord's flock without its shepherd," while the cardinals, " the hinges and columns of the Church," are, each of them, seeking to be Pope.[3]

This eloquent diatribe was no doubt directed against the cardinals who were opposing his schemes, and especially against those in Rome with whom he was furious as he could not make headway against them. Already in May his generals had been operating against the States of the Church in the Duchy of Spoleto and in the March of Ancona, endeavouring to take Narni, Reate, and Ascoli.[4] In July, he himself with a large army appeared before Rome, hoping to surprise it or carry it by storm.[5]

Frederick fails to take Rome, 1242.

---

[1] *Ib.*

[2] Ep. of May (?), 1242, ap. H.-B., vi, 44.

[3] Ep. of July, 1242, ap. *ib.*, p. 59 ff. " Ecce siquidem perdente Christo vicarium, princeps Apostolorum perdidit successorem, et pastorali regimine grex dominicus est privatus."

[4] Ric. of S. Germ., an. 1242.

[5] *Ib.*

But the Senator, Matteo Rosso, was a match for Frederick. We have seen how he seized the mausoleum of Augustus, the fortress of the Emperor's partisan, cardinal John of Colonna. He, moreover, formed alliances with the local communes, Perugia,[1] Narni, Alatri,[2] and others (March, 1242) ; led his troops against Tivoli, which was supporting Frederick (May) [3] ; and, when the Emperor's troops began to assemble, he reminded his allies of the injuries which they had suffered from the imperial forces. He informed them that, " to defend the liberty of the Church of God," the Romans would soon go forth to battle against him, and he called upon them to come forth and help them when they took the field.[4]

The measures of the Senator were effective. Whether as the result of an actual defeat in the field,[5] or because he foresaw that such a result would follow any attempt

[1] Gregorovius (v, p. 219) says that the alliance with Perugia " was ratified in S. Maria on the Capitol on March 12, 1242 ", and he cites as his authority a document of the archives of Perugia, *Lib. Sommiss.*, vol. c, fol. 31.

[2] On the alliance with Alatri see documents in Liverani, *Spicilegium Liberianum*, p. 747 f.

[3] Ric. of S. Germ., an. 1242, p. 155. *Cf*. ep. Fred., ap. H.-B., vi, 95 f. *Cf*. the letter full of idle brag which the Emperor addressed to the Senator and people of Rome on the occasion of this expedition of theirs. It begins " Preterite culpe ", and was doubtfully assigned to Dec., 1243, by H.-B., vi, p. 145. But with Gregorovius (*Rome*, v, 221) we may preferably assign it to June, 1242. His victorious sword " which has never known defeat " is going definitely to subdue Rome. If he cannot be everywhere himself, his power extends to the ends of the earth. As usual his eagle is victorious.

[4] Ep. of June 14, 1242. " Matthæus Rubeus Dei gratia almæ Urbis senator nobilibus viris potestati et consiliariis Alatrinis . . . salutem." Ap. Liverani, p. 747. The cities promised to support Rome, " salva fidelitate D. Papæ." *Cf. ib.*, p. 748.

[5] The words of the continuator of Gervase written by him under the year 1241 would appear to refer to this time. " Fredericus . . . obsidens Romam cum magno exercitu, turpiter a senatu et Romanis fugatus est." Gervase, ii, p. 201 *R. S.*

to storm the City, Frederick again withdrew from it in August.[1]

Meanwhile the cardinals had not ceased to urge him personally, and through his minister, Peter della Vigna, to release their imprisoned brethren.[2] Their prayers, when heeded, were at first but half answered. Only Otho was released (Aug.),[3] and the election of a new Pope was as far off as ever. The need, however, of a Pope was being more and more strongly felt, especially now in France.[4] If we are to trust Matthew Paris, the French sent a solemn embassy to the cardinals to give them plainly to understand that, if they did not quickly " provide the universal Church with the comfort of a Pastor " they would themselves, relying on the *fact* (?) of Pope Clement I. having given the apostolate of the West to St. Denis, elect a Pope whom they would obey.[5] This embassy is supposed to have been preceded by a strong letter from St. Louis to the cardinals.[6] The

Cardinals Otho and James released, 1242-3.

---

[1] Ric. of S. Germ., *ib.* *Cf.* Frederick's letter to St. Louis of France. Ap. H.-B., vi, 95 ff., June, 1243. He said he had devastated the neighbourhood of Rome in order that " *victrices imperii aquilas . . .* formidarent ".

[2] *Cf.* a letter written by a cardinal to Peter at the beginning of August, 1242. " Tociens vobis incassum preces effudimus pro karissimis fratribus nostris et aliis qui adhuc in carcere principis detinentur, utinam nunc nobis exaudicionis optate janua panderetur. Rogavit enim pluries universitas cardinalium quod matri filii redderentur ". Ap. H.-B., vi, 61. The writer then asks for more humane treatment for the prisoners, especially for card. James ; calls attention to the fact that Frederick had long before offered to release the two cardinals ; and concludes with a beautiful eulogy on royal clemency in the style of " the quality of mercy is not strained ".

[3] Ric. of S. G., an. 1242. *Cf.* ep. Fred. of June, 1243, ap. H.-B., vi, 90 f. The inaccurate statements of Mat. Par., *Chron. Maj.*, iv, 239–40, can be corrected by the authorities here cited.

[4] Mat. Par., *ib.*, p. 226 f. ; and 249.

[5] *Ib.*, p. 249, an. 1243.

[6] Ap. H.-B., vi, 68 ff. The authenticity of this letter is as stoutly affirmed by H.-B. (*Introduction*, p. ccciii) as denied by Berger, *St. Louis*, ap. *Reg.*, ii, p. v. The latter at any rate shows the views of *some*

writer of the letter in question, whoever he was, blames the cardinals, "the hinges of the world," for keeping the see of Peter so long vacant, inasmuch as the Papacy is "the head, the rule, and the glory of the world". Then, while nominally ascribing the long vacancy to the Roman greed of gold and office, he makes it plain that he knows that there is a Prince who is exercising pressure upon them. He therefore exhorts them to do their duty regardless of the threats of this Prince, as they can rely upon all the resources of France.[1]

However, despite all the pressure that was brought to bear upon Frederick and the cardinals, the whole of the year 1242 passed by without a Pope being elected, and without the release of cardinal James Pecoraria, whilst the government of the Church was carried on by the cardinals as best they could.[2]

Frederick again ravages the neighbourhood of Rome.

With the advent of the new year, Frederick had great hopes of subduing the whole of Italy to his will. As he told a friend "his victorious eagles were going to tear to shreds the relics of rebellion". His son Enzio was to conduct the campaign in Lombardy, and he himself that in the neighbourhood of Rome, whilst his fleet was ready to co-operate wherever it was required. Moreover, the death of cardinal Romanus, "an enemy

contemporary. The fact that Frederick *c.* June, 1243, sent a full explanation of his actions to Louis (ap. H.-B., vi, 95 ff.) is some support to the genuiness of the letter in question.

[1] "Nec pro tuenda ecclesiastica libertate de Francorum subsidio dubitetis, quia regnum, personas et pecunias vestre committimus." The writer goes on to say that he knows not how to designate this Prince : " cum rex esse postulet et sacerdos." The next letter, also in H.-B., vi, 70 ff., denounces the cardinals for leaving " mother Church " so long deprived of her glory.

[2] *Cf.* one of their letters, ap. Mat. P., iv, 250. " Nos autem, penes quos potestas residet, apostolica sede vacante, etc." From the signatures attached to this document, it appears that cardinal John of Colonna had been released by the Romans, and was acting with his brethren.

of us and the Empire," gave him reason to hope that a Pope would be elected who would prove a lover of justice, and would benefit " both us and all who love the Empire ".[1]

But things did not work out as he had hoped. His " victorious eagles " found " the relics of rebellion " too tough. He himself, indeed, overthrew a few towers and did some damage in the open country round Rome.[2] But he was not able to effect anything of decisive importance ; and, at length, making a virtue of necessity, and hearkening to the counsels of the count of Toulouse, of the emperor Baldwin, of the cardinals, and of others, he released cardinal Pecoraria (May), who was received by his brethren with the greatest joy.[3]

Now that, at last, their brethren had been released, and Frederick had once more withdrawn from the neighbourhood of Rome,[4] the cardinals assembled at Anagni, and did not take very long to choose a Pope. They

The election of cardinal Fieschi, June, 1243.

---

[1] Ep. of May (?), 1243, ap. H.-B., vi, 87. *Cf. Chron. de rebus,* p. 190.

[2] Ric. of S. G., an. 1243, p. 155. *Cf.* Frederick's letter to St. Louis, June, 1243, ap. H.-B., vi, 96 ; Mat. Par., *Chron. maj.,* iv, p. 240 f.

[3] See the contemporary life of Pope Gregory X., ap. *R. I. SS.,* iii, pt. i, p. 599. The biographer adds that Innocent was " straightway " elected, and the Church received a spouse, prudent, merciful, indefatigable and experienced as the times required.

[4] Ric., *ib.* In his letters to Baldwin and other sovereigns (*c.* begin. June) Frederick declares, with perfectly extraordinary bombast, that the annals of the world cannot show any act of magnanimity equal to his in freeing his enemy cardinal James : " Stupebunt profecto ut credimus principes bellicosi viri fortes, Cesarum memorie incomparabilibus decorate magnificentiis in libris scripte veterum annalium et chronicorum evolvantur et perscrutentur, . . . nihil tale a Deo inspirate clementie equale nobis quisquam inveniet diligens indigator." Ep. to Baldwin, ap. H.-B., vi, 90. *Cf.* epp. to other kings, ap. *ib.,* pp. 93 ff. and 95 ff. ; and *Chron. de rebus,* p. 190. During the vacancy of the Holy See, says the *Continuator Sancruc.,* Frederick " civitates et castella R. ecclesie subjugabat ". Ap. *M. G. SS.,* ix, p. 641. It is to these wars that the *Ann. Mellicences,* ap. *ib.,* p. 508, attribute the long vacancy of the Holy See.

unanimously elected on June 25, cardinal Sinibaldo
Fieschi.[1] No doubt the cardinals of the imperial party
voted for him because he had been friendly to Frederick,[2]
and their adversaries because of his talents and firmness
of character.   The new Pope, so we are assured, inasmuch
as " he wished to live in peace and innocence, was called
Innocent ".[3] A few days after, on the eve of SS. Peter
and Paul, he was consecrated bishop, and crowned
(June 28) ; and, on the following day, he himself preached
to the people,[4] as he did on subsequent occasions also.[5]

The new
Pope.
The new Pope, says his biographer, " was a Genoese,
of noble birth, but of more noble character, and well
endowed with learning [6] and virtue.   He was the son of
Hugh, count of Lavagna," [7] and a member of that
family of Fieschi (de Flisco) which is eulogized by James

---

[1] Carbio, c. 6 ; *Chron. de reb.*, *ib.*, " cardinales omnes insimul " ;
Ric. of S. G., " Sinibaldus . . . in papam . . . creatus est de voluntate
et consensu omnium cardinalium " ; Ep. of Inn. IV., of July 2, 1243,
ap. Rod. ii, p. 1 ; and epp. of Frederick and another king, ap. H.-B.,
vi, 98 ff. and 101 ff. ;   Mat. Par., iv, 450.

[2] " Quia imperatori aliquantulum familiaris erat, papa effectus
est."   Richer, *Gesta Senon.*, iv, c. 9, ap. *M. G. SS.*, xxv, p. 303. *Cf.*
Chron. Rythm. Colon. Frag., ap. *M. G. S.S.*, xxv, p. 374.   " Quem
velut antiquum dum Cesar sperat amicum " ; and Innocent's own
words at the Council of Lyons, ap. *Ann. Cossenat.*, ap. *R. I. SS.*,
xiv, p. 1100.

[3] Menko, *Chron.*, ap. *M. G. SS.*, xxiii, p. 537.

[4] " Regnum induit et in eorundem festo populo sollempniter
predicavit." *Chron. breve fratris Theutonicorum*, ap. *ib.*, xxiv, p. 154.
The account of these and immediately subsequent events in Matthew
Paris is as usual with his accounts of events abroad all wrong.

[5] Salimbene, *Chron.*, p. 174 ; and the historian, Ricobaldi of Ferrara,
who heard him as a boy when he came to Ferrara.   *Hist.* ap. *R. I. SS.*,
ix, p. 132.

[6] This particular assertion of Innocent's contemporary is endorsed
by modern writers. Figgis, *The divine right of Kings*, p. 343, ed. 1914,
speaks of him as " the dominus canonistarum, the master of the
Decretalists, a man never to be ignored in the history of thought ".

[7] Carbio, c. 6.   *Cf. Ann. Parmenses*, ap. *M. G. SS.*, xviii, p. 670,
" Synibaldus de Alavania."

of Voragine [1] for giving to the world " in about thirty-six years two Popes and several cardinals ". But, though he was a Genoese, both he and his family were closely connected with Parma. He himself made his early studies there,[2] and was for a time a canon of Parma [3] ; his sister Margaret was married to one of its principal citizens ; its bishops, Albert and Abizzo de Lavania, were his nephews (barbanis) ; and he was distantly connected by marriage with that gossip so often cited in these pages, the friar, Salimbene of Parma.[4]

Granted that Innocent was partial to his nephews His and other relatives,[5] he was certainly not the heartless, character. unprincipled, grasping, and arrogant person that the narrative of Matthew Paris would lead one to suppose. But the words of that inaccurate and prejudiced writer, who had no personal knowledge of Innocent, cannot be accepted in opposition to those of men who were in a much better position to know the Pope's real character, or in opposition to deeds performed by him which speak for themselves. In the very first set of important letters which he wrote, those, i.e., in which he announced his election to the Catholic world, he laid it down that

[1] *Chron. Jannense*, Pars xii, c. 8, ap. *R. I. SS.*, ix, p. 52. Another Pope of the Fieschi was Hadrian V. (1276), a nephew of Innocent IV.

[2] " Iste Papa studuit Parme in gramaticallibus, et maritavit tres sorores suas in Parma." Later on, all but one of his nephews born of these sisters helped him. *Cf. Chron. anon.*, ap. *Notices et extraits des MSS. de la bib. nat.*, 1896, t. xxxv, p. 366.

[3] " Cujus (the church of Parma) nos alumpnum fuisse recolimus." *Reg.* i, n. 4. *Cf.* Salimbene, *Chron.*, p. 61.

[4] Sal., *ib.*, and pp. 69, 195.

[5] *Ib.*, p. 62. " Multum enim dilexit propinquos suos, . . . quos (nepotes) optime prebendavit." *Cf.* p. 176, and *Chron. de rebus*, p. 195. It has, however, been pointed out that " he was far above the vulgar weakness of pushing them into functions to which they were not equal ". Smith, *Church and State*, p. 231. One of Innocent's nephews, Albert Arcilis, was rector of Hugate, in the diocese of York. *Cf. Cal. of P. Reg.*, i, p. 496.

the bearers of them, the papal messengers (cursores
d. Papæ) were not to be given money,[1] as he had suitably
provided for them.[2] Salimbene, who was personally
acquainted with him, speaks more than once of his
liberality.[3] His natural graciousness is often alluded to,[4]
and bishop Grosseteste vouches for his personal holiness.[5]

Innocent a
lawgiver,
and a writer
on law. That Innocent possessed considerable intellectual
powers is universally conceded. He had a remarkable
memory,[6] and distinguished himself, if not so much as
a lawgiver, at least as a writer on law, and as a patron
of legal studies.[7] His title to be considered a lawgiver
rests on certain Decretals which he added to those of
Gregory IX., and on the decrees which, with the constitution " Romana ecclesia ", he promulgated at the
Council of Lyons.[8] These documents, which are often
found hard to understand on account of their subtlety
and brevity,[9] he transmitted to the archdeacon of
Bologna with an injunction that they were to be
incorporated in the body of the Canon Law ; that they
were to be explained to the Masters and scholars of the

[1] Ep. of July 2, 1243, ap. Rod. ii, p. 1.

[2] *Reg.*, i, n. 43, p. 11. " Cum alias a nobis ipsis congrue sit pro-
visum."

[3] *Chron.*, pp. 53 and 61, " Curialis homo erat valde et liberalis."
Pg. 53. Even according to Matthew Paris, he was " largus in datis ".
Chron., v, 237.

[4] *Cf.* the preceding note, and " Hic Papa fuit plurimum gratiosus
et præclarus omnibus habebatur ". *Chron. Pont. et Imp. Mantuana*,
ap. *M. G. SS.*, xxiv, p. 216.

[5] " Scimus autem d. Papæ sanctitatem." Ep. 106, an. 1244,
p. 315. *R. S.* Carbio even says that miracles were worked at his
tomb. *Vit. Inn.*, c. 42.

[6] Salimbene, p. 61.

[7] Potthast, vol. ii, n. 15128.

[8] According to Mat. Par. (*Chron. maj.*, v, 246), Innocent published
this collection of Decretals in 1251. Geoffrey de Courlon, *Chron.
Senon.*, p. 520, ed. Julliot, says that his constitutions were read in
the schools. " Fecit constitutiones que modo in scolis leguntur."

[9] *Cf. Notices et extraits*, vol. xxxii, pt. ii, p. 209.

University ; and that, without a special mandate from the Apostolic See, no others under his name were to be admitted into the courts or the schools.[1] In due course Boniface VIII. incorporated many of them in his *Liber Sextus Decretalium*. But Innocent's legal reputation rests on his *Apparatus seu Commentaria in quinque libros decretalium*,[2] which he contrived to write, or at least to revise, amidst the cares of his pontificate, and to publish soon after the Council of Lyons. Despite some obscurities and contradictions, its intrinsic worth, and the rank of its author gave the *Commentary* a great authority. It was largely quoted by John of Athon, the first of our English canonists, as well as by his successors, Lynwood and the rest [3] ; and it earned for its author the substantial praise of imitation, and the title from subsequent jurists of " Father of Law ".[4]

Passing over the other works of lesser importance, of which Innocent was the author,[5] we may turn to his

Innocent a patron of learning.

---

[1] Ep. of Sept. 9, 1253, ap. *Reg.*, iii, p. 458, n. 7756, or Potthast n. 15129. " Principia constitutionum et epistolarum decretalium . . . quas edidit et in corpore juris contineri decrevit . . . transmittit." His Decretals, as a whole, have apparently never been printed.

[2] Printed at Strasburg in 1477 and often in Venice and elsewhere in the fifteenth and sixteenth centuries.

[3] No little praise is bestowed upon the work by Schulte, *Geschichte der Quellen des canonischen Rechts*, ii, 92. *Cf.* Tiraboschi, *Storia della letter. Ital.*, lib. ii, c. 5, n. 16 ; and Sarti, *De Professor. Bonon.*, vol. i, p. 422 ff., ed. 1888–96.

[4] " Quem (his book) Canonistæ magni imitantur. Erat enim jurista magnus valde." So says the monk, Martin of Fulda (fl. c. 1379), *Chron.*, ap. Eccard, *Corpus*, i, 1709. It is William Durand, " the author of the *Speculum*, and the chief authority on procedure " (Smith), who is credited with calling him " Pater Juris ".

[5] For instance, his *Liber de jurisdictione Imperatoris et auctoritate Pontificis*, a reply to Peter della Vigna's work on the authority of the Pope and of the Emperor. This is said to exist, along with other works of his, in MS. in the Vatican Library. Sarti, *l.c.*, p. 426, who deals with Sinibald, as a professor of Canon law.

patronage of learning. He was not content with being learned himself. He strove to promote learning. Writing (August 3, 1245) to the bishops of our own country, he tells them that, as he is anxious specially to advance the English, he would have them exhort their clergy, and those who were aspiring to enter the clerical state, especially the sons of the nobles and magnates, earnestly to devote themselves to the acquisition of learning and virtue.[1] Should they do so, he was ready to help them by " ecclesiastical provision ", and by allowing the more distinguished among them to hold more than one benefice.

Moreover, besides thus encouraging scholars by holding out to them the hope of reward, he encouraged religious to devote themselves to higher studies by approving of the action of their superiors in sending some of their monks to the University of Paris [2] ; and he encouraged a high standard of studies by insisting that at Oxford only properly qualified persons should be permitted to lecture.[3] Then, too, he strove to protect students in

---

[1] Ep. ap. Mat. Par., v, p. 520. " Universitatem vestram . . . hortamur . . . quatinus . . . inducatis ut . . . scientiæ litterarum et virtutum cultui ferventer intendant." According to the same author, *ib.*, p. 427 f., Innocent, finding that for the sake of gain, many scholars were neglecting the rudiments of grammar and the study of classical authors and philosophy, and were devoting themselves to the study of law, issued an instruction on this subject to the bishops of Christendom. This instruction, beginning *Dolentes*, is, as we have said above, of doubtful authenticity. However, supposing *Dolentes* not to be genuine, there is no reason why Paris' statement should not be well founded, and why Innocent should not have found it necessary to legislate against evils which may have resulted from the study of law which he greatly promoted. But even if the whole item is merely another of Paris' mistakes, it is matterless as nothing turns upon it.

[2] Ep. of Jan. 5, 1245, ap. Denifle, *Chartular. Univ. P.*, i, p. 175. *Cf.* ep. of Sept. 4, 1245, *ib.*, p. 183.

[3] Ep. May 20, 1246. *Ib.*, p. 189. Lyte, *A hist. of the University of Oxford*, citing *Munimenta Academica*, pp. 26–30, notes (p. 45),

every way he could from being oppressed either by force
or by fraud. He aimed at securing for them exemption
from tolls in going to the University,[1] and at preventing
them from being overcharged for their lodgings,[2] and from
being molested by the powerful, whether in Church or
State.[3] Finally, in his zeal for learning, Innocent
greatly favoured the development of the University
movement, so characteristic of the age. He had no
sooner settled down at Lyons, than he instituted a school
of theology and of canon and civil law in connexion
with his own court.[4] He did the same at Naples, and,
indeed, wherever the papal court established itself.[5]
Then, rejoicing that the Kingdom of Valencia had been
snatched from the Saracens, and that James I., King
of Aragon, was anxious to establish a University in the
city of Valencia, he approved of his plans, and granted
the privileges he desired.[6] A few years later he founded
a University at Piacenza, in the hope that a great crowd
of men would flock there to drink of the waters of learning
—granting to it,[7] and to the University of Toulouse,[8]

that : " In 1254 he took the University under his special protection,
confirmed its different immunities and privileges, and directed the
Bishops of London and Salisbury to guard it from evil."

[1] Ep. of March 18, 1251, Den., *ib.*, p. 221. *Cf.* epp. June 5, 1252,
ib., p. 237 f.

[2] Ep. May 30, 1252, *ib.*, p. 232.

[3] Ep. June 26, 1246, *ib.*, p. 191 ; May 30, 1252, *ib.*, p. 233 ; epp.
May 31, 1252, *ib.*, p. 235 f. ; June 1, 1252, *ib.*, p. 236 f. The reader will
find the special importance of some of these decrees (especially of those
exempting students from being cited to courts at a distance from
Paris—the " privilegium fori ") brought out by Rashdall, *The
Universities of Europe*, i, p. 343. See also documents of Jan. 12, 1253,
and Sept. 9, 1253, ap. Sarti, *l.c.*, ii, p. 174 f., regarding the University
of Bologna.

[4] Carbio, *Vit.*, c. 16. It became the University of the Roman Court.

[5] *Ib.*, c. 41.

[6] Epp. July 10, 1245, ap. *Reg.*, i, p. 210 f.

[7] Ep. Feb. 6, 1248, ap. Denifle, *Chart. U. P.*, i, p. 208.

[8] Epp. Sept. 11, and 22, 1245, ap. *ib.*, pp. 184–5.

all the privileges enjoyed by that of Paris.[1] Indeed, it may be said that very few men have done more for the advancement of learning than Sinibaldo Fieschi.

Innocent
and Art.

Nor was he deaf to the claims of art. During the comparatively brief period of his residence in Rome, whilst his mind was occupied, according to his biographer, " with pious and holy works," he renewed in splendid style (opere sumptuoso) the *Confession* and high altar of St. Lawrence-outside-the-walls ;[] for, says Carbio,[2] he was ever most devout to that Saint.

To the right of the entrance of that basilica is one of the very few tombs " that have survived to us from the first three quarters of the thirteenth century in Rome ".[3] It is that of the nephew of Innocent, cardinal William Fieschi († 1256), and consists of a fine ancient sarcophagus ornamented with bas-reliefs representing a marriage. It is surmounted by a mediaeval canopy " whose general style accords with that which covers the high altar ", and hence may have been the work of the artist employed by Innocent. Beneath the canopy is a fresco showing our Lord enthroned, to whom St. Lawrence is depicted as presenting Innocent IV., and St. Stephen as presenting

---

[1] And even for Paris, the model of so many Universities, Innocent greatly strengthened its corporate life by granting it for ten years the use of a seal of its own. Epp. May 30, 1252, *ib.*, p. 234 f. *Cf.* ep. May 31, 1252, *ib.*, p. 235.

[2] Carbio, c. 34. It would appear that to justify Mr. Smith's remark : " Innocent does not seem to have touched at any point the literature or art of his age" (*Church and State in the Middle Ages*, p. 243), it will be necessary very much to limit the meaning of "literature " and " art ", and of " at any point ". In the last chapter of his book, whence this passage is taken, Mr. Smith would appear to have abandoned the critical attitude displayed by him in the preceding part of his book. When he comes to speak of the personal character of Innocent, the carefully weighed judgment of the historian is replaced by the rhetoric of the lecturer. He draws his character of Innocent by imputing ulterior motives to all that he did, and by not troubling to support his statements by reference to documents.

[3] Davies, *Renascence Tombs of Rome*, p. 237.

cardinal Fieschi. Behind them stand SS. Eustace and Hippolytus. Innocent, moreover, added to the Vatican palace several beautiful rooms, and a very elegant tower.

As connected with art through the picturesque, we may here record Innocent's grant of the red hat to the cardinals. By this period, the cardinals had become the most important persons in the Church after the Pope himself. Subject to him alone,[1] they were regarded as the foundations of the world, as the hinges upon which rested the Catholic faith.[2]

Innocent gives the Cardinals a red hat.

The story goes that Margaret, countess of Flanders, and daughter of Baldwin II., Latin emperor of Constantinople, when on a visit to Innocent, was annoyed on afterwards discovering that she had saluted a mere abbot as a cardinal, and had greeted a cardinal as if he had been only an abbot. She accordingly begged the Pope to order that cardinals should be distinguished by the wearing of red hats when they went abroad.[3]

Whether this was the determining factor or not, contemporary evidence makes it certain that it was Innocent IV. who bestowed upon the cardinals the distinguishing sign of the red hat. Carbio gives us the exact date. " In the second year," he writes, " after the Council, Innocent went to Cluny to have an interview with the King of France and his brothers. It was there that, in accordance with a regulation made at the Council

---

[1] Pope Gregory IX. (1227) states " Cum cardinalis non nisi summi pontificis jurisdictioni noscatur de jure subesse ". See his letter to the dean and chapter of Lincoln, ap. *Register of St. Osmund*, i, p. 385 f., *R. S.*

[2] Grosseteste, *Epist.*, p. 125 ff.

[3] " Impetravit ut deinceps inter Cardinales et ceteros Prælatos discretio fieret, quod videlicet ad dignitatis evidentiam eorum pileos ex scarleto cardinales deferrent." F. Pippinus, *Chron.*, l. ii, c. 45, ap. *R. I. SS.*, ix, 666. The chronicler gives as his authority for this story Peter of Colonna, who became card. deacon of S. Eustachio in 1288.

itself, the cardinals received their red hats for the first time." [1]   Carbio's memory for dates occasionally played him false.   The Council of Lyons and the interview both took place in the year 1245.   Hence it may be regarded as certain that it was in 1245 that the red hat was first bestowed on a cardinal.

Though it is quite uncertain when the giving of the hat was first connected with a special ceremony, and came to be regarded as the chief act in the making of a cardinal, it is clear from a letter of Pope John XXII. to the King of France in 1316 that by that date " to bestow the hat and to promote to the cardinalate were regarded as equivalent expressions ". [2]

Innocent and money.

Unfortunately, however, Innocent's impecuniosity, and, on the other hand, slanderous gossip, industriously recorded by the rancorous pen of Matthew Paris, have resulted in the undue tarnishing of his reputation.   He succeeded to a legacy of debt which, despite his efforts, [3] he was unable to liquidate. [4]   His need of money was

[1] C. 21, p. 97. " Ubi d. cardinales primo capellos rubeos receperunt." Cf. William de Nangis, Chron., an. 1252, who adds that Innocent meant to insinuate by the colour that in the cause of faith and justice, " the Roman Church, which is head of all the others, should be especially ready, if necessary, to offer her head to be stained red with her blood." The cardinal's red hat is also mentioned in a poem written about 1263. Cf. Liber—carmen—de statu curiæ romanæ, ed. H. Gravert (Mag. Heinrich der Poet), Munich, 1912.

[2] Thurston, " The Cardinal's Hat and its History," in The Month, p. 8, June, 1899, quoting the letter from the Historisches Jahrbuch, vol. xxvi (1905), p. 103. Thurston's article is the foundation of what is here said on the red hat.

[3] The efforts he made were so considerable that Vincent of Beauvais, Spec. hist., xxx, c. 152, declared that he succeeded in clearing the Holy See of its debts—" a tempore P. Gregorii (IX.), multis ut fertur, debitis obligatam." Cf. Mat. Par., iv, 427 f., writing that Innocent complained : " quod aere alieno ecclesia Romana fere irrestaurabiliter obligata prægravaretur." Cf. his Reg., i, n. 22, p. 6 ; and Carbio, c. 7.

[4] Cf. supra, vol. xiii, p. 307 f.

even greater than that of his predecessor Gregory, who
had had to saddle the Apostolic See with ruinous debts.
The terrible ravages of Frederick round Rome just before
Gregory's death, and during the long vacancy of the
Holy See,[1] had still further reduced its resources, while
the long exile of Innocent only increased its needs.
Money therefore, was a pressing need of the Roman
Curia. As we shall see, Innocent himself was dunned
by its creditors. He was therefore driven even to
extend the use of the unsatisfactory means of raising
money, and of rewarding his servants then in vogue.[2]

The practice of Provisions was increased, and the calls Provisions.
for money on the clergy of England and France became
more frequent. The burden naturally fell most heavily
upon these two countries, inasmuch as, for one reason
or another, money was not readily obtainable from
other countries. In the countries of the North there
was not much of it. Frederick was able to a great extent
to cut off supplies from the Empire and Sicily, whilst
Lombardy and Spain needed so much for their wars
that they had little to spare for other purposes. These
demands for money, and the vexatious methods often

---

[1] See Frederick's letter of June, 1243, ap. H.-B., vi, p. 96, where
he boasts of the towers he has levelled with the dust and the crops
he has destroyed. He expressed a hope that the Romans would
learn sense " cum pulveres labentium turrium, segetes quoque ac
predia ferro flammaque vastata, . . . pre foribus Urbis aspicerent".
Cf. again Grosseteste's letter (n. 119) of 1246, in which he notes that
our spiritual father and mother, the Pope and the Church, were
" exilio relegatos . . . patrimonio suo spoliatos, de proprio, unde,
ut decet, sustententur, non habentes ". Innocent himself (ep. Nov. 3,
1253) ascribed many of the abuses to the evil times : " propter malitiam
temporum " (ap. Mat. P., Addit., vol. vi, p. 261), and he noted that,
in the time of Gregory, the Emperor had seized " nearly the whole
of the patrimony of the Church ". Ep. of Aug. 26, 1243, ap. H.-B.,
vi, pp. 113–14.

[2] Cf. supra, vol. xiii, p. 304 ff.

employed in its collection,[1] were naturally calculated to render the Pope not very popular. Moreover, when the history of Innocent's taxation is set forth by such a cantankerous writer as Matthew Paris, one is disposed to conclude from his narrative, highly seasoned too with anecdotes, which are in the main quite devoid of foundation, that that Pontiff was nothing but an unfeeling money-grubber. The truth, however, is that Innocent, though he knew, and regretfully acknowledged the abuse of Provisions, did not, as we have seen, always realize the extent to which his agents abused the commissions entrusted to them. But he was very tolerant of disagreeable truths being brought home to him by such really zealous bishops as Grosseteste of Lincoln [2]; and, as time went on, he issued various decrees which tended partially at least to remedy the evils complained of. After the complaints made to him at the Council of Lyons, he issued a series of decisions by which, for instance, he agreed not to give away more than twelve additional English benefices, and confirmed to patrons of benefices their rights of presentation (Aug. 3, 1245).[3] Some, however, of these privileges were not made absolute. They were to hold good " unless special mention be made of this indult ". The consequence was that the abuses continued; though, in the year before he died, in a bull addressed to the ecclesiastical and lay patrons of benefices in England, Innocent

[1] E.g., those of the nuncio Martin in 1244–5. From Grosseteste's ep. 106 and Mat. Par., iv, 419, 420, 431, it is clear " that Martin was understood to have exceeded his instructions, and that the responsibility for his extortions was attributed rather to the rapacity of the Roman Court than to the Pope himself. Stevenson, *Rob. Grosseteste*, p. 243 f.

[2] His protests to Innocent will be noticed when the affairs of England are treated of.

[3] Mat. Par., iv, 519–22; and Rymer, *Foedera*, i, 262, for the dates. *Cf.* ep. Aug. 8, 1245, ap. *Cal. of Papal Reg.*, i, 220; and Mat. Par., iv, 550, 598, 604; vi, 133, 289.

definitely recognized in principle, at least as far as
foreigners were concerned,[1] the position of these patrons,
and removed all obstacles to the exercise of their rights
of collation, election, and presentation (Nov. 3, 1253).[2]
The terms made use of by the Pope in proclaiming
these rights, show that he was conscious of the abuse
to which he was contributing, but that, while bitterly
regretting it, the importunities of suitors, and the
financial and other difficulties with which he was
surrounded had hitherto made it almost impossible for
him to remedy it. From the time when, he wrote, the
Providence of God had called him to rule the Church,
he had ever had at heart to do what was right ; and,
in making Provisions, to work for the good of churches
and places of religion. " That the very reverse of this
has happened at times, owing to the days being evil
and to suitors being excessively importunate, has oft
brought us sorrow, and overwhelmed our heart with
grief." The fact that, after long resistance, he has granted
Provisions quite against his will, has made him anxious
" for the peace of his mind ", and for the good of the
churches to apply a suitable remedy to these irregularities.
On condition, therefore, that the existing incumbents
were in no way interfered with, he fully restored their
rights to the patrons of benefices. In concluding his
decree on this matter, Innocent even went so far as to
say that the patrons, acting as his ministers, might
even tear up any letters of his or his legates which might
be presented to them in contravention of the said decree.[3]

---

[1] He was dealing with prebends, etc., " quæ optinentur a
quibuscunque oriundis extra regna, in quibus habentur . . .
præbende."

[2] Potthast, n. 15162. In full ap. Mat. Par., *Addit.*, vi, pp. 260–4.

[3] " Licitumque sit vobis universis et singulis, tanquam nostris
in hac parte ministris, nostras seu legatorum nostrorum lacerare
literas, si quæ statuto ipsi contrariæ vobis aut alicui vestrum fuerint

However much, then, Innocent may have abused his powers in the matter of Provisions, he, at any rate, in this most manly letter, openly acknowledged his fault, and in a most practical manner guarded against any recurrence of the evil, as far at least as he and England were concerned. He could not, of course, bind his successors ; and the abuse of Provisions broke out again after his death. But if succeeding Popes had observed his decree, there would not have been any Statute of Provisions in England in the fourteenth century, and there would have been one weapon less for the enemies of the Papacy to turn against it.

If then, after this, it must necessarily be admitted that Innocent was not so lost to shame in the matter of obtaining money for himself or his dependents, as Paris would have us believe, it has, on the other hand, been asserted by some modern authors that, though in this death struggle between the Empire and the Papacy, the latter " won and deserved to win ",[1] still Innocent's

præsentatæ." *Ib.*, p. 263. With his usual striking want of fairness when dealing with the Popes, Matthew Paris speaks of this whole-hearted concession as a slight redress, *aliquantulum mitigatoriæ*, vol. vi, p. 260. *Cf.* Mr. Smith's exposure of the unfairness of Paris in his whole account of the negotiations connected with the letter just quoted.

[1] Smith, *Church and State*, p. 213. " Both Empire and Papacy embodied a true unity among the nations of Christendom, but the latter was unity in a deeper sense, and for this reason the Papacy won and deserved to win." But this same able writer also asserts (p. 212) that " circumstances made Frederick the more scrupulous of the pair . . . " and that (p. 213) " of the two men (Fred. and Inn.) Frederick had almost the whole right on his side in the immediate circumstances of the struggle ". How blind to all this must have been their earnest and virtuous contemporaries, seeing that, as the same author (*ib.*) continues, " we must yet recognize that behind him (the Pope) were ranged greater religious and moral forces than the Empire could muster ". But the moral men of Frederick's age were not in the least blind to the merits of the case. One of our own countrymen proclaimed that the cause of the quarrel between Frederick

repeated rejection of Frederick's overtures for peace,
stamps his conduct as vindictive. Without in the least
attempting to justify all that Innocent did, the course
of our narrative has, we believe, already shown
conclusively that Frederick's word was wholly unreliable.
Recalling simply his conduct in seizing the Fathers
summoned to Gregory's council, and his behaviour
during the vacancies of the Holy See after that Pontiff's
death, we may safely assert that Frederick's measure
of right was what he had the power to accomplish.
It was no more possible for the Popes to make treaties
with Frederick than it was for the Parliamentarians
with Charles I., on whose word no man relied. There
was only one way of treating with both of them, and that
was absolutely to deprive them of the power of breaking
agreements by crushing them. If the Parliamentarians
could scarcely be called vindictive in beheading Charles I.,
Innocent can scarcely be called vindictive in waging
war against Frederick to the bitter end. In his struggle
with the Emperor, Innocent displayed the qualities
of a resolute man. He was wary of entering into the
quarrel. He did not do so till he had proved that
Frederick was as faithless to him as he had been to
Honorius III. and to Gregory IX. Then, when he had
entered into the quarrel, he resolved so to conduct himself as to make his adversary beware of him. We need
not, however, believe our countryman, John of Walling-
ford († 1258), who declared that Innocent strove to
bring it about that there should never be another
emperor, " in order that the Roman curia might be
supreme," and that he regretted that it had raised up

and the Popes was the effort of the former to destroy rights which
the latter were peacefully holding at least by prescriptive right.
" Quia . . . imperator consuetudines et libertates quas antiquitus
Romana ecclesia pacifice possiderat, conabatur adnichilare." Barling's
Chron., ap. *Chrons. of Edward* (*I. and II.*), vol. ii, p. cxiii, *R. S.*

William of Holland, as he had succeeded in becoming master of Germany.[1]

As another of our countrymen, Gervase of Tilbury, told Frederick's predecessor, Otho IV., the Empire was meant to be a support to the Papacy, not to be its lord.[2] Now it was precisely Frederick's effort to dominate the Papacy that Innocent resisted with all the power at his command. And if at times the fight seemed to be merely whether the Pope was to be a temporal ruler,[3] and was to remain suzerain of Sicily, both combatants knew that they were contending for objects of much greater moment. Innocent, in fighting for his rights as a temporal sovereign, was fighting to maintain not merely those privileges of general direction of the affairs of the West, which the reverence and gratitude of Europe, and the working of the feudal system had placed in the hands of the Popes,[4] but also to secure that measure of personal power and liberty without which the Papacy, in his days at least, could not act fully even as spiritual sovereign.[5]

[1] *Chron.*, ap. *M. G. SS.*, xxviii, p. 508 f. " Ut de cetero sola curia Romana dominaretur. . . ."

[2] *Otia imperialia*, ap. *M. G. SS.*, xxvii, p. 363 f. " Porro sacerdocio regnum se noverit adesse, non preesse, adici non prefici, in execucionem dari per adjutorium ; non in majoritatem efferri per dominacionis auctoritatem. . . . Utrorumque ergo creator et Dominus (Christus) clericos in funiculum sue vocavit portionis, et laicos in corporale venire voluit ministerium execucionis."

[3] " Le patron, le protecteur de l'Église, pour lui (Frederick) n'est autre que le maître absolu de l'Église." E. Gebhart, *L'Italie mystique*, p. 152. The same writer shows how Frederick imposed an absolute monarchy on Sicily, and strove (p. 180) to deprive the Pope of his social supremacy in Europe. He would be sole ruler of Christendom.

[4] *Otia, ib.*, " Dum unctio sacerdotalis immutata semper et uniformis in capite persistit, ad virgam (the kingly rod of power) pertinet directionis."

[5] It may then most justly be denied that " the aim of petty territorial princedom in Italy " on the part of the Popes was one of " narrow selfishness and of a character wholly political ". Smith, *l.c.*, p. 2. If, at the present moment (Dec. 1915), Italy were fighting on the side of the Central Powers, none would wish more keenly for the territorial independence of the Pope than we Englishmen.

On his side it was the aim of " the most wicked emperor
Frederick " [1] to lord it over the world as had done the
emperors of pagan Rome, and over the Church as did the
Basileus of Byzantium. The struggle waged by the
heads of the Church against such a man as Frederick II.
could only be a combat *à outrance*.[2]

To return now to the early career of Sinibaldo Fieschi, Continuation
who was born at least before the year 1207.[3] It was of the early
under Honorius III. that the canon of Parma came to Innocent.
Rome, and was made *Auditor* of the *literæ contradictæ*
(1226).[4] By Gregory IX. he was immediately appointed
vice-chancellor of the Roman Church, and at the first
promotion of cardinals made by that Pontiff, he was
nominated cardinal-priest of St. Lawrence in Lucina
(1227, Sept.).[5]

The *Audientia Litterarum Contradictarum* was a depart-
ment of the papal Chancery in which the letters were
finally examined before being dispatched to their

---

[1] Thus does the Chronicle of Melrose speak of him, *Chron. Mailros.*,
an. 1245. But to Mr. Smith, p. 243, Frederick's personality
" embodied every form of culture, was full of the joy of life, of art,
of *friendship* (think of his treatment of his wives, of his gross sensuality,
of his treatment of Peter della Vigna !), and presents to us a nature
that if it sometimes repels, more often attracts, and is always full of
a strange fascination, a nature so powerful, rich, and manifold, that
by contrast the figure of the Pope is cold, narrow, unlovable, even
inhuman ". Is then the wanton form of Pleasure to be preferred to
the severe figure of Duty ; and the painted picture of unbridled lust
to be loved more than the cold marble sculpture of Chastity ?

[2] Later on, at least, Frederick himself proclaimed this. He wrote
in 1247 (ap. H.-B., vi, 516–17). " Quumque, rebus ut nunc se haben-
tibus, papam istum aut quemlibet alium futurum processui nostro
contrarium incommutabiliter crederemus."

[3] Henry III. was born in 1207, and the Pope in a joking letter
addressed to that King says he was older than he. Ep. of Dec. 18,
1253, ap. Rymer, *Foedera*, i, p. 496.

[4] *Cf.* Potthast, ii, 679, for his signature as such. *Cf.* Alberic T. F.,
ap. *M. G. SS.*, xxiii, p. 920.

[5] *Ib.*, p. 939.

destination. The work of the *Auditor* was to decide
whether there was any " contradictious " matter in the
letter presented to him, anything which might cause
injury to anyone, and, if there was, to see that it was
emended before it was sent to the *bullator* to be sealed.[1]

A poem on the Roman Curia, written a few years after
Innocent's death, tells us that the Vice-Chancellor was
the Pope's second hand ; that it was his special business
to present to him the letters that had to be submitted
to him personally ; and that, as a furnace heated hotter
than the rest, it was his duty finally to perfect all that
came before him.[2]

Sinibaldo,
Rector of
the March
of Ancona,
1235-40.

Gregory's *Register* shows that Sinibaldo was indeed
one of Gregory's hands. He was constantly appointed
to preside over causes that were submitted to the Holy
See,[3] and was at length nominated to the difficult post

---

[1] *Cf.* the poem on the Roman Curia written by Master Henry in
the days of Urban IV. (1261–4). Our quotations are taken from
those portions of the poem published by Poole, *The Roman Chancery*,
p. 163 ff.   But it may be read in full, ap. H. Grauert, *Magister Heinrich
der Poet in Wurzburg*, Munich, 1912, and less well, ap. Mabillon, *Vet.
Analecta*, p. 369 ff., in the fol. ed. of 1723.

> " Contradictarum certus sedet arbiter illic,
>   Officio cujus discucietur opus.
> Si res est simplex, et non prejudicat ulli,
>   Expediet cursus absque labore suos.
> Si vero talis fuerit quod forte gravari
>   Inde potest aliquis, altera forma subit.
> Tunc sub dissimili ponetur judice causa,
>   Nec poteris ventis ad tua vota frui.
> Sic enim servat sua Curia jura cuique,
>   Ne quisquam vere possit ab Urbe queri.
> Cum fuerit concors convencio facta, repente
>   Mittitur ad bullam carta refecta sacram."—P. 164.

The distinguished Englishman, Rob. Summercote, who died a cardinal
in 1243 was at one time (1238) " papal subdeacon and auditor of papal
litere contradicte ".   Bliss, *Calendar*, i, 168.

[2] *Ib.*, or ed. Grauert, p. 79.

[3] *Reg. Greg. IX.*, vol. i, pp. 54, 602, 1187, 1280 f. ; ii, 160, 812 ff.

of Rector of the March of Ancona (1235).[1] The letters addressed to him by Gregory in this capacity give some insight into the military, civil, and ecclesiastical duties that the cardinal had to perform. He had by force of arms to put down private wars, and to co-operate with other Rectors in punishing cities which had inflicted injuries on the Patrimony, and in general had to fulfil the duties which fall to the lot of a civil and an ecclesiastical head of a province.[2] In December, 1240, he paid a visit to Rome, where Gregory decided to keep him for the time " on account of urgent and important business "—business no doubt connected with the General Council which he had summoned to meet in the following year.[3]

Sinibaldo was then in Rome on the death of Gregory ; General rejoicings on his election, and was, as we have seen, elected Pope in 1243. Great was the rejoicing at his election, not merely in Genoa 1243. because a compatriot was raised to the first position in Christendom,[4] but throughout the whole Catholic world. " Who can tell," wrote our distinguished countryman, the Franciscan, Adam Marsh, " with what prolonged joy the Catholic world offered praise to our most merciful Saviour who placed in the supreme position of the Apostolic See a Vicar of His own, a Successor of Peter to oppose the great evils of the time, and to reform the world. He has given us a Pope whom, by His special divine mercy, He has endowed with a majestic presence (magnificæ majestatis excellentia) and with a fearless constancy ; with remarkable industry and untiring

---

[1] Potthast, epp. of Oct. 17, 1235, nn. 10032 ff.

[2] Ib., and Reg. G., ii, pp. 385, 960, for epp. of May 5, 1236, and Apr. 1, 1238, and vol. iii, p. 189, and pp. 277, 337, epp. July 4, 1240, and Oct. 22, 1240 (concerning the foundation of the episcopal see of Recanati).

[3] Epp. of Dec. 12, 1240, ap. Rodenberg, i, p. 702.

[4] Ann. Genuen., l. vi, ap. R. I. SS., v, p. 504.

watchfulness ; with an affection strong as death, and a
zeal as hard as hell (*Cantic.*, viii, 6) ; . . . with the muni-
ficence of a generous heart, and with the great soul that
comes of illustrious birth—qualities so much thought of
in the world. Hence does the Church rejoice, and,
thanking God for the many excellencies of the Pope,
say with the Most High, ' I have found a man after
mine own heart.' " [1]

Men were glad because again there was one " to whom
all the faithful, all over the world, could have healthy
recourse in all kinds of necessities ". They rejoiced
because once more there was one to give " to all the
nations of the earth " a rule of life, justice, and the true
mode of worship.[2] Nowhere was the rejoicing at the
election of the new Pope greater than in England, because
it was thought that our nation had a special claim upon
the Pope's care. " Never shall it be doubted," it was
said to him, " that among all the parts of the habitable
world, you will embrace with more fatherly affection
the most excellent King, the pious clergy, and the
faithful people of England, which is more especially
bound to the Papacy by the bond of a trusty covenant ;
and that you will ever incline towards them the height
of your supreme majesty, so that you may powerfully

---

[1] See an address to Innocent seemingly drawn up at the request of
the Archbishop of Canterbury, and sent to him on the occasion of
King Henry's assuming the cross, which he did on March 6, 1250.
Ap. *Mon. Francis.*, c. 3, p. 422 ff., *R. S.* This description of Innocent is
not such as would be gathered from the carpings and gossip of Matthew
Paris. After it, Adam addresses an exhortation to the Pope in the
words of St. Bernard to Eugenius III.

[2] Marsh, *ib.*, pp. 428–9. " Per quem (the Pope) . . . omnibus sæculi
nationibus prærogatur forma vivendi, dirigitur censura judicandi,
sancitur ritus colendi." *Cf.* 435 where he says that " Augustine, sent
by blessed Gregory, gave the form of faith (formam fidei) to the English ",
and he asks, " Will the ruin of faith be reformed except in accordance
with that Apostolic form which first fashioned it."

protect them . . . wisely instruct them, gently correct them, and lovingly cherish them. . . . For in them is recognized more than in all the others who are subject to your most sacred sway, the holiness of divine worship, strong Catholic faith, devotion to the Apostolic See, and ready obedience." [1]

A day or two after his consecration, Innocent announced his election to the Catholic world, and asked its prayers.[2] Letters of congratulation soon began to pour in upon him. Among the first to felicitate the new Pope was Frederick. Later authors, indeed, declare that, when the Emperor heard of the election of Sinibaldo, he said : " We have lost a great friend. Now that he has become Pope he will manfully defend what the Church maintains to be her rights against us." [3] In any case, there is no doubt that, hitherto at least, he had regarded him as a friend, and, on that assumption worked for his election.[4] Hence, throughout the kingdom of Sicily,[5] he ordered thanks to be given to God for the election, and sent

Innocent announces his election.

[1] *Ib.*, p. 429. " Nempe super omnes sanctissimæ ditioni vestræ subjectos in illis indubitanter agnoscitur . . . fortitudo fidei Catholicæ, sedis Apostolicæ devotio, etc." *Cf.* p. 431, where he says that King Henry is a more devout son of the Pope than any other King ; and, very finely, that as becomes such a great Catholic Prince, he intends to strive " terra marique *jus imperii Christiani* distendere."

[2] Ep. of July 2, 1243, ap. Rod. ii, p. 1 ff. *Cf.* Mat. Par., iv, 257.

[3] Jacobus de Aquis, *Chron. imaginis mundi* (it extends to 1290), ap. *Mon. hist. patriæ, SS.*, iii, p. 1584. *Cf.* Dandolo, *Chron.*, l. x, c. 5, p. 354, ap. *R. I. SS.*, xii, and F. Pipinus, *Chron.*, l. ii, c. 34, ap. *R. I. SS.*, ix, 657. The author of the pamphlet (June, 1245) against Frederick, generally ascribed to Albert von Behaim, says that Frederick was very angry at the election of Innocent, p. 64, ed. Höfler.

[4] Ep. ap. H.-B., vi, 516.

[5] Ric. of San. G., *Chron.* sub. fin. " Gavisi sumus gaudio magno " at Innocent's election, so Frederick told the King of Hungary in July, 1244. Ep. ap. H.-B., vi, 204. *Cf.* also the letter of the unknown King (July), ap. H.-B., vi, p. 101 ff. " Canite igitur tuba et cithara, canite Deo nostro qui suum prosequendo negotium papam concessit populo, patrem filiis, virum vidue, pastorem ovibus, et in altis habitans respexit humilia, largitus mundo perituro rectorem."

a most important embassy [1] to Anagni to present to the
new Pope the imperial letters of congratulation, and to
arrange terms of peace. By heaven-sent inspiration,
he wrote, has the name of Innocent been given to you,
because by you what is *noxious* will be destroyed, and
innocence will be protected. "To us, you have come
from out the noble sons of the Empire as an old friend
now made into a new father, through whom the Empire
has full confidence that its desire for peace and for its
rights will be for ever listened to." He concluded
by assuring the Pope that his envoys were commissioned
to place at his service, "saving the rights of the Holy
Roman Empire," the Emperor himself and all that
was his.[2]

Congratula-
tions of
Grosseteste.

Among the other distinguished men of his age who
wrote to congratulate Innocent on his accession was the
light of our own hierarchy, Robert Grosseteste, bishop
of Lincoln.[3] "Our Blessed Lord," said the bishop,
"who after the storm brings the calm, and after its
mourning brings joy to his Church, long terribly assailed
by the storms of many great tribulations, and long flooded
with sorrows like the cheeks of a widow wailing with tears
by night (*Lament.*, i, 2), has provided Her with a spouse
to wipe away her tears, to relieve her of her tribulations,
and to turn a defensive shield against those who are
assaulting her. With so noble a spouse the Church

----

[1] Including Peter della Vigna, and Master Thaddeus of Sessa (Suessa).
Cf. Ep. Fred., ap. *ib.*, p. 205.

[2] Ep. of July, 1243, ap. H.-B., vi, p. 104 f. *Cf.* his letter of June 25 to
the Duke of Brabant (seemingly a circular letter) in which he announces
the unanimous election of card. Sinibaldo "well disposed towards
himself—pro nobis tam verbo quam opere semper se benevolum
obsequiosum præstiterit." See also his letter, full of misrepresenta-
tions to the King of Hungary. July, 1244, ap. *ib.*, p. 203 f. Even in
March, 1244, Frederick still spoke of Innocent's zeal for peace and
justice. *Ib.*, p. 168.

[3] Ep. iii, p. 328, *R. S.*

which has long sat in mourning, rightly throws off her
widow's weeds, and puts on the garments of joy. The
sheep, which, long without a pastor, have narrowly
escaped being driven off by robbers . . . now hearing the
voice of their shepherd calling them by name (S. John, x,
3) . . . will find pasture, and under his pastoral authority
and care, will enjoy long desired peace and quiet. . . . So
I, your Holiness's servant (the least in fact, but in my
affection the most devoted) giving thanks to God . . .
throw myself with all humility at the feet of your
paternity and commend my insignificance to your
Holiness's power ; entreating you to deign to take
me to your paternal arms, and begging that your care of
all the churches and of the salvation of souls will deign
to bestow some attention on my affairs, which are
concerned with the salvation of souls or my episcopal
charge. . . . May God long preserve you to his holy Church."

The first thought of the new Pope was one of peace. Peace
He was so anxious to end the strife between the Church negotiations
and the Empire that " on the very day of his consecra- Pope and the
tion " he took counsel with the cardinals on the subject.[1] 1243.
As a result of their deliberations, there were dispatched
to the Emperor, Peter, afterwards (1244) cardinal-bishop
of Albano, and then archbishop of Rouen, William,
abbot of St. Facundo, and soon to be cardinal priest
of the basilica of the Twelve Apostles,[2] and Nicholas,
bishop of Reggio,—all, we are assured, men of great
standing and prudence, and all favourably disposed
towards Frederick.[3] As Nicholas died soon afterwards

[1] Carbio, c. 7 ; Albert v. B., p. 64.

[2] He received his new dignity at Innocent's first promotion of
cardinals in 1244.

[3] Carbio, *ib.* Of Nicholas in particular this is confirmed by Salimbene,
Chron., p. 27. " Gratiam habuit imperatoris Frederici et Romanæ
curie." *Cf.* also the assertion of Innocent himself. Ep. of July 17,
1245, ap. Rod., ii, p. 89.

at the court of the Emperor,[1] his place in these peace negotiations was taken by Albert of Savoy, bishop of Modena, who became cardinal-bishop of Sabina in 1244. The Pope instructed the envoys to insist, as a preliminary to the negotiations, that the Emperor should release the rest of those whom he had captured at sea,[2] as he had promised " before our promotion ". They were to inquire what satisfaction he was prepared to make in connexion with the causes of his excommunication ; to state that the Pope was ready to call together Princes both secular and ecclesiastical to arbitrate on the differences between them ; and to inform the Emperor that peace must also be granted to the friends of the Church.[3] Frederick received the ambassadors favourably, and made many promises,[4] but took no steps either to obtain release from excommunication for himself or for his chief counsellors or to release the captives.[5] Accordingly when his envoys, Peter della Vigna and the others, reached Anagni,[6] the Pope would not receive them, or at any rate would not accept them as intermediaries to treat of peace, seeing that they were under sentence of excommunication

---

[1] Salimbene, p. 175.

[2] On Aug. 26, 1243, Innocent had to complain that Frederick was still detaining the prisoners. Ap. H.-B., vi, 114.

[3] The articles of peace, ap. H.-B., vi, 112 f. *Cf.* Carbio, c. 7, who adds that the Pope insisted that the Emperor should grant free access to Rome—" apertionem viarum quas idem clauserat imperator." With no little assurance Frederick informed his subjects and friends after the Pope's flight to Genoa that Innocent had offered him satisfaction (it is true on the award of a general council) for the wrong done to him by Pope Gregory. " Per quos (Innocent's envoys) pacem nobis obtulit, vel vocatis nuntiis regum et principum et prelatis ad concilium generale, emendationem offense *nobis per predictum papam G. irrogate*, nec non receptionem satisfactionis cum misericordia et Ecclesie lenitate." See the important letter of July, 1244, ap. H.-B., vi, 206.

[4] Carbio, *ib.*

[5] Ep. Inn., ap. H.-B., vi, 114.

[6] Richard of S. G., p. 156, says they were sent off in July, 1243.

for having communicated with Frederick.[1] On his side, Frederick thereupon complained to the papal envoys, as they informed the Pope,[2] that their master had sent a legate into Lombardy ; that he took proceedings against heretics at a distance but not against those in Lombardy and Tuscany ; that he had refused to receive his envoys, etc.[3]

Innocent had no difficulty in brushing aside these trivial objections ; but, to facilitate the peace negotiations he instructed his legates (Sept. 2) to absolve the envoys of the Emperor who were to be sent to him again.[4]

Frederick, however, only wanted peace on his own terms. He was determined not merely not to include in the peace the Lombards whom Innocent properly refused to abandon ; but not even to give up the papal territory which he had seized. As he said himself,[5] though in justice he ought to have reannexed to the Empire territory which the wrongs inflicted upon him by Pope Gregory had compelled him to take back, still he had offered to surrender it again to the Pope, on condition that the Church enfeoffed it to him for an annual tribute.[6] Surprised that the Pope, " who was well aware that his future spiritual power depended in great measure on

Failure of the negotiations, Sept., 1243.

---

[1] Ric., *ib.*, says they were well received and took back a favourable reply to the Emperor. But Frederick, ep. of July, 1244, *ib.*, p. 205, says "legatos nostros . . . Petrum de Vinea, etc., *non* admisit." So also says the Pope. See Innocent's letter of Aug. 26, *ib.*, p. 115 ff.

[2] *Ib.*, p. 113.

[3] *Ib.*

[4] Ep. ap. *ib.*, p. 118.

[5] Ep. apol., ap. H.-B., vi, 205–6.

[6] See also the *Chron. Estense*, ap. *R. I. SS.*, xv, p. 310. "Cum imperator fere totam Italiam possideret in superbiam elevatus, verba quædam blanda dicebat (et) . . . proponebat Ecclesiis jurisdictiones et possessiones Villarum et castrorum quibus erant ab Imperio prædotatæ." The generosity of German Kaisers with regard to other people's territory is exactly as great to-day (1915) as it was in the thirteenth century !

the restoration of the lost provinces," [1] should refuse
his offer, Frederick declared that he was nevertheless
seeking a shorter road to peace than any proposed by
the Pope, when word reached him that Cardinal Rainer,
" his special friend," as he sarcastically called him, had
seized Viterbo. [2] This gave him the excuse he needed ;
he refused to listen to the Pope's terms ; and, in
accordance with their instructions, [3] the papal legates
returned to the Pope, and Frederick's envoys left him. [4]
War between the Papacy and Empire was reopened.
Frederick gave his attention to the affair of Viterbo,
and Innocent instructed his energetic legate in Lombardy,
Gregory of Montelongo, to stir up the devotion of the
partisans of the Church, and to assure them that he
would make no peace without them. [5]

Innocent
enters Rome,
Oct. 1243.

Three or four weeks after the dispatch of this letter,
Innocent left Anagni for Rome, about the time when
the Popes were wont to return to the city after the
heats of the summer had passed away. He was received
with the enthusiastic joy with which the Romans and
their senate were wont to welcome the return of a Pope
to Rome after any lengthy absence had reminded them
that their material prosperity depended on his presence. [6]

[1] Kington, *Life of Fred. II.*, ii, p. 323.

[2] Fred's. manifesto after the Pope's flight, July, 1244, ap. H.-B.,
vi, p. 206. " Nobis autem viam pacis tanquam breviorem (than the
Pope's scheme of arbitration) eligentibus . . . ille . . . specialis
amicus et devotus noster (cardinal Rainer) civitatem Viterbii . . . a
nostro dominio revocavit."

[3] " Quod si forte se monitionibus vestris . . . humiliter non inclinet,
volumus . . . ad nos protinus redeatis," wrote the Pope on Aug. 26,
ap. H.-B., vi, p. 116. *Cf.* Carbio, c. 7.

[4] Ep. Inn. to Gregory of Montelongo, " our subdeacon and notary and
legate " (in Lombardy). Sept. 23, 1243, H.-B., vi, p. 123.

[5] *Ib.*, *cf.* ep. Inn., Sept. 27, to the Commune of Treviso, ap. Rod.,
ii, p. 21.

[6] Carbio, c. 17, Ric. of S. G., p. 156—unfortunately the last entry
in his useful chronicle. Mat. Par., *Chron. maj.*, iii, 407, tells us how the
Romans felt the loss of money caused by the absence of the Pope from
the city.

VITERBO, LOGGIA AND STAIRCASE OF THE PAPAL PALACE.
Thirteenth Century.

[to face p. 38.

But, says his biographer,[1] he was treated by the He is dunned for money. Romans as our Lord was treated by the Jews, who one day laid down their garments before him and a few days afterwards stripped him of his own. Innocent had scarcely returned to the city, ere a number of merchant-bankers with a gang of followers poured into the Lateran palace, and with loud cries demanded the immediate repayment with considerable interest of a loan of sixty thousand marks which Gregory IX. had borrowed from them. They continued their importunities for days, but at length had to be content to depart with a great deal less interest than they had hoped for. And now, leaving Innocent paying off other debts due from the Holy See,[2] we must devote a little space to the Viterbo incident which furnished Frederick with an excuse to break off the peace negotiations with the Pope.

Among the other cities which surrendered to Frederick Viterbo throws off Frederick's yoke, 1243. on the occasion of his last attack on Pope Gregory[3] was Viterbo, Feb., 1240.[4] Its people soon found that the easy suzerainty of the Pope was one thing, and the iron rule of Frederick quite another. He set over them a governor Simon, count of Chieti, built a fortress palace to overawe them, and did exactly as he thought fit.[5] Roused at length by the oppressions of the imperial

---

[1] C., c. 7.

[2] *Ib.*

[3] " Eodem anno (1240) Fredericus . . . contra d. papam innumera mala tanquam desperatus faciebat, et cepit Biterbum, et quasdam alias civitates et munitiones, ita quod in brevi totam marchiam Guarneri et totam vallem Spoleti papa abstulit." Alberic Tri. Font., *Chron.,* ap. *M. G. SS.,* xxiii, p. 948.

[4] " Recipit (the Emperor) tunc etiam Viterbium eodem mense (Feb., 1240) " Ric. of S. S., p. 152.

[5] *Ib. Cf.* Lanzillotto (*supra,* vol. xi, p. 7), *Croniche di Viterbo,* p. 246 f. " Et gia e facto el dicto imperatore signore de Viterbo, e disponiva quello che voleva." Of the palace the substructions were laid bare in 1888. *Cf.* P. Egidi in his notes to Lanzillotto, and also in his *Viterbo,* p. 19, Naples, 1912.

officers, the people rose, drove out many of the imperial
officials (Sept. 5, 1243), sought the help of the Romans,
and invited Cardinal Rainer Capocci, the Pope's legate
in Tuscany, to come and take up his residence among
them.   The cardinal came at once from Sutri (Sept. 9),
was installed in the new palace, and assisted in the attack
on the remnant of the imperial force which was shut up
in the citadel.[1]   Before the close of the month, Frederick
appeared before the town with a large army, and an
appeal was at once made by the citizens to the Pope
and to the Romans for men and money.   Innocent was
very loath to have anything to do with the affair.   He
declared that he did not want war, and did not wish to
spend money over it.   However, when it was pointed
out to him that the lives of the people of Viterbo would
be in danger if they fell into the hands of the enemy, he
sent the cardinal two thousand five hundred ounces of
gold.[2]   With this and with the support of the Romans,
the people of Viterbo proved too strong for the Emperor.
He was compelled with great bitterness of heart to raise
the siege (Nov., 1243).[3]

[1] Mat. Par., iv, 266 ; Lanz., p. 300 ff. ; Ric. of S. G., p. 156 ; Carbio,
c. 8 ; and especially a number of letters from Tineosus and others who
were shut up in the citadel asking Frederick for help. " Civitatem
vestram laudabilem subverterunt nonis septembris potestate et ceteris
officialibus vestris cum armis acriter infugatis. Vocantesque de longin-
quo cardinalem Raynerium, etc." writes the knight Tineosus, ap. H.-B.,
vi, 125. According to Count Simon, ep. ib., p. 129, the cardinal had
only 200 men.

[2] Ep. of Oct. 7, ap. ib., pp. 130–1.

[3] Ric. of S. G., l.c., Frederick's version of the Viterbo incident in his
apologetic letter of July, 1244 (ap. H.-B., vi, pp. 206–7) only differs
from the above in this, that he declared that, when he withdrew from
the city, the agreement made with him was not kept, and that when he
complained to the Pope about the matter, Innocent said that he
would like to see justice done, but that he feared to lose the city :
" quod libenter hec omnia faceret emendari nisi quod civitatem timebat
amittere." Cf. ib., p. 211.

Whether or not Innocent was guilty of any diplomatic error in having anything whatever to do with the rebellion of Viterbo whilst peace negotiations were in progress, the incident was closed before the definitive negotiations for peace were opened by the Emperor.[1] Moved especially, as he said, by the entreaties of Raymond VII., count of Toulouse,[2] who had left France on the failure of his last revolt against Louis IX. (1243), or perhaps, really, because his affairs in Lombardy were not going well,[3] Frederick again opened negotiations for peace. At length, after much discussion,[4] the Emperor, on Holy Thursday (March 31, 1244), through his agents, Raymond, Peter della Vigna, and Thaddeus of Sessa,[5] in the Lateran palace before the Pope, the cardinals, Baldwin, emperor of Constantinople, and " a very great number " of bishops and others, swore, that he would, in a word, stand by the ruling of the Pope in

[1] This is clear from Frederick's own words in the above letter, p. 207, " Hec (the Viterbo affair) ante tractatam et firmatam inter nos et Ecclesiam concordiam contigerunt."

[2] *Ib. Cf.* Ric. of S. G., *Chron.*, p. 156, who tells of Raymond's going to Rome " tractans inter ipsum (the Pope) et imperatorem bonum pacis ". It would seem that Raymond went to Frederick because the Emperor was with him and our King Henry III. against Louis. *Cf.* Vaissete, *Hist. gén. de Languedoc*, iii, p. 434, relying on the terms of alliance between Raymond and Henry in Rymer's *Fœdera*, vol. i.

[3] *Cf.* Marchetti-Longhi, *La legaz. di G. da Monte Longo*, n. 8, p. 163.

[4] *Cf.* epp. of Fred., ap. H.-B., vi, 146 f. ; p. 167 ff., and the long apology, p. 207 f. *Cf.* Carbio, c. 10. It is to be specially noted that the Viterbo incident notwithstanding, Frederick in March, 1244, considers the Pope as " a lover of peace and justice ". He is " pastor ydoneus . . . quem pacis et justitie credimus zelatorem, secum ad salutaris concordie redire proponimus unitatem ". *Ib.*, p. 168. *Cf.* ep. of Inn. (Jan. 3, 1244) ap. Potthast, 11215, to the Bolognese authorities to come and take part in the peace discussions. This letter furnishes another proof that Frederick's subsequent contention that it was *understood* that the Lombards were not to be included in the peace was unfounded.

[5] Ep. of March 28, 1244, of Fred., giving these commissioners authority to swear " in anima sua ".

most of the matters in dispute between them.[1] The
details of the treaty of peace are furnished us by Matthew
Paris,[2] and are set forth with certain omissions by the
Emperor himself in his lengthy statement to his subjects
and friends of the events which preceded the Pope's
flight.[3] By the terms of this treaty, Frederick, in the
first place, agreed to give up " all the territory " possessed
by the Church and its adherents at the time of his
excommunication.[4] He next agreed to let the world know
that, in not heeding the sentence of excommunication
pronounced by Gregory, he had no intention of showing
contempt for the power of the keys ; but he had been
advised that, as the sentence had not been announced to
him directly, he was not bound to observe it. Still he
acknowledged that he had not acted properly in this
matter, as he " firmly believes that the supreme pontiff,
even if, which God forfend, he be a sinner, has full power
in spirituals as well over him as over all Christians, kings,
and princes, clergy and laity ".[5] For this he was prepared to make all the satisfaction which the Pope should
award ; as he was also with regard to the plundering
of the property of the prelates who had been seized
when going to the council, and with regard to the injury
he had done to churches. He further undertook to
forgive the offences committed against him by all those who
gave in their adhesion to the Church, after the outbreak

[1] Carbio, *ib.*

[2] *Chron. maj.*, iv, 332 ff.

[3] Ap. H.-B., vi, pp. 204–21.

[4] These important details are omitted by Frederick. On these
omissions Huillard-Bréholles, *ib.*, p. 207 n., says that he dare not say
whether they were made of set purpose, or merely for shortness sake.
The reader must decide for himself.

[5] " Cum bene sciat et credat fideliter, quod tam super eum quam
super omnes Christianos, reges et principes, clericos et laicos, habet
summus pontifex . . . in spiritualibus plenitudinem potestatis." Mat.
Par., *l.c.*, p. 332.

of the quarrel; to leave to the decision of the Pope and the cardinals the case of those who had offended him before the outbreak of the dispute with the Pope; to release the prelates and others captured in the galleys, as well as other captives taken since the issue of the sentence of excommunication; to permit exiles to return to their homes; to give security to the legate, Gregory of Montelongo, etc., etc.

Frederick at once hastened to express his satisfaction that peace had been at length concluded. He told his son Conrad that his agents had in his behalf " sworn to obey the commands of the Church in accordance with Canon Law " [1]; and bade him proclaim the good news throughout Germany. He further told him that, after interviewing the Pope, he intended to betake himself " with a powerful force—potenti brachio " (ominous words !) into Lombardy, and he instructed him to hold himself in readiness to attend a diet which he was going to hold at Verona. Besides the Emperor, others also spread about the news that the peace between the Church and the Empire for which all longed had at length been established.[2] And the Pope himself, too, gave thanks to God and St. Edmund, whose aid he had invoked,[3] for the happy consummation of the affair.

Frederick expresses his satisfaction at the conclusion of peace, 1244.

But rejoicing over the peace was premature. Difficulties arose the moment the scope of some of its articles began to be considered. The Pope, not unnaturally it would seem, contended [4] that the terms of the peace implied

He immediately withdraws from it.

---

[1] " Parituros nos mandatis Ecclesie secundum disciplinam ecclesisticam juraverunt." Ep. of April, 1244, ap. H.-B., vi, p. 176.

[2] *Cf.* a letter of a subject of Frederick, ap. *ib.*, p. 177.

[3] Mat. Par., iv, 336.

[4] Fred. pretends that the Pope only put forward the Lombard question in private and by means of others. " Quod (the settlement of the time, etc., of his absolution from excommunication) ab eo (Innocent) occasione Lombardorum . . . , licet de ea non palam sed clam et per alios faceret mentionem, nullatenus potuit obtineri." The Emperor's

that what was said about the adherents or partisans
of the Church in general naturally included the Lombards
(seeing that no exceptions or limitations were put to the
word adherents), and hence that in their case matters
were to be restored to the state in which they were
before the dispute between Frederick and the Church,
viz., that in their regard the peace of Constance, and the
compacts of Neuss and Eger should be respected.[1] The
Emperor, however, declaring that he was not prepared
to give up the rights of the Empire in regard to
Lombardy,[2] said that, if the Pope were honest, he must
acknowledge that it was agreed before the signing of the
peace that the Lombards were not to be included in it,
" repented in his pride " of the agreement to which he
had sworn, and unhappily refused the satisfaction which
he had once offered in a spirit of lowliness.[3]

Frederick
violates the
treaty, and
tries to
overreach
the Pope.

Coming from Matthew Paris, these words may be
taken as a clear indication of the public feeling that the

apology, H.-B., vi, p. 211. The Emperor implies that the Pope had to
speak in secret about the whole Lombard question because, as he
declared, the imperial envoys before swearing to the peace had expressly
insisted that Lombard prisoners taken before their master's excommunication would not be unconditionally surrendered, and because the
Pope had allowed their exception to pass.

[1] *Cf. supra*, vol. x, p. 247 f., vol. xi, p. 179 f., and vol. xiii.

[2] " Papa motus propterea quia nolebamus in eum super negotio
Lombardorum de juribus scilicet et regalibus nostris compromittere
negat et differt absolutionem nostram." Fred.'s apology, *l.c.*, p. 210.
From pp. 215 and 217 it is clear that the Emperor was not prepared to
accept the Treaty of Constance, " cum sit promissum et firmatum per
principes imperii quod predictam pacem tanquam factam in evidens
prejudicium juris et honoris imperii non debeamus observare." P. 217.

[3] Mat. Par., iv, p. 337. *Cf.* p. 353. " Frethericus, superbiæ stimulis
exagitatus pœnitere cœpit quod se ecclesiæ . . . obligasset." See
the letter of Innocent (Apr. 30, 1244) to Henry, Landgrave of Thuringia.
" A quo (the peace) non post multos dies elegit resilire." Ap. Rod. ii,
p. 46, and his statement at the Council of Lyons : " postmodum
quod juraverat, non implevit." Ap. Mat. P., iv, 448. See also
Carbio, c. 10.

breach of the peace was due to Frederick, and not to the Pope. This same anti-papal historian, after re-affirming his assertion that Frederick broke the peace, adds that he began to lay " snares and hidden traps for the Pope which, however, were afterwards exposed ". Innocent, however, he continued, avoided " the fox-like meandrings " of the Emperor, nor did " he trust either Frederick or his counsellors, since he knew them all, and prepared for the future by knowledge of the past ".[1] Some of these " fox-like meandrings—vulpinos mæandros " we can ascertain from different sources. Considering that he was the party who had to offer satis-faction, Frederick should have at once begun to give up the captives and the Papal territory which he had seized. Instead of this, however, he simply " played with " the Templar and the others whom the Pope had sent to him at Acquapendente to receive the captured territories and prelates [2] ; and he endeavoured to secure the inaction of Innocent by proposing that one of his nieces should marry his son Conrad.[3] It was also discovered that he or his agents were fomenting disaffections in Rome against the Pope [4] ; and, though the Emperor stoutly denied the charge,[5] it was found that he had certainly revived an old scheme to obtain undue influence in the city. He had terrified Henry Frangipane, " the count of the Sacred Lateran Palace," and his son into making over to him their rights over half the Colosseum with

[1] *L.c.*, p. 353–4.

[2] Carbio, c. 10.

[3] *Ib.*, c. 11.

[4] *Cf.* letters (*c.* April) of " a certain cardinal " to the emperor Baldwin, and to Frederick himself, ap. H.-B., vi, p. 183–6. In the letter to Baldwin the cardinal points out the harm these intrigues are doing to the cause of peace to which the Pope was inclined in the interests of the Holy Land and the Empire of Constantinople. P. 184.

[5] Ep. *c.* April, ap. *ib.*, p. 186. These letters are not dated so that it is not quite certain that they refer to this period.

the Palace adjoining it which they held of the Church as a fief. This grant, as wholly illegal, Innocent promptly annulled.[1] Finally Frederick was also discovered to be trying to induce Peter, the Prefect of the City, to acknowledge him as his immediate superior instead of the Pope, just as his grandfather Barbarossa had done.[2] With these proofs of Frederick's insincerity in front of him, Innocent on April 20 informed the Landgrave of Thuringia that, " a few days after his oath, the Emperor had withdrawn from it," [3] and, as we may suppose, in disgust at Frederick's want of good faith, he allowed copies of the articles of peace to which the Emperor had proved false to be sold for six denarii apiece.[4]

The Pope makes new cardinals, May, 1244.

Still further to strengthen his position, Innocent determined to create a number of new cardinals, as the number of the Sacred College had now fallen to seven. Accordingly, on the eve of Trinity Sunday (May 28), he created in St. Peter's twelve new cardinals, three of whom were bishops, three priests, and six deacons.[5] Among them was master " John of Toledo " or (John Tolet), an Englishman by birth ; and the rest were " of distinguished family and character, from different parts of the world ".[6]

Frederick still feigns a desire for peace.

It did not, however, suit Frederick's policy that it

[1] *Cf.* Epp. of April 16 and 19, ap. Rod. ii, p. 43 f.

[2] Hence his anger with the Pope for thwarting his schemes, and his unfounded assertion that the Prefect had always received his dignity from the Emperor. " Recipiens prefectum . . . qui omni tempore imperii fuit et dignitatem ab imperio recepit." Ep. apol. H.-B., vi, p. 219. *Cf. supra*, vol. xi, p. 47. Again it cannot be said that it is quite certain that this reference to the Prefect has reference to the Prefect of Rome.

[3] Ep. ap. H.-B., vi, p. 189 f.

[4] Frederick accused the Pope of want of good faith in this matter ; but the text would seem to explain the situation. Ep. Apol., *l.c.*, pp. 218-19.

[5] Carbio, c. 12.

[6] Mat. Par., iv, 354, Vincent of Beauvais, *Spec. hist.*, xxx, c. 152.

should be realized by the world that he was making
no effort to get freed from his excommunication, and
that therefore Innocent would be justified in confirming
the sentence passed upon him by his predecessor. He
knew that, by German law,[1] the fact of a person remaining
for a length of time—a year and a day—under sentence
of excommunication meant a deprivation of dignity
for that person. He accordingly urged that " proximity
of bodies may help to bring about union of wills ",
and that consequently it was desirable that he should
have a conference with the Pope.[2] To this Innocent
at length agreed, and it was arranged that a meeting
should take place at Narni.[3] If, however, we are to
believe Carbio and others, the object of Frederick in
proposing an interview was really to get possession
of the Pope's person,[4] or at least so to get him in his power
as to hinder his communication with the outside world.
It was then, perhaps, the discovery of the Emperor's
treachery, or at least a strong suspicion of it, which
caused the Pope to decline to proceed to Narni, which
was too near Interamna (Terni) where Frederick was
staying, and to take up his quarters in the strong
city of Civita Castellana (June 7),[5] preparatory to

---

[1] Such at any rate was the declaration of the Saxon and Suabian
thirteenth century codes, concerning which Mr. E. Jenks, *Law and
Politics in the Middle Ages*, p. 48, London, 1898, writes that they " came
to be accepted in Germany as law, although men must have known them
to be the work of private jurists ". *Cf. supra*, vii, p. 104. It is likely
enough that Innocent was calling attention to this law when he stated
in his sentence of deprivation against Frederick at the Council of
Lyons (1245) that " a year and more " had now elapsed, and yet he
had not troubled to make satisfaction. " Cum anno et amplius jam
elapso, nec ad ipsius ecclesiæ gremium revocari potuerit."

[2] Ep. Apol., p. 214. *Cf.* other imperial letters ap. H.-B., vi, pp. 177
and 194.

[3] Ep. apol., p. 214.　　　　　　　　[4] Carbio, c. 12.

[5] As to the fact of his going to C. C., *cf.* Carbio ; Mat. Par., iv, 354,
and the ep. Apol., p. 214.

making an effort to get clear from Frederick's power altogether.[1]

Accordingly, whilst keeping up negotiations on the Lombard question [2] with the envoys [3] whom the Emperor sent to him, Innocent, convinced of Frederick's insincerity,[4] dispatched a Franciscan, one of his relatives, to the Podestà of Genoa and to his numerous kinsmen in that ity, cbidding them send to Civita Vecchia a number of galleys to escort him to their city.[5]

Word at length reached the Pope that the galleys which he had requested, and which, with several of his nephews on board, had sailed with the greatest secrecy, had reached Civita Vecchia. Accordingly on June 27, he left Civita Castellana, as though to celebrate the feast of SS. Peter and Paul in the Cathedral at Sutri which, like that of Civita Castellana, had, not long before, been beautifully decorated by the Cosmati, mosaic workers from Rome.[6] When Innocent arrived at Sutri, orders were given to make all the needful preparations for a papal Mass on the twenty-ninth.

[1] Carbio, c. 13.

[2] On his side Frederick writing to the King of France (ep. begin. of June) told him that he had written to ask the Pope to send him one of the cardinals as he had altogether new terms to propose which would bring peace. " Cui (the cardinal) intima cordis nostri intendimus reserare, que nondum in aures cujuspiam de nostri pectoris thalamo descenderunt . . . quod pacem indubitanter credimus proventuram."

[3] Peter della Vigna and Walter of Sora. The Emperor insisted on the impossible conditions that the Lombards " should dissolve their League and renounce the Peace of Constance ". Ep. Apol., p. 215. Cf. p. 216, where it is clearly stated that in all negotiations on the Lombard question there must be no question of the observance of the Peace of Constance : " Deducta expressim de compromisso pace Constancie."

[4] " Videns se illudi ab Imperatore verbis et promissionibus fraudulenter." Chron. Estense, 1244, ap. R. I. SS., xv, p. 310.

[5] Carbio, c. 13 ; Chron. Sic., ap. H.-B., i, pt. ii, p. 907 ; Ann. Genuen. ; Lib. vi, ap. R. I. SS., vi, p. 505.

[6] Cf. Frothingham, The Monuments of Christian Rome, pp. 132-3, 368-9.

These little ruses [1] were the more necessary that the Pope was unable to make armed resistance to Frederick who had blocked most of the roads, and was in possession of most of the papal territories. It is true that, in the March of Ancona, he had not yet got possession of Ancona itself, nor of Assisi, Narni, Rieti, and one or two more places in the Duchy of Spoleto, nor of Perugia, Orvieto, and Radicofani in the Patrimony, nor of " Mons Asula " in the Sabina. But, says Carbio, who gives us this information, these places were so beset by Frederick that they were not even able to help themselves let alone the Pope.[2]

At length, when night was bringing to a close the vigil of SS. Peter and Paul, there issued forth from one of the gates of Sutri, a small company of eight mounted men in the dress of the gentry of the period.[3] Of these one was the Pope, " having again became Sinibaldo," as Matthew Paris expresses it. The rest of the party was made up of William, the cardinal deacon of S. Eustachio, one of Innocent's nephews ; of " brother Nicholas Carbio, a priest, chaplain, and confessor to the Pope, of the Order of the Friars Minor, and afterwards bishop of Assisi ",[4] and Innocent's biographer ; of two more of the Pope's nephews ; of Godfrey " de Preseratis ", papal chaplain and afterwards bishop-elect of Bethlehem, and two of the Pope's chamberlains, a Templar and a Hospitaller. Riding hard, but making their way by devious paths over the hills, the august company, worn

[1] " Sciens quod est scriptum, quod ars deluditur arte," says the contemporary annalist of the house of Este. *Chron. Estense*, an. 1244, ap. *R. I. SS.*, xv, p. 110. *Cf.* Richer, *Gesta Senon.*, iv, c. 9, ap. *M. G. SS.*, xxv, p. 303.

[2] C. 13.

[3] " Papa et pater noster . . . accinctus gladio in habitu militari Sutrium exiverat," says Fred. in his apology, ap. H.-B., vi, p. 221.

[4] So Carbio, *l.c.*, describes himself. Godfrey is called " de Præfectis " in Eubel, *Hierarch. Cath. Med. Ævi*, p. 135.

out with fatigue, reached Civita Vecchia about "the ninth hour" on June 29.

This hurried flight was necessary as Frederick, if he had not heard of the arrival of the galleys, had got wind of the Pope's intended departure, and had at any rate sent some three hundred Tuscan knights to seize him or to prevent his flight on the very night on which he fled, "as Innocent was afterwards wont to declare."[1]

On the day after the Pope's flight, five of the cardinals, including the Englishman, John Tolet, followed him to Civita Vecchia, whilst seven others journeyed north to await him at Susa. Four others, in obedience to his orders, remained behind—Stephen, cardinal-priest of S. Maria in Trastevere, as the Pope's Vicar in Rome (in Urbe Vicarius) ; the energetic cardinal-deacon Rainer, as Legate in Tuscany, the Duchy of Spoleto, the March

---

[1] So says Mat. Par., iv, 354. I am not wont to attach the least weight to the words which Paris puts into the mouths of the Popes ; but in this instance he states what at least appears to be a fact. The assertion that Frederick endeavoured to seize Innocent on this occasion is borne out by the words of Innocent himself at the council of Lyons : "Timeo laqueos (of Frederick) quos vix evasi." (Mat. Par., iv, 437) ; by Carbio, c. 12 ; by the *Annals of Genoa*, ap. *R. I. SS.*, vi, 535. The Emperor " laboravit stringere eum, et ad carcerationem ejus milites C. C. mandavit apud Tuscanellam ; by Albert von Behaim, p. 66, ed. Höfler, p. 66, who says that from April 7 to June 29, Frederick worked to bring about a conference at Narni or Rieti in order to seize the Pope ; and by John " de Columpna " (b. 1298), *Hist.*, ap. *M. G. SS.*, xxiv, p. 283; and is supported by such phrases in connexion with the Pope's flight as " imperatoris timens insidias " of the *Annals of Waverley*, iii, *R. S.*; and " insidias multas et injurias perpessus " of Menko, *Chron.*, ap. *M. G. SS.*, xxiv, 537 ; " timore imp. Fred." of the *Annals of Parma*, ap. *ib.*, xviii, 670 ; " persecutionem imperatoris declinans " of the *Annals of Scheftlarn*, a contemporary source quite favourable to Frederick, ap. *ib.*, xvii, p. 342, and " Fredericus . . Papam . . . in Sutrio teneret obsessum ", of James of Voragine, *Chron. Januense*, ap. *R. I. SS.*, ix, pp. 13, 48. On the latter page, James tells us that he became a Dominican the very year that Innocent came to Genoa.

of Ancona and the Patrimony [1]; Riccardo Annibaldi, cardinal-deacon of St. Angelo, as Count of Campania and the Maritima ; and, seemingly as an adviser to them, Rinaldo Conti, cardinal-bishop of Ostia.[2]

On the evening of the day following his arrival at Civita Vecchia,[3] Innocent, who had found over twenty Genoese warships and transports awaiting him, went on board along with his suite, and, at early dawn, set sail for Genoa. The fleet encountered very bad weather, and the miseries of the voyage made such an impression on Carbio that he could not think of it years after " but with tears ".[4] The storm, however, was not the only thing that the fugitives had to fear. Its violence forced them to take refuge and pass the night in the harbour of the island of Capraria, which belonged to the Pisans. " On the morrow, however," writes Matthew Paris,[5] " when all had been absolved from their sins, and had heard the Mass of the Blessed Virgin, being in great dread of the Pisans, they spread all sail, and, making one hundred and twenty-four miles in a day, they reached an island belonging to the Genoese "— probably Gorgona. After an enforced rest here, and then, later, one of a few days in the picturesque bay of Porto Venere, the fleet made for Genoa, which it reached on July 6.[6]

The Pope sails for Genoa.

---

[1] One legate for four provinces shows how little territory there was left for him to rule over. *Cf.* Innocent's letter of July 8, to him, ap. H.-B., vi, 200.

[2] Carbio, c. 13.

[3] So says the Pope himself. Ep. of July, ap. H.-B., vi, 201.

[4] C. 14.

[5] *Chron.*, iv, pp. 355–6.

[6] Ep. Inn. of July 8, ap. H-B., vi, 201 ; Carbio, *l.c.* ; Mat. Par., *l.c.* ; and *Ann. Gen.* (here the work of an excellent author, Bartholomew the Scribe, writing between 1225–48), *l.c.* E. Ferrando has written *L'itinerario di P. Inn. IV. da Roma a Lione*, 1910, a book which I have not been able to procure.

Reception in
Genoa.
When the galleys carrying the Pope and the cardinals entered the grand harbour of the city, they were gaily bedecked with silk and cloth of gold, and, on his landing, he found the streets decorated in the same way. He was met " by the Archbishop, the military, the ladies, and all the people ", and was, with every demonstration of joy, escorted to the palace of the Archbishop.[1]

Illness of the
Pope, July–
Oct., 1244.
The anxieties and hardships of his flight nearly proved fatal to Innocent. He had been at death's door during the confinement that preceded the election of Celestine IV.,[2] and, soon after his landing in Genoa, he found himself in the same condition. Then, acting on the advice of his physicians, he went to the Cistercian abbey of St. Andrew of Sestri Ponente, a little way out of the city, in order that he might enjoy a larger air,[3] and there he remained three months.

It was in this monastery that Innocent exposed his plans to the Podestà and other eminent Genoese. " My children," said he, " it is my wish with the help of Jesus Christ to go to Lyons, and before my death to show all Christians, all princes, and all prelates the distress in which is now the Church of God, and the injustice under which she labours. If I cannot go there on horseback, I will be carried there." At once the Genoese declared their devotion to him, and offered at their own expense to convey him with a fleet to the Rhone. They endeavoured to dissuade him from going by land on account of the nobles who in their fortresses had no respect for any man. But the Pope, still suffering from the effects of his recent voyage, repeated his intention of proceeding by land, and then resigned himself to wait till his sickness would permit him to move.[4]

---

[1] Carbio, *l.c.*, and especially the *Annals of Genoa*, *l.c.*
[2] Carbio, c. 5.   [3] *Ann. G.*, *cf.* Carbio.
[4] *Ann. Genuen.*, ap. *M. G. SS.*, xviii, p. 215. Innocent's motives in going to Lyons are well brought out in the *Gesta Episcop. Virdun.*, ap. *ib.*, x, p. 524 f.

Meanwhile, when the facts connected with the Pope's flight reached Frederick, who in the course of the month of July had gone to Pisa, the rival of Genoa, we are told by Matthew Paris that " he gnashed his teeth like a satyr ", and "upbraided the guardians of his ports and cities for their carelessness and sloth in permitting his enemies to slip past them ".[1] He did not, however, at once openly proclaim that the negotiations for peace had broken down ; but, " in the hope of deceiving the Pope, sent to tell him that he was astonished at his departure, and that he wished to conform to his will." [2] In a letter to some of the cardinals, he even declared that he would agree to any form of peace of which they might approve, provided, he was careful to add, that " the dignity of the Empire was not diminished ".[3] He again employed the Count of Toulouse as his agent, who, however, did not go to Genoa but sent his envoys to Innocent from Savona. After the experience he had had of Frederick's promises, Innocent would not listen to the count, but resolved to go to Lyons, and to lay the whole case between the Emperor and himself before " the Princes and before the Prelates of the Church ".[4] Frederick now " declared himself the open enemy of the Pope ".[5] He ordered all the roads leading from Genoa to be most strictly watched, and proclaimed to the King of Hungary and to the whole Empire that " the unthought of, nay unthinkable, departure of the Pope " [6] had put

---

[1] L.c., p. 356.

[2] Ann. Gen., ib.

[3] Ep. of Aug., 1244, ap. H.-B., vi, p. 222.

[4] Ann. Gen., l.c. " Quibus (the envoys of the Count) quum nullam fidem daret d. Papa, eo quod tenuerat ipsum in verbis, et promissa non curaverat in adimplere, statuit ire Lugdunum, et ibi Principes et Prælatos Ecclesiæ convocare."

[5] Mat. Par., l.c.

[6] Frederick's words to the people of Mantua. Ep. of July 7, 1244, ap. H.-B., vi, 200.

an end to all hope of peace. He reminded the former
that his letters had already often made known to him
" with what reluctance, like a lamb led to the slaughter,
he had been dragged into the present war ",[1] of which
Gregory IX. was the cause, and of which " the wickedness
of persons or of the times " had prevented the close.
This letter was accompanied by the long apologetic
version of his relations with Innocent from his election
to his flight which he had addressed " to all his beloved
subjects and friends " and which we have already so
often cited.[2] In it Frederick declared that the cause of
the collapse of the peace negotiations was Innocent's
undue attachment to the cause of the rebellious
Lombards,[3] and not, of course, his own disregard of the
obligation of the Treaty of Constance, which, he said,
he had been advised that he ought not to observe, seeing
that " it had been drawn up in obvious prejudice of the
rights and honour of the Empire ".[4]

[1] Ep. of July, ap. *ib.*, p. 202 ff. " Quantum autem et qualiter ad
presentis guerre discrimen tanquam ad occisionem ovis et agnus ad
victimam tracti sumus inviti, etc." Anyone familiar with the public
utterances concerning the present awful war (Feb., 1915) of the Hohen-
zollern William II., will see how closely they resemble those of the
Hohenstaufen Frederick II., and what little truth there is in either
of them.

[2] Ap. *ib.*, pp. 204–31. This letter is a good example of what Albert
von Behaim called the " exquisita commentorum figmenta " with which
" he seduced nearly the whole world ". P. 64, ed. Höfler.

[3] " Alias etiam in favorem rebellium Lombardorum voluntatem
suam valde detexit, causam ipsorum manifeste defendens." *Ib.*, p. 219.

[4] *Ib.*, p. 217. Even after the Pope's flight, during the desultory peace
negotiations, which were then carried on, Frederick still refused to be
bound by the " Peace of Constance ". *Cf.* ep. Inn., Apr. 30, 1245,
ap. Rod., ii, 78. " Excepitque pacem Constantie, quam semper se asserit
excepisse." As history certainly does at times repeat itself, we may
say, in the German diplomatic language of to-day, that the " Peace of
Constance ", guaranteeing the rights of the Lombards, was, like the
" Treaty of London " which guaranteed those of the Belgians, " a scrap
of paper " which was found to be disadvantageous to the interests of
the German Empire in the thirteenth century.

In his endeavour to show that the blame for the failure of the peace negotiations rested on Innocent, he enumerated a number of reasonable compromises on the Lombard question which he had offered to him, but which, because he would not submit its settlement to him absolutely, were rejected one after the other. For instance, he had offered, he said, to submit the said question to papal arbitration, provided that the basis of its settlement was, not the Peace of Constance, but the terms which the Lombards had themselves offered at the time of their defeat at Cortenuova, and, moreover, the resignation by the Pope of his position as patron of the League.[1] He complained that the Pope put off drawing up the list of obvious injuries for which he required compensation from him ; and that he did not consult the cardinals. The Emperor further put forth as a grievance that his rights and dues [2] in the March of Ancona, the Duchy of Spoleto, and the other territory held by the Church had never been defined ; and, reverting again to the Lombard difficulty, stated that Innocent had told the envoys of the French King that, even if he absolved him, he would still help the Lombards against him, were they not granted an unconditional peace (pacem plenariam).[3] Finally, he professed to be utterly astonished at the Pope's flight in the very midst of negotiations which might have led to peace, and he expressed his belief that he was about to go possibly beyond the Alps, " in order, if he could, to injure us and the Empire." [4] The apology closed with the state-

---

[1] P. 217. " Ita tamen quod prius omnino rumpatur promissio protectio et quelibet obligatio habita inter eum et Ecclesiam ex una parte, et Lombardos ex altera, quia non deceret nobis compromittere de negotiis imperii . . . in protectorem rebellium Lombardorum."

[2] " Videlicet de cabalcata et parlamento et mercato et procuratione que nos tanquam advocati, patroni et defensores Ecclesie habere debemus." P. 218.

[3] P. 219.   [4] P. 221.

ment that it was clearly impossible for him to submit his
great cause to the arbitration of so prejudiced a judge
as the Pope.

Meanwhile, seemingly a short time before the issue of
this elaborate defence of the imperial action, which
Innocent's ill-health may have afterwards prevented
him from answering, the Pope made a brief statement
of his position to the people of Brescia. He told them
that many had blamed the spirit of mildness in which
he had hitherto defended the interests of the Church.
He had, however, he continued, found that his clemency
had done more harm than good ; and, at length, inasmuch
as he had not been allowed to have free communication
with those devoted to the Church, he was compelled
to commit himself blindly to the guidance of Providence
(dispositioni divinæ), rather than to continue to allow
himself to be cribbed, cabined, and confined to the loss
of ecclesiastical freedom. Forced then " by the malice
of the times ", he had fled to Genoa, and was now at
last in a position wherein he could attend to what concerned " the exaltation of the faith, the good estate of
the Church and the tranquillity of the whole of
Christendom ".[1]

---

[1] Ep. of July, ap. H.-B., vi, 201 f. Mr. A. L. Smith in his *Church and
State in the Middle Ages*, when treating of the character of Innocent IV.,
says that " from this latter (i.e. lying) he did not shrink on occasion,
as in the peace negotiations of 1244 " (p. 235). He may be correct in
his contention, but he gives no reference, and I can only say that
I have not been able to detect the lie, unless indeed, Mr. Smith would
define the language of diplomacy as a display of lying as a fine art.
I certainly do not consider the mere assertion of Frederick sufficient
to prove that Innocent " aliud in corde gereret quam voce proferret".
See his *Apology*, ap. *ib.*, p. 212. Some of the best modern authors agree
that Innocent was forced to fly from Frederick. The editor of Innocent's
Register, E. Berger. (*Reg.*, vol. ii, pp. i and ii) notes that it was with
difficulty that the Holy See maintained against the Empire a struggle
of which no one could foresee the issue, and that Innocent " was forced
to fly from Italy to escape Frederick II." ; Stevenson, *Rob. Grosseteste,*

For some time, however, Innocent was not in a position to do much for any of these great ends ; for, as we have seen, serious illness confined him for three months in the monastery of St. Andrew.   At the end of that period, feeling somewhat better, he gave his blessing to the Podestà and people of Genoa, and went to Varazze (Voragine), a coast town which gave its name to the author of the *Golden Legend* (Oct. 5).   Thence, followed by the Podestà and nobles of Genoa, he had himself conveyed in a litter, with but a small personal suite, to Stella.   He was escorted to this stronghold among the mountains by Manfred, marquis of Carretto, with a strong force, " on account of the snares set for him by his enemies." [1]   But he had evidently not been in a fit state to move.   He had a serious relapse, and for days his life was despaired of.   He recovered, however, and, as soon as he was fit to move, he resolved to proceed without delay to Lyons,[2] to which city he had, with a view to carrying out the intention of Gregory IX., determined to summon the Bishops and Princes of the world to judge between himself and Frederick.   His great namesake (Innocent III.) had seen his treatment of Otho IV. justified by the approval of Christendom, and, conscious of the justice of his cause, he was desirous of submitting it to the same august tribunal.

Accordingly, on October 24, he quitted the mountain fortress of Stella, and made his way in a litter or carriage to Carcare.   Thence after a few days rest, he rode to Cortemiglia in a sort of pannier (in quadam cabia lignea) on a mule.   So weak was he, that he was again compelled

also says, p. 245, that he fled " in order to procure his independence " ; Balzani, *The Popes and the Hohenstauffen*, p. 207, " He (Frederick) did certainly aim at obtaining the absolution without keeping the conditions."

[1] Carbio, c. 15.

[2] *Ann. Genuen.*, *l.c.*, p. 506.

to rest, but managed to reach S. Stefano in the valley
of the Belbo on November 2. Here he was met by a
large body of troops sent by the Marquis of Montferrat,
who escorted him to S. Ambrogio, a place in the Val
di Susa belonging to the great abbey of Chiusa, where
too had halted Calixtus II. in his entrance into Italy,
and the Emperor Barbarossa in his flight from Italy in
1168. Thence he boldly made his way to Asti, a city
then under the sway of Frederick. On his arrival
(Nov. 6), the officials shut the gates in his face, and he
retired to the abbey of the Apostles. But that an insult
should be offered to the Pope was not to the mind of
the people at large. They rose against the authorities,
and flocked to Innocent to beg his forgiveness for the
outrage which had been offered to him. From Asti the
suffering Pontiff journeyed to Susa (Nov. 12). Here he
found the six (seven?) cardinals who in their overland
route had managed to evade the imperial guards who were
watching the roads between Sutri and the north. Hither,
too, eluding Frederick's guards, came from France Odo,
cardinal-bishop of Tusculum, and Hugo, cardinal-priest
of St. Sabina, who, so Carbio adds, were on this occasion
given "their cardinalitial rings".[1] From Susa began
the ascent of Mont Cenis,[2] and we read without wonder,
as the winter snows had set in among the Alps on
November 1, that the Pope had many hardships to
endure during the crossing of the pass, which mounts
up to nearly seven thousand feet. Still under the
protection of Thomas II., the lord of Piedmont, and the

---

[1] It is from Carbio, c. 15, that we get all these particulars of Innocent's
flight to Lyons. "Qui in eo castro Segusie sui cardinalatus anulos
receperunt." Nicholas is not at all clear as to the numbers of the
cardinals in his narrative of these events. Odo de Castro Radulfi
(otherwise Eudes of Châteauroux) and Hugo de S. Caro (or St.-Cher)
were both destined to play an important part in the history of their
times. Cf. Mat. Par., iv, 393.

[2] Chron. Reg. Colon., contin. v, pp. 285-6, Mat. Par., iv, 393-5.

ancestor of the present House of Savoy, and especially
under that of Philip, Thomas's brother, Innocent
proceeded from the mountain by La Chambre and
Chambéry to the celebrated monastery of Hautecombe
on the pretty Lac du Bourget. Thence, by boat down
the rapid Rhone, the Pope and his party were conveyed to Lyons in three days.[1] So " all the papal powers
were transferred " [2] to that ancient city, " the first see
of the Gauls " (Dec. 2, 1244),[3] which gave the exhausted
but undaunted Pontiff a most enthusiastic welcome.[4]

---

[1] *Ib. Cf. Ann. S. Rudbert*, ap. *M. G. SS.*, ix, p. 788; Mat. Par., *Addit.*,
vi, p. 444 ; and the *Annals of Dunstable*, iii, 166, which add that
the Pope's safe arrival in Lyons was largely due to the help of *Baldwin*
(they should have said Philip) of Savoy, bishop-elect of Lyons, and
brother of Thomas of Savoy. Innocent could not but be grateful to
the House of Savoy for the assistance given to him by it at this the
most critical moment of his life. But, with regard to Philip, the *Annals*
immediately add : "Quem statim cassavit." Thus freed from the clerical
state (he had not taken major orders) Philip became, by marriage,
Count of Franche Comté, and later of Savoy itself.

[2] " Et sic omnia jura papalia Lugdunum sunt translata." Menko,
ap. *M. G. SS.*, xxiii, p. 537. *Cf. Ann. Parmenses major.*, ap. *M. G. SS.*,
xviii, p. 670.

[3] Vincent of Beauvais, *Spec. Hist.*, xxxi, 1. It would not be Matthew
Paris if he did not introduce money into Innocent's flight. Hence we
find him insinuating (" à tort sans doute ", Berger, *Reg. d'Inn.*, ii,
p. xvii) that Innocent's object in crossing the Alps was to get Cisalpine
money. *Chron.*, iv, pp. 354 and 394.

[4] Carbio, c. 15 ; ep. Inn., Feb. 14, 1257.

CHAPTER II.

INNOCENT AT LYONS (1244–51), PART I (1244–5)
THE THIRTEENTH ECUMENICAL COUNCIL (1245).
DEPOSITION OF FREDERICK.

Why Innocent chose Lyons. THE primary reason why Innocent elected to retire to Lyons was its independence.[1] Nominally, indeed, it was subject to the Empire ; but, in practice, it was more independent than Milan. It was to all intents and purposes a free city under its Archbishop. It was moreover on the borders of France, so that the Pope could, in an emergency, either procure help from St. Louis, who was determined never to suffer him to be subjected to physical force or fly into his dominions. Lyons, too, could easily be visited by the bishops of France, England, and Spain, who were independent of Frederick ; and, what was of great importance, the wealth of those countries, of which the Pope had naturally great need, could easily be conveyed thither.

He was sure of the good-will of Louis. Of the good dispositions of Louis towards him, Innocent had again recently been assured. Understanding that it was the intention of the King to be present at the General-Chapter of the Cistercians (Sept., 1244), the

---

[1] The hostility of Pisa to Genoa, and the power of Frederick rendered the latter city unsafe for Innocent. Mat. Par., iv, 356. *Cf.* ep. of Inn., Feb. 13, 1251, where he speaks of Lyons : " Civitatem . . . titulo nobilitatis insignem . . . et situ loci communem et habilem universis." Ap. Raynald, *Annal.*, 1251, n. 16.

Pope had written to the brethren to ask them to beg Louis, in accordance with the ancient traditions of his country, to help the supreme Pontiff against the attacks of Frederick, and, if need be, receive him into his kingdom, as in times past his ancestors had received Alexander III. and St. Thomas Becket. Accordingly, when accompanied by his mother, Blanche [1] of Castile, and by many of the great nobles of his kingdom, Louis entered the chapter-house of Citeaux, some five hundred abbots on bended knees implored him to succour the Pope. Bending in turn the knee to them, Louis declared that, as far as honour allowed, he would repel from the Church the injuries offered to it by Frederick, and, if his nobles were agreeable, would receive the Pope himself if he were compelled to go into exile.[2]

We have here an indication of the policy which St. Louis pursued in all his relations with the Pope and the Empire. The position he took up towards the Papacy was that of a " benevolent neutral ".[3] He did not wish to offend Frederick, because he did not wish to lose such influence in the cause of peace as he possessed ; and he knew that the interests of the Crusades which he had profoundly at heart, were bound up with the existence of peaceful relations between the Papacy and the Empire. Still, though he was not prepared

The policy of Louis towards the Papacy.

[1] She had obtained a special dispensation to enter the monasteries of the Cistercians.

[2] Mat. Par., *Chron.*, iv, 392. He adds that Frederick had sent special envoys there to prevent the demands of the Pope from having any effect.

[3] The saint was " plein de déférence et de dévouement envers le Saint-Siège ". Berger, *Reg. d'Inn.*, ii, p. v. Hence Innocent declared to Louis that the Holy See had always found him ready to sustain it in its needs, and had always regarded him as the chief defender of the faith, and of the Church's liberty. Ep. of Dec. 12, 1243, ap. *ib.*, p. xii. Merely as the editor of Innocent's Register alone, the authority of Berger is necessarily great.

to suffer the Pope to encroach upon his own rights as a temporal sovereign, he was certainly less prepared to allow the Emperor to crush the Church with which were all his sympathies; and, as we shall see, he showed Frederick that he was prepared to fight for the liberty of the Pope even to death.

Lyons was Innocent's voluntary selection.

Were we to trust Matthew Paris, we should have to believe that Innocent elected to take up his abode at Lyons because he was refused admittance into France, Aragon, and England, though, through some cardinals, he had expressed a special wish to see "the delights of Westminster and the riches of London".[1] But it has been pointed out that neither Spain nor England would have been a suitable centre from which to carry on a struggle against Frederick, and that the story of this refusal rests solely on the authority of one who was very hostile to Innocent. Resting, then, on the words of the Pope himself, it seems just to conclude that Lyons was his deliberate and free choice.[2]

Innocent's home in Lyons.

Innocent took up his abode in the great fortified monastery of St. Just, in which, some sixty years later, Clement V. was proclaimed Pope. The monastery was protected by the Rhone and the Saône and by the escarpments of Pierre Seize, and proved its strength by holding out against the attacks of the citizens of Lyons some twenty-five years later. We may presume that

[1] *Chron. maj.*, iv, 410; *cf.* p. 422. The Pope expressed his wish (d. Papa procurante), we are told, through some money-loving cardinals: "quidam cardinalium qui solius erant amatores pecuniæ." In that edition of the *Chronicle* of Mat. Par. which is assigned to *Matthew of Westminster*, Innocent is said to have asked permission to fix his see at Rheims, then without a bishop.

[2] " Mathieu de Paris, si hostile à la cour de Rome, est seul à rapporter ce fait (viz., the choice of Spain; but it is equally true of France and England). . . . La nouvelle capitale qu'il se choisit (Lyons), probablement de son plein gré, etait aussi sure et bien autrement commode." Berger, *l.c.*, p. xx.

the various pontifical bureaux were grouped in buildings around the monastery. At any rate we read of the burning of a building in which was the Pope's wardrobe.[1]

Despite occasional brawls between individual servants of the Pope and individual citizens,[2] the stay of Innocent at Lyons brought a considerable increase of prosperity to it. A great improvement in the city's trade was caused by the influx of people who came to visit the Pope. He himself, on the other hand, advanced the building of the cathedral and of the bridge over the Rhone which had to replace the one which in 1190 gave way under the march of the crusading hosts of Philip Augustus and Richard Cœur-de-Lion. He gave an indulgence to all who contributed money for the cathedral,[3] and not only raised money for the bridge, but took under his special protection the Friars-pontiff who were building it.[4] "The bridge-maker (pontifex) of souls, constructed a bridge of stones," says a line of the inscription which, dedicated to him, was placed in

Innocent a
benefactor of
Lyons.

---

[1] Mat. Par., *Hist. Anglorum*, ii, p. 501, *R. S.*, and *Chron.*, iv, 431 and 417. In the latter place, Paris, after his wont, insinuates that the wardrobe was set on fire purposely "in order that the Pope might have a pretext for extorting money from the prelates who were coming to the council" of Lyons. I am weary of recording Paris' enumeration of the deeds which Innocent did for money. If the reader assumes in future that Paris invariably states that greed of money was the motive power of Innocent's acts, he will nearly always be right. It should, however, here be noticed that, in his *Hist. A.*, Paris attributes the disaster to the carelessness of the papal servants, and adds that, to excuse themselves, they said that the fire had been caused by emissaries of the Emperor, who wished to burn the Pope. *Cf.* T. Sprott, *Chron.*, p. 72, ed. Hearne.

[2] Mat. Par., iv, 418.

[3] Ep. (Apr. 27, 1247) to all the faithful. He consecrated the high altar himself. Potthast, n. 12496. *Cf. Reg.*, i, n. 2569. He endeavoured to procure help for the rebuilding (opere sumptuoso) of the cathedral of Osnabrück. *Cf.* ep., of Nov. 13, 1254.

[4] See a bull of Apr. 27, 1247, ap. *Reg.*, i, p. 389, n. 2607 : "Fratribus apud pontem Rodani Lugduni constitutis."

the tower at the east end of the bridge.[1] Moreover, says
Carbio, " that all might freely rejoice in the general
plentitude, he founded a school (studium generale) in
connexion with the pontifical curia, for the study of
theology and of canon and civil law. It was destined
for the instruction of the ignorant, and for the advancement of the learning of the wise." [2]

Not content with all this, Innocent gave large alms to
the poor and sick of the city,[3] and, in the last year of his
stay at Lyons, took its people under his special protection,
" for never could the Apostolic See forget with what
veneration their city had received him, and with what
earnestness it had striven to honour him." [4]

The hard
work of the
Pope.

Having at length found rest in a city where order
was kept by one of the energetic princes of the house
of Savoy, Philip, bishop-elect of Lyons, " the guardian
of ecclesiastical peace," [5] Innocent was able to devote

---

[1] We give the whole inscription from Berger, p. lxiv :—
    " Ave Maria, gratia plena, Dominis tecum.
    Virtutum Capa, Vitiorum framea, Papa
    Progenie magnus, ferus ut Leo, mitis ut Agnus,
    Innocuus vere dictus, de nolle nocere.
    Posset ut hic fieri Pons, sumptus fecit haberi,
    Pontem Petrarum construxit Pons animarum
    Ut Plebis nemo partem portaret utramque.
    Tanto Pontifici quisquis benedixerit isti,
    Aesque sibi carum dabit ut pons crescat aquarum,
    Integer annus ei, quadragenaque sit Jubilæi.
    Summi Pontificis opus est Pons nobilis iste.
    Istius artificis tibi grata sit actio, Christe,
    Quando nomen ei privatio dat nocumenti,
    Qui pro laude Dei facit haec manifesta videri."

[2] Carbio, c. 16.   [3] *Ib.*, c. 29.

[4] Ep. Feb. 14, 1251, ap. Potthast, n. 14188. *Cf.* 14186-7.

[5] So he is called by Matthew Paris, iv, 418. Philip was never in
major Orders. He was a most loyal protector of the Pope during his
journey to Lyons from Genoa, during his stay in Lyons, and during his
return to Italy. According to the assertion of his steward he on one
occasion spent a thousand pounds over the expenses of guarding the
Pope. Mat. Par., *Addit.*, vi, p. 444. *Cf. ib.*, iv, 426.

himself to clearing off the arrears of work which had
accumulated since the death of Gregory IX., and to the
needs of those who " from all parts of the world " flocked
to Lyons " as to another Rome ". According to his
biographer, the Pope spent his time " in raising the
oppressed and humiliating the oppressor ", settling,
" by his industrious wisdom," in a remarkably short
space of time, cases which, from various causes, had been
dragging on for a lengthy period.[1] All this time, too,
as we shall see later in some detail, he was engaged in
sending envoys and missionaries " with solemn letters "
to bring men back to the unity of the See of Rome,
or to convert them from paganism.[2]

Meanwhile, the differences between him and the
Emperor were drawing to a head. When he found that
the Pope could not be diverted from his resolve to place
himself out of reach of the imperial power, Frederick
immediately threw off the mask. His first effort was to
frighten the Pope's friends. Through his agent Walter
of Ocra, he explained to a council in London that while
he was ready to obey the Church, the Pope insisted that,
before he was absolved from excommunication, he
should hand over to him certain cities the ownership
of which was doubtful, and should release certain traitors.
The English were then urged not to send money to his
rival, and he promised that, if they would conform to
his wishes, he would by force free them from the tax
which Innocent III. had imposed upon them. But, if
they would not, he threatened to seize any money which
they might send to the Pope, and to wreak vengeance
on any Englishmen whom he found in his dominions.[3]

Frederick still treats of peace.

---

[1] " Utpote discretione preditus, mente pius, scientia præclarus et
sapientie plenitudinis titulo decoratus." Carbio, c. 16.

[2] *Ib.*, c. 17.

[3] Mt. Par., iv, 371 f. " Addidit d. Imperator, cum quadam etiam
comminatione adjuncta, quod omnia transmissa in auxilium d. Papæ

Still further to convince the Pope that he was resolved
to go to all extremities against him, he gave his daughter
in marriage to Vatatzes, the emperor of Nicæa, " a man,"
says Matthew Paris, " hateful and disobedient to the
Roman Church and hence a schismatic." [1]

But with the close of the year (1244), Frederick again
found cause to speak of peace. He was most anxious
that the merits of his quarrel with the Pope should not
be laid before the impartial tribunal of Christendom.
Accordingly he heard with anxiety that Innocent had,
on the feast of St. John the Evangelist after Christmas,
when preaching to the people at the cathedral of Lyons,
publicly announced that a General Council was to be held
on June 24, 1245. On the same occasion the Pope had
solemnly cited Frederick himself to appear before it in
person or by proxy, in order that he might state his case,
and hear its verdict. He had added that the Emperor's
malicious conduct did not permit of any other mode of
citing him. [2]

A few days later (Jan. 3), he had informed the archbishop of Sens and the King of France that he had
decided to call together " the Kings of the earth, the
prelates of the Churches, and the other Princes of the
world " to consider, among other things, the relations
between the Papacy and the Empire (inter ecclesiam
et principem). He had also begged them to be sure to

---

fuerint addita imperiali thesauro." On the date of this letter, of
which we only possess the abstract given us by Mat. Paris, see Berger,
Reg. d'Inn., ii, p. xvi ff. He and others think, rightly as we believe, that
this letter was written before Innocent left Italy.

[1] *Ib.*, p. 357. *Cf.* pp. 299–357.

[2] Carbio, c. 18. " Cum, ejusdem malitia faciente, non posset ad
ipsum alia citatio pervenire." Later on he pointed out that this mode
of citation, as it was public, and certainly brought to the Emperor's
notice (et cum alias ad ipsum pervenire tute non posset), was legitimate.
Ep. ap. Albert von Behaim, p. 89. *Cf.* the next note.

be present in person, and had informed them that he had already in a sermon cited the Emperor to appear.[1]

Perturbed by these unmistakable evidences of the Pope's intention to lay the history of their quarrel before the world, Frederick made use of the services of Albert Rizzato,[2] patriarch of Antioch, whom " he had long regarded as one of his principal friends " [3] to reopen negotiations for peace with the one " whom divine Providence had made father of the world ".[4] In his reply which he addressed to the Patriarch of Antioch, Innocent said that he was willing to accept the terms previously agreed to by Frederick, if he released the partisans of the Church, and restored its property before the assembling of the Council.   If not, the whole question would have to be left to its decision.[5]

But as the Emperor, who had meanwhile begun his march to Lombardy with a great army and a large amount of treasure conveyed by camels and dromedaries, showed no readiness to restore anything,[6] and even instituted fresh proceedings against certain relatives of Innocent,[7] the Pope renewed the excommunication already issued against him by Gregory IX.[8] He also made it plain that the dispute would have to go before the Council. Frederick, accordingly, at once sent

Peace negotiations again broken off.

---

[1] Epp. ap. Rod., ii, 56 ff. As an evidence of his care for others he admonishes the archbishop not to be a burden to his Church by coming to the council with too large a suite. *Cf.* his letters to the four cardinals who remained in Italy. He wants them to come to him in good time before the Council, or at least by the fixed date (June 24). Epp. of Jan. 31, ap. *ib.*, p. 63 f.

[2] Carbio, c. 18.

[3] See Fred's. letter to the Pope, March, 1245, ap. H.-B., vi, 266.

[4] *Ib.*

[5] Ep. *c.* April, ap. *ib.*, p. 271 ff.

[6] " Cum nollet satisfacere de offensis." Carbio, c. 18.

[7] According at least to Mat. Par., iv, 406.

[8] Apr. 13, 1245. *Ib., Annal. Wormat.*, an. 1245 ; and *Annal. Placent. Gibel.*

plenipotentaries to Lyons to appeal from " the unjust procedure " of Innocent to God, to a future Pope, to a General Council, to the Princes of Germany, and generally to all Kings, Princes, and Christian peoples.[1]

Diet at
Verona, June,
1245.
Moreover, with a view to counteract as far as might be what he felt would be the adverse influence of the coming General Council, Frederick held at Verona the Diet of the Empire of which he had spoken to his son Conrad in the April of 1244.[2] It was attended by Conrad and a number of German nobles, and by " Ezzelino da Romano and many other nobles and powerful men (from Lombardy) who favoured the cause of the Emperor ". The Diet lasted several weeks, but is said to have led to nothing.[3]

Innocent is
urged to
depose
Frederick.
It was now clear that there was nothing for it but a fight to the finish, and to this the Pope had long been urged. Whilst he was at Genoa, many of the Lombards had come to him and begged him not merely to convoke a general council, but to depose the Emperor.[4] Moreover, when he reached Lyons, long letters came to him from Italy enlarging on the Emperor's crimes, and conjuring him not to make peace with Frederick at any price since his crimes were worse than any punishment could be.[5] He had been guilty

---

[1] Ep. *c.* June to the Cardinals, ap. H.-B., vi, 275 ff.

[2] Ep. ap. H.-B., vi, p. 177.

[3] " Nec videbatur hæc tanta imperatoris cura certum aliquid stabilire." Rolandinus Patav., *Chron.,* v, c. 13, ap. *R. I. SS.,* t. viii, pt. i, p. 80 new ed. One reason assigned by Rolandinus for the failure of the Diet was the distrust felt by Ezzelino for the Emperor. *Cf.* Alb. v. B., p. 68, who says that Frederick wished this Diet to be regarded as a sort of council, " ut suis conciliabulis dissolvat, si poterit, concilium ecclesiasticum sacrosanctum."

[4] " Lombardi . . . multos ambaxatores ad d. papam direxerunt postulantes ut imperatorem deponeret." *Chron. de rebus* or *Ann. Placent. Ghib.,* p. 193. *Cf.* Mat. Par., iv, 394.

[5] Epp. of June, 1245, ap. H.-B., vi, 277 ff. and 285 ff., or ap. Höfler, Albert von B., 61 ff. and 73 ff. Frederick is called " eversor ecclesiastici

of high treason against his overlord over and over again, and so, *ipso facto*, had deprived himself of all right to the Empire or the Kingdom of Sicily. It devolved upon the Princes to choose a new Emperor[1]; for it was impossible to treat with the present one as he did not regard any promise as binding.[2]

From Germany itself also came the same request. Before Easter, the archbishops of Mainz and Cologne appeared before the Pope, and, after denouncing Frederick in strong terms, assured Innocent that, if he would depose the Emperor, they would name a King favourable to the Church.[3]

All these representations made the greater impression on Innocent seeing that they coincided with his own view of the situation. At the very close of the month of January, he signed the encyclical summoning the prelates to the Council. In it he set forth that the Church had been established in " order that, through it, justice might reign, and in order that the whirlwind of war having been lulled, peace and quiet might descend upon the world ". Now that the Church is in difficulties, they must come to its help, so that it may once more be held in honour ; that relief may be sent to the Holy

The Pope calls a general Council, 1245.

dogmatis atque cultus . . . crudelitatis magister . . . terræ malleus universæ ". P. 61. The writer insists quite unanswerably on Frederick's breach of faith towards the Popes considered as his temporal overlords for the kingdom of Sicily. " Ligium solvens . . . d. Gregorii . . . sui domini temporalis." P. 62. " Verumtamen isto modo (his final treatment of Gregory IX.) quam aliis hic scelestus quantum crimen læsæ majestatis incurrit," etc. P. 63. " Cum quater et ultra crimen læsæ majestatis commiserit." P. 71. *Cf.* p. 77.

[1] *Ib.*, p. 71.

[2] " Quibuslibet cautionibus artari poterit quin agat post concilium pejora prioribus, cum apud ipsum omnia juramenta sint vacua, promissiones frivolæ." *Ib.*, p. 71 f. *Cf.* p. 78.

[3] *Ann. Wormat.*, ap. *M. G. SS.*, xvii, p. 49. After their interview with Innocent we are told (*ib.*) that the archbishops returned to Germany, to work against Frederick, and to find a suitable person as a candidate for the imperial throne.

Land, to the Latin Empire of Constantinople, and to the countries oppressed by the Tartars ; and that the dispute between the Church and the Emperor may be considered. The prelates were to appear in his presence on the Festival of St. John the Baptist (June 24).[1]

The bishops and magnates at Lyons. By the assigned date, there had assembled at Lyons " venerable prelates from almost the whole extent of Christendom, or their suitable proxies ", as well as the representatives of the Kings of France, England, and Spain and of many other princes and states.[2] Hungary, however, which had been cruelly devastated by the Tartars, did not send any deputies ; and, owing to the power of the Emperor, to the fact that some of them were at his Diet in Verona, and to the struggle against him which had already begun in Germany, only a few prelates came from the Empire or the Kingdom of Sicily.[3] But though, on account of the great peril in which it was, no deputies had been summoned from the Holy Land, it chanced that Waleran, bishop of Beyrout, " the general envoy of the whole of Syria, and the sindic of all the Christians of the Holy Land," made his way to Lyons, bringing a lamentable account of the ruin of the Holy Land.[4]

---

[1] Ep. Jan. 30, ap. Mat. Par., iv, 410 ; *Chron. de rebus*, p. 194 f. *Cf.* Epp. of Jan. 31, ap. Rod., ii, pp. 56, 63.

[2] Mat. Par., iv, 430 f., and Carbio, c. 19. A document (ap. H.-B., vi, 317, is extant showing the signatures of bishops from France, England, Ireland, and Scotland, Italy, Spain, Portugal, Bohemia, Sicily, and the Empire (Liège).

[3] *Cf.* Alb. Stadt, *Chron.*, ap. *M. G. SS.*, xvi, 369, and Mat. Par., *l.c.*, p. 431.

[4] Mat. Par., *l.c.*, p. 431. The same author tells us that " a great number of prelates who did not attend gave, through their agents, sufficient and lawful reasons for their absence". P. 430. *Cf.* p. 413 ff., where a letter of Innocent (May 20) to King Henry III. is cited in which, in accordance with his requests, the Pope excuses a number of English prelates from attendance. He refuses, however, to except the Archbishop of York, for " as he is a distinguished member of the Church of God, we consider his presence necessary to the Council".

When, says Matthew Paris, one of the important authorities for the proceedings of this council,[1] " the Pope saw that a great many of the prelates, but not all of them," had arrived in Lyons, he gathered them together for a preliminary meeting in the refectory of the monastery of St. Just in which he had taken up his abode.[2] " There were present, besides the cardinals, two patriarchs, the patriarch of Constantinople,[3] wrongly said to have been also patriarch of Antioch, and the patriarch of Aquileia,[4] who was also patriarch of Venice ; the emperor of Constantinople, the count of Toulouse, and, as proxies from England, Earl Bigod

---

[1] Among other authorities for it, not yet noticed, we may mention the anonymous *Brevis notitia eorum quæ in primo concilio Lugdunensi generali gesta sunt.* It is found in Mansi, *Council,* t. xxiii, p. 610 ff., and in the other principal editions of the *Councils.* It is also embodied in the *Annales Cesenates,* ap. *R. I. SS.,* xiv, p. 1098. An anonymous imperialist wrote a satirical account of this council in verse, representing the members of the Council as different kinds of birds, and its head, the Pope, as a peacock (pavo). This satire, of little historical value, its author entitled *Pavo.* Its ascription to Jordan of Osnabrück does not appear to have any foundation. It was first printed by Karajan in 1851. Comparatively recently Mr. W. E. Lunt (ap. *Eng. Hist. Rev.,* 1918, p. 72 ff.) has called attention to another source for the story of this Council, " written probably not more than thirty-five years after 1245." Printed in 1844 by Sir H. Cole (*Docs. illustrative of English History,* p. 351 ff.), the document is important because " wherever (it) . . . throws light on the divergencies between Matthew Paris and the *Brevis Nota,* it is the *former which suffers from the illumination.* The reasons for the belief that Matthew's account must be used with great caution are increased ", p. 78. These words of Mr. Lunt go to support the general assertion of Döllinger, *Hist. of the Church,* iv, p. 63 n., that Matthew's narration " where it is not supported by contemporary writers or by documents, merits little or no belief ".

[2] *Chron.,* iv, 431.

[3] Nicholas of Piacenza, formerly bishop of Spoleto. As Albert Rizzato, patriarch of Antioch, was still alive for some time after this, the statement that Nicholas was also patriarch of Antioch is another of the mistakes of Mat. Par. *Cf.* the document of July 13, ap. H.-B., vi, p. 317, and the *Brevis notitia, l.c.*

[4] Berthold of Meran.

and some of his fellow nobles, and a hundred and forty archbishops and bishops." [1] After the Patriarch of Constantinople had called attention to the danger of extinction which, through the steady advance of the Greeks, the Latin Empire of Romania was in, and after it had been decided to leave aside for the moment the question of the canonization of St. Edmund, that of the relation between the Empire and the Papacy came up. Frederick's cause was ably upheld by Thaddeus of Sessa, an eloquent jurisconsult. He assured the assembled Fathers that peace was the great desire of his master. If that were granted, Frederick would bring back the Greek Church to the unity of the Roman Church, to which he would restore its possessions, and he would oppose both the Tartars and the Saracens. Splendid promises, replied the Pope, made to delude the Council, and to turn aside the axe now laid to the root of the tree. Let him keep the promises to which he swore on his soul. If his request were now to be granted, who would compel him to keep his promises. The Kings of England and France, answered Thaddeus. That will not do, retorted Innocent. If he withdraws from his agreement, and one must suppose he will, as he has so frequently done before, the Church will have to fall back on the two Kings, and so, as they would not welcome the task of fighting for her, she will have three enemies instead of one. [2]

The first Session of the Council, June 28. Two days later was held the first formal session of the Council in the new cathedral of St. John the Baptist " in pede montis " as it is described, i.e., at the foot of the heights of Fourvières, further up the right bank of

---

[1] Mat. Par., *l.c.* Evidently then, there were more bishops afterwards present at the Council. The *Chronicle of Erfurt* speaks of 250 bishops, p. 239 ed. Holder-Egger ; and the *Chron. reg. Colon., Contin. V.*, p. 287, gives 150 as the number of bishops.

[2] Mat. Par., *l.c.*

the Saône than the monastery of St. Just. Innocent, accompanied by all the prelates in full pontificals, made his way from his monastic home to the cathedral in great state,[1] while the road along the slow-rolling river was kept by companies of Knights Templars and Hospitallers whose shining armour and white and black cloaks added much to the picturesqueness of the scene.[2] After Mass, the Pope took his place on a raised dais. On his right was the Emperor of Constantinople, and on his left were a number of lay Princes, the cardinal-deacons and the secretaries, including the vice-chancellor, Master Marinus of Naples, the notaries, the *Auditor* and the *Corrector*, and the papal chaplains and sub-deacons. On a lower level were the great mass of the Prelates. Opposite the Pope, seats were placed for the Patriarchs of Constantinople, Antioch, and Aquileia. But the first two Patriarchs had ordered the seat of the third to be overturned, saying that the Patriarch of Aquileia ought not to sit near them, as he was not one of the four great Patriarchs. However, to avoid a scandal, the Pope ordered that the Patriarch of Aquileia should be allowed to take the place prepared for him. To the right of the Patriarchs were the cardinal-bishops, and on the other side the cardinal-priests and the arch-bishops. In the nave sat the bishops, abbots, proctors of chapters, the envoys of kings and of the Emperor Frederick and others. After the singing of the " Veni

[1] It was probably on this occasion that the Pope was struck by the beautiful orphreys (aurifrisia) worn by the English prelates ; and, on learning that they were made in England, he bade the Cistercians send him some for the ornamentation of his chasubles and copes. " Truly," said Innocent, " England is our garden of delights. It is an inexhaustible well, and where there is much, much can be drawn." But all this is only Mat. Par., *Chron.*, iv, 546–7. *Cf. supra*, vol. ix, p. liv.

[2] It is the *Brev. notit.*, ap. *R. I. SS.*, xiv, p. 1100, which tells us that the knights had sent many armed men to guard the Pope and the Council.

Creator Spiritus ", and the recital of various prayers, the Pope pronounced a most moving discourse on the five wounds which were distressing the Church as His five wounds had distressed our Lord.[1] The wounds were the sins of certain of the higher and lower clergy and the spread of heresy ; the aggression of the Saracens, who had again taken Jerusalem ; the schism of the Greeks and their attacks on the Latin Kingdom ; the savage inroads of the Tartars ; and the persecution of the Church by the Emperor. He had pretended that he was not attacking the Church, but only Gregory IX. He had, however, continued to attack it even during the vacancy of the See, and, that too, although he was bound to be the chief guardian of its secular affairs and its protector—summus sæcularium yconomous et protector ecclesiæ. Enlarging on the grievances against the Emperor, Innocent called attention to his having built a city for the Saracens (Lucera) in the midst of a Christian country, and to his inordinate intimacy with their Princes, their superstitions (ritibus et superstitione), and their women. Further, by the production of the Emperor's letters in which he acknowledged that he held Sicily as a fief from the Church, that episcopal elections in that Kingdom were to be free, etc., etc., Innocent showed that he was guilty of perjury.

On the conclusion of the Pope's address, which was often interrupted by outbursts of grief on the part of his hearers, Thaddeus of Sessa arose, and " seemed

---

[1] All the above is from the *Brevis notita.* Its author says the Pope's text was Psalms xciii, 19, " According to the multitude of the sorrows of my heart, thy comforts have given joy to my soul." Mat. Par., however, says it was Lamentations i, 12, " O all ye that pass by the way attend, and see if there be any sorrow like to my sorrow." He describes the effect of the Pope's preaching (satis eleganter) : " Cunctos audientes dolore compassionis salubriter sauciavit. *Exitus* enim *aquarum deduxerunt oculi* ejus (Ps. cxviii, 136), et singultus sermonem proruperunt." *Chron.*, iv, 434–5.

to excuse the Emperor in a marvellous manner ".[1]
He even produced papal letters which seemed to give
the lie to what the Pope had just said. But, as Matthew
Paris takes occasion to observe, there was no real con-
tradiction, as " the letters of the Pope were only con-
ditional . . . and the breach of faith appeared to be clearly
on the side of the Emperor, who, although he had
positively promised everything, had never fulfilled
any of his promises ".[2] With regard to the charge of
heresy, Thaddeus asserted that that could only be
proved by the confession of the Emperor. He therefore
asked that the proceedings might be delayed in order
that he might have time to beg the Emperor to come in
person before the Council, or to ask for more powers.
As for the Saracens, said Thaddeus, the Emperor had
only had intercourse with their rulers from motives of
prudence, and with their women to be amused by their
performances. However, to be above suspicion, he had
finally dismissed the women. According to the *Brevis
notitia* the first session terminated with a triumphant
reply to " the sugared words "[3] of Thaddeus by the
Pope.

In the second session a great impression was made
on the Council by the strong attack on Frederick
developed by the Spanish bishops, who occupied an
impartial position. They called on the Pope to take
proceedings against Frederick, and offered to defend
him with their goods and with their lives.[4] Thaddeus

The second Session, July 5.

---

[1] *Brev. not.*

[2] *Chron.*, iv, 435. " Et apparuit læsio fidei manifeste ex parte
imperatoris, qui cum omnia absolute promiserat, nec inde aliquid
secundum promissa compleverat."

[3] Menko, *Chron.*, ap. *M. G. SS.*, xxiii, p. 538, speaks of " verbis
dealbatis " of the handsome envoy.

[4] " Surrexit archiepiscopus de Hispania . . . promittens quod
ipse et alii prælati Hispaniæ, qui multum magnifice, et generaliter
melius quam alia natio ad Concilium venerant, Papæ assisterent,

was at last driven to such sorry makeshifts of arguments
to defend the action of his master in the seizing of the
prelates going to the Council summoned by Gregory IX.,
that the Pope declared that the deposition of Frederick
was necessary.[1] Thereupon the English begged that the
sentence of deposition might not fall upon Henry and
Matilda, the children of the Emperor by Isabella, the
sister of their King Henry III.[2] Further, on his side,
Thaddeus begged that the holding of next session might
be delayed as long as possible to give Frederick the
opportunity of reaching Lyons, for he knew for certain
that he was on his way thither.[3] His request was
vigorously opposed by many of the prelates, as they had
naturally no faith in Frederick or his ministers, and
especially by the Templars and Hospitallers, as
they were maintaining a great number of men-at-arms
in the city for the protection of the Council.[4] But the
Pope, who was very anxious for peace, agreed to a delay
of twelve days. This was certainly not a long proroga-
tion in itself ; but, under the circumstances, considerable,

---

in personis et rebus juxta suum beneplacitum voluntatis." *Brev.
notit.* In his defence of himself to the English, Frederick endeavoured
to discount the action of the Spaniards by urging that their country
was far from Italy, and that, in their ignorance of the real state of
things, they had been deceived. Ep. of July 31, 1246, ap. Mat. Par.,
iv, 540.

[1] Mat. Par., iv, 439. The sophistries of Thaddeus regarding the
drowning of innocent ecclesiastics on their way to the Council are
strangely parallel with those to which we were recently treated in
connexion with the sinking of innocent women and children on board
of the *Lusitania.* Both Frederick II. and William II. seem to think that
to give notice that one is about to commit a crime, excuses its
committal.

[2] M. P., *ib.*

[3] *Brev. not.* If Thaddeus was not lying, he was certainly deceived,
as Frederick did not quit Verona till July 8. *Cf.* Rolandinus Pat.,
Chron., v, c. 14. The Genoese annals say he was merely pretending to
be going to the Council. *Cf.* Böhmer-Ficker, *Reg. Imp.*, v, p. 621.

[4] *Brev. not.*

and long enough if Frederick had been in earnest, and if, as the Council was led to believe, he was in or near Turin.[1]

In the interim, with a view to showing the claims of the Roman Church to the territories which Frederick had seized, and his duties to it, as its vassal for Sicily, the Pope caused to be transcribed all the privileges which Emperors and Kings had given it at different times. Then on July 13 he caused the transcription to be signed by some forty of the most distinguished bishops to guarantee its conformity with the originals.[2] *The interval between the last two Sessions.*

Also, in the interim, word was sent to Frederick that the last Session of the Council had been put off to give him an opportunity of presenting himself before it. But, according to Matthew Paris, he contented himself with observing that the Pope had called the Council together simply to humiliate him for seizing his relatives, "Genoese pirates," along with the prelates at sea, and that it was not becoming the imperial dignity to abide by the sentence of a synod, especially of a hostile one.[3] When this reply was made known to the Fathers, and it was clear that he was not prepared to submit *The third Session, July 17.*

---

[1] *Ib.* "Et quia d. Papa hoc quamplurimum affectabat, ut possent inter eos pacis fœdera reformari, usque ad diem Lunæ post octavas secundæ sessionis . . . contra multorum Prælatorum voluntatem prorogavit Tertiam Sessionem." Mat. Par. asserts that the Pope granted the delay at the request of the envoys of the Kings of England and France, who pitied the disgrace of Frederick, and that it was granted "to the detriment of many who were waiting at Lyons". *Chron.*, iv, 437. As usual Paris is inaccurate in his presentment of the proceedings of the Council.

[2] *Brev. not.*, and the signatures ap. H.-B., vi, 317. This valuable collection consisting of 82 documents upon 17 rolls of parchment, was deposited by the Pope in the archives of Cluny, and is known as the *rouleaux de Cluny*. One of the original rolls is still extant in Paris, but the others have disappeared. *Cf.* Berger, *Reg.*, i, p. xlvi ff. The collection was, however, made in duplicate, and Leopold Delisle discovered the copy kept by the Pope in the Vatican. *Cf. ib.*, ii, p. lxxxvii n.

[3] *Chron.*, iv, 437.

to what was right,[1] they were very indignant, and blamed the English particularly for their intercession on the Emperor's behalf. Whether all this is so or not, it is certain that the Emperor did not come to the Council.

The first business to which the Council devoted itself was the publication of a number of decrees concerning legal procedure, the piling up of debts on church property, the raising of money for the needs of the Holy Land and the Empire of Constantinople,[2] the resistance to be offered to the awful ravages of the Tartars,[3] etc., etc. Then, after discussion on papal taxation had been deferred to a more suitable time,[4] the all-important question of the conduct of the Emperor was again brought forward. Thaddeus did all in his power to avert from his master an adverse sentence, the more so that Frederick's fiancée, an Austrian princess, had declared that she would not accept him if he were not freed from excommunication—a decision to which she in fact adhered.[5] Seeing, however, that neither his eloquence nor his subtleties were likely to prevail, he declared that any sentence against the Emperor was null and void, as he had not been legally cited ; and as the Pope was a partial judge, he appealed against him to a future Pope and to a really ecumenical council.[6]

---

[1] " Quod scilicet sic dicens noluit juri pariturus accedere." *Ib.*

[2] The Holy See itself engaged to give a tenth to the Holy Land and then a tenth to the Empire. " Nos vero de obvertionibus Ecclesiæ Romanæ, deducta prius ex eis decima succursui terræ deputanda prædictæ, decimam prædicti pro subventione imperii plenarie tribuemus." Can. 14. Ap. Hefele, *Concil.*, t. v, pt. ii, p. 1652.

[3] The Holy See was to be at once warned of the approach of the Tartars, so that it may organize help to be sent by itself and all Christendom. Can. 16.

[4] This matter will be treated of later.

[5] Mat. Par., *l.c.*, p. 440.

[6] *Brev. not.*, M. P., *l.c.*, and especially H.-B., vi, 318, for the appeal of Thaddeus, " Procurator ad hoc specialiter constitutus." With regard to the " citation " the Continuator of the *Gesta Regum* of our own historian Gervase of Canterbury, pertinently remarks that Frederick

As due attention had been given to all that could The Pope
be urged in Frederick's defence,[1] Innocent delivered his pronounces
sentence of
sentence against him at great length. After reviewing deposition
the whole course of his dealings with Frederick, he against
Frederick.
charged him with perjury in connexion with his engage-
ments regarding peace ; with sacrilege in seizing the
Fathers of the Council ; with heresy, and with treason
in connexion with his fief of Sicily.[2] The Emperor
had, moreover, ignored the excommunication pronounced
against him ; had seized and, with few exceptions,
was still holding possession of the States of the Church;
had, despite his oaths to the contrary, grievously
oppressed and robbed the Church in Sicily, keeping
a great number of its sees and abbacies vacant [3] ; and
had maintained discreditable relations with Saracens
and Greeks. For these and other unspeakable excesses,
the Pope declared that Frederick had rendered himself
unworthy to reign, and that consequently, in God's
name, he declared him deprived of all honour and dignity.
All who had taken the oath of fidelity to him were
declared to be absolved from their allegiance, and all

knew quite well that his contumacy and rebellion against the Church
were the chief cause of the summoning of the Council, to which, though
cited, he had refused to come.   ii, p. 202, R. S.

[1] "Deliberatione prehabita diligenti," says Carbio, c. 18. Cf. the
Pope's statements in his sentence of excommunication, ap. Mat. Par.,
iv, 454 ; and especially in a letter of his to the chapter of the Cistercians
(Sept., 1245), in which he justified his action. "We do not remember
any cause to have ever been discussed so deliberately . . . so much so,
indeed, that in our private meetings some of the cardinals (aliqui
fratrum) took the role of advocates for him, and some, on the other
hand, pleaded for him . . . as is the custom in the schools . . . in
order that the truth of the question might be thoroughly sifted out."
Ib., p. 480.

[2] "Juramentorum . . . violator, non sine proditionis nota, et
læsæ crimine majestatis." M. P., iv, p. 449.

[3] In the two pamphlets against Frederick of June, 1245, printed with
the letters of Albert von Behaim, the number is given as over fifty.
Cf. pp. 69 and 75 ed. Höfler.

were forbidden, under pain of excommunication, to recognize him as Emperor or King. Finally, those to whom the right of election belonged were informed that they were free to choose a successor to the excommunicated sovereign, while the Pope himself and his cardinals would arrange in due course for the future of the Kingdom of Sicily.[1]

The profound impression which the reading of this indictment made on all who heard it was, we are assured, changed into dread when the drastic sentence was pronounced, and then approved by the assembled Fathers extinguishing the lighted tapers which they held in their hands.[2]   On hearing the sentence of deposition, Thaddeus cried out : " This day is a day of wrath, a day of tribulation and distress " (Sophonias, i, 15). Then, with his fellow-envoys, he left the Cathedral, whilst the chanting of the Te Deum was bringing this memorable Council to its close.[3]

[1] Mat. Par., iv, pp. 454–5.

[2] *Ib.*, pp. 445, 456, 473, and 479. *Cf.* Rolandinus Pat.,*Chron.*, v, c. 14. " Sentenciavit (the Pope) ob justas causas eum amodo privatum ab imperio et corona." *Cf.* Carbio, c. 19.   Even the Ghibelline *Annals of Piacenza*, p. 196, acknowledge that the sentence was only pronounced " post dilationes multas datas imperatori ".   The *Ann. Spirenses*, ap. Böhmer, *Fontes*, ii, 156, say that the Emperor " communi sententia destitutus est ".   The *Gesta Epp. Virdunensium*, ap. *M. G. SS.*, x, 524–5, say that Innocent deprived Frederick of his sceptre " universalis ecclesiæ judicio ". The *Ann. Blandin.*, an. 1245, ap. *M. G. SS.*, v, say " culpis clarescentibus dampnatus est, et ab imperio deficitur . . . culpis suis exigentibus ".   Will. of Puylaurens, c. 47, ap. *M. G. SS.*, xxvi, p. 600, says Inn. deposed Fred. : " per sententiam diffinitivam." *Cf.* the contemp. *Chron. rythmicum*, ap. *M. G. SS.*, xxv, p. 361, and Salimbene, ap. *M. G. SS.*, xxxii, p. 201, who says that at the Council of Lyons " Frederick's malice was made known to all " ; *cf.* p. 342. Without going into further detail we may state that, as a body, the contemporary chroniclers of Europe assert that Frederick was condemned by the general verdict of the Council, and that the verdict was just.   Moreover, the general tenure of their words shows that they believed that the General Assembly of Europe had the right to deprive the head of Christendom of his position if he was false to it.

[3] *Brev. not.*

CHAPTER II.

PART II (1245–51). INNOCENT AND THE EMPIRE FROM THE DEPOSITION TO THE DEATH OF FREDERICK II., AND THEN ON TO THE DEPARTURE OF THE POPE FROM LYONS.

FREDERICK, meanwhile, pretending to be making for Lyons with his son Conrad, left Verona for the west, and had reached Turin when word was brought him of the sentence of deposition which had been pronounced against him.[1] Beside himself with rage at the news, he is said to have called for a diadem and, after having placed it upon his head, to have cried : " I have not yet lost my crown, nor will I be deprived of it by Pope or Council without a struggle even unto blood. Has his vulgar pride so puffed him up as to dare to hurl from the height of the imperial dignity one who is the Prince of Princes, who is second to none, to whom indeed no one is equal ? . . . Now at any rate am I free from any kind of obligation of keeping the peace with him." And we are further assured that he was as good as his word, and that henceforth he strove with greater energy to injure the Pope in his goods, and in his relations and friends.[2]

Frederick's action on hearing of his deposition.

Whether or not there is any truth in that part of these statements of Matthew Paris regarding Frederick's crowning of himself, there is no doubt about the truth of the latter part of them. There is no doubt that he now

---

[1] *Mon. Patav., Chron. (Ann. S. Justinæ)*, ap. *R. I. SS.*, viii, p. 681, *Chron. reg. Col., Cont. V.*, p. 287, etc.

[2] Mat. Par., iv, 475. Regarding Frederick's cruel treatment of Innocent's relatives, *cf. ib.*, pp. 406, 613, and v, p. 65. If Innocent came to hate Frederick II. personally, it is as easy to understand as it is to understand the hatred of the relatives of the victims of the Scarborough bombardment (1915), and of the sinking of the *Lusitania* for William II.

threw himself into the struggle against Innocent without any restraint. He first endeavoured by a series of letters (in the summer of 1245 and the spring of 1246) to persuade the other Princes that his cause was theirs. If he could be deposed, so could they. He also strove to arouse their cupidity. The Church was too rich. The Princes should take from her what they had formerly bestowed. He accordingly addressed to the King of England and other Princes what even Matthew Paris styled a " very reprehensible letter in which he vomited forth the long-concealed poisonous designs of his heart ".[1] In the opening of this document he averred that " the presumption of Innocent IV. in daring to depose him who wore the imperial diadem menaced all kings. " It is not his affair to exercise any severity against us in temporal matters, even if just causes for severity existed." It is the money which the Church is receiving from nations which are impoverished for its benefit that is causing it to run riot. Then, in his rage, completely revealing his intentions, he informed the Princes that his agents would make known to them in secret what plans he had for making, " through great mediators," at least " a superficial peace " with the Church ; and for stripping the Pope of his position in Christendom as judge of kings, and lord of the isles of the Ocean.[2] They were also told with what great forces, " all ready for war," he intended in the coming spring " to oppress

[1] iv, 475. This letter, which Paris assigns to the year 1245, is really of the first part of the year 1246, as is clear from the words about the coming spring which occur in it. Nothing, however, turns on the exact date of this letter. On the contrary, the fragment of Frederick's letter to the King and Barons of France, which H.-B. (vi, 389) refers to February, 1246, really belongs to the period immediately after the Council.

[2] This, at any rate, I take to be the import of the words that the imperial agents are to explain to the Kings : " Quid de regum communibus specialibusque negotiis disponere proponamus ? quid super insulis Oceani fuerit ordinatum ? "

his oppressors, even though the whole world should oppose him ".[1] Our imperial greatness is not bent by the papal sentence, but, with you, will strip the clergy of their superfluous wealth.

At the same time the princes of the Empire were strictly forbidden to receive any papal envoys or letters.[2]

According, however, to Matthew Paris, this violent attack on the Pope and the Church quite failed to accomplish its object, as " it appeared clearer than light to the magnates of France and England that Frederick was striving with all his might to annihilate the liberty and grandeur of the Church which he himself had done nothing to augment. And thus rendering himself suspected of heresy, he wantonly extinguished by his thoughtless impudence every spark of the good opinion of him hitherto entertained by people generally ".[3]

Frederick loses caste.

But Frederick did not confine himself to letter writing. He frankly appealed to force. He would take up the hammer, and devote himself to the grand and final remedy of force. With his sword which was gasping to subdue for good and all the last of the rebels against

Frederick's proceedings against the Churches and the Communes.

---

[1] " Quantis viribus quot virorum qualiter instructorum ad bella in hoc ipso vere quod instat (the spring of 1246), omnes illos, qui modo nos opprimunt, opprimere posse speremus, etsi se nobis totus mundus opponeret." How strangely familiar to us in this year of grace 1916, is this German imperial bombast. *Cf.* his letter to the English, ap. *ib.*, iv, 538 ff. (Turin, July 31), in which, when animadverting on the sentence pronounced against him at Lyons, he declared that none of the princes of Germany " on whom our rank and deposition depend, have confirmed it by their presence or counsel (consilio) ". He did not tell the English that even before the Council, the archbishops of Mainz and Cologne (two of those " a quibus assumptio status et depressio nostra dependent ", *ib.*, p. 543) had approached the Pope, and told him that if he would depose the Emperor they would name a King who would be favourable to the Church. *Cf. Ann. Wormat.*, an. 1244, ap. *M. G. SS.*, xvii, p. 49. See also another variety of Frederick's epistolary attack on the Pope, ap. H.-B., vi, 347 f., Sept.

[2] *Ann. S. Rudbert.*, ap. *M. G. SS.*, ix, 788. *Cf.* epp. Fred., ap. H.-B., vi, 393, and 394.

[3] *Chron.*, iv, 477 f.

him, he would cut away all the putrid parts of the body
politic.[1]   To do this, he taxed the Churches, demanding
a third of their revenues [2] ;   raised troops against the
Milanese whom he at once proceeded to attack [3] ; expelled
Bernardo Rosso, " a very near relative of the Pope,"
from Parma and destroyed his house [4] ; and treated
such of his enemies as fell into his hands with the greatest
cruelty.[5]

Frederick
and the Pope
seek the
friendship of
Hakon.

At the same time he did not disdain to try to win
to his side by diplomacy those whom he could not coerce
by the sword.   A little reading between the lines of even
an Icelandic Saga will let us see that, in their great
struggle both Frederick and the Pope tried to secure the
material or moral support of the influential men of

---

[1] *Cf.* three letters of Sept. to his partisans, his justiciaries, and to his
son, Enzio, ap. H.-B., vi, 357 ff. " Sequitur igitur ut . . . mallei . . .
officium resumamus . . . tanquam supremum et grande remedium
nos ad potentialis medele suffragium convertamus." P. 358. " Restat
itaque mederi per gladium putres partes et audacter abscindere."
P. 360. " Pro conterendis finaliter rebellium nostrorum reliquiis, ad
quorum exitium gladius noster solerter invigilat et hanelanter aspirat,
etc." P. 361.

[2] *Ib.*

[3] Epp. ap. *ib.*, p. 362 f., and 364. *Cf. Ann. Placent. Gib.*, p. 206,
and *Annal. Mediol.*. ap. *R. I. SS.*, xvi, 652.

[4] *Ann. Med.*, *l.c.* Bernard is often mentioned by Salimbene ; *cf.*
Chron., p. 75.   Bernard is said to have afterwards plotted against
Frederick's life. *Cf. Chron. de rebus*, pp. 207–8.

[5] *Chron. de reb.=Ann. P. G.*, p. 207 ; ep. of the notary Roland on
the hanging of thirty-two citizens of Corneto, ap. H.-B., vi, 367 ff., and
a letter (Nov.) of Frederick himself about the beheading of a number
of the people of Reggio, ap. *ib.*, p. 375. The notary gave vent to his
feelings in verse in order that " the impious cruelty of the deposed
Frederick might be known to all, and that his name might be held in
reproach for ever ". P. 368. In conclusion the poet called upon the
people to resist the author of the conflict (Frederick), and assured them
that their hope of liberty was in Innocent. P. 372.

> " Eidem resistite qui est auctor litis.
> Liberi poteritis esse si velitis.

> Per quem (Innocent IV) gentes subdite dantur libertati
> Et Cometum subditum Dei majestati.''

Christendom. The Saga of King Hakon IV. of Norway shows us the Emperor constantly engaged in endeavouring to secure the friendship of that enlightened monarch. From the earliest days of the Norse King's reign, missions and presents kept coming to him from Frederick.[1] Innocent, however, appears to have made more headway with Hakon than the Emperor. Expressing a hope that his favours would increase the King's love of God and devotion to the Roman Church, he dispensed him from the consequences of his illegitimate birth; granted him, for crusading purposes, a tenth of the church revenues for three years; and, saving the rights of others, subjected to his sway such heathen tribes as he might conquer and Christianize.[2] Moreover, at the King's request, he sent William, cardinal of Sabina, to crown him. Arrived in Bergen the cardinal first settled a dispute in the King's favour between him and the bishops of Norway who wished their sovereign to take an oath giving them control of the royal succession. This demand Hakon was unwilling to concede; and the cardinal decided: " It seems to me that the King has the truth more on his side than those who ask another thing; and therefore I wish that you should know that I will ask naught else henceforth, but crown the King as freely as beseems the kingly honour."[3] The cardinal gained further influence with the King by acceding to his wishes in connexion with various reforms[4]; and, naturally, by crowning him with great pomp. " Praised be God," said the cardinal on the eventful day of the coronation, " that I have this day fulfilled that errand which was charged on me on behalf of holy Rome and the lord Pope and all the cardinals. Now your King is crowned and

[1] Saga, cc. 191 and 243, pp. 177 and 247, *R. S.*
[2] Cf. *Diplomatarium Norvegicum*, ed. C. Lange, Christiana, 1849, Vol. I, n. 38, p. 29; n. 40, p. 31. Cf. nn. 47 and 46, p. 35.
[3] *Ib.*, c. 251, p. 254. Cf. *Dip. N.*, nn. 64a–65, p. 52 ff.
[4] *Ib.*, c. 252, p. 255.

thoroughly honoured so that no King can have gotten such honour before in Norway." [1]

The cardinal also increased papal influence with the Norse King by another very important act. The Kings of Norway, and Hakon IV. was no exception to the rule, had always been desirous of subjecting Iceland to their sway. It had been colonized by men from Norway, and so they regarded it as just that their authority should be recognized there. Cardinal William agreed that their contention was well founded, and so in the words of Hakon's Saga : " Then was that order made as to Iceland with the advice of the cardinal that the people who dwelt there should be subject to King Hakon : for he called it unfair that that land should not be subject to some king like all others in the world." [2]

Action of the Pope against Frederick. Meanwhile the Pope was not idle in other directions. Soon after the closing of the Council, he dispatched Philip, bishop-elect of Ferrara, into Germany to urge the Princes to elect a new king [3] ; and about the same time (Aug. 21) freed the King of Hungary (Bela IV.) from the oath of allegiance which he had taken to Frederick, on the ground that it had been taken on the strength of help promised against the Hungarians which had not been given.[4] He also strove by letters to counteract the influence of those issued by Frederick. By one of them in which he declared that, after the most careful consideration of the case, it had not been found possible to deal with Frederick in any other way, and that he

[1] *Ib.*, c. 255, p. 258. Cf. *Dip. N.*, nn. 30-2, p. 25 f.

[2] *Ib.*, c. 257, p. 262.

[3] Ep. of Phil. ap. H.-B., vi, 346, and *Chron. reg. Colon., Contin. V.*, pp. 287–8. Through the help of the archbishop of Cologne, the envoy was introduced to Henry Raspe, Landgrave of Thuringia, whom Innocent is believed to have already approached on the subject of his becoming King of the Romans. See ep. Inn., Apr. 30, 1244, ap. H.-B., vi, 189; and Mat. Par., iv, pp. 356–7, *cf. ib.*, 268–9. But there is evidently some confusion in M. Paris.

[4] Ap. H.-B., vi, 345.

and the cardinals were ready to die for the cause, he won over to his side the whole Cistercian Order. " They abandoned the cause of the Emperor Frederick," we are told, " and wonderfully inclined to that of the Pope." [1]

The then very influential Order of St. Dominic also declared against Frederick. In one General Chapter after another (1246, –47, –48), it was decreed that the brethren must not, under pain of severe punishment, criticize adversely the acts of the Pope, or show any manner of favour to Frederick. [2]

Despite his blustering appeal to his victorious sword, facts such as those just enumerated, as well as the going over of his relative, the son of the King of Castile, to his enemies, [3] the doubtful loyalty of the important city of Parma, [4] and the growth of the party against him in Germany gave some anxiety to Frederick. He would try, therefore, to secure a peace more or less on his own terms through the mediation of St. Louis. Accordingly " on account of his special love for France and its King ", he wrote to tell the French people that he was prepared to commit the matter (causam) between " us and the supreme Pontiff " to their King. Then, knowing the zeal of Louis for the cause of the Cross, he offered to co-operate with him in the Crusade which

Frederick strives to secure the mediation of the King of France.

---

[1] Mat. Par., iv, 480. The letter of Innocent to the Cistercians was written about Sept. 14, 1245, the date at which the Cistercians held their General Chapter. Will. of Nangis also notes the care that was taken in examining Frederick's position, and adds that he gives the chief reasons for his excommunication that it may not be thought that Innocent acted through spite : " ne dictus papa invidiæ ductus livore vel odio fecisse videatur." *Vit. Ludov.*, ap. *R. F. SS.*, xx, p. 548.

[2] *Acta capitulorum gen. Ord. Prædic.*, vol. i, ed. Reichert, Rome, 1898 : " Vel Frederico deposito in aliquo verbo vel facto auxilium prebere."

[3] Ep. of Fred. (August), ap. H.-B., vi, 340, to the young prince's father.

[4] Cf. *Chron. de rebus*, p. 205, and two privileges of Fred. (Sept. 1245), by which he strove to retain the loyalty of Parma, ap. H.-B., vi, 352 ff.

he was contemplating, if the desired peace was brought about. But, at the same time, he showed that it was a peace on his own terms that he wanted when he declared that the peace between himself and the Church would have to be followed by the submission of the Lombards, or by their abandonment by the Church.[1]

Although, to use the words of Berger,[2] St. Louis was not deceived by Frederick's statement of his case, he was so anxious to clear the way for his Crusade that, in the hope of effecting at least some working arrangement, he begged the Pope to meet him at Cluny.[3]

The interview at Cluny, 1245. Contemporary chroniclers have told us much of the magnificence of the gathering in the immense monastery of Cluny, Nov. 30. They have told us the names of the great nobles who accompanied St. Louis and his mother Blanche of Castile, and of the cardinals who, wearing their red hats for the first time, attended on the Pope.[4] But they have not told us for certain anything that was discussed at the private conferences which took place between the Pope and the King and Queen Blanche. "William of Nangis," says Berger, "who belonged to the wise school of St. Denis where historic truth was so much respected, has not told us anything about what was discussed at the interview, because he did not know anything; but Matthew Paris, that intemperate narrator who was fond of contrasting his characters, and of retailing sayings and anecdotes,

---

[1] " Pace per hoc (viz. Frederick's amends to the Church) inter nos et Ecclesiam *procedente* et reliquiis Lombardorum . . . vel ad mandatum nostrum . . . redeuntibus, vel prorsus ab Ecclesie defensione seclusis. Ep. Sept. 22, 1245, ap. H.-B., vi, 349 ff.

[2] *Reg.*, ii, p. cix.

[3] Mat. Par., iv, 484.

[4] Will. of Nangis, *Vit. Lud.*, ap. *R. F. SS.*, xx, p. 352 f. Louis also had a great desire to see the Pope : " flagrans desiderio videndi summum pontificem." See also the *Chronicon Cluniacense*, ap. Potthast, 11965 ; or *Bibliotheca Clun.*, p. 1666, cited by Berger, *l.c.*, pp. cix ff., and Carbio, c. 21.

has shown himself less restrained." He has made two interviews out of one, and told us a great deal of what was not known to anyone.[1] We may, however, without accepting any of Paris' details, believe that the subjects which were discussed included the dispute between the Empire and the Papacy, the Crusade, the continuation of the peace between France and England, and certainly the projected marriage between Louis' brother, Charles of Anjou, and Beatrice of Provence.

The Pope was anxious about this marriage. On the death of her father Raymond Berenger, count of Provence (Aug., 1245), his daughter Beatrice became the Lady of Provence, and as such was eagerly sought in marriage. Among others who aspired to her hand was Raymond VII., count of Toulouse, an ally of Frederick II. It was obviously not to the interest of Innocent that the Emperor's position should be strengthened by a union of Toulouse and Provence under Raymond, but it was to his advantage that France should be strengthened. He accordingly granted Charles of Anjou, who was related to Beatrice in the fourth degree, a dispensation.[2] The two were married in January, 1246, and the strong government which Charles at once inaugurated in Provence [3] was supported by the Pope.[4]

The interview of Cluny, then, from which Frederick had hoped to gain some advantage against the Pope,

---

[1] Cf. Mat. Par., iv, 484, 504, and 523. Among other things, he ventures to say that Louis left the Pope in anger because he found no humility in him. The fact is that he left the Pope after having received his blessing and humbly taken his leave of him. Will. of N., l.c., p. 354. Berger, Reg., ii, p. cxiv, has shown that there was only one interview at Cluny.

[2] Cf. Innocent's letter (March 1, 1246) to our Henry III., printed in full, ap. Berger, l.c., p. cxiv f. ; Mat. Par., iv, 545 f. ; Annal. S. Victor. Massil., ap. M. G. SS., xxiii, p. 5 ; Will. of N., l.c., p. 354.

[3] Thos. of Tuscany, Gesta imp. et pont., ap. M. G. SS., xxii, p. 520.

[4] Ep. Inn., June 1, 1246, ap. Reg., n. 1886, printed in full, ap. Berger, ii, p. cxxi.

resulted in the final loss of imperial influence in the Rhone valley, and in the definite establishment therein of that of France, to which Innocent, even at the risk of offending England, contributed so much.[1]

The election of Henry Raspe, May, 1246.

But the efforts of Innocent against Frederick did not end with this substantial success. Not only did he continue to issue encyclicals in answer to the epistolary attacks " of the precursor of Antichrist " who ungratefully spurned the Church who had brought him up from his infancy,[2] but he encouraged resistance to Frederick in the Kingdom of Sicily,[3] and pushed forward the election of a new King. He reminded the world that in attacking the Church the Emperor was attacking Christ Himself; and that a son who would not defend his mother when attacked was not worthy of the name. The world, therefore, should rise against him " whose hands are against all men's ", and take up arms for the defence of the Church.[4]

In April the Pope sent various letters to the German Princes " who had the power of electing the King of the Romans ".[5] He urged them to elect as their new

---

[1] Cf. Mat. Par., iv. 505 f., and the letter already quoted of Inn. (March 1, 1246), whence it appears that Henry III. laid claim to certain castles in Provence. Among the benefits conferred upon France by Innocent, Berger, ii, p. ii, places first: "Il favorise le mariage de Charles d'Anjou avec l'héritière de la Provence." Cf. ib., p. ccliii, for Innocent's care of Charles' interests whilst he was absent with his brother the King on Crusade.

[2] Cf. ep. c. the end of March, 1246, ap. H.-B., vi, 396 ff.

[3] Epp. of Apr. 26, ap. ib., p. 411 ff.

[4] Ib.

[5] Since the election of the emperor Lothaire II. (1125), the choice of the head of the Empire began gradually to fall into the hands of a few of the Princes. A small number of them exercised the right of prætaxation, or that of selecting the candidate and presenting him to the others for approval. In 1240 Abbot Albert (Annal. Stadenses, ap. M. G. SS., xvi, 367), names as original electors ("ex prætaxatione principum et consensu ") the archbishop of Trier, Mainz, and Cologne. (Trier elects, he says, by reason of its antiquity—licet de Alemannia non sit), the

King, Henry Raspe, the Landgrave of Thuringia, " as
he was prepared to assume the burden of the Empire," [1]
pointing out that the peace of the world, destroyed by
Frederick, absolutely required a new Emperor.[2] At
the same time he instructed his envoy, Philip, the bishop-
elect of Ferrara, to bring spiritual and temporal pressure
to bear on bishop and baron to make them submit to
the new King of the Romans.[3]

Accordingly after preaching a crusade against " the
deposed Emperor ", the archbishops of Cologne and
Mainz elected Henry Raspe, Landgrave of Thuringia,
King of the Romans (May 22, 1246).[4] Success
immediately attended the new King. He defeated
Frederick's son King Conrad, and received large sums

Count Palatine of the Rhine, because he is the standard-bearer, the
Duke of Saxony because he is the marshal, the Margrave of Brandenburg because he is the chamberlain. The King of Bohemia, who is the
cup-bearer, does not elect because he is not a German. (*Cf.* the *Sach-
senspiegel*, iii, c. 57, § 2). A note in Mat. Par., iv, 455, replaces the
archbishop of Trier by the archbishop of Salzburg, who certainly never
became a regular elector, and gives the lay electors as the Dukes of
Austria, Bavaria, Saxony, and Brabant. Innocent wrote on this
occasion (H.-B., vi, p. 401) to the King of Bohemia (who at any rate
ultimately became an elector) to the Dukes of Bavaria, Saxony, and
Brabant, to the Marquises of Brandenburg and Meissen (who was
an elector in 1257, *cf.* Mat. Par., v, 504), and to the Bishop of Wurzburg.

[1] Ep. of Apr. 21, 1246, ap. *ib.*, p. 400. *Cf.* the next two.

[2] Innocent calls attention to the terrible wars Frederick has caused :
" Quanta commotione guerrarum velut fervens pacis emulus. quam
plures provincias christianorum quassaverit, et concutiat incessanter."
Ep. of Apr. 21, 1246, to the King of Bohemia and others, ap. *ib.*, p. 401.
Cf. the striking phrase of Conrad of Hostaden (*Catal. arch. Colon.*,
ap. *M. G. SS.*, xxiv, p. 353), who speaks of Frederick : " pacem tocius
orbis invadens."

[3] Ep. of Apr. 22, 1246, *ib.*, p. 402.

[4] *Chron. reg. Colon.*, *Contin. V.*, pp. 288–9; Mat. Par., *Chron.*, iv, 495,
544 ; *Annal. Ephord.*, p. 100 ; Menko, *Chron.*, ap. *M. G. SS.*, 539.
Cf. Raspe's letter to the Milanese announcing his election, in which
with much exaggeration, he says he was elected by the princes :
" concordi et unanimi voluntate." Ap. H.-B., vi, 429 ff., *cf.* also letters
of Innocent of June 9, in which the same is said. Ap. Rod., ii, pp. 144–5.

of money (some 25,000 marks) from the Pope to buy support. He proclaimed that " he had taken up the sword in behalf of the Christian people out of reverence for God and his holy mother the Church ".[1]

Frederick expresses a wish to clear himself of heresy, 1246.

When to these difficulties in Germany, there was added rebellion in the Kingdom of Sicily,[2] Frederick again thought of the Pope. In the month of May, therefore, he sent the archbishop of Palermo and other ecclesiastics to Innocent to inform him that he had cleared himself of the charge of heresy before the envoys whom he was sending to him. Innocent, however, was not a man to be caught by any device of that kind.[3] He pointed out that the said envoys had not received any commission or directions as to the conduct of an inquiry into Frederick's religious beliefs, and that " they were members of his court, and subject to his power or rather tyranny ".[4] Their evidence was therefore worthless. However, if Frederick would come to Lyons himself with but a small unarmed retinue, and, as he had offered to do, there clear himself of the charge of heresy, Innocent declared his readiness to listen to him.

Irritated at his failure to cajole the Pope, Frederick by circular letters told the world that " the immense pride " of the Pope was concerned not with peace but with crushing us for ever (circa nostrum exterminium sempiternum). He, therefore, bade the other Princes realize what would happen to them if the Pope succeeded in his present intention with regard to him.[5]

---

[1] Ep. cit. of Raspe. *Cf.* Mat. Par., iv, 544, 577.

[2] *Chron. de rebus* = *Ann. Placent. Gibel.*, pp. 207–8, and epp. Fred., Apr. 25, ap. H.-B., vi, 402 ff., and that of Walter of Ocra, *ib.*, p. 457.

[3] As Berger, *Introduc., Reg.*, ii, p. clxxi, points out, Frederick did not suppose that Innocent would be deceived. His object was " ménager les bonnes dispositions des autres souverains, et tout particulièrement du roi de France ".

[4] Ep. of May 23, 1246, ap. H.-B., vi, 425 ff.

[5] Ep. ap. H.-B., vi, 428 f.

Concluding his angry note with a declaration that he had no fear of the Pope's " nefarious intentions ", he devoted himself to crushing the conspiracy which had sprung up even in the midst of the Kingdom which he was ruling with a rod of iron.   In this he was successful. The plot, initiated by the Lombards, was betrayed to him ; and he punished its authors as, " by the continuous hammer of our power," they gradually fell into his hands, with the utmost severity.   Asserting that they had intended to kill him, he not only killed or blinded the conspirators themselves, but killed even their wives and children.[1] Then, in informing the English how the conspiracy had but added to his power and wealth, he accused the Pope of having inspired the plot against his life.[2]

Frederick crushes the Sicilian conspiracy.

It will be seen that the struggle between the Church and the Empire was now being urged with greater vigour and with more personal acrimony.   Frederick was not disposed to refrain from the use of any weapon that came to his hand.   But if he had some success in the southern half of Italy,[3] his power in Germany was on the wane.   Innocent lent all the weight of his authority to Henry Raspe.   He bade the German bishops preach a Crusade against Frederick,[4] and his legates Philip

The cause of Frederick loses ground in Germany, 1246–7.

[1] This last statement rests on the *Chron. Siculum*, ap. *ib.*, i, pt. ii, p. 908. *Cf. Chron. de reb.*, pp. 207–8, and epp. Fred., Apr. 25, ap. H.-B., vi, 402 ff.

[2] *Cf.* the letters of Apr. 25, H.-B., vi, 402–11, and epp. of July 21, *ib.*, pp. 438, 440–2, 457.   See also the letter of March 14, 1247, of Innocent IV., *ib.*, p. 5018, making grants of land to some of the conspirators.

[3] He appears to have had some success against cardinal Rainerius Capocci and the people of Perugia and Assisi. *Cf.* the epp. of Apr. 25, *ib.*, pp. 406 and 409.   Against this, however, may be set a Saracen rebellion in Sicily a little later. *Cf.* Frederick's letters of Aug., 1246, ap. *ib.*, pp. 456–71.

[4] Ep. of June 27, 1246, ap. *ib.*, p. 432.   And many we are told " on account of the great indulgence offered by the Pope took up arms against the *quondam* emperor ". *Ann. S. Rudberti*, ap. *M. G. SS.*, ix, p. 789. *Cf. Ann. S. Georgii*, ap. *ib.*, xvii, 297.

and the energetic Albert von Behaim, whose words we
have so often cited, ably carried out his wishes. They
excommunicated the bishops who would not support
Henry,[1] and strove to detach the powerful princes from
Frederick's side. They impressed upon them that " the
lord Pope wished in every way to preserve the Roman
and German Empire (imperium Romanum et Alamannie)
to the illustrious lord Henry, now elected King of the
Romans ; and that he would not draw back from his
intention if the stars fell from heaven and the rivers
were turned to blood ".[2]

As a result of these earnest efforts Henry's party
increased, and he was able about the middle of August
to announce that he had inflicted a severe defeat on
Conrad,[3] and, a month or two later, he was in a position
to state that he would soon be ready to treat of the
affairs of Lombardy.[4]

Death of
Henry
Raspe, 1247.

Despite a new attempt on the part of St. Louis to
bring about a peace in the autumn of 1246,[5] fighting

---

[1] Ep. of Philip, Aug. 13, *ib.*, p. 449.

[2] Ep. of Albert v. Behaim, ap. *ib.*, p. 446, to Otho of Bavaria. See
the eulogy on the loyalty of Philip to the Roman Church pronounced
by the *Mon. Patav., Chron.*, ap. *R. I. SS.*, p. 682.

[3] See his letter ap. *ib.*, p. 451. *Cf.* various *Annals*, e.g. those of
Colmar, ap. *M. G. SS.*, or Böhmer, *Fontes*, ii, p. 3. " Conradus rex
Teutonie victus ab episcopis " ; and those of Strasburg (*Annal.
Argentinenses*) ap. Böhmer, *ib.*, p. 108, and of Worms, *ib.*, p. 185.

[4] Ep. of Nov. 30, ap. H.-B., vi, p. 470.

[5] Ep. of Inn., Nov. 5, 1246, ap. *ib.*, p. 463. He observes that having
in vain worked with all his might for peace (" toto ingenio, totaque
sollicitudine ") right up to the Council of Lyons, he had now no hope of
peace. He would, however, receive the Emperor if he made sincere
advances. On hearing of this reply, Frederick again tried to induce
Louis to act with him. Ep. ap. *ib.*, p. 472. Others besides the Pope
himself chronicle his sustained efforts for peace : " Post magnum
tractatum de pace " says the *Memor. potestat. Reg.*, ap. *R. I. SS.*,
viii, p. 1113. *Cf. Chron. Estense*, an. 1242, ap. *ib.*, xv, p. 18 new ed. ;
and *Liber Regiminum Paduæ*, ap. *ib.*, t. viii, p. 315 new ed.

between the Guelfs and Ghibellines [1] went on both in Germany and Italy where also papal legates were at work against Frederick. [2]

Most disastrous, of course, were the results of this internal warfare. " Wickedness," we are told, [3] " prevailed ; the people of God were without a ruler; Rome was desolate ; clerical decorum (decor clericalis) perished ; and the people of God were divided. Some took the Cross (against Frederick) ; while others followed Frederick, formerly Emperor, insulted the divine religion, and were

[1] It is only about this time that these party names appear in Italy. In the form of " Welf " and " Waiblingen " they are supposed to have originated in Germany, and were first heard as battle cries in 1140, in a fight (Weinsberg) between the rival families of Welf (Dukes of Bavaria) and Hohenstaufen, who took their rallying cry from their castle of Waiblingen. Italianized as Guelf and Ghibelline, they are first used by the Italian historians of this period. Benvenuto da Imola, *Coment. in Infer. X.*, vol. i, p. 339 ed. Lacaita, says that in the time of Frederick II. "istæ partialitates fuerunt in magno fervore in Italia, et specialiter in Tuscia, et specialissime in Florentia, Unde vidi literam in qua Fredericus lætatur quod ghibelini de Florentia amici sui expulerunt Guelphos ", and he adds, p. 346, that the Florentines are more given to factions than any other Italian people. (See the fantastic account of their origin in Saba Malaspina, *Hist.*, i, c. 1, ap. *R. I. SS.*, viii, p. 787. *Cf.* p. 788.) In the main, when these rallying cries were living forces, the Guelf party was that of the Church, and the Ghibelline that of the Emperor ; though in the swirl of party politics among the city-states of north Italy nothing was stable for any great length of time. To checkmate a rival city a Ghibelline city would fight for the Pope almost as readily as for the Emperor, and a Guelf city that had one day been almost annihilated for its attachment to the Pope, would, for the same end, fight side by side with those who had tried to destroy it. In the last passage quoted above from Malaspina we are told how party zeal for Pope or Emperor divided all Italy : " Quicunque in terra propria poterat aliquid, necessario de parte Imperii aut de parte nominatim Ecclesiæ censebatur." *Cf.* Butler, *The Lombard Communes*, p. 193 f.

[2] See Innocent's letters about the legatine commission of cardinals Stephen de Normandis and Rainer Capocci for Italy and Sicily, ap. *Reg.*, i, nn. 1972–87, p. 292 ff., Apr. 16, 1246.

[3] *Annal. Schefflar.*, ap. *M. G. SS.*, xvii, p. 342.

excommunicated. . . . Great sorrow and lamentation sprang up everywhere ; mercy, justice, and truth left the earth, and many of the clergy said Mass against the interdict."

The authority we have just quoted is for the most part referring to the state of things in Germany. Salimbene draws an equally gloomy picture of the condition of affairs in Italy. " In those days (c. 1247) there was the fiercest war which lasted many years. Men could neither plough, nor sow, nor reap, nor cultivate the vine, nor gather the vintage, nor dwell in the villages, especially in the neighbourhood of Parma, Reggio, Modena, and Cremona. Hard by the cities themselves, however, men tilled the ground under the guard of the city militia, who were divided into sections corresponding with the number of the gates. . . . This was necessary on account of the highwaymen, thieves, and robbers who were multiplied exceedingly and seized men and carried them off to dungeons to be ransomed for money. The cattle they drove off, and ate or sold them. Such as were not ransomed (were tortured)—for their (gaolers) were more cruel than devils. . . . Wild animals increased beyond measure—pheasants, partridges, and quails, hares, roebucks and fallow-deer, buffaloes, wild boars, and ravening wolves (which last) crept into the cities by night and devoured men, women, and children who were sleeping under the porticoes or in waggons." [1]

The quarrel intensifies.

Meanwhile the obstinacy and cruelty displayed by Frederick were hardening the heart of the Pope. In the beginning of the year 1247, he stated publicly that he would never make peace with Frederick as either Emperor or King [2] ; and a few months later he included

[1] *Chron.*, p. 190 f.
[2] Ep. of Jan. 28, 1247, ap. H.-B., vi, p. 489.

Frederick's sons in this resolve.[1] The quarrel between the Papacy and the house of Hohenstaufen was now fairly ablaze, and was not to be extinguished till the last of a line which had so oppressed the Church had perished on the scaffold.[2]

But the power of Frederick was not yet broken. On the contrary, Fortune seemed to smile more sweetly upon him than ever in the beginning of the year of his fall. Master of the situation in Sicily, he informed his partisans that he was now " more free to take the sword to crush the rebels of Lombardy ".[3] It is true that the King of Cyprus was absolved by Innocent from allegiance to him,[4] but just before this (Feb. 17) his powerful rival, Henry Raspe had died—" perchance," was the reflection of Abbot Menko, " because God wished still further to punish and to try His Church." [5]

Although this was a serious blow, it did not unman the Pope. He told the Milanese that his trust was in God, and that, if death carried off Princes who were a support to the Church, " the constancy of the Church was not thereby shaken. . . . For never will the Church lack the aid of Him who is the life and salvation of all, and to whom all powers are subject." [6]

Reception of the news of Henry's death.

---

[1] Ep. of May 4, 1247. " Promittimus . . . nec etiam pacem aliquatenus cum præfato Frederico reformabimus ita quod ipse vel aliquis filiorum suorum rex aut imperator existat."

[2] Cf. infra, an. 1268, under the *life* of Clement IV.

[3] Ep. Fred., Jan., 1247, ap. H.-B., vi, 491. Cf., ep. of Feb., ap. ib., p. 497 ff. " Nos in manu forti et copia thesaurorum sic *ad ultimum exterminium* nostrorum rebellium . . . partes Italiæ (i.e., as usual Lombardy) magnifice repetemus." P. 500. See similarly boastful and savage letters to our King Henry, and to the people of Cremona (ib., pp. 502 and 505, c. same date).

[4] Ep. Inn., March 5, ib., p. 506.

[5] *Chron.*, ap. *M. G. SS.*, xxiii, p. 539. He died " in omnipotentia sua regnans ", say the *Ann. Ensdorfenses*, an. 1247, ap. *M. G. SS.*, x.

[6] Ep. March, ap. H.-B., vi, 510.

On his side Frederick rejoiced at the news, and conceived the plan of ridding himself of his second and more formidable rival by seizing the Pope at Lyons. Accordingly, to keep the Lombards quiet, he gave out that he was most anxious to be reconciled with the Church, entered Lombardy " as meekly as a lamb " (April), and convoked a diet to meet at Cremona.[1] But at the same time to alienate French sympathy from the Pope, he again, in letters to the King and to the nobility of France, accused Innocent of having conspired against his life,[2]—declaring that the evidence that the Pope really had done so was known to all, whereas the evidence that he in his turn had attempted the life of the Pope rested merely on trumped-up stories.[3]

The Emperor proclaims his intention of marching on Lyons.

Frederick held the diet of his Italian partisans in due course at Cremona (May, 1247), and then, as he had by money and other personal considerations, secured the allegiance of the Counts of Savoy and other lords who had control of the Alpine passes and their approaches,[4] he boastfully proclaimed his intention of clearing himself

---

[1] *Chron. de reb.*, p. 209 f. ; and *Annal. Genuen.*, ap. *R. I. SS.*, vi, p. 571.

[2] Ep. of April. He said that his first enemy was Gregory IX. : " gregis Ecclesie disgregator," as he facetiously describes him. Ap. H.-B., vi, p. 514 ff.

[3] *Ib.* " Nec per ficta tormenta clamantium, a quibus extorta dicitur subornata confessio quod per quosdam ex nostris mortem pape fuerimus machinati." P. 516. Matthew Paris tells more than once of Frederick's sending assassins to kill the Pope, but adds that some asserted that the accounts he gives were mere inventions to counterbalance Frederick's story that the Pope had conspired against his life. *Cf. Chron.*, iv, p. 585 ; p. 605 for a second attempt, and p. 607 for a third. Paris adds that after the third attempt the Pope caused his palace, which he seldom left, to be guarded by fifty men day and night. But as Carbio does not accuse Frederick of having tried to procure the assassination of the Pope, we may safely conclude that Paris is, as so often, only repeating gossip, and may leave Frederick to accuse the Pope of having thought of playing the assassin.

[4] Details are furnished by Berger, *Reg.*, ii, p. clxxxi f.

before the Pope of the charges laid against him with the aid of an army.[1] Moreover to divide the French he called upon the French nobles who had recently exhibited a strong anti-clerical bias to meet him in arms, in order to assist him in carrying out his intention.[2]

This news naturally struck no little fear into the hearts of the Pope and his *entourage*.[3] There were, moreover, other serious reasons to cause Innocent grave anxiety at the moment. In Germany after the death of Henry Raspe, the power of King Conrad was steadily increasing, as no Prince, as a successor to Raspe, immediately came forward to oppose him.[4] Frederick's allies in the Alps were preventing Octaviano degli Ubaldini, cardinal-deacon of S. Maria-in-Via-Lata,[5] from passing into Lombardy with the troops which the Pope had

---

[1] *Cf.* his letters of July, 1247, (1) to Louis IX., ep. H.-B., vi, ii, p. 554, and (2) to a Sicilian official, ap. *ib.*, p. 555 f., in which he declared that it had been his intention : " cause nostre justitiam presentialiter et potenter in adversarii facie coram transalpinis gentibus posituri." *Cf.* Salimbene, *Chron.*, pp. 53, 211, and 189. At the last place (p. 189) " Ibat (Fred.) enim Lugdunum, ut caperet cardinales et papam." *Cf. Chron de reb.*, p. 210, and *Ann. Genuen.*, ap. *R. I. SS.*, vi, p. 511 ; Mat. Par., iv, 637.

[2] See his letter to Hugh de Castillione (Châtillon), count of St. Pol, one of the four nobles who formed the executive of the French baronial league against the clergy, ap. H.-B., vi, pt. ii, 528–9. On this league, to which we shall return, see Mat. Par., iv, p. 590 ff.

[3] See a letter of Archbishop Boniface of Savoy, ap. Mat. Par., vi, 133.

[4] Archbishop Boniface wrote to his brother : " Versus partes Germaniæ nullus stat pro ecclesia, nec cum ecclesia post mortem Landegravii, sed omnia cedunt voluntati regis Conradi." Ap. Mat. Par., vi, p. 132–3.

[5] He had been named legate for Lombardy and Romagna in March, 1247. *Cf. Reg.*, i, p. 450 ff., n. 2998 ff., March–May. On the blocking of the passes against Ottaviano, *cf. Reg.*, n. 4099, Nov. 9, 1247 ; and n. 5342, June 9, 1251. Carbio, c. 23 ; Mat. Par., iv, 624 f. ; Fred. epp. ap. H.-B., vi, ii, p. 556, and p. 570.

raised for the help of the League.[1] Added to all this, there were rumours of treachery at home.[2]

Innocent appeals to the French for aid, May, 1247.

Innocent, however, " was not shaken ; as calm and as firm in danger, as his adversary was prompt in attack, he prepared to receive him, and found the protector he had need of." [3] He at once appealed for help against " the disturber of the age " to the clergy and laity of France, and especially to its King (May, 1247).[4] He told them that Frederick had given out that he was coming to Lyons " to clear himself of the charges against him ", but that this statement, instead of bringing joy to him, had filled him with distrust, because Frederick was coming with an army, and without any preliminary negotiation with the Church, which he still continues to despise.[5] St. Louis promptly responded to the Pope's appeal. The armies of France were at his disposal.[6]

The revolt of Parma.

Confident that at length success was about to crown his efforts, Frederick set out for Turin and the passes of

---

[1] To the authorities in the preceding note add *Ann. Genuen.*, ap. *R. I. SS.*, vi, p. 511 f. " Papa fecit soldari . . . milites MD, quos in subsidium Parmensium et aliorum Lombardorum destinabat, quibus Comes Subaudiæ transitum prohibuit seductus a d. Frederico."

[2] Salimbene, *l.c.*, p. 189.

[3] Berger, *Reg.*, ii, p. clxxxv.

[4] His letter of May 28, 1247, to the archbishop of Narbonne is given in full by Berger, *l.c.* It is on the same lines, and, for the most part, in the same words as his letter (May 30) to the abbot of Vendôme, ap. H.-B., vi, 536. *Cf.* a document ap. Mat. Par., vi, p. 106.

[5] *Ib.*, ep. May 28.

[6] Carbio, c. 24. *Cf. Chron. rythm. Colon.*, p. 309 :—

> " Sic parat invasum papam, sed eum cito casum
> Noscens, Francorum Ludewicus rex dominorum
> Surgit ab opposito, collecto milite trito
> Obviat et pape mandat, constanter habere,
> Se papam scire sibi succurrendo venire,
> Augustum mire faciens cepto retroire."

Cf. Innocent's warm letters of thanks to Louis and his mother. Epp. June 17, 1247, ap. H.-B., vi, 544 ff., and the letter of July 2, to certain cardinals, ap. *ib.*, pt. ii, pp. 551–2, of which we merely know the contents.

the Alps on his way to Lyons (May). But, to use the words
of Balzani,[1] " a mysterious power seemed to shatter every
effort he made to recover his old fortune." He had, as
he says himself, reached " the foot-hills of the Alps, the
roots of the mountains (radices montium) ",[2] when word
was brought that Parma was lost to him (May 16).[3]
He had for some time past been concerned about its
loyalty. He had, therefore, banished many of its chief
men, the Pope's relatives and others, and as late as
August, 1246, had caused its Podestà to be seized.[4] But,
taking advantage of King Enzio's [5] being engaged in an
unimportant siege, the exiles suddenly returned, roused
the people, killed the imperial officials, called upon the
legate Gregory of Montelongo and upon neighbouring
Guelf cities to help them, and made feverish preparations
for a siege.[6]

Furious at this serious check to his plans, Frederick
turned back at once, ordered all his forces and those of
his allies to meet him at Parma, and in his usual style
informed the world that he was bringing his victorious
powers to bear on the place which he intended to capture
forthwith.[7]

[1] *The Popes and the Hohenstaufen*, p. 209.

[2] Ep. of July, ap. H.-B., vi, pt. ii, p. 554.

[3] The revolt of Parma says Salimbene " was the cause of his complete ruin : fuit causa totius ruine ipsius ".

[4] See his letter of Sept., 1246, ap. H.-B., vi, 460. *Cf. Mon. Patav.,
Chron.*, ap. *M. G. S.*, viii, 683.

[5] The imperial *legatus* in Italy (i.e. Lombardy).

[6] *Mon. Pat. = Ann. S. Justin., l.c.*, " Velociter munientes ad defen-
sionem se fortiter paraverunt." *Cf.* Salimbene, p. 180. *Ann. Parmenses*,
an. 1247, pp. 13–14 new ed., and the letters of Frederick to be quoted
in the foll. note.

[7] Ep. of July to Louis IX., ap. H.-B., vi, ii, p. 554. " In ejusdem
(Parma) eversionis precipitio indubitalem fiduciam obtinentes quod
cum civitas ipsa locus sit penitus immunitus, etc. . . . in brevi eam
. . . nos recognoscere suum dominum oportebit." " In obsidionem
Parme victricia signa nostra convertimus." Ep. to the Capitaneus

Siege of
Parma, and
defeat of the
Emperor.

(The election
of William,
Count of
Holland)
1247.

The formal siege of Parma commenced in the beginning of July, but month after month passed by, and the poorly fortified city inspired by Montelongo, still held out.

The ill-success of Frederick before Parma encouraged his enemies in Germany. After the death of Raspe there was, to begin with, a difficulty in securing a suitable candidate to succeed him, although the nobility were steadily falling away from Frederick. First one noble and then another was elected, but each in turn declined the dangerous honour.[1] Among others who were asked to accept the imperial crown was the powerful Hakon IV. (1217–63), King of Norway. To render him amenable Innocent legitimatized him, and consented to his coronation by cardinal William of Sabina (July 29, 1247). But, no sooner was he crowned, than he declared that he was indeed ever ready to make war upon the enemies of the Church, but not upon all the enemies of the Pope.[2] At length, however, through the energy of the devoted legate, cardinal Peter of St. George, a number of bishops and Princes met near Cologne, and on October 3 elected a successor to Henry Raspe in the person of William,

regni Siciliæ, ap. *ib.*, p. 557. " Ad obsid. P. *victoriose* processimus," so he writes to one of the Ghibelline cities of Tuscany, which he wishes to send aid " to his fortunate army ", " cujus est jam *presto victoria* ", ap. *ib.*, p. 558. See other letters, *ib.*, pp. 558–61, 564, and in ep. of September, ap. *ib.*, p. 569. So are now boasting (the first weeks of March, 1916) the Hohenzollerns before Verdun.

[1] Mat. Par., v, p. 201.

[2] That this remark was made we may believe even though it comes from Matthew Paris (*ib.*), because he states : " This the said King declared to me, Matthew, who wrote these pages, and attested with a great oath." Cf. *ib.*, p. 222 ; and *Reg. Inn.*, i, p. 325, nn. 2185, 2947, for the appointment of Will. as legate (Oct. 30, 1246), and n. 2217, and Carbio, c. 17, for the decree declaring Hakon (Haquinus as he is called in the document) legitimate. Cf. *Saga Hakonar Gamla* of Sturla Thordson, †1284. The mission of cardinal William to Norway, the most important since that of Nicholas Breakspear, is treated of in cc. 247–58 of this Saga, p. 250 ff. of the English trans., ap. *Icelandic Sagas*, vol. iv, R. S. The Icelandic original is in vol. ii. Cf. *supra*, p. 85 f.

count of Holland, quite young, but judged to be equal to the position to which he was elected. He was solemnly crowned at Aix-la-Chapelle after its capture by him on November 1, 1248.[1]

About the time of William's election, Frederick unable to carry Parma by storm, founded close to it a city to which he gave the boastful name of Victoria, and by which he proposed to replace the hostile town. He tried, moreover, by cruel treatment of prisoners to terrify the rebellious people into surrender.[2] It was all in vain. The Parmese, in constant receipt of assistance of all kinds from the Pope,[3] took reprisals on such partisans of the Emperor as were in their hands, and, by keeping a careful watch, were enabled, at length, to take the Imperialists by surprise. "The day that frowned on Frederick"[4]; which avenged Cortenuova; the day from which he never recovered, was February 18, 1248.[5] His ally, Cremona, lost its Carroccio, and Frederick, besides losing thousands of men, including the famous Thaddeus of Sessa, lost his new city, his treasure, and all prestige

Great defeat of Frederick, 1248.

---

[1] *Chron. reg. Colon., Contin. V.*, p. 291; *Ann. Erphord.*, p. 102, where (as in the *Chronicles* generally) an excellent character is given to William; Menko, *Chron.*, ap. *M. G. SS.*, xxiii, 541; *Gesta Abbat. Horti S. Mariæ, ib.*, p. 602; and especially the *Chronicle* which goes under the name of John de Beka, a canon of Utrecht. But the earlier portion of the *Chronicle* (698–1303) is the work of an anonymous author which the canon continued to 1346. Ap. Böhmer, *Fontes*, ii, p. 432. For a full list of authorities on this election, see Böhmer-Ficker, *Regest. Imperii*, v, p. 918 ff.

[2] On Frederick's regime of "frightfulness" before Parma, see Mat. Par., iv, 648, and Salimbene (*Chron.*, p. 197) who was in Parma during a long period of the siege.

[3] "P. Inn. a principio usque ad finem vite sue fecit omnia bona quecumque potuit pro defensione civitatis Parme, et fuerunt bona et auxilia infinita et inextimabilia." *Chron. Parmen.*, ad. an.

[4] Dante, *Purg.*, xvi.

[5] The *Chron. Siculum*, ap. H.-B., i, ii, p. 808, sums up the affair very well. "Turpiter devictus fuit, multis de suis ibidem captis et inter fectis, et multo rubore confusus, infirmus in regnum rediit."

in Lombardy.[1] His enormous imperial crown was found
by a man, who on account of his mean stature was known
as Short-step (Curtus-passus). Holding it as one holds a
hawk, he walked with it through the city, " showing it
to all who wished to see it in honour of the victory they
had gained, and to the eternal disgrace of Frederick." [2]
" From that day," says Rolandinus, " his victorious
career walked backwards like a crab." [3]

Frederick
remains in
Lombardy
for over a
year longer,
Feb., 1248–
Apr., 1249.

Although the defeat of Frederick naturally gave great
satisfaction to the Pope who, according to Matthew
Paris, on hearing the news, cried out : " Oh Victory
(*Victoria* in allusion to Frederick's destroyed new foundation) for the honour of Christ, thou hast been vanquished,"[4]
still he knew that Frederick was not crushed.   He
accordingly exhorted all the Guelf cities not to allow the
defeat of Frederick to lull them to sleep, and impressed
upon them that though God had indeed shortened the
days of the oppression of the liberty of Italy, they must
stand by Parma, on which still rested the hope of the
country.[5]

[1] Cf. *Vita Ricciardi Comitis*, ap. *R. I. SS.*, viii, p. 132. Its author
sarcastically notes that after this defeat Frederick was never again
distinguished by the performance of any " royal crime—nullo postmodum regio insignis facinore ".   See also the other Italian Chronicles
in the same vol. : *Chron. Parm.*, ap. *ib.*, ix, p. 15 ff. new ed. ; Carbio,
c. 26, and Thos. of Tuscany, Menko etc. in *M. G. SS.*, xxii, and xxiii,
and many letters of Frederick himself and others, ap. H.-B., vi, p. 588 ff.
For the fullest details of the siege see the *Chronicle* published, ap. H.-B.,
vi, pp. 924–33. It is really an extract from Salimbene.

[2] Salimbene, p. 203. *Cf.* p. 343. Frederick had also to bewail the
loss of " camera nostra cum auree bulle typario et regni nostri sigillo ".
Ep. Fred. ap. H.-B., VI, ii, p. 596.

[3] *Chron.*, l. v, c. 22. This remark about " the crab " is a hit at
Frederick's astrology. *Cf. ib.*, c. 21.

[4] " Ad laudem Christi Victoria victa fuisti." *Chron.*, v, 15. *Cf.* ep.
of card. Rainer, ap. H.-B., VI, ii, p. 603 ff.

[5] " Videntur siquidem breviari miserante Domino, dies mali quibus
tranquilitas ecclesiastice et Italicæ libertatis per iniquam persecutoris
rabiem lacessitur etc." . . . . " In defensione civitatis predicte de qua
pendet potissimum revelatio status Italie."   Ep. of March, 1248, ap.
ib., p. 599 ff. *Cf.* ep. ap. *ib.*, p. 601 f.

Innocent had correctly gauged the situation. For more than a year after the defeat of Parma, Frederick remained in Lombardy, moving about from place to place, and, in conjunction with his son Enzio, burning and destroying. and giving way more and more to his heartless cruelty.[1]

He also encouraged a paper warfare against the Pope, by lending his support to a certain brother Arnold, a Dominican. This man, about whom nothing is known, called for the reform of the Church in head and members, on account of the " heresies " of the Roman Church and Pope Innocent.[2] Addressing all the faithful, Arnold explained how, in his zeal for reform, he had approached " the lord Frederick, the most serene Emperor, . . . as the principal defender of the Church". The Emperor had rejoiced when the friar's plan for the reformation of the Church was explained to him, for he was concerned on account of the injury done to the faithful " in things spiritual, corporal, and temporal by Pope Innocent IV. and all his followers ".[3] The Pope was " quite opposed to Christ ", and so were all his partisans. Arnold then accuses them of all the vices under twenty-five heads, of which the last is the heresy of disobedience, committed by their despising the warning voice of the lord (emperor). Hence must the faithful cut themselves off from the Pope, and his party and adhere to Arnold and those who think with him.

In his next pamphlet, anticipating the malicious

(marginal note:) Frederick encourages a paper warfare against the Pope, 1248.

---

[1] Cf. Chron. de rebus = Annal. Placent. Gib., p. 217 ff. On his cruel execution of three bishops, cf. the indignant letter of card. Rainer just quoted, ap. H.-B., ii, 603 ff. Cf. ep. Inn., Apr. 18, ap. ib., p. 614 ff.

[2] Fratris Arnoldi, O.P., De correctione ecclesiæ epist., ed. E. Winkelmann, Berlin, 1865. Arnold is perhaps also the author of the Libellus de Innocentio IV., P.M. Antichristo, published ib., pp. 20–2.

[3] With the same concern as is felt and expressed by the present emperor, William II., for the injury being done to Europe by the Allies (1916).

absurdities of some of the reformers of the sixteenth
century, Arnold gave as a very special reason why all
should abandon the Pope, the fact that he was Antichrist,
for he had the number of the beast, i.e. 666 (*Apoc.*, xiii,
18). "Innocent(c)iu(v)s Papa" gave the required
figure. I (1) N (50) N (50) O (70) C (100) E (5) N (50) C (100)
I (1) V (5) S (200), gives 632. So far so good. To get the
remaining 34, Arnold fell back upon the fact that P
is the sixteenth Greek letter and A is the first, and
St. John wrote the Apocalypse in Greek.   Therefore
P (16) A (1) P (16) A (1) equals 34. Pope Innocent IV.
then was clearly Antichrist !

Renewed
excommuni-
cation of
Frederick,
1248.

But the brutal violence of Frederick and of his savage
Saracens of Lucera,[1] and the rabid pen and ink
ravings of such pamphleteers as brother Arnold, only
put new vigour into the resistance of the Pope and the
Lombard League.   On April 16, Innocent renewed the
excommunication of Frederick and his supporters,[2] and
then encouraged opposition to him in Germany and
Palestine.[3]   Strong in the support of the Pope, and in
that of Conrad of Hochstaden, the powerful archbishop
of Cologne, who was the soul of the papal party in
Germany, the new King, William of Holland, was steadily
strengthening his position, and in April was able to
commence the siege of Aix-la-Chapelle.[4]   Accordingly,
in order to gain time for the arrival of the men and

---

[1] *Cf.* the present savage conduct of the Germans and their Moslem
allies, whose recent awful massacre of the Armenians will never be
forgotten.

[2] Ep. cit., and ep. of Apr. 27, 1248, ap. *ib.*, p. 618.

[3] Epp. of May 15 and 25, ap. *ib.*, pp. 622 and 623 ff.

[4] *Chron. reg. Colon., Contin. V.*, p. 292. *Cf.* ep. of W. of H., *c.* Sept.,
1248, ap. H.-B., vi, ii, 654. *Ann. Argentin.*, ap. Böhmer, *Fontes*, ii,
109, and *Chron. Erphord.*, *ib.*, p. 405. The strength of character of
Innocent is well seen in his resistance to the exactions practised by his
great supporter, Archbishop Conrad. *Cf.* Menko, *Chron.*, ap. *M. G. SS.*,
xxiii, p. 537.

money which he was hoping to draw " from the fatness " of his realm of Sicily, as he expressed it,[1] Frederick again tried to induce St. Louis IX. in the interests of his approaching Crusade, to work for the removal of his excommunication.[2] But, whatever steps were taken by the French King, Innocent in a short letter gave him to understand that, although he was most anxious for peace with the former Emperor, it would have to be a peace honourable to the Church, and one which would ensure " the safety of those who are known to have stood by her in this crisis ".[3] Moreover, he must take it as irrevocable that no peace would be made which included the return to imperial power of Frederick, or of any of his descendants.[4] The real difficulty in the way of peace, as Frederick himself at this time declared to our King Henry, was, and always had been, the Lombard question.[5] Innocent was determined to stand by the Peace of Constance and his allies the Lombards ; Frederick was resolved to disregard the Peace and never to cease fighting the Lombards till he had subdued them. He must be lord of Italy and of the Church in it.

[1] *Cf.* a letter of Fred. (March, 1249) where he speaks of " habilem succursum pecunie de regni nostri pinguedine ". Ap. H.-B., VI, ii, 704. *Cf.* epp. of May and June, 1248, ap. *ib.*, pp. 633–6, 933 ff.

[2] *Ann. Genuen.*, ap. *R. I. SS.*, vi, 515. *Cf.* ep. Fred., July 24, 1248, ap. H.-B., vi, 638 f.

[3] Ep. July, 1248, ap. H.-B., *ib.*, p. 641. " Tractatum pacis . . . nullatenus admittemus nisi cum . . . illorum salute qui sibi (the Church) adhesisse in hac parte noscuntur."

[4] " Ceterum pro constanti teneas quod qualiscumque pacis tractatus emergat, dictus Fredericus aut aliquis de sua progenie numquam de cætero ad imperii regimen assumetur." *Ib. Cf.* ep. Inn., Aug., 1248, ap. *ib.*, pp. 643–4.

[5] Ep. of August, 1248, " Sed iste bonus pastor Ecclesie (Innocent) nullum ad jus et honorem imperii nec ad nos coluit habere respectum sed totum sue subjicere potestati pro Lombardorum negocio, qui pacis tractatui semper hactenus impedimenta pararant, et pacem quam debebat exquirere, turpiter profugavit oblatam." Ap. H.-B., *ib.*, p. 645.

Continuation
of the
struggle in
1248.

The death struggle accordingly went on. Again Innocent proclaimed the aim of his pontificate. It was " in God to pacify with the world the disturber of the public peace; or, if he persisted in his hardness of heart, then would he with the help of God take his stand for the people, and boldly face the implacable pestilential Prince who stirs up the deadly blasts by which the world is wearied. It is absolutely fixed in my heart either to tear the evil roots of discord from the people of Christendom, or to destroy the cause of these evils, the tryanny of that malignant Prince, once Emperor, by which the whole world is falling to ruin, the orthodox faith o'erthrown, and the glory of ecclesiastical liberty uprooted ". Hence must Stephen, cardinal-priest of S. Maria Trastevere, cause the Cross to be preached in Rome, Campania, and the Maritima, and after due warning, place under the interdict all, cleric and lay, who in the Kingdom of Sicily support Frederick. " It must no longer be that among a Christian people the sceptre of power should remain with Frederick, or be handed over to any of the viperish offspring of one whom prosperity has so inflated that, seemingly forgetful that he is sprung from men, he rages inhumanely against them." [1]

St. Louis
makes a
second
attempt to
make peace
between
Frederick
and the
Pope.

This was written by Innocent after the failure of the effort on the part of St. Louis, just spoken of, to make peace between the Emperor and the Pope. Frederick, as we have said, promised the holy King to help him in his Crusade if he succeeded in inducing the Pope to remove the sentence of excommunication which he had inflicted on him.[2] In the forlorn hope of being able to bring about so desirable a co-operation, Louis interviewed the Pope on his way to embark for Cyprus. But Innocent would not agree either to abandon the cause of the Lombards or to

---

[1] Ep. of Aug. 30, 1248, ap. H.-B., vi, ii, p. 646 ff.
[2] *Ann. Genuen.*, l. vi, p. 515, ap. *R. I. SS.*, vi.

recognize Frederick as Emperor.[1]   Whether Louis was really disappointed, or not, it may well be doubted with Berger [2] if he ever said to the Pope on learning his decision : " If the expedition to the Holy Land is not successful, the blame will be laid on you." [3]

The year which witnessed the departure of St. Louis on his ill-starred Crusade (August 28, 1248), and the solemn crowning of William of Holland at Aix-le-Chapelle (November 1), came to a close with a little more talk of peace on Frederick's part.[4]   But whilst he was thus talking, he was once again endeavouring to secure his power in Piedmont,[5] and Innocent, in behalf of the freedom of the oppressed church of Sicily, was denouncing the ambition of one whom " the whole world could not satisfy ", and of one who " thought he had but little if he had sway only over the things of this world, and if the things of the spirit escaped his control ".[6]

For over four months longer did Frederick remain in Lombardy, endeavouring in vain with the aid of his bastard sons,[7] Enzio and Frederick of Antioch, to make headway against the free cities of Lombardy.   While continuing to boast as usual of his intention of crushing " with the sword of his power " such as had rebelled

The struggle in 1249. Frederick gets more violent as his fortune wanes.

---

[1] *Cf.* epp. July, 1248, of Innocent, probably to William of Holland, ap. H.-B., VI, ii, p. 641, and of August, ap. *ib.*, p. 643, and ep. Fred., *ib.*, p. 645.

[2] *Reg.*, ii, p. ccxxii f. " Il y a certainement dans ce recit (of Matthew Paris) beaucoup d'exagération et l'on est en droit de se demander par qui les paroles de St. Louis et d'Innocent IV. auraient bien pu rapportées a Mathieu de Paris."

[3] Mat. Par., v, p. 22.

[4] Ep. Fred. to the counts of Savoy, Nov. 8, ap. *ib.*, p. 657.

[5] Epp. Fred., ap. *ib.*, pp. 642, 658 ff., 674. *Cf. Chron. de reb.* = *Ann. Placent. Gib.*, p. 218.

[6] Ep. Inn., Dec. 8, ap. H.-B., *ib.*, p. 676 ff.

[7] " Cruelty, treachery, and lewdness are the three blots that can never be wiped away from the memory of Frederick the Second," says his biographer, Kington, i, p. 474.

against his authority—on this occasion various cities of Tuscany [1]—he could not fail to realize that Fortune was turning her back upon him. Like all lustful tyrants, he began to suspect everyone, and to give full reign to his cruelty. [2] He caused his hitherto much trusted and able minister, Peter della Vigna, to be blinded, and was contemplating an ignominious public disgrace for him when the unfortunate man put an end to his life, April, 1249. [3]

Unable, despite his intrigues round Lyons, to lay hands on the Pope, [4] as he had on his favourite, Frederick did not blush again to accuse him to the Princes of the world, as he had already done, of plotting his death. It was given out that, like Peter della Vigna, the Pope had tried to have him poisoned, " because he could not bear an equal, and was impatient of a consort." [5] Frederick could, however, lay hands on those who were carrying out the Pope's commands in his dominions, and he accordingly ordered the officials of the Kingdom of Sicily actually to *burn* such Dominicans and Franciscans as were found acting against him by the introduction of

[1] Ep. Fred., Feb., 1249, ap. H.-B., *l.c.*, pp. 698-9. He announces his intention of proceeding to Tuscany " ut incauta nostrorum corda rebellium, de quibus finalis et desiderata victoria nostre potentie gladio reservatur sicut in absentia nostra gloriati sunt hactenus, sic ex vicenitate nostre potentie terreantur." *Cf.* ep. of March, *ib.*, p. 703 f.

[2] *Cf.* the old French Chronicle of Rheims, which dates from the second half of the thirteenth century : " Adont (Frederick) se commencha a douter de traïson, et entra en une grande mescréandise telle qu'il ne crévit nului. Et fist occire une grant partie de sa maisnie, ou fust à droit ou fust à tort." Cited by H.-B., *Pierre de la Vigne*, p. 57.

[3] *Chron. de reb.*, p. 218 f., Ep. Fred., 1249, ap. H.-B., VI, ii, p. 708 f. ; and Mat. Par., *Chron.*, v, 68 f. The obscurities that hang about the death of P. d. V., are discussed at length by Huillard-Bréholles, *Pierre*, pp. 55-91.

[4] From the passage of Matthew P., just cited, it appears that Frederick had not abandoned hope of seizing the Pope. *Cf.* Mat. Par., v, 146.

[5] Ep. of March, ap. H.-B., VI, ii, p. 705 ff. The Princes should prevent the clergy from interfering in secular affairs.

papal letters or otherwise. He even decided that those
of his subjects who killed them at sight were not to be
brought to judgment.[1] Even according to Matthew Paris [2]
the deadly stench of such deeds irritated all the faithful.

But the walls of destiny were closing in on Frederick. The action
Innocent continued to give his support to William of of Innocent
in 1249.
Holland,[3] who, on his side, swore to protect the rights
and possessions of the Roman Church.[4] Thus regularly
supported by the moral and material assistance of the
Pope, William continued to strengthen his position in
Germany, despite Conrad's despairing effort to hinder the
progress of his adversary by encouraging the heretics of
Suabia.[5] Moreover, at the Council or Diet of Muldorf
(1249) held by Philip, elect of Ferrara, Otho II., the fickle
duke of Bavaria (1231-53), was for the moment at least
" both by sentence of excommunication and by the
material sword forced to return to the Roman Church,
and to adhere to it against Frederick ".[6] In Lombardy
also, after the Emperor had left it, the tide of events
continued to run against him. His favourite Enzio was

[1] Epp. of March, ap. H.-B., *ib.*, pp. 699 and 701. Even Frederick
himself appears to have been afraid of the effect of these atrocious
orders becoming generally known. " Fidelitati tue (the count of
Caserta) modis omnibus inhibemus ut mandati hujus non fias in
populo publicus delator." P. 701. *Cf.* C. Lazzari, *Guglielmino Ubertini*,
p. 3 ff., for the cruel death inflicted by Frederick II. on Bishop
Marcellinus.

[2] *Chron.*, v, 60, an. 1249.

[3] Epp. of Jan. and Feb., 1249, ap. *ib.*, pp. 690 and 691.

[4] Ep. Feb. 19, 1249, ap. *ib.*, p. 692 f. The possessions are thus
enumerated : " Ad has pertinet tota terra que est a Radicofano usque
Ceperanum, exarchatus Ravenne, Pentapolis, marchia Anconitana,
ducatus Spoletanus, terra comitisse Mathildis, comitatus Bertenorii,
cum adjacentibus terris expressis in multis privilegiis imperatorum a
tempore Ludovici. . . . Adjutor etiam ero ad retinendum et defen-
dendum Ecclesie Romane regnum Sicilie."

[5] Alb. Stadensis, *Chron.*, an. 1248. *Cf.* for Will's. success, *Chron.
Erphord.*, 1249, ap. Böhmer, *Fontes*, ii, 405.

[6] *Ann. S. Rudbert.*, ap. *M. G. SS.*, ix, p. 790.

captured by the Bolognese, and confined to a prison whence he was never to emerge.[1] It was to no purpose that Frederick threatened Bologna " della Chiesa ".[2] The Bolognese replied that God destroyed those " who trusted in might rather than in right ", and that, as they were not reeds, they cared not for Frederick's windy words. They had got possession of Enzio, and would keep possession of him, and if Frederick wanted him, he had better try to take him by force. But, with all his power, he must not forget the proverb that a boar is often held by a little dog.[3]

Frederick returns to the kingdom, 1249. The capture of Enzio broke the spirit of his father. He had not the courage to face the Lombards again, but returned " sad and anxious " [4] to his kingdom of Sicily, to drown, say some, his sorrows in the pleasures of sense (May, 1249). " For," says one of his modern admirers,[5] " despite his advanced age, and doubtful health " he was at this time in that condition which an historian of the time characterized by an expression pre-eminently Italian—he was *innamorato*." [6] It is certain, however, that he did not wholly give himself up to pleasure. He took some revenge on the Pope by attacking the pontifical city of Benevento and destroying

---

[1] *Chron. de rebus*, p. 219.

[2] Ep. of June, ap. H.-B., *ib.*, p. 737.

[3] Ap. H.-B., VI, ii, p. 739. This short letter is the most spirited in the whole *Hist. Diplom.* of Fred. II. " A cane non magno sepe tenetur aper." Again, one is forcibly reminded of contemporary events. " The boar," William II., was well held by the little dog Belgium, as Frederick II. was by Bologna.

[4] John of Victring, † 1347, *Hist.*, p. 191 ed. Schneider.

[5] Huillard-Bréholles, *Recherches sur l'hist. des Normands et de la maison de Souabe dans l'Italie mérdid*, p. 103. But he seems to be relying here solely on the forged *Diurnali* quoted in the following note.

[6] " Et però si dice che non va più (in Lombardy) per questo anno, et si dice ancora che sta innamorato." Matteo di Giovenazzo, *Diurin.*, §20, a sixteenth century forgery, quoted *ib.*

its walls,[1] and continued to indulge in acts of cruelty which rendered him odious,[2] and made Innocent more determined than ever not to listen to proposals of peace with such a tyrant.[3]

The opening of the last year of Frederick's life saw him well nigh at the end of any resources in the West, which were available to make the balance of parties in Lombardy incline in his favour. He accordingly turned to the East, and prevailed upon his son-in-law, John Vatatzes, to agree to send him a body of troops with which, and with his own new levies he proposed in his usual boastful language, to set out for Lombardy in the spring " for the final extermination of those who have rebelled against us, and for the complete destruction of those who through papal malevolence are in opposition to us." [4] But the Greek troops did not come. A papal mission consisting of a number of Franciscans and Dominicans, among whom was the pure-minded general of the former, John of Parma, had meanwhile arrived in Nicæa. Their mission was not in the least political, but it had the effect of again directing the mind of Vatatzes towards thoughts of reunion with Rome. Hence the idea of sending troops to the help of Frederick was abandoned,[5] and there was nothing left to Frederick but to reproach Vatatzes for

The death of Frederick, 1250.

[1] *Ann. Cavenses*, ap. *R. I. SS.*, vii, p. 927. *Cf.* Ep. Inn., Aug. 23, 1252, ap. Rod., iii, p. 134, n. 156.

[2] H.-B., *ib.*, p. 104.

[3] Hence he would not listen to St. Louis IX. again, pleading for Frederick, because he had sent provisions to him at Cyprus at the end of 1249. Mat. Par., *Chron.*, v, 70.

[4] Ep. of Feb., 1249, to Michael II. of Epirus, ap. *ib.*, p. 759. *Cf.* the foll. ep. *Cf.* Salimbene, *Chron.*, pp. 304, 321, 324 ; *Catal. General. O. F. M.*, ap. *M. G. SS.*, xxxii, p. 662.

[5] Miss Gardner in her valuable book, *The Lascarids of Nicæa*, is mistaken in supposing (p. 175) that the Greek troops really arrived in Italy. She supposes that *Pergamene* soldiers fought in north Italy, relying on the words of a letter of Frederick (ap. H.-B., *ib.*, p. 792) : " robustorum Pergamensium." But these words refer to the men of Bergamo, the Bergamese. *Cf. Chron. de rebus*, p. 227.

dealing with Innocent, who was constantly calling the Greeks heretics.[1] However, with a view to induce the Greek Emperor not to attach himself to the weaker side, he continued in his letters to belittle the Pope, and to assure Vatatzes that " we are daily defeating our enemies, and everything is being done in accordance with our directions." [2] Month after month the same story was told to Vatatzes, who, despite the successes of William of Holland,[3] was assured that in Germany also, by the victories of his son Conrad, his enemies could not find a hiding place.[4]

But Frederick's subtle mixture of falsehood and truth had no effect on Vatatzes. His archers remained in Nicæa, and the struggle in the West went on with such forces as Frederick and his allies had at their disposal. At length, however, in the very last month of the year, " the pernicious discord between the Empire and the Papacy was to some degree assuaged " [5] by the death of Frederick (Dec. 13, 1250), which took place at Fiorentino (or Firenzuola), a few miles from Lucera.

The death-bed of Frederick.

Great is the divergence among contemporary historians as to the manner in which " the wonder of the world, the last of the emperors ",[6] prepared to meet his Maker. According to one class of writers, he died impenitent, and " went down to hell taking nothing with him but

---

[1] Ep. to Vatatzes, c. May or June, 1250, ap. H.-B., ib., p. 771 ff.

[2] Ib.

[3] Ann. Wormat., 1250, ap. Böhmer, Fontes, ii, 187.

[4] Ep. c. August, ap. H.-B., ib., 790. " Qui tamen simili errore in Alemannia ad novitates surrexerunt et in reprobrum sensum vertuntur, de loco in locum per potentiam. . . . Conradi viriliter profugati, invenire locum ubi latitent non jam possunt." Cf. ep. of Sept., 1250, ib., p. 791. Cf. on Frederick's success, Mat. Par., v, 145.

[5] Chron. Erphord., ap. Böhmer, ib., ii, 410.

[6] " In hoc imperium Romanum cessasse videtur." Annal. Norman., ap. M. G. SS., xxvi, p. 515. Cf. James de Voragine, Chron., ap. ib., xxiv, p. 71.

a sack of sins ".[1] Whereas, according to another class, he died in good dispositions after having confessed his misdeeds [2] ; and it is possible that the latter, if smaller, class has preserved the truth. At any rate Frederick's illegitimately born son, Manfred, who was with him when he died, informed his brother Conrad that " with a contrite heart, as one zealous for the true faith their father humbly recognized his mother the Holy Roman Church, and ordered complete restitution to be made for the injuries which he had inflicted on churches, perchance against his will, or, rather under provocation ".[3] This is confirmed by Frederick's will,[4] and by Matthew Paris, whose testimony in this instance seems to be reliable, as he declares that he had been informed " by the positive statement " of Frederick's friends that the Emperor had humbly assumed the Cistercian habit before he died. He adds that, as he promised satisfaction for his faults, he was duly absolved.[5]

However all this may be, Frederick's body was buried at Palermo (Feb. 25) where his red porphyry sarcophagus,

---

[1] *Mon. Patav.*, ap. *R. I. SS.*, viii, 685 ; Carbio, c. 29 ; *Hist. Sic.*, *ib.*, p. 780 ; Saba Malaspina, *ib.*, p. 788 ; *Vit. Ricciardi, ib.*, 132 ; Rolandinus, *ib.*, p. 942 ; *Ann. of Waverley*, iii, 343, etc., etc.

[2] *Cf. Ann. Austriæ, contin. Garstens.*, ap. *M. G. SS.*, ix, p. 599. He died " sub penitentia cordis et confessione oris et recognoscentia sue culpe ".

[3] Ep., Dec., 1250, ap. H.-B., vi, ii, 810 ff. *Cf.* a letter of Conrad, March 20, 1251, ap. *ib.*, p. 892, which is not quite so positive as to his father's dispositions with regard to the Church.

[4] In his will dated Dec. 10, 1250 (ap. H.-B., vi, ii, p. 805 ff. The version of it given by Mat. Paris, v, 216, is very inaccurate). Frederick orders restitution to be made to the Templars and to churches, and that the churches of Lucera and others injured by his officials should be restored. His language with regard to the Roman Church is ambiguous. Its rights are to be restored if it restores those of the Empire. " Item statuimus S. Rom. ecclesie matri nostro restituantur omnia jura sua, salvis . . . jure et honore imperii . . . si ipsa Ecclesia restituat jura imperii."

[5] *Chron. maj.*, v, 216. *Cf.* p. 404.

under a granite canopy supported by six pillars, may still be seen in the cathedral.

The Papacy
more than a
match for
Frederick.
By his death, at any rate, Frederick's dream of world-power came to an end ; and to one who has taken the trouble to read the preceding pages there is no need of repeating that it was the Papacy that saved the liberties of Europe from the destroying hand of Germanic Cæsarism. This fact is well brought out in a story of Frederick's early years preserved by an author, other-wise of no great repute, who flourished at the close of the thirteenth century. "When Frederick was four years old," says James of Aix, "we are told that he once cried out in his sleep : ' I cannot. I cannot.' When he awoke and was questioned as to what he was dreaming about, he replied : ' It seemed to me that I was engaged in eating the countries of the world, and had eaten several when I tried to eat up a very large one. I could not swallow it, and it nearly choked me. Hence I cried out.' " Needless to say, " the very large one " was the Papacy, for, continues James : " this was verified when the Pope excommunicated him, and deprived him of the Empire." [1]

The end of
the Hohen-
staufen, and
the con-
demnation
of Frederick.
The death of Frederick was, as the sequel of this work will show, followed at no great interval by that of his offspring either on the field of battle or on the scaffold, and his principal English biographer assures us that " there are not many instances in history of so awful a downfall as that of the Hohenstaufens ".[2] The same author adds that in the strife between them and the Papacy " Rome won the battle ; and we need not regret

[1] Jac. Aquensis, *Chron. maj. mundi.* (to 1290), ap. *Mon. histor. pat. SS.*, iii, p. 1572.

[2] Kington, ii, 514. We may add also that there are not many families whose chiefs have been so often struck with personal excommunication by the Heads of the Church as that of the Hohenstaufen. " The Heads of the Church " whom the same author (*l.c.*) speaks of as those " Papal giants of the thirteenth century, ever ready to march in the van of public opinion, shrinking from useless crimes ".

it [1]; for " the impartial inquirer will hesitate before he
pronounces that the fall of the House of Suabia was a
blow to the interests of mankind ".   Whatever Frederick
II. may incidentally have done for the advancement of
material civilization, he has been judged severely in
these pages, because " he was personally cruel,[2] luxurious,
and perfidious, and because he drew from force and fraud
the most powerful weapons of his government " [3]; and
because we accept the considered judgment of the most
distinguished of all the students of the doings of Frederick
II., Huillard-Bréholles :   " We must," he says in the
last words of his *Introduction* to his *Historia Diplomatica*,
" be on our guard against that fatal optimism which
displays too great indulgence towards material progress
secured by violence and injustice ; and we must continue
to believe that in the collective life of peoples, as in the
career of individuals, nothing is really meritorious but
honour and justice." [3]

---

[1] *Cf.* Oscar Browning, *Guelphs and Ghibellines*, p. 11. " The success
of a Ghibelline emperor meant the subjection of Italy to Germany, the
binding of north and south together in an unnatural union, the establishment of a great power in Europe fatal to the freedom of the nations."
Hill, *A Hist. of European Diplomacy*, i, p. 344, speaks to the same effect.
As I record these testimonies to the danger of the German Empire of
the thirteenth century to the liberties of Europe, the present European
war (1914 ff.) is bringing out wonderfully the work done by the Popes
for these liberties. At this moment it is taking some fifteen million
men, and treasure beyond calculation, to do the work done by the
Popes, whose biographies we are writing, i.e. to preserve the freedom
of the nations from the iron militarism of Germany.

[2] " Cestu emperor, quy fu mout cruel home de cuer et sans pité,
et fu mout contraire et persecutor de sainte yglise, et por ce li meschut
ala à nient, luy et ces hairs." *Les Gestes des Chiprois*, p. 143, n. 243
ed. G. Raynaud, Geneva, 1887.

[3] H.-B., pp. Dlvii f.

CHAPTER III.

INNOCENT RETURNS TO ITALY. HIS SOJOURN AT PERUGIA,
ASSISI, AND ROME. HIS EFFORTS TO SAVE SICILY
FROM CONRAD. HIS DEATH.

1251–4.

The aims of Innocent in contrast with those of Frederick and Conrad.

FROM the will of Frederick II., and from the subsequent action of Conrad, two things are clear. It was the joint aim of father and son first to make the Empire hereditary in the family of Hohenstaufen, and then permanently to attach the Kingdom of Sicily to the Empire. Both these objects were unconstitutional. The entire history both of the Holy Roman Empire, and of the Empire of Old Rome which was its model, proves that the Emperor was to be elected not born.[1] Nor is there any doubt that for generations the Kingdom of Sicily had been universally recognized to be a fief of the Roman Church,[2] and was therefore subject to the feudal laws that regulated fiefs. Now it was the duty of the Popes as the acknowledged arbiters of Europe at this period [3] to see that its public laws were observed ; and it was, moreover, their interest, as Head of the Church, to strive that the Head of the State, that is the Emperor, should remain an elective Prince. Even Frederick himself, as we have noted, had declared that the Emperor was the Advocate of the Church. It was then but natural that the Church

[1] Hence Innocent's plain statement to the Duke of Saxony : " Ipsi (the sons of Frederick) nullum jus habeant in imperio, cujus *non successione* set *electione* dignitas obtinetur." Ep. Feb. 19, n. 67 ap. Rod. iii, p. 54. *Cf.* n. 74.

[2] Hence Saba Malaspina, *Hist.*, i, c. 3, could write : " Licet regnum Siciliæ foret ad dispositionem Ecclesiæ Romanæ cujus juris et proprietatis extitit, libere devolutum, etc."

[3] Hence St. Louis spoke of the Curia Romana " in qua solent arduæ causæ et difficiles terminari ". Mat. Par., iv, 647.

should have some say at least in the choice of its Defender. It had its opportunity if the Empire remained elective. Further, as the temporal ruler of the centre of Italy, it was obviously the interest of the Pope to maintain his prescriptive rights over Sicily in order to save himself from being crushed between the upper and nether millstone. This he would be wholly unable to do if the Kingdom of Sicily became an hereditary appendage of the Empire.

There was then nothing for it but for Innocent to continue the struggle against the Hohenstaufen who had unmistakably shown that it was their intention to make both the Empire and Sicily hereditary, and that too in the person of the same Prince. William of Holland must, therefore, be supported in his candidature for the Empire against Conrad IV., and Sicily must be prevented from falling into his hands. On his side Conrad showed no disposition to forego his claims both to Empire and to the Kingdom of Sicily.

Accordingly as soon as the death of Frederick came to the knowledge of Innocent, he lost no time in taking steps to recover control over Sicily. That he had the strictest right to do this, is well brought out by Mr. Sedgwick, who shows that the question was one purely of feudal law, inasmuch as Frederick had solemnly declared himself the Pope's vassal for Sicily. " By feudal law and feudal custom the obligations inherent in that relation (of lord and vassal) were clear and definite. Among the vassal's duties to his lord were these : to do him homage, to acknowledge his rights, to do him no wrong, and to pay the tribute that had been fixed. On the vassal's fidelity depended his title to his fief. If he turned heretic, or if he turned traitor his fief was forfeit.[1] . . . Every code based on the feudal system

The prompt action of Innocent regarding Sicily.

---

[1] Mr. Sedgwick here cites the cases of Raymond of Toulouse who was dispossessed of his fief for heresy by the Fourth Lateran Council,

accepted and confirmed these principles.[1] . . . Most of
the offences charged against Frederick were matters
of common knowledge. He had not paid his feudal
tribute for years, etc. . . . By consent of all, the King of
Sicily was guilty of fatal breaches of duty towards his
suzerain lord " [2]; and his suzerain lord now took steps
to recover his fief.

An
encyclical
to Sicily,
1251.

Accordingly, when the death of Frederick, which was
kept secret for some days, became known in Lyons,
Innocent addressed an encyclical to all the clerical and
lay magnates of Sicily. " May the heavens and the
earth rejoice," he wrote, " now that the fearful tempest,
by which the dread Majesty of God has allowed you to be
afflicted for a long period, would appear by His great
mercy to have been changed into a dewy breeze, since
he has taken from your midst, one who unceasingly
attacked you especially of all the faithful with the
hammer of persecution, and who greatly harried the
whole Church of God, but you most particularly in
many ways. All this you can easily perceive from the
fact that we in sighs and groans had to leave the Apostolic
See for distant lands in order that we might be able to

and a case from Greece decided by the King of France, where a vassal
was declared deprived of his fief for making war on his lord.

[1] Reference is here made to the *Assize of Jerusalem*, the feudal code
of the Latin kingdom of the Holy Land, and to the causes (such as
failure to appear at the lord's court to answer a charge of treason) which
justified the forfeiture of a fief. Mr. Sedgwick also cites Bracton (*c.* 1256)
the great commentator on English Law, and especially Frederick's
own Sicilian Code of 1231, Lib. iii, tit. 18 and 19, ap. H.-B., iv, p. 131.
" Vassals shall not be privy in plot, consent or knowledge to their lord's
losing his land, rather they shall warrant and defend it to the utmost
of their power against everybody," etc. " Non erunt (vasalli) in arte
consilio vel consensu qualiter domini terram quam habent amittant ;
immo eam ipsis contra omnem hominem defendere pro posse curabant."

[2] *Italy in the Thirteenth Century*, vol. i, c. 22, p. 312 ff. *Cf.* Saint-
Priest, *Hist. de la conquête de Naples par Charles d'Anjou*, i, p. 26. This
author gives a useful summary of the previous history of the relations
of the Popes with Sicily.

put a term to the afflictions of many, but most of all
to your difficulties." He accordingly exhorted his corre-
spondents not to allow anything to prevent them from
returning to the bosom of the Church in order there to
enjoy peace and liberty. He would, he concluded,
send envoys to them, and come himself as soon as he
could in order to make suitable arrangements for their
future welfare.[1]

A little later he ordered his legate Peter, cardinal-
deacon of St. George in Velabro, by offers of certain
baronies to induce, if possible, Berthold of Hohenberg
and the Count of Caserta to return to the allegiance of
the Church, and to give up the fortresses of the country
into his hands.[2] About the same time, with a view to
prevent fresh German efforts against Sicily, he bade
the Archbishop of Cologne and his suffragans proclaim
the greater ecclesiastical penalties against any such as
made any attempt against that Kingdom "which
specially belonged to the Apostolic See".[3]

Innocent's efforts to recover the States of the Church.

Among the envoys whom Innocent sent into the
Kingdom was the Dominican, brother Roger of Zentini.
He gave him a free hand, and bade him arrange with
the barons what was necessary "for the honour of the
Apostolic See, and for the peace and tranquillity of the
land".[4]

Desirous as he was to return to Italy and to Rome,[5]
in order to be the better able to work for the recovery
of Sicily and the States of the Church [6] which Frederick

His action against Conrad.

[1] Ep. Jan. 25, 1251, ap. Rod., n. 32, vol. iii, p. 24 f.

[2] *Ib.*, n. 37. " Ac munitiones et roccas ipsius regni tibi restituant
et assignent." *Cf.* n. 106.

[3] *Ib.*, ep. Feb. 7, n. 50.

[4] *Ib.*, epp. of March 7, nn. 85–7 and 91, March 10.

[5] " Licet utile plurimum . . . videretur nostrum versus Urbem
accelerare regressum, disposuimus tamen non ante redire quam de
imperii Romani negotio, sicut convenit, ordinemus." Ep. Jan. 27,
n. 41, *ib.*, p. 31. *Cf.* nn. 95 and 104.

[6] *Cf.* ep. Jan. 25, 1251, n. 39, *ib.*, p. 28 f. *Cf.* n. 97.

had seized, his anxiety about the future of the Empire detained him in Lyons for some months. He took at once most vigorous steps against Conrad,[1] and in behalf of his rival William of Holland. He pointed out to the magnates of Germany that birth did not give a right to the Empire. That right, he reminded them, was to be obtained by election [2]; and he declared that in any event would he never consent to a descendant of Frederick becoming King of the Romans, Emperor or Duke of Suabia.[3] At the same time he pushed forward the preaching of a crusade against Conrad,[4] whose own evil doings as well as those of his ancestors rendered him, so Innocent wrote, unworthy of honour.[5]

On the other hand, he strove to secure the general recognition and success of William of Holland by personal appeals to different German magnates ; by the dispatch of envoys to others [6]; and by endeavouring to secure a rich wife for him.[7] He also promised to crown him Emperor in the immediate future,[8] and wrote to him and to other leading men in Germany bidding them come to Lyons to arrange what was best to be done.[9]

The counter-action of Conrad and Manfred.

If, however, on the death of Frederick, Innocent acted with remarkable vigour in order to recover his

---

[1] A distinctly bad character is assigned to Conrad by Will. of Tyre, *Hist.*, l. xxvi, c. 3, p. 1042, ap. *P. L.*, t. 201.

[2] *Cf.* epp. nn. 67 and 74.

[3] Ep. March 29, n. 100. *Cf.* n. 101 and n. 186, where Innocent declares that in this he is ratifying the decision of the Diet of Frankfort.

[4] Ep. Feb. 5, n. 48. *Cf.* nn. 54 and 101, and Mat. Par., v, 259.

[5] Ep. March 31, n. 101. Hence our own *Dunstable Annals*, iii, p. 181, *R. S.*, set down Conrad as " an imitator of his father's vices ". *Cf.* Mat. Par., iv, 634.

[6] Ep. of Feb. 18, n. 66. *Cf.* nn. 65, 67–76.

[7] Ep. of Feb. 18, n. 64.

[8] Ep. Feb. 15, to William himself, n. 60. *Cf.* n. 74, etc.

[9] Ep. Jan. 27, n. 41. Not many of the German Princes, clerical or lay, appear to have hearkened to the Pope's summons to meet him at Lyons. *Cf. Gesta Trev., Cont. V.*, ap. *M. G. SS.*, xxiv, p. 412.

rights, Conrad and Manfred were not inactive in their efforts to uphold what they considered to be their just dues. By Frederick's will [1] Conrad had been constituted his heir to the Empire and Sicily, and Manfred whom he named Prince of Taranto, had been appointed regent (balium) of Lombardy and Sicily in the absence of Conrad from Italy. Manfred, the son of Frederick by the attractive Bianca Lancia, though born out of lawful wedlock had, so it is said by some, by the merciful law of the Church, become legitimized by the subsequent marriage of his mother with the Emperor. [2] Very like his father in his good and bad qualities, [3] Manfred, in many ways the best of Frederick's descendants, [4] was a failure for the same reason as his father. His bad qualities were those of character, and thus stood in the way of his real success either as a man or as a ruler. A contemporary has left us of him what is a comparatively rare thing for a mediaeval writer, to wit, a character sketch. Manfred, says the chronicler to whom we refer, [5] " was a man eager for empty glory, astute and circumspect ; but his courage was small, and so when the hope of fame led him to think of great things, his weakness of character made him recoil from the prosecution of them. This weakness, however, he so carefully concealed that many thought him a man of great heart. He was only formidable to the fearful, and he readily checked his onslaught when he encountered resistance. He made his way by threatening rather than by fighting ; and when he could not work his will by violent threats

[1] Ap. H.-B., vi, 806.

[2] Andrew of Hungary († 1272), *Descriptio Victoriæ*, c. 5, ap. *M.G. SS.*, xxvi, p. 561, says : " Pia mater ecclesia . . . numere materno, licet tacite, legitimavit eundem."

[3] H.-B., vi. *L'hist. des Normands*, p. 114.

[4] "M. . . . respective *lucifer* dici poterat in tota posteritate Caesarea," Saba, i, c. 3.

[5] *Chron. Pont. et Imp.*, ap. *M. G. SS.*, xxxi, p. 221 f.

he would try to accomplish it rather by talk than by
the sword." Hence, on the death of Frederick II.,
he aspired to be King of Sicily himself instead of regent
for Conrad. Accordingly he opened negotiations with
Innocent in his own interests, and it appears from one
of that Pontiff's letters,[1] that, if he had been willing to
make such concessions as the regent desired, he would
have thrown off all allegiance to his elder brother. As
it was, however, finding that Innocent was bent upon
taking Sicily into his own hands,[2] and hearing that Conrad
was making preparation to make good his claims to the
Kingdom, Manfred decided for the time at least to accept
the rôle of regent that had been assigned to him in his
father's will. Therefore, acting more or less promptly
in his brother's interests, he at once set about reducing
the towns of Apulia, such as Andria, Foggia, and Barletta,
which, on the death of Frederick, had thrown off the
Hohenstaufen yoke.[3] Apulia was soon subdued ; but
it was a different matter when the cities of the west
such as Naples and Capua, which had also returned
to the Pope, had to be dealt with. Manfred failed to
recover Naples, and was compelled to return to Apulia
to await the coming of Conrad.[4]

[1] Of July 25, 1251, to his legate Peter, cardinal of St. George in
Velabro, ap. Rod., n. 119, iii, p. 99. *Cf.* Salimbene, *Chron.*, p. 347,
and Villani, *Cron.*, vi, 44, ap. *R. I. SS.*, xiii, who says that Manfred
was wrath (cruccioso) at Conrad's coming, " as he had intended to be
the lord of the said Kingdom."

[2] For Salimbene notes (p. 224) that on Frederick's death " regnum
ipsum debuit ad ecclesiam reddire (*sic*)," and that on Conrad's death
Innocent did for a brief space get it into his own hands : " Eo mortuo
(Conrad) rediit (regnum) ad ecclesiam, que ipsum modico tempore
tenuit."

[3] *Ib.*, p. 115 f. *Cf.* Jamsilla, the panegyrist of Manfred, *Hist.*, ap.
R. I. SS., viii, p. 497–503 ; and Bartholomew de Neocastro : " Post
mortem Caesaris, Neapolis, Capua etc. . . . . rebellionis spiritum
assumentes, nomen Romanae matris ecclesiae invocarunt, et deposito
nomine Conradi regis, etc."

[4] Jamsilla, p. 503 f.

Meanwhile that "unspeakable son of an unspeakable father (nefandus nefandi)", as Matthew Paris calls him,[1] who, had been driven out of Germany by William of Holland [2] (1248), had returned to it, and had in turn gained some advantage over William (1250).[3] On hearing then of his father's death, he at once began to prepare to make a descent on Sicily. For this he needed money ; and his principal preparation for the Sicilian expedition would appear to have consisted in following the example of his father by further alienating the possessions of his house in order to procure that all-important implement of war.[4] He was ready to march in the autumn (1251) ; and in October descended with a large army into Lombardy. After a brief stay there while he held "a parliament" with the Ghibellines,[5] he left it in December to go to Apulia by sea.[6] Landing

Conrad comes to the Kingdom, 1252.

[1] iv, 634. The same author speaks of his cruelties to friars and others whom he seized on their way to the Pope, iv, 278 ; and to the followers of Henry Raspe, iv, 611. On Conrad's imitation of his father's vices, cf. Thos. of Tuscany, Gesta imperat., ap. M. G. SS., xxii, pp. 515–16.

[2] Mat. Par. with his wonted inaccuracy would seem to imply that Conrad was twice driven out of Germany. Cf. iv, 634, and v, 27. But cf. Gesta Trev., Contin. V., ap. M. G. SS., xxiv, p. 411, and Gesta Abbat. Horti S. Mariæ, c. 61, ap. M. G. SS., xxiii, 602. Unfortunately we are very much in the dark as to the doings of Conrad between the close of 1248, and his departure from Germany for Apulia in October, 1251.

[3] According to Mat. Par., v, 90, towards the close of the summer, 1249 ; but the victory would seem to have been in August, 1250. Cf. ep. Fred. of Sept. 1250, ap. H.-B., vi, ii, 794, and Ann. Wormat., ap. Böhmer, Fontes, ii, 187–8. Cf. Ann. Aust., Contin. Garst., ap. M. G. SS., ix, 599, ad an. 1250.

[4] It is the Annals of St. Rupert, ap. M. G. SS., ix, 792, which, after calling Conrad his heir, tell us of this alienation of Frederick's German possessions : "occupatis et distractis per infoedationem sive per obligationem possessionibus suis." Cf. Ann. Neresheim., ap. ib., x, 24, which say that Conrad entered Italy "exhaustis viribus et sumptibus".

[5] Chron. de reb., p. 235 ; Ann. Veron., ap. M. G. SS., xix, 14 ; Ricciard. vit., ap. R. I. SS., viii, p. 132.

[6] On his way, Roger, archbishop of Spalato, would not receive him at that city on account of his excommunication. Cf. Thomas, Hist.

at Siponto (Jan., 1252), he was received with honour by
Manfred, who at once resigned his regency into his hands.[1]
Then, soon after, showing himself wholly harsh towards
Manfred (perhaps because he had discovered his negotiations with the Pope), and without the slightest reference
to the rights of his overlord, the Pope, Conrad began with
the aid of his Germans, energetically to reduce the
mainland of the Kingdom under his authority.[2]

Innocent
returns to
Italy, 1251.

Innocent had also meanwhile come into Italy. He
had waited in Lyons to meet William of Holland. When
it was known that William had arrived, and that the
Pope was about to return to Italy, so many people from
all parts came to see him in Holy Week (1251) " that
the city of Lyons could not hold them ". In order,
however, says the papal biographer, that the people
might gain the indulgences which they sought, and get
his blessing, the Pope on Holy Thursday rode out of
the city accompanied by " the King of Germany, the
most Christian William ", who in accordance with
ancient custom held the bridle of his horse.

After he had preached to the assembled multitude,
granted them various indulgences, and blessed them,
he returned to his monastic dwelling, said Mass,
excommunicated Conrad once more,[3] and then sat down
to eat with the King and the cardinals (Apr. 13).[4] A few
days later, when he had come to a complete understanding

Salon., c. 47. Hence, when lodged in the episcopal palace by the people,
he searched the archbishop's papers in the hope of being able to convict
him of treason : " versando scrinii cartulas." *Ib.*

[1] Jamsilla, p. 505.

[2] *Ib.*, and p. 506. *Cf.* Carbio, c. 31 : " Occupavit regnum Apulie et
Sicilie in jacturam et dispendium Ecclesie, cum esset *de jure* ipsum
regnum ad manus Ecclesie devolutum."

[3] Mat. Par., v, 248.

[4] Carbio, c. 31. He also preached to the people in their own dialect
on the following day, supported by the archbishop of Treves and the
King. *Cf. Gesta Trev.*, *l.c.*

with the King, the two left Lyons together (Apr. 19),
the King with cardinal Hugo of S. Sabina for Germany,
the Pope with his whole court for Italy and Rome.[1]
At Vienne the papal party embarked on galleys, sailed to
Orange, and proceeded thence by land to Marseilles,
Susa, and Genoa. Everywhere as he went along Innocent
was received with the utmost honour by the people.
As before, his reception at Genoa was especially splendid.
The whole city was gay with tapestry, and the Pope
was escorted to his residence beneath a specially made
canopy (May 18).[2]

The first thing that Innocent did in Genoa was to
summon the Guelf cities [3] to send envoys to him, so that
an effort might be made to keep them on good terms
with each other ; and, in view of the coming of Conrad,
to renew the Lombard League. To keep the cities
in north Italy at this period from fighting each other
was a task beyond the power of man ; but the words
of the Pope reinforced later by the actual arrival of
Conrad in Lombard, were not without effect ; and, under
the auspices of the legate, cardinal Octavian, the Lombard
League was renewed at Brescia (March 8, 1252).[4]

The Gulf cities send envoys to the Pope, 1251.

[1] *Ib.*, and *Annal. Genuen.*, ap. *R. I. SS.*, vi, 518.

[2] Carbio, c. 31 : " Coopertis plateis . . . pictis tapetibus . . .
Fecerant quoque sibi . . . contra solis estum quoddam umbraculum
innectentes captibus quatuor perticarum pecias de serico artificiose
insitas."

[3] *Ib.* "' Vocatis ad se ambaxatoribus de societate fidelium Ecclesie
omnium civitatum Lombardorum et Mediolanensium." *Cf.* ep. of
March 15, 1251. He had already (Feb. 7, 1251, ap. Rod., iii, 40) urged
the Ghibelline cities of Cremona, Pavia, Padua, etc., to be reconciled
with the Church.

[4] The *Pacta et conditiones* of the League will be found ap. Muratori,
Antiq. Ital., iv, p. 487 ff., ed. Milan, 1741. *Cf. Vita Ricciard. comitis*, ap.
R. I. SS., viii, p. 132. " Octavo Idus Martii conventum omnium in
episcopio Octavianus habuit, in quo omnes se foederatis Lombardiæ,
Marchiæ, et Romaniolæ pro opibus affuturos et amicos cujusque pro
amicis, hostes pro hostibus habituros juravere." This time the League
did not last long. We are told that the last document which mentions

Innocent's
triumphal
tour through
Lombardy,
1251.

Meanwhile, as soon as Innocent had finished his diplomatic interviews with the Lombards, he informed them of his anxiety to get to Rome in order that he might deal more effectively with the Sicilian question. Knowing, however, what an influence for the promotion of unity in Lombardy the presence of the Pope would have, they begged him to defer his southern journey till he had visited the chief cities of the Lombard plain. As their request was strongly supported by the legates Octavian and Gregory of Montelongo, Innocent gave way. Leaving Genoa on June 26 he made a triumphal progress through Lombardy, and then through Romagna to Perugia, visiting Milan, Brescia, Ferrara, Bologna, Cesena, and Fano. After receiving at Alessandria the submission of Thomas of Savoy,[1] he proceeded to Milan where he met with such a glorious reception that the pen of Carbio could not describe it. To save him from fatigue from the heat of the sun, and from being oppressed by the crowd, the Milanese had prepared a sort of canopied howdah for his horse ; and to honour him they met him with a procession which stretched for miles. Emboldened by the presence of the Pope in their midst, the people of Milan before he left their city captured Lodi, one of the cities which stood for the Emperor.[2] Wherever he went Innocent addressed the people,

the League is dated Jan. 1, 1253. (E. Jordan, Les orig. de la domination Angevine en Italie, p. 53.) External German imperial pressure brought the League into existence, but nothing short of that was capable of keeping it in existence. As soon as it became clear that Conrad was not able to exert that pressure, the League died a natural death, and the cities having no external foe to fight, continued to fight among themselves, and at length wearied with strife, began soon after this to give themselves into the hands of despots for the sake of peace.

[1] Carbio, c. 30. Cf. ep. June 22, 1251 of Innocent on his absolution. Potthast, 14, 341 ; and also Mat. Par., v, 255, who tells us, moreover, that Innocent gave Thomas one of his nieces in marriage with a fine dowry.

[2] Carbio, ib.

and two historians have left it on record that they heard him preach at Ferrara.[1] Moreover, wherever he went some new kind of honour was shown him, and we read of the people of Bologna by some "wondrous contrivance" causing the standard of their *carroccio* to bend down to the Pope's feet when he approached it.[2]

In the words of Berger [3] : "Innocent (had indeed) returned in triumph to the land whence seven years before he had left as a fugitive. During his stay at Lyons he had by his skill and constancy re-established the fortunes of the Holy See, had worn out, discomfited and destroyed his adversary, and was, moreover, ever the same, bold and indefatigable, more than ever resolved to resist the enemies of the Church, but also always ready to receive those who wished to return to him."

On November 5, Innocent reached Perugia where, after having been received with great honour, he remained about a year and a half, and where among other acts, he made three cardinals (Dec., 1251), of whom one was his relative, Ottobono Fieschi, afterwards Pope Hadrian V.[4] Why the Pope suddenly stopped at Perugia, and did not continue his journey to Rome is not told us by his biographer. But a reason is supplied by Matthew Paris. He says that Innocent had been given to understand that if he went to Rome, the Romans would attempt by force to wring a large sum of money from him. Hence, although the Romans desired his

Innocent arrives at Perugia, 1251.

---

[1] Salimbine, *Chron.*, p. 165, says he was touching the Pope when at Ferrara he preached from a window of the bishop's palace. *Cf.* pp. 174–360. Ricobaldi of Ferrara also heard him, *Hist. Imp.*, ap. *R. I. SS.*, ix, p. 132.

[2] Carbio, c. 31. The different local annals all make mention of the arrival of the Pope at their respective cities.

[3] *Introd.*, p. cclviii, *Reg.*, ii. *Cf.* note on the following page.

[4] *Ib. Cf.* Mat. Par., v, 274.

presence (for they were bankrupt without it), he would not put himself " in their net ".[1]

Settled in Perugia, and convinced that parties were so balanced in Lombardy that there was no danger of the imperialists becoming ascendant in the north, Innocent turned his whole attention towards the Kingdom of Sicily,[2] which he endeavoured to bring under direct papal control. He did all in his power to encourage the disaffection towards the Hohenstaufens which the oppression of Frederick II. had rendered universal throughout the mainland. His bull of December 13, 1251, granting privileges to the city of Naples which had professed its allegiance to the Holy See is an illustration of his procedure. He denounced Frederick, " who had long depressed the Kingdom beneath the yoke of affliction," as worse in his harshness, impiety, and cruelty than Pharao, Herod, and Nero, and he pointed out that his sons, " heirs of their father's wickedness," and of the same viperous blood, were endeavouring to continue their father's evil work. He praised the resistance that

---

[1] *Ib.*, p. 206. *Cf.* pp. 372, 418. A little later, *ib.*, p. 237, he says that the Milanese on the occasion of his visit to them, endeavoured to get money from him, and that this experience had such an effect on him that " he would not enter a large city . . . (but), not sparing his horse's sides, he made all haste on his journey till he reached Perugia ". How false all this is the text has demonstrated. The more Matthew Paris is studied alongside other historians, the more unreliable is he seen to be. Unfortunately Innocent IV. is known in this country from the caricature of that historian.

Matthew also states that in 1250 the Romans had with threats urged the Pope as their bishop and pastor to return to Rome, v, 146. *Cf.* the letter of the Senator of the city to him begging him to return even in 1246. " Romana . . . funditus desolata sedeat civitas, expers papæ . . . facta est quasi vidua domina urbium . . . et, quod timeri potest, Cæsari sub tributo." Ap. *Albert v. Behaim*, p. 139.

[2] Letters to Innocent from his Lombard legate, cardinal Octavian degli Ubaldini, show that it was thought by the Guelfs there that he was neglecting them. Epp. of 1252, ap. *Registri dei card. Ugolino e Ottaviano*, pp. 159, 164, 166, and 175 especially.

the great city was offering to these sons, and, in accordance with its wishes, took it under the direct authority of the Holy See " like Campania or the Maritima ", and undertook in the future not to yield any rights over it to any one.[1]

Two weeks after the dispatch of this document Conrad landed at Siponto, and with the aid of his Germans soon put an end to all Innocent's hopes of bringing Sicily under his personal rule.[2] Meanwhile, however, as the King did not show the slightest intention of submitting his claims to Sicily to the Pope,[3] Innocent again excommunicated him and his adherents.[4] Thereupon, whether in the real hope of coming to terms with the Pope, or simply to gain time, Conrad sent to Innocent a number of ambassadors, among whom was that Walter of Ocra whom his father had often sent to England and other places on similar errands. They boldly asked Innocent to recognize their lord both as Emperor and as King of Sicily. Their request was of course refused[5]; and while Conrad at once devoted himself with energy to establishing his authority firmly over the Kingdom, Innocent, convinced that he could not bring it under his direct authority, resolved to offer it to some powerful and friendly Prince.

Successes of Conrad there, 1252.

[1] Ap. R., iii, p. 105. *Cf. ib.*, p. 96.

[2] Will. of Nangis, *Gesta Philip. III.*, ap. *M. G. SS.*, xxvi, p. 673. Conrad " sui patris sequendo prava vestigia, illud regnum (Sicily) presumptione temeraria occupavit ".

[3] Conrad " regna Sardaniæ, Siciliæ, Apuliæ et Calabriæ violenter et sine Romanæ Ecclesiæ assensu sibi appropriaverat ". Mat. Par., v, 256.

[4] Carbio, c. 31.

[5] *Ib., cf.* Mat. Par., v, 284, 300–2. According to the latter author, negotiations would seem to have been going on even in June, 1252. He also asserts that they were hindered by an attempt being made to poison Conrad, who accused the Pope of being the author of the attempt. *Ib.*, pp. 284 and 301.

Innocent
offers Sicily
to a foreign
prince,
1252-3.

As time pressed, he offered it almost simultaneously to two Princes. Perhaps the first person to whom Innocent turned was our own wealthy Richard, earl of Cornwall, brother of Henry III. About the feast of St. Martin (Nov. 11) there arrived in England one Albert, a pontifical notary, who, in the Pope's name and in accordance with previous papal communications,[1] offered Richard " the Kingdom of Apulia, Sicily, and Calabria ".[2] But, not being particularly warlike, Richard declined to oppose Conrad,[3] as he had already declined to oppose his father Frederick.[4] Under the circumstances, he is reported to have said, that the Pope might as well have offered him the moon.

However, the King, his brother, " mindful of all the . . . favours he had . . . received from the Roman Church," warmly thanked Innocent for having made choice of Richard " before all the other princes of the world for the throne of the Kingdom of Sicily ".[5]

Innocent
sounds
Charles of
Anjou, 1253.

Innocent next addressed with the same proposal a very different person, the able and warlike Charles of Anjou, the youngest brother of St. Louis IX.,[6] and urged his brothers, St. Louis IX. and Alphonsus, count of Poitiers, to persuade him to accept the proffered throne.[7] Charles was ambitious, and there seemed to be

[1] On Aug. 3, 1252, Innocent wrote to Henry III., begging him to induce his brother to accept the Kingdom. Potthast, 14680. *Cf.* Mat. Par., v, 347.

[2] M. P., v, p. 346 f. ; Carbio, c. 31.

[3] *Ib.*, 457 ; *cf.* pp. 361, 680.

[4] *Ib.*, p. 201.

[5] Rymer, *Fœdera*, i, 288, ed. 1846.

[6] Carbio, c. 31. According to Carbio, however, it was Charles himself who first approached the Holy See " offerendo personam, terram et omnia sua bona servitio Romanæ ecclesie". *Cf.* also Andrew of Hungary, *Descriptio victoriæ a Carolo . . . reportatæ*, c. 9, ap. *M. G. SS.*, xxvi, p. 563. Andrew († 1272), chaplain of Bela IV. and Stephen V., kings of Hungary, dedicated his *Descriptio*, which is strongly opposed to Manfred, to Peter, count of Alençon († 1284).

[7] Potthast, nn. 14681-2, Aug. 5, 1252.

more hope in that quarter. Accordingly when Albert
left England (1253),[1] he was commissioned by Innocent
to do all in his power to induce the lord of Provence to
accept the proffered throne. For when on "account
of the importance of the task that had been committed
to him "[2] the nuncio was raised to the dignity of a
legate (June 7, 1253), the Pope must have been full of
anxiety on account of the situation in the Kingdom.

He had quite failed to check Conrad's victorious Innocent's
career there by any action he had been able to take against action
against
him elsewhere. He had instituted proceedings against Conrad.
his great ally in Lombardy, the formidable Ezzelino da
Romano on the charge of heresy.[3] In the kingdom
of Sicily itself he had annulled all the acts of Frederick
or his predecessors against the rights of the Church,
and had restored to the Churches what had been taken
away from them [4]; and in Tuscany he had sent two
cardinals to put down factions the very existence of
which was hostile to the interests of the Church.[5] But it
was in Germany especially that he had endeavoured
to bring pressure to bear on Conrad. He had ratified
the confiscation of all his property which had been
ordered by the Diet of Frankfort [6]; had stirred up
preachers against him throughout Germany [7]; and he
had ordered his legates to take steps against such clerics
as favoured him.[8] Further he had confirmed the sentence
decreed by the aforesaid Diet of Frankfort by which

[1] Mat. Par., v, 457. He left about Apr. 25.

[2] Ep. June 7, 1252, n. 6806, ap. *Reg*., iii, 274. *Cf*. the foll. epp. to 6819.

[3] Epp. of June 16, 1251, ap. R., iii, n. 113, and June 23, 1252, *ib*.,
n. 143.

[4] Ep. Aug. 23, 1252. What effect this declaration actually produced
is difficult to imagine.

[5] Ep. Aug. 26, 1252, n. 158.

[6] Ep. July 20, 1252, Potthast, n. 14669.

[7] Epp. Feb., 1253, nn. 187 ff., ap. R., iii, p. 156 f.

[8] Ep. June 4, 1253, *ib*., n. 205.

those were to lose their fiefs who failed by a fixed date to accept them from the hands of William of Holland.[1] He had, moreover, authorized the raising of money from ecclesiastical property for him [2]; and had called upon the Dukes of Brabant and Austria, and the King of Bohemia to support William.[3]

Success of
Conrad,
1252–3.

But neither any one nor all of these measures had had the effect of distracting Conrad from the work he had in hand ; and before Albert had been named legate he had subdued all the mainland of the Kingdom except Naples, and had begun its siege in May or June (1253).[4]

Terms
arranged
with Charles
of Anjou,
1253.

Under the circumstances, Innocent was naturally desirous of coming to terms with Charles, and he authorized Albert to raise money for the prosecution of the affair even at exorbitant interest.[5] He begged Charles to have full confidence in him, and assured him that he would do far more for him in the matter than he had asked.[6] Charles on his side was equally anxious to accept the offer of the Pope, and readily accepted the terms on which he was to be invested with the kingdom of Sicily, the Duchy of Apulia, Capitanata, and Calabria, the Principate of Capua, and all the territory between the Pharos and the boundaries of the lands of the Church, except Benevento.[7]   He agreed to hold Sicily

---

[1] Ep. Dec. 2, 1252, Potthast, 14793.

[2] Epp. Apr. 11 f., 1253, ap. R., iii, n. 198. *Cf.* Mat. Par., v, 439.

[3] Ep. March 11, 1253, ap. *ib.*, n. 194 ; and ep. July 5, n. 217.

[4] *Ann. Cavenses*, ap. *R. I. SS.*, vii, p. 927. *Cf.* B.-F., *Reg. Imp.*, n. 4596a.

[5] Ep. June, 1253, *Reg.*, n. 6810. " Mandamus quatinus . . . recipias nostro et Ecclesie Romane nomine mutuum, etiam, si oportuerit, sub gravibus usuris, quantumcumque et a quibuscumque poteris invenire." *Cf.* n. 6811.

[6] *Ib.*, n. 6812. In the following letters he thanks various bishops and others for what they have done to forward the negotiations, and begs them to continue their good offices.

[7] See the conditions, ap. *Reg.*, iii, p. 278 ff., or R., iii, 178.

as a fief of the Church in such a way that it should never be attached to the Empire, to respect the liberties of the Church therein, and of those who had adhered to the cause of the Popes. He was also to give the Roman Church at least a thousand ounces of gold each year, and a sound and handsome white palfrey every five years, as a sign of the Pope's overlordship.[1]

With these terms it appears that Charles himself was quite content, but that some of his advisers were not. Upon this, Innocent, to oblige the Count, suggested to his legate a way out of the difficulty which did much more credit to him as a lawyer and a diplomat than as a Pope. Albert was to promise in his name that he would agree to such recommendations on the disputed points as should be made to him by two prelates and a knight nominated by Charles. But the Count was previously to give the legate an undertaking in writing that the said promise was to be without real effect.[2] But the advisers of Charles were not satisfied ; and as he could not get his own way with them, he was compelled this time to decline the Pope's proposals.[3] *Failure of the negotiations with Charles.*

The exigencies of the situation, however, soon forced Innocent to try again. In October, Conrad entered Naples, destroyed its walls, and displayed genuine *The Sicilian throne offered to Edmund of England, 1253-4.*

[1] The Pope on his side was to lend Charles 400,000 pounds Tournois until the Kingdom was conquered. However, as the Pope has no money, and will have to borrow the money, Charles must pledge the Kingdom in payment of the debt, less what monies the Pope may receive from the churches of France and Provence.

[2] Ep. July 11, 1253, ap. *Reg.*, n. 7755. Charles had asked the legate to obtain from the Pope that the articles objected to by his advisers should be modified—" non tamen ut fiat, sed ut habeatur erga eosdem consiliarios excusatus." The Pope then suggested a way in which Charles' wishes could be met.

[3] Carbio, c. 31. " Licet ipse comes hoc multum in corde gestaret, collateralium tamen suorum devictus consilio, hoc donum . . . recipere non temptavit." On these negotiations with Charles, see Berger, *Reg.*, ii, p. cclxxvii ff.

Hohenstaufen cruelty towards its brave but unfortunate inhabitants.[1]   He was now practically undisputed master of the two Sicilies.   Fearful lest he should consolidate his power, Innocent again looked to England, and this time through Albert offered the Sicilian throne, now harder than ever for a stranger to grasp, to Henry's second son, the boy Edmund.[2]   Henry lost no time in replying to Albert.   "Since we and our ancestors," he wrote, "have received many honours and benefits from our Mother the Holy Roman Church, it is fitting that we should show ourselves obliging in all that concerns the honour and advantage of the lord Pope and the afore-said Church."   Accordingly, he accepted the crown for his young son ; and agreed to accept such subsidies and such conditions as Albert, cardinal Ottobono, and other plenipotentiaries whom he named, should fix.[3]

[1] Carb., c. 31. He declares that Conrad was more cruel even than his father. *Cf.* Jamsilla, p. 506 ; Saba, i, c. 3 ; *Ann. Cavenses*, *l.c.*

[2] Ep. Dec. 20, 1253, ap. a *relatio* of the Sicilian affair made by Albert to Alexander IV. on Oct. 23, 1256, ap. Rod., iii, 406. *Cf.* Mat. Par., v, 457 f. and 470.

[3] Ap. *ib.*, p. 407. He accepted what the Pope and the plenipotentiaries should agree to : "tam super subsidio nobis faciendo ad predictum negotium prosequendum . . . quam super aliis conditionibus omnibus apponendis et removendis duxerint ordinandum." This letter is dated Feb. 12, 1254, from Bazas in Gascony where Henry then was. *Cf. ib.*, various letters of March 6, 1254, including letters of Innocent to Edmund.   The plenipotentiaries were, besides cardinal Ottobono Fieschi, Philip of Savoy, archbishop-elect of Lyons, Peter, bishop of Hereford, counts Thomas and Peter of Savoy, brothers of Philip and uncles of Queen Eleanor of England, John Mansel, provost of Beverley, and Peter Cachapor, archdeacon of Wells. Albert, *ib.*, p. 408, gives great praise to Henry as a loyal son of the Roman Church : "Princeps catholicus inclitus et verus adleta ecclesie in fervore perpetue subjectionis, devotionis et obedientie Romane ecclesie perseverantia inconcussa persistat." With regard to the subsidy, the Church was to advance 100,000 pounds Tournois or £25,000 (Potthast, 15382, and 15784), and to grant the King certain tithes from the church property of England and Scotland ; but Henry had to repay the loans, and we find Alexander IV. demanding in consequence 135,541 marks sterling, Potthast, n. 15784.

On May 14 Innocent confirmed the formal grant of the Kingdom to Edmund which had meanwhile been made by the legate [1]; begged Henry through Albert to send Edmund to Sicily as soon as possible,[2] and to be very economical himself in the meantime.[3] He also urged the archbishop of Canterbury, at the new King's request, to borrow money for him on the security (nomine) of the Roman Church and the churches of England.[4]

Meanwhile, despite all his efforts, Innocent had not been able to offer any substantial direct resistance to Conrad, although he had ordered the continuance of the preaching of the Crusade against him, and had granted indulgences of all kinds to William of Holland and to his followers.[5] However, in the midst of the chagrin caused to Innocent by the little advance made by William in Germany, and by the slowness of Henry III. in taking action for his son, word reached him that the second of his great enemies, Conrad IV., had died suddenly when only twenty-six years of age (May 21).[6] Conrad, who was accused before Innocent of having poisoned his nephew Frederick,[7] and by some of having even poisoned his brother Henry,[8] is stated on good authority to have

Death of Conrad IV., 1254.

[1] Potthast, n. 15364.

[2] *Ib.*, n. 15365.

[3] Rymer, i, 515. Epp. of May, 1254.

[4] *Ib.*, n. 15363. These letters may be read in full, ap. Rymer, *Fœdera*, i.

[5] Epp. of Feb. 16, 17, 22, nn. 259–62 ; n. 274 of Apr. 5 ; and n. 285, May 14, ap. Rod., iii.

[6] Jamsilla, pp. 506–7 ; Mon. Pat., *Chron.*, p. 689. The date of his death is given wrongly by Mat. Par., as is all the story of the offer of Sicily to Edmund. *Chron.*, v, 457–60 and 470.

[7] See the *responsio* of Conrad's advocate made " in presence of the lord Pope, of his brethren (the cardinals) of the Senator, and of the council " to the charges made against him. Ap. Mat. Par., *Additamenta*, vi, p. 299 ff. Conrad had not been formally cited, but " being zealous for his good name " had sent at once to clear himself.

[8] Mat. Par., v, 449 ; Bartholomew, *Hist. Sic.*, c. 1. According to Paris, Innocent concocted the story of Conrad's having killed his brother Henry through the agency of John the Moor, in order to inflame

himself been poisoned by Manfred, who was also accused
of having hastened the death of Frederick II.[1]

At any rate, it is certain that, even to the end, Conrad
did not trust Manfred ; but, passing him over, named
as Regent for his infant son Conradin, Berthold, marquis
of Hohenburg, a relative of his wife,[2] Moreover, he
gave orders that Conradin was to be committed to the
hands and favour of the Apostolic See.[3] We are, however,
assured,[4] that when envoys came from the Regent to
beg the papal interest for Conradin, Innocent, knowing
that the action of Conrad had been dictated "more from
a feeling of weakness than from a sense of devotion",
replied that he intended to take over the rule of the
Kingdom himself, but that he would consider Conradin's
claims when he came of age.[5]

the King of England against the murderer of his sister's son. *Cf. ib.*,
p. 459. This assertion affords another proof of the malignity of Paris ;
for in the official document (the *responsio*) just cited, to which he refers,
there is only question of the imprisonment of the young Henry. *Cf.
ib.*, pp. 432, 448.

[1] Saba Mal., i, c. 4. Mat. Par., v, 460, says Conrad died " ut dicitur
veneno propinato impellente ". *Cf.* Salimbene, *Chron.*, pp. 205, 470,
472. Thos. of Tuscany, ap. *M. G. SS.*, xxii, p. 516, offers proof that
Manfred at least contemplated killing Conrad.

[2] Saba, *ib. Cf.* Jamsilla, p. 507, who ascribes Berthold's success to
German scheming.

[3] " Cum inter alia, quæ. . . . Conradus de filio et regno suo in ultima
voluntate disposuit filium suum manibus et gratiæ sedis Apostolicæ
submittendum esse mandasset, etc." As this is said by Manfred's
panygerist *Jamsilla, ib.*, there can be no reason to doubt its accuracy.

[4] *Ib.*

[5] Jamsilla, *ib.* The account of the unrestrained joy that, according to
Matthew Paris, v, 460, Innocent manifested on the news of the death
of Conrad, is utterly unworthy of notice. Paris pretends that the
Pope's joy was the more intense that he had just heard of the death of
Robert Grosseteste. At this part of his *Chronicle* Paris gives more rein
to his imagination or to the free introduction of the most absurd and
groundless gossip than almost at any other. In the most sober manner,
he describes the bishop's appearing after his death to the Pope, upbraid-
ing him and striking him, etc., etc.

TOWERS OF THE CAPOCCI. ROME.

[Photo: Mosrioni.

[face p. 138.

When Innocent heard of Conrad's death, he was residing at Assisi. He had descended from Perugia at the close of April, 1253, and had passed the summer of that year at Assisi in the monastery of St. Francis. Whilst there, he had consecrated the wonderful church begun in honour of that Saint by Elias of Cortona, and had twice visited the dying St. Clare, the companion and " the little flower of St. Francis ",[1] and, as her biographer calls her, " the special disciple and daughter of the Roman Church." [2] " Would to God," exclaimed Innocent as he gave absolution to the sweet saint, " that I had no more need of forgiveness." [3]

On Conrad's death Innocent leaves Assisi for Anagni, 1254.

Meanwhile in the preceding year (1252), the Romans, dissatisfied with the internal condition of the city, had decided to introduce a Senator from without. Accordingly, in 1252, they elected the Bolognese, Brancaleone degli Andalo, Senator for three years, and gave him increased powers.[4]

The new Senator of Rome, Brancaleone.

He proved an able and energetic ruler ; and for the time being curbed the lawlessness of the Roman nobility.

[1] Carbio, c. 33, and the contemporary *life* of St. Clare, pp. 64–6, Eng. trans. by Fr. Paschal Robinson.

[2] *Life*, p. 62.

[3] *Ib.*, p. 66. On this visit see also the *Legenda Aurea* of James de Voragine, p. 225 ff. Eng. trans., ed. O'Neill, Cambridge, 1914. When the Pope had left her, the Saint who had on the same day received Holy Communion " said to her Sisters with tears : Praise the Lord, my little daughters, that on this day Christ hath vouchsafed me a favour so great that heaven and earth would not suffice to repay it. This day I have merited to receive the Most High Himself, and to behold His Vicar ". *Ib.* Innocent attended the Saint's funeral, *ib.*, p. 73 f., and instituted an inquiry into her life with a view to her canonization. *Cf.* Bull of Oct. 18, 1253. On Aug. 9, 1253 he confirmed the rule of the Poor Clares by a bull, the original of which is still extant, and which bears on it some words in Innocent's own handwriting. Cozza-Luzi has given a facsimile of it in his *Un Autografô di Innocenzo IV. e memorie de S. Chiara*, and Fr. Robinson a translation of it (p. 99 ff.) in his book just cited, *The Life of St. Clare*, London, 1910.

[4] Cantinelli, *Chron.*, an. 1252, p. 7 new ed., Mat. Par., v, 358 ; Carbio, c. 34.

But before many months of his rule had elapsed, he provoked the opposition of the Pope. Indulging the Romans in their wishes to make the neighbouring cities directly subject to their Senate instead of to the Pope, he attacked Tivoli, and then wanted to force Terracina to show its submission to Rome by sending deputies to its public games. This continued aggression roused Innocent. He commanded Brancaleone to desist from his attempts,[1] and instructed the cities of Campagna to help Terracina against the Romans.[2] Thus adjured, and finding that force was going to be met with force, Brancaleone left Terracina alone, and turned his attention to inducing Innocent to come back to Rome. Realizing that Rome without the Pope was but a body without a soul, the new Senator tried hard to compel the Pope to return to his See; for, he urged, he was bishop of Rome and not of Lyons or Perugia. It is even said that the Romans threatened to destroy first Perugia and then Assisi if the Pope was allowed to remain in either of those cities.[3] Accordingly, not indeed without misgiving, Innocent returned to Rome from Assisi in October, 1253. He received, however, a most magnificent welcome.[4]

Innocent receives an embassy from Conrad, 1254. The chief business transacted by Innocent in Rome was the reception of an embassy from Conrad to arrange terms of peace. According to Carbio, however, the embassy was simply sent to endeavour to debauch the loyalty of the Roman people. This time German gold had no effect, and on Holy Thursday (Apr. 9),

---

[1] Ep. of May 7, 1253, Potthast 14, 964.

[2] Epp. May 5, *ib.*, 14958 ff.

[3] Mat. Par., v, 372 and 417. There is obviously confusion in Paris's account of the Senator's action.

[4] Mat. Par., v, 417; Carbio, c. 34. According to Carbio, Brancaleone had been elected through the influence of Conrad, and acted in his interests.

" the day on which the penitent are wont to be reconciled, and the wicked to be anathematized," Innocent preached to the people in the square in front of the Lateran, and renewed the excommunication already pronounced against Conrad (1254).[1]

" And because," says Carbio,[2] " the Popes are wont to leave the city in the summer time, Innocent left Rome at the end of this same month (Apr.) for Assisi. He intended to pass the summer there, in the hope that his stay might do something to restore its prosperity, as it had suffered more grievously at the hands of Frederick and his savage Saracens than any of the neighbouring cities.

It was whilst at Assisi that, as already said, Innocent heard of Conrad's death. He instantly determined to take possession of the Kingdom, and in order to be nearer the scene of action, he left Assisi (June, 1254), commended his enterprise to the Romans as he passed through the city, and took up his abode at Anagni.[3]

Arrived at Anagni, Innocent formally called upon the Regent, Berthold, and the magnates of the Kingdom of Sicily to hand it over into his hands.[4] In obedience

Innocent summons the Regent of Sicily to deliver it up to him.

[1] The atrociously cruel tyrant, Ezzelino da Romano, was also excommunicated on this occasion. *Cf.* Rod. iii, n. 278, and Carbio, cc. 35 and 36. " Ipse d. Papa in platea Lateranensi, ut moris est pontificum Romanorum sermone proposito verbo Dei, excommunicavit . . . Conradum." C. 36. Like his father on a similar occasion, Conrad appealed against this sentence to God, to a future Pope, a General Council, the Princes of Germany, etc. See his letter to the cardinals, ap. Baluze, *Miscel.*, i, p. 194 ed. Lucca, 1761.

[2] C. 37.

[3] *Ib.*, c. 38. " Ut ibi (Anagni) commodius de negociis regni Apulie ordinaret." Innocent was at Anagni on June 9.

[4] Carbio, c. 39. About the same time, in order to effect a general settlement, he ordered the bishop of Mantua to make great efforts to bring about peace in Lombardy (Rod., iii, n. 294, June 22, 1254) and he exhorted William of Holland to come into Italy in order to receive the imperial crown about Christmas. Potthast, 15475. *Cf.* John de Beka, *Chron.*, ap. Böhmer, *Fontes*, ii, 446.

to this summons, Manfred, Walter of Ocra, and others
came to Anagni to discuss the situation. According to
Carbio, terms had practically been agreed upon after
negotiations had gone on for fifteen days, when the
magnates suddenly repudiated the agreement, retired
to San Germano where Berthold had taken up his
residence, and summoned to arms the Saracens from
Nocera, and the Germans who were in different parts of
the Kingdom.[1]

On his side, Innocent began to collect an army, and
on August 15 summoned Berthold, Manfred, and the other
nobles in opposition to him to give up the Kingdom of
Sicily into his hands under pain of excommunication.[2]
As they paid no heed to his summons, they were duly
excommunicated on Sept. 8[3]; and an army[4] under
William Fieschi, cardinal-deacon of St. Eustachio, a
man of learning and prudence, appeared before San
Germano. The opposition to the Pope collapsed.
Ambassadors were dispatched to the cardinal and
to Innocent, and "in the palace of the lord
Matthew" at Anagni, they made their submission to
the Pope.[5]

An immediate result of this surrender was that Manfred
was received into the Pope's favour. His possessions
were confirmed to him, and he was named Vicar of the
greater part of the mainland of the Kingdom with a

---

[1] *L.c.*

[2] See n. 4, p. 141.

[3] Ep. of Sept. 12 to Will. of H. Innocent summoned Berthold, etc.
"ut . . . regnum predictum et civitates, castra, villas, roccas et alia
ipsius loca Romane ecclesie, ad quam regnum ipsum . . . totaliter
pertinere dinoscitur, libera . . . dimitterent." Ap. Rod., iii, pp. 283–4.

[4] Brancaleone had tried to prevent the Romans from sending
provisions, men, or money, to Anagni, whereas the Pope, says Carbio,
c. 40 : " oblitus injurie illorum " made peace for them, when they
were in difficulties with Tivoli.

[5] Carbio, *ib.*

yearly revenue of eight thousand ounces of gold [1] ; for
Berthold had already resigned the regency (Bajulatus
officium) into the hands of the Pope or of the nobles.[2]

When these preliminary settlements had been made,
Innocent left Anagni (Oct. 8) for Ceprano in order to
enter the Kingdom as its suzerain. At the bridge there
over the Garigliano, he was met by Manfred and the
magnates of the realm. Acting as his squire the Vicar
led the Pope's horse over the bridge ; and a magnificent
reception was accorded to him.[3]

Innocent might now seem to have accomplished his
task. He had saved the temporal position of the Papacy,
and would seem to have secured the freedom of the Church
in Germany and in Sicily. In the former country a
king favourable to the liberty of the Church was only
opposed by a baby of two years old,[4] and in the Kingdom
of Sicily he was himself the overlord. But according to
Manfred's historian *Jamsilla*, a portent showed that his
triumph was to be short-lived. The Cross which

---

[1] Epp. to Manfred of Sept. 27 ap. Rod., iii, pp. 287 f. and 289 f. *Cf.*
Saba, p. 792, who calls him "Capitaneus in Apulia". At the same time
he conferred privileges on Galvano Lancia, and other nobles. R., *ib.*,
pp. 291–6. A little later, Oct. 7, 20, etc., followed privileges for the
clergy and cities, *ib.*, p. 296 ff. The Pope gives the boundaries of his
vicariate as : "a Faro usque ad flumen Sileris (Sele) et ab eodem
flumine infra per terram Beneventanam et comitatum Molisii usque
Trignium (the River Trigno), excepto justitiariatu Aprutii," pp. 289.

[2] Jamsilla, pp. 508–10. Manfred is always spoken of by the author
known as Jamsilla as *Princeps*. According to J., Berthold placed the
regency in the hands of the nobles, by whom it was given to Manfred.
But according to Saba M. (p. 792), it was resigned by Berthold into
the hands of the Pope. This is no doubt the fact, as it is in accord with
the Pope's letters, and with Berthold's known antipathy to Manfred ;
" Marchio (the Marquis B.) in manibus d. Papæ bajulatui et Corradini
tutelæ cessit in totum." Alexander IV., however, speaks as though
Berthold had resigned the regency directly into Manfred's hands. Ep.
of Feb. 15, 1255, ap. R., iii, n. 382. " Balium regni Siciliæ nobili viro
Manfredo principi Tarentino cessisti (Berthold)."

[3] Carbio, c. 41.   [4] Conradin was born March 25, 1252.

" according to custom " was being carried before him
slipped from the hands of the one who was carrying it,
and fell to the ground just as the Pontiff crossed the
bridge and set his foot on the soil of the Kingdom.[1]

The inten-
tions of
Innocent
with regard
to the future
of the
Kingdom.

For a brief space, Innocent was the recognized
immediate ruler of the Kingdom of Sicily ; and it is
an interesting question whether it was his intention,
if possible, to remain so. It appears to us that it was
not. His own direct assertion, supported by that of
several historians, seems to show that he was prepared
to consider some adjustment of the future claims of the
baby Conradin, and his letters to England prove that
he was always ready immediately to hand the Kingdom
over to Edmund as soon as he should come to claim it.

On September 27, he proclaimed " to all the faithful
of Christ " that he confirmed to the child Conrad (i.e.
Conradin) the Kingdom of Jerusalem, the Duchy of
Suabia, and such other rights as he might have in the
Kingdom of Sicily and elsewhere. Hence all those who
had to take the oath of fidelity to the Pope were to do
so " saving the rights of the child Conrad ".[2] Moreover,
not merely before but after Conrad's death, did he urge
Henry III. to send his son as soon as ever possible to
take possession of the Kingdom.[3] In his last letter to
Henry, written a few weeks before his death, he urged
him to send someone into Apulia as soon as possible,
" because the Church, on account of the mildness and

[1] P. 512. We may here note that picturesque details of events in
southern Italy at this period to be found in Cherrier, in Huillard-
Bréholles, etc., are taken from *Matteo di Giovenazzo* whose *Diurnali*
has since their time been proved to be a forgery.

[2] Ep. ap. R., iii, p. 290. It was the duty of the Church to look after
the poor and the orphan. *Cf.* Jamsilla, p. 508, and Saba. M., p. 792.

[3] *Cf.* Potthast, epp. of May 15, 22, and 25, nn. 15, 369 ; 15, 379 ;
15, 388 ; of June 9, n. 15, 420. In the last cited letter he tells Henry
that the death of Conrad must not cause him to relax his efforts, but
that he must send his son quickly.

gentleness of its sway, could not long maintain its domination over it." But he must understand that the Church cannot wait long. It will have to grant the fief to another, if he delays much longer.[1]

Whatever were the intentions of Innocent with regard to the governing of Sicily, Manfred had never really ceased to scheme for it for himself. We have seen how his first attempt to become the ruler of the Kingdom was thwarted by Innocent's refusal to fall in with his wishes and by the prompt arrival of Conrad. However, he never ceased his efforts to curry favour with the nobles of Apulia ; and with the aid of a superior intelligence, reinforced by grace of person and an unscrupulous will, this bright star (Lucifer) of the Hohenstaufen became very popular.[2] It was soon common talk among many that they would have no other ruler but Manfred. They would have no clergy over them. The Roman Church might keep her spiritual power, but it must leave temporal sway to the Prince.[3]

Manfred's successful rebellion, 1254.

Nevertheless, with all his ambition, it is probable that Manfred would not have immediately rebelled

Manfred defeats the papal army.

[1] Epp. of Nov. 17, 1254, ap. P., n. 15, 558, from Rymer's *Fœdera*, i, 190. Though this letter is not noticed by Gasquet, *Henry III. and the Church*, pp. 351–2, still see his work on these negotiations. Meanwhile, Henry had done nothing to advance his son's cause, but contented himself with styling himself " Guardian (tutor) of Edmund, King of Sicily ". Ep. of Oct. 14, 1254, ap. Rymer, i, p. 310 ed. of 1816. *Cf.* Mat. Par., *Chron.*, v, 459.

[2] Saba M., p. 792. Whatever papal sympathies Saba had, he has always praise for the accomplishments of Manfred. " Qui (Manfred) licet quantum ad communem opinionem in suscepto capitaneæ officio nomen Ecclesiæ profiteretur . . . nihilominus tamen Apulorum corda . . . ad devotionem et amicitiam suam quantum poterat attrahebat, in amore Sarracenorum de Luceria . . . potissime se involvens." G. de Cesare's *Storia di Manfredi*, 2 vols., Naples, 1837, is more than favourable to Manfred.

[3] *Ib.* It is clear even from Jamsilla (pp. 511–12) that Manfred's submission to the Pope was merely a temporary expedient to allay the suspicion of his enemies.

against the Pope's authority but for an accidental combination of circumstances. He was in the midst of a very heated quarrel concerning a fief with a powerful noble, Borello of Agnone (or Anglone) when, accompanied by a large number of his followers, he encountered Borello unarmed or with but a small troop. A fight ensued, and Borello was slain, seemingly by Manfred's orders,[1] but, according to *Jamsilla*, by Manfred's followers on their own account (October 18).[2] However that may be, Manfred furnished an immediate assumption of his guilt by taking to flight,[3] and that too despite the advice of a number of his followers to submit himself to the known justice of the Pope.[4] His panegyrist has given us a long description of the rapid flight of the Prince to Lucera. Doubtful of receiving any support from any Christian nobles or cities, he fled to his father's Saracen colonists at Lucera. These alien infidels, conjecturing, no doubt justly that, if the rule of the Church was thoroughly established in Apulia, their career of violence would be brought to an end with their lives, welcomed Manfred with enthusiasm (November 2), and handed over

---

[1] *Cf.* Saba, l. i, c. 5, p. 793. *Cf.* Carbio, c. 41, *Chron. de rebus*, p. 238, and *Chron. Suessanum*, ap. Pellicia, *Raccolta di varie Croniche*, i, p. 54. According to Jamsilla, pp. 512–13, Manfred was also irritated because the papal legate, William Fieschi, acted in a high-handed manner, regardless of his rights and those of Conradin.

[2] " Non ex ejus mandatis." Pp. 514–15. He was slain near Teano, where the Pope was from Oct. 16–19.

[3] J., p. 517. *Cf.* ep. of Alex. IV. to Berthold, Feb. 15, 1255, ap. R., iii, p. 342. " Qui (Manfred) postquam a Tiano propter mortem condam Burelli de Anglone ab ecclesia illicentiatus recessit, rebellionis spiritum assumpsit."

[4] So, at least, writes Jamsilla, p. 521. " Cujus (the Pope) est proprium æquitatis viam omnibus esse." Alexander IV. (ep. March 25, 1255, ap. Winkelmann, *Acta Imperii*, ii, p. 727) says that Manfred would not stand his trial : " idem princeps stare justitie noluit, licet . . . Innocentius . . . vellet in hoc antiquas regni Sicilie constitutiones observari."

to him the treasures which Frederick and Conrad had stored up there.[1] With this accumulated wealth, Manfred soon raised troops, taking especially into his pay the Germans whom Conrad had brought into the country. With these tried troops and with the Saracens and, according to some, helped by treachery, he defeated the papal army under the legate William and Berthold at Foggia (December 2).[2]

This defeat, and the flight of William and Berthold, gave the death blow to Innocent the Magnificent.[3] He had been ill at Teano, and some weeks after he had taken up his abode at Naples [4] in a house that had belonged to Peter della Vigna, he was seized with an attack of pleurisy.[5] The disaster of Foggia aggravated it. His hour had come. His physician, the white Cistercian cardinal, the Englishman, John Tolet,[6] could not save him.[7] With great devotion he received the last Sacraments at the hands of Cardinal Rinaldo, who was soon to succeed him ; and he who for about eleven years and a half " had been on his feet fighting ",[8] gave up the ghost, towards the hour of vespers on December 7.

Death of Innocent IV. Dec. 1254.

All during the night his bier was watched by the clergy both secular and regular singing the Office for the Dead.[9]

---

[1] Saba, i, 5, p. 793 ; Jam., pp. 530–3 ; Carbio, c. 41.

[2] Carbio, *l.c.* ; Jam., p. 539 ; Mat. Par., v, 430, 471, 474 ; etc.

[3] This title is given to Innocent by the Mon. Pat., *Chron.*, c. 2, p. 689.

[4] He entered it Oct. 27.

[5] *Cf.* Jams., p. 514 ; Mat. Par., v, 430.

[6] For English medical history it is an interesting fact that the physicians of Gregory IX. and Innocent IV. were Englishmen.

[7] Mat. Par., *ib.*

[8] *Chron. Hugonis contin.*, ap. *M. G. SS.*, xxiv, p. 100.

[9] This shows that the assertion made by Eccleston that, when Innocent was dying, he was abandoned by his whole household except by the Friars Minor, is false. *De adventu Minorum*, collat. xv, p. 119 ed. Little. *Cf.* what we have said about the death of Innocent III., *supra*, vol. xii, p. 301 n. Of course, the story is repeated by the gossip

On the following morning the body of the late Pope was solemnly conveyed by the clergy and people to the Cathedral of St. Restituta, where he had decided to be buried. There was it laid to rest in a splendid tomb, and there, adds Carbio,[1] by the mercy of God were sick people cured of their infirmities.

The tomb of Innocent IV. At the end of the left transept of the cathedral of San Gennaro [2] the visitor will see a large sepulchral monument of five stories, probably belonging to three different periods. The plain marble tomb at the bottom with its rim of inlaid marbles in the Cosmati style is original, and contains Innocent's body. On the top of it is a heavy recumbent figure of a Pope wearing a tiara ornamented with three crowns. This is evidently later than the tomb, and may have been the work of archbishop Humbert of Montoro (1308–20), who brought the original tomb from the cathedral of St. Restituta, and who composed the epitaph which occupies the fourth story of the monument. The inscription on the third story is the work of archbishop Annibale (1578–95) who, as he says in it, restored the epitaph. The monument is crowned by a piece of sculpture, also later than the tomb, showing Innocent and archbishop Annibale kneeling by a seated figure of

Salimbene another Franciscan. *Chron.*, p. 420. I need scarcely say that I attach no credence to the rubbish given by Mat. Par. concerning Grosseteste's appearing to him and giving him a blow in his side which helped the pleurisy to kill him, v, 429 ; nor to the vision " of a certain cardinal " who saw him condemned to hell for ruining the Church, v, 471 ; nor to that of Alexander IV. who is said to have seen him condemned to hell or purgatory, *ib.*, 491 ; nor to Thomas of Cantimpré († c. 1270), lib. ii, c. 10, n. 21. *Bonum universale de apibus*, Douay, 1627. These friars repeated gossip against Innocent because he legislated against them.

[1] C. 42, Carbio tells us here that he was with the Pope till his death : " usque ad ipsius obitum familiariter secum."

[2] To this church (begun by Charles I of Anjou, but only completed in 1316), which succeeded that of St. Restituta as the cathedral, was the tomb of Innocent transferred by archbishop Humbert.

Our Lady with the infant Saviour in her arms. The upper epitaph [1] sets forth that it was the work of Humbert, and states that : Here lies the kindly Pope of the house of Fieschi (de Flisco) who, worthy of heaven, called a council to reform the world by the renovation of ancient laws. Under him heresy was destroyed as well as that snake Frederick, the enemy of Christ. Genoa is proud of her illustrious son, and beautiful Naples, to whom he gave much, also extols him.

As the lower inscription states, this epitaph was renewed by archbishop Annibale of Capua, to whom I believe we owe the three upper stories of the monument.

---

[1] See the illustration in this vol. The reader who cannot make out the original of the inscriptions from the illustration will find them in Duchesne, *Liber Pontif.*, ii, p. 454, and Gregorovius, *Tombs of the Popes*, p. 50 f., Eng. ed.

CHAPTER IV.

France and the Crusades.

Sources.—The different biographies of St. Louis and the Chronicles relating to his reign will be found ap. *R. F. SS.*, vols. xx–xxiii. Specially important are the *Mémoires di Sire de Joinville* (1245–70), ed. N. de Wailly, Paris, 1874, and the *Vita Ludovici IX.*, by Geoffrey of Beaulieu, ap. *R. F. SS.*, xx. The former work has been edited very frequently. An English translation of it will be found ap. Bohn's *Chronicles of the Crusades.* Ethel Wedgwood has given *A New English Version* (slightly abridged), London, 1906.

Modern Works.—There are a great number of *Lives* of St. Louis. That of Le Nain de Tillemont (†1698), *Vie de S. Louis*, ed. J. de Gaulle, 6 vols., Paris, 1847 ff., will always be valuable, as it contains extracts from works now lost. In addition we may note the *Hist. de S. L.*, by the Marquis de Villeneuve-Trans, 3 vols., Paris, 1839 ; *Saint L.*, by H. Wallon, Tours, 1878 (valuable) ; *Saint L.*, by A. Lecoy-de la Marche, Tours, 1894 ; *Saint L.*, by L. Sepet, Paris, 1900 ; and *Saint L., the Most Christian King*, by F. Perry, London, 1901. For our purpose, of the first importance is the study of É. Berger, which we have already mentioned. *S. L. et Inn. IV.*, étude sur les rapports de la France et du Saint-Siège. Useful also are such biographies as *Guillaume d'Auvergne* by N. Valois, Paris, 1880, and the brief one of *Jean de Bernin*, by U. Chevalier, Paris, 1910. Innocent's relations with the great abbey of St. Denis are told by J. Cordey, *Guillaume de Massouris, abbé de S.-Denis*, ap. Luchaire, *Mélanges d'hist. du moyen-âge*, Paris, 1904. Labande's *Avignon au XIIIe siècle*, Paris, 1908, gives us information about bishop Zoen Tencarari, the legate whom Innocent used in his pacification of the South of France.

France and the Holy See from the days of Innocent III. to Innocent IV.

WHILST the Empire was wearing itself out in its struggle with the Lombards and the Holy See, the monarchy of France, preserving the most friendly relations with the Popes, was steadily strengthening its position. At the expense of England and of the great feudal nobles, it was surely increasing its power over that splendid country which we now know as France. After the territorial

additions to the French crown made by Philip Augustus
(† 1223), nothing of any particular note in that direction
was accomplished by his son, Louis VIII. († 1226). It was
reserved for his famous son St. Louis IX., both to show
himself one of the most distinguished sovereigns not merely
of France, but of the world, and to add undying lustre
and solid strength to the house of Capet. During his
minority, his heroic mother, Blanche of Castile, guided
by the legate Romanus Bonaventura, cardinal-deacon
of Saint-Angelo,[1] proved too strong for various coalitions
of nobles who strove to recover the power they had lost
under his grandfather.[2] Romanus, aided in his turn by
the Popes, was almost as valuable a support to the little
Louis and to the Regency as the legate Gualo had been
to Henry III. and his Regency. Through him, in spite of
the opposition of the nobles, was the young Louis
crowned,[3] and through him was the war against the
Albigenses, which was not over when Innocent III. died,
pushed to a final conclusion. Obtaining letters from
Honorius III. forbidding the King of England to attack
the French King " whilst he was engaged in the service
of the Pope and the Church of Rome ",[4] Romanus caused
the campaign to be prosecuted with such vigour that in
1229 the count of Toulouse, Raymond VII., was glad to
sign the Treaty of Paris which practically put an end
to the Albigensian war.[5]

Naturally enough, the legate was not always successful
in giving the best advice to Blanche. On one occasion,
for instance, after a " town and gown " row (1229) by

[1] Sent into France by Honorius III. *Cf.* Roger of Wendover, *Chron.*,
ad an. 1226, and Will. of Puylaurens, *Chron.*, c. 32 al. 34. Will. justly
calls Romanus " vir magne discretionis ".

[2] Langlois, *Hist. de France*, iii, pp. 7–10. Speaking of the death of
Philip Augustus (ad an. 1223), Geoffroy de Courlon, *Cronica*, says that
he " superbos deprimens . . . regni sui fines quam plurimum dilatavit."

[3] Roger of W., *ib.*   [4] Roger, *ib.*

[5] See the documents ap. *Regist. Greg. IX.*, iii, p. 1265 ed. Auvray.
Cf. Will. of P., c. 37, al. 39.

supporting her strong measures against the students of
the University of Paris, and ordering its seal to be
broken,[1] he nearly caused the city to lose its University.
Still both he and the Popes deserved well of the learned
world of France ; for on other occasions he did good
service to the University of Paris,[2] and he won the
highest praise from that of Toulouse. He was, said its
authorities, " their Moses, their leader, and protector,
and, after God and the lord Pope, their founder." [3]

Eulogy of
the Church
of France.

In general, we may say that the relations between
Honorius III. and Gregory IX. with the Church of France
were most friendly, and the latter Pope, in whose
pontificate Louis IX. came of age (1234), declared : " We
freely ackowledge that the French Church (ecclesia
Gallicana) is after the Apostolic See, as it were a model
for Christendom, and an unshakable foundation of the
faith, inasmuch as, in its Christian fervour and devotion
to the Apostolic See, it does not follow the other churches,
but, to speak without offence to them, leads them." [4]

Gregory's
aim to keep
France at
peace.

The great aim of Gregory IX. was to keep the peace
during the minority of St. Louis, and of this aim his letters
are a lasting memorial. Writing (Nov. 29, 1229) to
the archbishop of Lyons, and reminding him that the
harassing of a minor is always considered very mean, and

---

[1] Mat. Par., *Chron.*, iii, 166 f. *Cf.* ep. Inn. IV., Oct. 30, 1246, ap.
Denifle, *Chart. Univer. Paris*, i, n. 165, p. 194 (*cf.* n. 45, *ib.*) ; and
ep. Greg. IX., ap. *Reg.*, i, n. 374, p. 226 ff.

[2] *Cf.* ep. Greg. IX., June 3, 1228, ap. Denifle, *l.c.*, n. 58, p. 113.
Cf. n. 89, p. 144.

[3] *Cf.* a letter (1229 c. fin.) of the professors of Toulouse to the other
Universities, ap. *ib.*, n. 72, p. 130 ff. Langlois, *Hist. de France*, iii,
p. 6, speaking of Romanus, says : " Ce n'était point un parvenu, un
diplomate, comme d'autres Italiens, fins et vers, qui ont gouverné
la France ; c'était un cavalier, un grand seigneur d'allures dédaigneuses
et cassantes." The vain efforts of Romanus to induce the Church of
France to adopt a scheme to help the papal finances have been noticed
in the biography of Honorius III. *Cf.* also *supra*, vol. xii, p. 294 ff.

[4] Ep. of July, 1227, ap. Raynald., *Annal.*, 1227, n. 60.

is really a breach of the duty of loyalty owed to him,
Gregory stated that he had been shocked to hear how
some of the magnates of the realm, setting at naught
the prohibition of the King, had in their hatred of one
another not hesitated to rend " the kingdom of France,
that kingdom of benediction and grace ". They had not
given a thought to the fact that their wars were causing
loss of property and lives, and were endangering the souls
of men and the prospects of the Holy Land. Especially,
as he told the Archbishop, had he urged the Duke of
Burgundy not to allow himself to be drawn into fighting,
but to lay himself out in every way he could to prevent
wars. He brought his eloquent letter to a conclusion
by exhorting the Archbishop to use his influence with the
Duke for the same purpose.[1]

When Sinibaldo Fieschi became Pope Innocent IV., The work
there was peace throughout the realm of France. The and aims of
power of the barons against the crown had been broken, Louis IX.
and the treaty of Lorris (Jan., 1243) had closed the
last important rising of the Albigenses,[2] or rather, more
accurately, the last effort of Raymond VII., Count of
Toulouse, to assert his complete independence of the

---

[1] Ep. No. 29, 1229, ap. *Reg.*, i, 378. One of those against whom
Gregory had to give special assistance to Louis was Pierre de Dreux,
surnamed Mauclerc, count of Brittany. *Cf.* Jager, *Hist. de l'eglise
cath. en France*, ix, p. 206 ff. Matthew Paris has much to say of this
pirate and turncoat. *Cf.* his letter of Oct. 21, 1229, to St. Louis,
ap. H.-B., v, 457, in which he says that among the kingdoms of the earth
France takes the lead for its work for Christianity. " Inter quae (the
kingdoms), sicut tribus Juda inter ceteros filios patriarche ad specialis
benedictionis dona suscipitur, sic regnum Francie pre ceteris terrarum
populis a Domino prerogativa honoris et gratie insignitur." Recalling
the work of France for the Crusades, etc., he concludes by praising
it for subduing the Albigensian heresy : " pravitatem hereticam que
in partibus Albigensium fere fidem extirpaverat *christianam*, totis
viribus expugnare non destitit donec ea quasi penitus confutata
fidem ipsam ad pristini status solium revocavit."

[2] *Cf. supra*, vol. xii, p. 259.

throne of France.   That throne was occupied by
St. Louis IX., a man, for he was now of age, who was
recognized by all to be a saint, a statesman, and a warrior.
He had taught the feudal lay nobles that they must
respect the law, he had impressed the duty of moderation
on the clergy, and, whilst displaying the utmost deference
to the Head of the Church, he had shown that he could
distinguish between the obedience he owed him as a
Christian and as a responsible member of the great
Christian commonwealth,[1] and the independence to
which he had a right as a man and a king.   His home
policy consisted in the dispensing of justice and charity,
in the promotion of peace, and in the suppression of
heresy ; his foreign policy, in work for the deliverance
of the Holy Land from the power of the infidel.[2]   Hence
in the great struggle between the Papacy and the Empire,
while giving his moral support to the former,[3] and affording
the Pope protection against physical force, he would not
furnish him with armed support against the Emperor.
He would but strive in season and out of season to bring
about peace between them, and when he saw that he was
powerless to effect this, he would not allow their differences
to interfere with his Crusading expeditions.   Perhaps
he might have done more for Christendom if he had
listened to the Pope's appeals for help against the

[1] For he fully acknowledged the Pope to be the arbiter of Christendom. Cf. Mat. Par., iv, 647.

[2] He first took the cross (December) after the Kharismians had
taken Jerusalem in 1244.

[3] Berger, Reg., ii, p. xxvi. " Ce souci des intérêts chrétiens, cette
sollicitude pour l'honneur du Saint-Siège, se retrouvent jusqu' à la
fin de sa vie et dans ses dernières instructions." Hence we find one of the
biographers of St. Louis saying : " Ipse enim negotia matris Ecclesiæ
plus quam propria reputans." Ap. R. F. SS., xx, p. 33. In his last
advice to his son he inculcates devotion to the Pope and the Roman
Church. " Care fili, doceo te quod tu sis semper devotus Ecclesiæ
Romanæ et summo pontifici." Gesta Ludov., ap. ib., p. 49.

oppressor of Europe, and never embarked on his ill-fated enterprises against the East.

At any rate, for what " the King of the Kings " [1] did for Innocent, that pontiff was not ungrateful. He not only spoke of Louis himself in the most flattering terms,[2] but to quote the words of Berger, " he helped forward the marriage of his brother Charles of Anjou, with the heiress of Provence, and was the first to think of placing a French King on the throne of the Two Sicilies ; he assisted as far as he could the Crusade of St. Louis, and after the King's departure, remained, despite some difficulties, on good terms with those who governed the Kingdom." [3] It was to please St. Louis that he received Raymond VII., count of Toulouse, into favour,[4] and that he agreed to consider offers of peace made by Frederick even though he was convinced they would lead to nothing.

Even with regard to the vexed questions connected with appointments to bishoprics, Innocent made every effort to oblige the French monarch. Writing to him in connexion with such an appointment he said : " As soon as ever an occasion offered we were at pains to satisfy your desire in this matter. Full of solicitude for all that can increase the honour of one to whom we are more attached than to any other prince, we urge your Highness to turn to us with confidence in the interests of your Kingdom, whenever you think it desirable. For it is our intent, by special privilege of grace and favour, to raise you higher than all other Princes." [5]

Innocent's deference for St. Louis.

The appointment of bishoprics.

[1] Such is the description given of him by Mat. Paris, v, 480.

[2] Ep. Dec. 12, 1243, Potthast, n. 11, 192 ; Berger, *l.c.*, p. xii.

[3] *L.c.*, p. ii.

[4] *Ib.*, p. x.

[5] Ep. Feb. 26, 1244, ap. *Reg.*, i, n. 511. *Cf.* Berger, *ib.*, p. xxix ff. *Cf.* ep. Apr. 26, 1245, ap. *ib.*, n. 1360. " Sane scire tuam excellentiam volumus quod, cum inter alios orbis principes te specialis dilectionis brachiis amplexemur, et exaltationem tue persone ferventi animo cupiamus, non solum jura regalia minui nolumus, sed ea per que

Troubles
between the
nobles and
clergy.

But if no serious differences came to a head between the Pope and the King or the successive Regents, Blanche of Castile, and his brother Alphonse, count of Poitiers, such was not the case between the Pope and the French nobility. Already in 1235 there had been trouble between a considerable number of the nobles of France and some of the higher clergy, principally concerning questions of jurisdiction. The former had protested to the Pope that the latter were unwilling to take their share in sitting in the King's court to judge temporal causes.[1] If any agreement was come to on this question after it had been referred to Gregory IX.,[2] it did not prevent the quarrel between the secular and the ecclesiastical nobility from continuing. It came to a head in 1246, after it had been diligently fomented by Frederick, who secured the adhesion of a number of the French nobles in his attack on the Church. Some of them even marched into Germany to the support of Conrad against the party of the Church.[3] Moreover, despite the fact that the council of Béziers (April, 1246) declared those excommunicated who made laws against ecclesiastical liberty,[4] a number of the great nobles formed a confederation against the clergy ; and, to make it effective, nominated an executive of four of their

---

dignitatis" regie provenire possit augmentum intendimus sollicite procurare."

[1] Berger, *l.c.*, p. xxxiii f., and Jager, *Hist. de l'église en France*, ix, 246 ff. On the general history of these conflicts between the French nobles and clergy at this time see Fournier, *Les officialités au Moyen-Age*.

[2] Gregory wrote (Feb. 15, 1236) some very strong letters on the subject to King Louis, to Thibaut, count of Champagne, and to the nobles of the Kingdom generally. *Cf.* Raynaldus, *Annal. Eccles.*, 1236, § 31–6. He called upon the King to annul all action taken against ecclesiastical liberty, and he quoted a bull of Honorius III. issued at the time of Frederick's coronation against the violators of that liberty.

[3] Ep. of Walter of Ocra ap. H.-B., vi, 57, or Mat. Par., iv, 575 ff.

[4] Can. 18 ap. Hefele, *Concil.*, v, p. 1696, 2nd French ed.

number.[1] In the most arrogant language they set
forth that the arms of the nobility had made the position
of the clergy, and now, sons of slaves, they dared,
according to laws made by themselves, to judge these
very nobles. They therefore ordained that if a clerk
or layman dared to cite anyone before an ecclesiastical
tribunal, except for heresy or matrimonial cases or usury,
he was to be liable to the loss of his goods and one of his
limbs. In fine, in imitation of the language of Frederick,
they declared that it was their object to bring back
the clergy to their condition in the primitive Church.[2]

Notice of this federation, which one of our historians,
John of Oxnead, calls " a destestable conspiracy against
the Pope and the Roman Curia, and a danger to the
Universal Church and the Christian faith ",[3] was soon
brought to the Pope. According to Matthew Paris,
though his words are not supported by any confirmatory
entries in Innocent's *Register*, the Pope at once sought

---

[1] The nature of the federation may at least be partially understood
when it is stated that one of the four was the pirate Peter Mauclerc,
once count of Brittany. On the rights and duties of the executive see
their letter, ap. H.-B., vi, 468, or Mat. Par., iv, 591.

[2] See their resolution ap. H.-B., vi, 467, or M. P., iv, 592.
"Credebatur hæc a consensu Fretherici emanasse." P. 593.

[3] *Chron.*, p. 117, *R. S.* John lived at the close of the thirteenth
century. Mat. Par., *Chron.*, iv, 614, says that even King Louis affixed
his seal to the proclamation of the barons. *Cf. ib.*, vi, 132. But, as
Berger points out (p. clxxvii), the King's assent is not affirmed either
by the barons themselves or by the Pope ; but he may at some other
time have made representations to Innocent based on representations
of the nobles, as he certainly did at the Council of Lyons with regard
to the papal taxation of France. *Cf.* his complaint put before Innocent
at the Council of Lyons in 1245, ap. Mat. Par., vi, 99 ff. In 1245 at
any rate, it is stated (*ib.*, p. 100) that the nobles do not obey the Church
except through fear of the King—"ipsi non obediant (obediunt)
ecclesiæ, nisi quantum hoc faciunt timore regiæ partis." Unfortunately,
this complaint (called *literæ* by Paris) is anonymous (though the writer
professes to put down what Louis had enjoined him—"dicturus quod
injunctum est mihi a d. rege Franciæ ") and undated.

to pacify the recalcitrant nobles by granting them and
theirs privileges of all sorts, after having failed to terrify
them by threats.[1]   However that may be, the instructions
issued by Innocent to his legate, Eudes of Châteauroux,
i.e., Otho, cardinal-bishop of Tusculum, show that he
was resolved to resist the barons.[2]   The Pope begins
by expressing his grief that, whilst the persecutor
Frederick was striving to absorb the Church,[3] it should
be attacked by its children, by the sons of the very men
who had done so much for it.   He pointed out that,
in giving civil jurisdiction to bishops, Charlemagne
had but followed Theodosius ;   and suggested that,
if the French barons had remembered that such as
establish laws against the liberty of the Church are
ipso facto excommunicated, they would probably not
have been so ready to act.   They must then be instructed
on this point, inasmuch as what they propose to do would
destroy " not merely ecclesiastical liberty but the condition of the whole Church ".[4]   The letter closed with
a series of instructions on the measures which Otho
(or Eudes) should adopt against the rebellious barons,

---

[1] iv, 593.

[2] Ap. H.-B., vi, 483 ; ep. Jan. 4, 1247.

[3] A very striking expression " qui (not que as H.-B. has it) ad
absorbendum eam per se ac membra sua totis viribus inhiat ". P. 483.

[4] " Cum per predicta ab eisdem baronibus attemptata videatur non
tam libertas ecclesiastica quam status totius Ecclesie immutari, etc."
P. 485. This justifies the resistance of the Church at this time to the
taking away by individual kings or others of the civil privileges which
had been granted her. If a civil authority proportionate to that which
gave the said privileges found it desirable to withdraw them, such an
authority no doubt might have the right to do so ; but certainly no
inferior authority. And, in any case, the withdrawal ought to be gradual,
in order that the existing *status* of the Church might not be injured.
Innocent added that it was believed that the action of the barons had
been brought about " by that enemy who was aspiring to the overthrow of the faith ".

and on the ecclesiastical punishments which had to be
meted out to them.

Though a similar letter urging them to resist was sent
to the French clergy,[1] the federation was still in existence
about May, 1247. At that period the papal Curia was
awaiting the arrival of its representatives, and it was
popularly said that their coming was awaited in no
laughing spirit,[2] as they had received more encouragement
from Frederick.[3] But the defeat of that Prince at
Parma was fatal no doubt as well to the French baronial
federation as to his own influence.

Although it is true that no differences caused any St. Louis
grave trouble between St. Louis or the Regents, Blanche has
difficulties
of Castile and then Alphonse, count of Poitiers, who ruled with the
Pope.
France in his absence, and Innocent, it was not because
there were no serious differences between them. The
question of pontifical taxation in France provoked
discontent in that country as it did in England. To
use the language of a Frenchman of the time, Innocent
was compelled in order to guard the liberty of the Church
(" pro tuicione ecclesiastice libertatis ") to impose heavy
taxes—first a twentieth and then a tenth—on the
Churches and monasteries, in order to subsidize soldiers,
and then to enforce payment by threat of excommunication.[4] The author of these words was evidently a wise
and considerate man, a man after the pattern of bishop
Grosseteste and St. Edmund of Canterbury.[5] But
the majority of the French clergy, like their brethren in

---

[1] *Reg.*, i, n. 2951.

[2] *Cf.* a chatty letter of archbishop Boniface of Savoy to his brother
Peter, ap. Mat. Par., vi, 132.

[3] See his ep. of *c.* April, 1247, ap. H.-B., vi, 514 ff.

[4] *Cf.* the author of the *Gesta Epp. Virdunensium*, ap. *M. G. SS.*, x,
p. 525. But at last God laid low the cause of the trouble, Frederick II.
" qui vehementi scismate turbaverat urbes, et regna concusserat ".

[5] *Cf. supra*, vol. xiii, pp. 306–8.

England,[1] were unable to appreciate the gravity of the cause for which Innocent was struggling. They were, however, well able to feel the great drain upon their resources caused by the papal impositions, and were able to resent the insolence of some of the papal tax-gatherers, and their drastic methods of enforcing payment.[2] The fiscal grievances of the French clergy at this period are known to us especially by two documents preserved by Matthew Paris. The first is a letter of our archbishop Boniface to his brother, Peter of Savoy [3] (May 4, 1247); and the second is an anonymous and undated memoir drawn up in obedience to the orders of King Louis. This more important document belongs to the latter part of the same year 1247.[4]

Taxation of
the French
clergy. In the beginning of May, 1247, there arrived in Lyons representatives of the episcopate and clergy of France, and Ferry Paté, marshal of France, representing its sovereign. Besides complaining of the Pope's grant of " provisions " to Italians in France, and of other things, they complained especially of the taxes raised for the Roman Church and the Eastern Empire, and of the conduct of those who collected these taxes.[5]

In reply to the representations made to him, Innocent, while naturally declining to interfere with those Italians already in possession of benefices, promised to revoke

---

[1] Cf. ib., p. 304, on papal taxation in general and in England in particular. Cf. also infra, p. 233 ff.

[2] As Berger notes, p. ii, " To save the Church Innocent imposed such heavy taxes on the faithful, that at times they were ready to revolt." Cf. ib., p. cxci.

[3] Ap. Mat. Par., vi, 131 ff.

[4] Ap. ib., p. 99 ff. It was provisionally dated by Luard 1245; but Berger, p. cxciii, has given arguments to show that the date given in the text is the correct one. To his arguments add the comparison between the statement on p. 106 that Innocent called upon the French clergy to send him troops to resist the expected attack of Frederick, with other letters to the same effect cited supra, p. 100.

[5] Ep. of Boniface, p. 131.

all grants that had been made to others in the matter of
future vacant benefices, and finally to recall the offending
collectors. But, with regard to the taxes for the Eastern
Empire and for the Roman Church, he undertook to
send envoys to the next French parliament, and there
to make satisfactory arrangements for the future. Not
content with these concessions, the deputation left
Innocent to urge the King to fresh action.[1]

Louis apparently listened to their representations,
and authorized the drawing up of the long and strong
memorial to which we have referred. The document
set forth that the patience of the King was exhausted,
and that he found it necessary to speak, seeing that the
devotion of the people to the Roman Church was turning
to hatred. The cause of this was the new taxes exacted
by the Pope.[2] Up to his time, the words " Give me so
much or I will excommunicate you ", had never been
heard. The result of this method of raising money was
that the Gallican Church was oppressed to a greater
extent than the Pope had any idea of. Moreover, the
granting of prebends not yet vacant was most reprehensible. Living canons had daily to look on men who
were awaiting their death. " Although," urged the
writer of the memoir, " you are not bound by any human
law, you ought to submit to the laws you have made,
just like our Lord Jesus Christ who owed no obedience
to any law, but still wished to be subject to certain
laws. . . . Wherefore if you do these and other such things
from a certain plenitude of power, nevertheless reason
and moderation ought to govern everything. . . . Although
the first see presides over the others, and doubtful
questions must be referred to it, it is not stated that

---

[1] *Ib*.

[2] The memoir ap. Mat. Par., vi, p. 100 : " A sæculo non est auditum
quod ecclesia Romana pro quacunque necessitate subsidium pecuniare
vel tributum de temporalibus suis exegerit ab ecclesia Gallicana."

the first see must rob the others, or take from them what belongs to them." [1] If it needs help it should procure it in such a way as not to oppress its subjects.

Then turning to the subject of " Provisions ", and making various historical blunders, [2] the author of the memoir declared that Innocent IV. had already given away more benefices than all his predecessors put together. The evils of this system were then pointed out, and the compiler concluded his task by stating that, although the King had a sincere affection for the Pope, and much compassion for his difficulties, he was bound to defend " the liberties and customs of the Kingdom that had been committed to him by God ".

Unfortunately this anonymous and undated document though voicing real grievances has no history. It is not known whether it was ever presented to Innocent, and hence nothing can be said with certainty as to any effect produced by it. " We do not know," says Berger, [3] " whether subsidies for the Roman Church continued to be levied in France after 1247, but the silence of the chroniclers furnishes ground to believe that, thanks to the opposition of the King, our country was not in this respect so heavily burdened as England."

St. Louis and the Holy Land, 1244–8.

But the one great concern of Louis IX. all this time was the Holy Land. Ayub, the son of El-Kamil, and sultan of Egypt, in order to make headway against Ismaʻil, sultan of Damascus, who was hand in glove with

[1] " Nam etsi prima sedes aliis præsit et ad ipsam debeant dubiæ quæstiones referri, non legitur tamen quod prima sedes alias debeat spoliare, vel eis auferre quod suum est." *Ib.*, p. 104.

[2] E.g., the author declares that Innocent III (instead of Innocent II. nearly a hundred years earlier ; *cf. supra*, vol. xiii, p. 161) was the first to practise the right of disposing of benefices.

[3] *L.c.*, p. ccxi. The Registers of Innocent abundantly prove that he granted a great many provisions, permitted a number of clerics to hold many benefices, and reserved many benefices not yet vacant for the benefit of such as he wished to favour.

the Christians, took into his service bands of Kharismian Turks who had been driven from their territories by the Tartars. In the summer of 1244, hordes of these horsemen overran Palestine, and Europe was once more shocked by the news that Jerusalem was again in the power of the infidel (Aug., 1244), and that at Gaza (Oct., 1244) the Christian arms had suffered a decisive defeat.[1] Towards the close of the same year King Louis of France was lying sick unto death. On his unexpected recovery he took the Cross, and no representations of his mother or of the statesmen of France could turn him from his design of striking a blow to free the Holy Land.[2] Before he could get ready, the state of affairs there had gone from bad to worse. The Tartars had reduced Bohemond V. of Antioch to pay tribute (1246), and in 1247-8 Ayub had begun to capture some of the few cities of Palestine remaining in Christian hands. However, it was at this juncture that he heard that a new Crusade had left Europe, and that St. Louis had landed at Cyprus (Sept., 1248), on his way to the East.

As soon as he had recovered his health, Louis at once began his preparations for his Crusade. Though he made every effort to bring about peace between the Emperor and the Pope in order to secure their aid, there is no doubt that he soon realized that he would have to rely chiefly upon his own efforts and resources if his expedition was ever to mature at all. It is true that, despite his difficult position, and his preoccupations "truly terrible", as Berger calls them, the Pope "did much to prepare the Crusade".[3] Soon after the news of the fall of Jerusalem reached Europe, his letters

The eighth Crusade, 1248.

---

[1] Cf. Mat. Par., iv, pp. 299 and 306, and letters of Frederick II., etc., ib., p. 300 ff.; and 307 ff.; 337 ff. In the *Annals of Burton*, i, p. 257, the last-named letter is addressed to Innocent IV.

[2] Joinville, c. 4; Mat. Par., iv, 397.

[3] Berger, *Reg.*, ii, p. cxxii.

called the nations to arm in defence of the Holy Land.[1] At the council of Lyons Innocent in his address to the assembled Fathers told them how " the detestable Kharismians had levelled to the ground the houses of the Templars and the Hospitallers, the City of Jerusalem, and many other Christian cities, and had shed a great quantity of Christian blood ".[2] Then " full of anxiety for the relief of the Holy Land ", he issued a number of decrees " with the approbation of the sacred council ", relative to urging Christians to take the Cross, and to assemble at suitable times and places " whence they might proceed to the help of the Holy Land with the Divine and the Apostolic blessing ".[3] To ensure the descent of this blessing on the Christian arms, the Crusaders were to be exhorted above all things to lead good lives ; and both clergy and people were ordered to be taxed to provide the necessary funds.[4]

Cardinal Eudes, or Otho, preaches the Crusade in France, 1245.

As soon as the Council had broken up, Innocent, in accordance with the request of Louis for a distinguished preacher,[5] sent into France a native of that country,

[1] Epp. of Dec. and Jan., 1244–5. *Cf*. Potthast, 11491, for the bull Terra Sancta Christi. That same bull was addressed to Henry III. on Jan. 23, 1245. *Ib*., 11561. *Cf*. 11562, and *Annales Stadenses*, ap. *M. G. SS*., xvi, p. 369.

[2] Mat. Par., iv, 434.

[3] Can. 17, ap. Mat. Par., iv, 456.

[4] *Ib*. After this a number of minute regulations were issued concerning the duties and privileges of Crusaders. *Ib*., p. 458 ff. and 473. They were the same as those which had been promulgated by Gregory IX. in 1234. *Cf. ib*., iii, p. 280 ff. Paris, *ib*., p. 473, pretends that the taxation clauses for the Crusade were disputed chiefly on the ground of the regulation that the taxes had to be levied by agents appointed by the Pope, " for the faithful have often complained that they had been cheated by the Roman Curia concerning money which they had contributed for the assistance of the Holy Land."

[5] M. P., iv, 416. A very rare little book, printed in the fifteenth century, of which a copy (n. 259, formerly 12360) is to be found in the Mazarin library in Paris, contains a treatise by Humbert de Romanis, fifth Master-general of the Dominicans (1254–63). It is entitled

Otho (or Eudes), cardinal-bishop of Tusculum [1]—a man whom a contemporary prelate regarded as second to no one in the world.[2] The legate applied himself to his task with the greatest self-devotion, and be it added, with the greatest success.[3] He was well supported by the Pope, who bade him choose preachers to send into " England, Germany, Scotland, Denmark, and Brabant ", in order to rouse the people to assume the Cross.[4] Innocent also exhorted him to raise the tenth which had been ordered for the King before anything was collected, either for the Roman Church, or for the Empire of Constantinople.[5] He moreover named him spiritual head of the Crusade,[6] and wrote to the prelates and Kings of Armenia, Cyprus, etc., to recognize him as such.[7]

Tractatus de prædicatione sanctæ crucis, and was written about 1267. It was a guide to those who had to preach the Cross. It set forth the objections which prudence was now raising against the Crusades, and showed by example how the cause of the Cross was to be proclaimed, how it was to be proved that, in the strong words of Master Prévostin, chancellor of the University of Paris, " the God of the Christians was not quite dead." This note is extracted from an article by A. Lecoy de la Marche, " La prédication de la Croisade au 13ᵉ siècle," ap. *Rev. des Quest. Hist.*, July, 1890, p. 5 ff.

[1] Vincent of Beauvais, *Spec. Hist.*, l. xxxi, c. 1.

[2] *Cf.* Lecoy de la Marche, *La chaire française*, p. 67, Paris, 1868 ; and Hauréau, *Quelques Lettres d'Inn. IV.*, p. 48 ff. The contemporary was Étienne Tempier, bishop of Paris, ap. de la Marche, citing *M.S. Lat.*, 16481, n. 128, in the Bib. Nat.

[3] *Cf.* one of the *lives* of St. Louis, ap. *R. F. SS.*, xx, p. 67 ; *Chron. Norman.*, ap. *ib.*, xxiii, p. 214.

[4] *Cf.* epp. of Nov. 6, 1246, ap. *Reg.*, i, nn. 2228–9, or in full ap. Hauréau, p. 53. Whilst he was legate the Pope entrusted him with a number of most delicate negotiations, besides the preaching of the Crusade ; e.g. the enforcing of his Provisions. Cf. ep. of Oct. 14, 1247, ap. *Reg.*, i, n. 3321, in full ap. H., p. 56.

[5] Ep. Oct. 29, 1247, ap. *Reg.*, i, n. 3383, or in full ap. H., p. 57. " Mandamus quatenus decimam in regno Franciæ omnium ecclesiasticorum proventuum . . . priusquam aliquid Ecclesiæ Romanæ vel imperii Constantinopolitani . . . colligatur." *Cf.* n. 3384.

[6] Ep. Feb. 23, 1248, ap. Raynaldus, *Annal.*, 1248, n. 28.

[7] *Reg.*, i, 3965, June 22, 1248.

How
Innocent
helped the
Crusade
forward.

In many other ways also, both directly and indirectly, did Innocent forward the interests of the Crusade which his legate was preaching with the best results. He refused, for instance, a request made by an envoy of the King of Aragon, to guarantee the King of Tunis from an attack by the Crusaders,[1] and through the famous Franciscan, Piano Carpini, he exhorted the great ruler of the Tartars, Manguchan, not to attack the Christians.[2] He also forbade trading with the enemy, at least in munitions of war.[3] Henry III. was also forbidden under pain of the heaviest ecclesiastical censures to attack the realm of Louis during his absence on Crusade.[4] As a rule, too, Innocent would not allow of the commutation of the vows of such as had promised to join in the Holy War,[5] and he insisted that those who had once taken the vow, should at all times wear the cross on their shoulders.[6] Especially did he help in the matter of money. The Council of Lyons had decreed that a tax of a twentieth of all ecclesiastical revenues should be raised for the Crusade. Innocent, however, authorized Louis to raise a tenth throughout his dominions,[7] and arranged for its collection by agents appointed by his authority. If, however, this arrangement had the advantage of saving the Church from State interference, it had the disadvantage of lessening the popularity of the Church of Rome which became more and more associated with taxation. At any rate, as far as Louis was concerned, the

---

[1] *Reg.*, i, 2011, July 19, 1246.

[2] Ep. March 13 (5), 1245, ap. *ib.*, n. 1365, or Röhricht, *Reg. Hierosol.*, n. 1134.

[3] *Ib.*, 7331, March 21, 1248.

[4] Mat. Par., v, 51 and 346.

[5] *Reg.*, i, n. 3054, July 5, 1247.

[6] *Ib.*, n. 3970, June 22, 1248.

[7] *Cf. Reg.*, i, nn. 2032-3, July 19, 1246 ; and 2492, March 27, 1247, and the " Rothelin " *Continuation of William of Tyre*, ap. *Hist. des Croisades, Historiens occident.*, ii, p. 567, cited by Berger, p. cxxxv.

action of the Pope brought him in large sums from his
own country.[1]   How far the twentieth was raised in other
countries and what monies were raised therein is not
known.   It was certainly raised in England, if under
some protest from King Henry [2] ; and, among the many
nobles who benefited by the funds assigned to them by
the Pope, was William Longsword, Earl of Salisbury,
"the hero of Mansourah." [3]   The tax was also collected in
Norway ; and, to induce its King, Hakon IV., to keep
his promise, and assist Louis in person, he was granted
its proceeds.[4]   But Henry and Hakon were both more
eager to finger money than to keep their royal word
untarnished, and it must be set down to them and not to
the Pope, if the English and Norwegians did not take
their proper share in the eighth Crusade.[5]

The same, however, cannot be said regarding the
Germans.   It was certainly largely Innocent's fault that
they did not partake in this Crusade.   But then he could
scarcely help himself.[6]   He was engaged in a life and

Innocent does not push the Crusade in the Empire.

[1] Incomplete returns show that he received some 14,500 pounds
tournois from the diocese of Chartres alone. *Cf.* the fragment of the
levy in France which has come down to us, *Triennis et biennis decima
ab anno* 1247 *collecta*, ap. *R. F. SS.*, xxi, 534, n. 1.   The collection
received this curious name because the tax originally granted (1247)
for three years was extended for another two (1247–52).   Mat. Paris
estimates that the tenth from England would reach more than
600,000 (marks ?), v, p. 282.

[2] Rymer, I, i, p. 155, ap. Potthast, 12559, June 12, 1247.

[3] Mat. Par., iv, 630. *Cf. Reg.*, i, n. 2758–9, June 6, 1247 ; 3723–4, etc.

[4] *Reg.*, i, n. 3439, Nov. 19, 1247.   On Hakon's connexion with the
Crusade, see Riant, *Expéditions et pélérinages des Scandinaves en
Terre Sainte*, Paris, 1865.

[5] Berger, *Reg.*, ii, p. clix.   In all this account of the Crusade we are
simply following Berger.

[6] Berger, *ib.*, p. clxii, observes : "Quelle que soit sa part de responsa-
bilité dans le combat décisif que se livraient le monde religieux et la
puissance impériale, Innocent IV., dans l'extrême danger que courait
la Papauté, ne pouvait disposer de ses forces pour secourir la Terre
Sainte."

death struggle with a cruel and powerful enemy, and it appeared to him that the future of the Church would be compromised, not by any success of Tartar, Turk, or Saracen, but by the victory of Frederick. The Emperor must then be fought by all the resources of Germany and Italy which he could bring to bear upon him. Most of Innocent's energy and money, therefore, had to be employed in combatting Frederick. He had to send subsidy after subsidy to Raspe and to William of Holland,[1] and, altogether, according to Carbio, his efforts against Frederick cost him more than two hundred thousand marks in silver, in seven years.[2]

While, therefore, in other countries, their inhabitants were exhorted to arm for the relief of the Holy Land, the people from the North Sea to the middle of Italy were urged to combat Frederick.[3] Innocent even actually forbade the preaching of the real Crusade in Germany,[4] and ordered certain sums raised there in connexion with it to be given to William of Holland.[5] Knowledge of this step on the part of the Pope, despite his efforts to keep his action secret, could not fail soon to reach Louis. However much he sympathized with the difficulties of Innocent's position, he was, of course, primarily anxious for the success of his own Crusade. Accordingly, he made some protest on the matter to the Pope (1247), and was so far successful that Innocent ordered that all that concerned the interests of the Crusade for the Holy

---

[1] *Annal. reg. Colon.*, an. 1246, p. 289; Carbio, c. 21-2; Mat. Par., iv, 545, 551.

[2] Carbio, c. 29.

[3] *Reg.*, i, n. 1993, June 27, 1246; n. 2945, Oct. 11, 1246; and *Reg.*, ii, n. 4509, May 14, 1249. *Cf. Annal. S. Georgii*, an. 1246, ap. *M. G. SS.*, xvii, p. 297. " Adulti signati sunt cruce contra Fridericum."

[4] *Reg.*, i, n. 2935, July 5, 1246. He, however, bade the Bishop of Tusculum to whom he gave the order to forbid the preaching, not to publish abroad that he had received it.

[5] *Reg.*, ii, n. 4510, May 14, 1249; and n. 4269 of Jan. 2, 1249.

Land should have free course at least in the dioceses of Liège, Cambrai, Toul, Metz, and Verdun.[1] The concession, it will be seen, was not extensive, and St. Louis was particularly hurt that the Pope allowed the gallant Frisians, who were making great preparations to co-operate with him, and whose support he had led the King to expect [2]; to commute their vows, and to take service with William of Holland.[3] It was necessary, wrote Innocent, that the cause of the Church should make marked progress in Germany.[4] It is a question (which Berger at any rate refuses to decide) whether this necessity was overwhelming enough to justify Innocent in relegating to a second place the needs of the Holy Land, and the requirements of his saintly benefactor, St. Louis IX.[5]

The French King had very early given notice to the Crusaders to assemble at Aigues Mortes, by the feast of St. John the Baptist (June 24), 1248, and, acting very differently to Frederick II. on a similar occasion, was there himself on the appointed day. Up to the very last we find Innocent co-operating with him, and ordering his envoys to compel all the French who had taken the Cross, either to go with the King, or redeem their vows by supplying him with money.[6]

St. Louis sets sail for the East, 1248.

---

[1] *Ib.*, i, n. 3384, Oct. 29, 1247 ; and n. 4065, Nov. 19, 1247 ; n. 3970, June 22, 1248. In the first letter Innocent wrote : " Animo ferventi desiderat carissimus in Christo filius noster L. illustris rex Franciæ ut possit . . . feliciter dirigi negotium Terre Sancte."

[2] For the Crusaders of Frisia, Holland, and Zealand had been commissioned in virtue of the Pope's orders to be ready to set out for the Holy Land in March, 1249. *Reg.*, i, n. 3967, June 22, 1248.

[3] *Ib.*, n. 4070, Nov. 17, 1247 ; and n. 4068, Nov. 19, 1247 ; and n. 3779, Apr. 8, 1248.

[4] See the last letter of the preceding note.

[5] Cf. Berger, *Reg.*, ii, pp. clxviii f. We attach special importance to Berger's opinions not only on account of his knowledge of his subject, but because being neither an ecclesiastic nor a Catholic, he is not likely to be suspected of prejudice.

[6] *Reg.*, i, n. 3975, June 22, 1248. *Cf.* 3976.

The last
meeting of
Innocent and
Louis, 1248. The last time that Innocent saw Louis was when the
King passed through Lyons on his way to embark.
When they met, Louis, in the interests of his undertaking,
made a last effort to bring about peace between Frederick
and the Pope. The Emperor's envoys came to the city,
and declared that " saving the honour of the kingdoms
over which he ruled ", their master was ready to make
peace, and to give such guarantees of his readiness to
make satisfaction to the Pope as Louis should think
sufficient.[1] But, according to Frederick, the Lombard
question as usual stood in the way of peace,[2] and no doubt
also Innocent's determination that the decision of the
Council of Lyons should hold good, and that neither
Frederick nor his son should wear the imperial crown.[3]
At any rate the negotiations came to nothing, and
Matthew Paris would have us believe that Louis thereupon told the Pope that his hardness would cause trouble
to France when he had gone away, and that he would
be responsible if the expedition failed. However, he
concluded, " guard France as the pupil of your eye, for
on its prosperity depends yours and that of all Christendom." This Innocent promised to do, and was then
entrusted by the King " with the reins of the government
of the kingdom of France ".[4]

After this conversation, Louis " made a careful confession to the Pope, and then having received the
remission of his sins and the papal blessing, the King
bade him farewell, left Lyons, and marched with his

[1] Ep. Fred. to Henry III., Aug., 1248, ap. H.-B., vi, ii, p. 645.

[2] *Ib. Cf. ib.*, p. 711, in a letter to Louis.

[3] *Cf.* epp. of Innocent to William of Holland or some other king, ap.
ib., pp. 641 and 644. *Cf.* Bartholomew the Scribe, *Ann. Genuen.*, an.
1248, ap. *R. I. SS.*, vi, 515 ; Mat. Par., v, 22.

[4] v, 23. There is Paris' usual exaggeration here (Berger, p. ccxxxii) .
but we know that Innocent did guard the interests of France in the
absence of Louis. *Cf.* Mat. Par., v, 23, 51, and 346.

army towards Marseilles ".[1] The host of the King of France embarked at Aigues Mortes on June 25, and at first sailed to Cyprus.

It is not for us to tell of the initial success which attended the armies of St. Louis against the Moslem by the capture of Damietta (June, 1249), nor of the disaster brought on them by the rash bravery of Robert of Artois, nor of the final failure of the expedition and the capture of St. Louis himself (1250).[2] After the conclusion of peace with the Moslems of Egypt, Louis sailed to Palestine where he remained nearly four years strengthening the strongholds of the Christians. It was in the last year of Innocent's life (1254) that Louis left Palestine to return to France (Apr. 24). We may, however, note that while Frederick gave some public assistance to Louis by supplying him with provisions,[3] Moslem authors tell us that he secretly warned the Sultan of Egypt that the French intended to attack that country, and bade him be prepared.[4] Their statements are borne out by

The failure of the eighth Crusade.

[1] *Ib.*, p. 23.

[2] *Cf. The Invasion of Egypt by Louis IX.*, by E. J. Davis, London, 1898.

[3] For which he received the thanks of Queen Blanche, who, says Paris, wrote strongly to the Pope urging him to lay aside his rancour against Frederick. If she did, she was a victim of Frederick's artful diplomacy. M. P., v, 70.

[4] *Cf.* Makrizi, *Description de l'Egypte,* p. 647, ed. Bouriant, and Ibn-Wasil (ap. Blochet in his translation of Makrizi's *Hist. d'Egypte,* p. 374, n.), who says that he got his information from the imperial official who took the news to Sultan Ayub. The same author states (*ib.*) that Frederick and his son were hated by the Pope " on account of their friendship with the Moslems ". Berger, *Reg.*, ii, p. ccxlix, quotes Bedr-Eddin Alayny, p. 201, ap. *Hists. des croisades, Hists. orient.*, ii, pt. i, to the same effect. *Cf.* Carbio, cc. 27 and 28. Joinville, too, mentions some facts which show this same friendship—" the vile Turk," Secedin, had been knighted by Frederick, and " bore on his banner the Emperor's arms ". Pt. ii, c. 9, Eng. trans. Joinville himself found favour in an Emir's eyes because " his lady mother was Frederick's first cousin ". *Ib.*, c. 14. Many of the Crusaders suspected

a letter of Ayub, the sultan of Egypt, who in reply to a request from Innocent for a truce, said that he could not make a peace without the consent of Frederick, his own and his father's friend, but that he had communicated with his ambassador at the Emperor's court on the matter.[1]

Consequently, it is not surprising that, after the news of the captivity of Louis and many of his nobles reached Europe, and Frederick had sent envoys to ask for their deliverance, Joinville should write : " I well remember that several said that they believed the emperor wished to find them still prisoners for they suspected that his motive in sending this embassy was to cause us to be more straitly confined and more heavily oppressed." [2]

Some blame the Pope for the failure of Louis, 1250.

When the news of the failure of the Crusade St. Louis (Apr., 1250) reached Europe, we are assured by Matthew Paris, that, though Innocent was " deeply grieved " at the misfortune, it did not prevent some people in France from throwing the blame of the catastrophy upon him, owing to his not having granted peace to Frederick.[3] At any rate Innocent at once wrote a beautiful letter to condole with Louis,[4] took steps to

the Emperor of treachery towards them, pt. iii, c. 3. *Cf.* Röhricht, *Reg. reg. Hierosol.*, n. 1163.

[1] Ep. of May 25, 1246, ap. Mat. Mar., iv, p. 566, where in true Eastern style Innocent is addressed as " the holy one, the thirteenth of the Apostles, the universal mouthpiece of the Christians . . . the judge of the Christian people, the leader of the sons of baptism, and the supreme pontiff of the Christians." *Cf.* Röhricht, *Regest. reg. Hierosol.*, n. 1142.

[2] Pt. iii, c. 3.

[3] M. P., v, 172–3. " Doluit vehementer." *Cf.* epp. Fred. II., ap. H.-B., vi, 770, 774.

[4] Ep. Aug. 12, 1250, ap. Raynaldus, *Annal.*, 1250, $ 11, note. He concludes by an exhortation to cease vain inquiry into the *why* of the sad event, and adds : " Confiteamur in humilitate spiritus Domino Deo nostro, benedicentes nomen ipsius . . . potestatis . . . et dicamus : Omnia quæ fecisti nobis Domine, in vero judicio fecisti."

have money forwarded to him,[1] and, in response to the King's appeal to him,[2] strove to rouse the English and others to go out to help him.[3] Indeed as far as the English were concerned, he did not cease throughout the whole of his life striving to rouse our useless sovereign, Henry III., to take his proper share "of the business of the Cross" (crucis negotium), which, after the disaster to Louis, "rested on his shoulders."[4]

But, especially as he was never in a position to give his undivided attention to the matter, Innocent failed to stir up another Crusade. The next attempt to save Palestine had again to be made by St. Louis, and that too once more only with the resources of his own country.

Innocent cannot rouse another Crusade.

---

[1] *Reg.*, ii, n. 4928–30, Nov. 29, 1250 ; nn. 5154–5, March 17, 1251.

[2] Paris (v, 175, 188–9) " un historien emporté par la haine " (Berger, p. ccli) says that Louis' brothers tried by threats to force Innocent to make peace with Frederick so that he might be free to help the King.

[3] *Ib.*, n. 4926, Nov. 29, 1250, *re* the French Crusaders ; n. 4927, *ib.*, *re* the Norwegians and Frisians ; and ep. of Nov. 16, 1250, ap. Mat. Par., vi, 201 f. Our weak and incompetent King Henry III. had taken the Cross on March 6, 1250, and the last cited letter was written by Innocent to discourage the English Crusaders from crossing the sea in driblets, and to urge them to cross together at an opportune time. *Cf.* epp. of Oct. 18,1251, and of 1252 to Henry III., ap. *Ann. de Burton*, pp. 293 ff. and 298. Mat. P., v, 274.

[4] Ep. just cited ap. *Annal. de B.*, p. 298 f. It is there dated 1252, but it must belong to 1250, as it speaks of the report of the *recent* disaster of Louis : " negotium crucis quod per miserabilem casum Christiani exercitus qui *nuper* in transmarinis partibus accidisse *dicitur*, etc." He tells Henry that all look to him to save the Christian faith. Berger, p. ccxlvii, n., gives a list of the letters written by Innocent to Henry to urge him to set out for the Holy Land.

CHAPTER V.

THE TARTARS, AND THE NEAR AND FAR EAST.

Sources.—On the Tartars see the letters of the Popes of the thirteenth century, and the various chroniclers of the same period. Of the first importance also are the narratives of the religious, commercial, and other travellers who visited them during the same century. Of these we may mention, in the first place, the Franciscan, John of Plano Carpini (a companion of St. Francis) who, at the bidding of Innocent IV. went to Kuyuk Khan (1245), and returned to Innocent at Lyons in 1247. He went through Poland and Russia, and was accompanied by another Franciscan, Benedict of Poland. John published an account of his travels,[1] and another was compiled from the narrative of Benedict, and published with that of John († 1252). John's voyage was " epoch-making ", and is the first of the splendid series of such narratives which the thirteenth century has furnished us.[2] Ap. Hakluyt, *Collection of the Early Voyages*, vol. i, London, 1829. *Cf. The Journey of Friar John of Pian de Carpine*, printed with *The Journey of William of Rubruck* for the Hakluyt Society, London, 1900, translated by W. W. Rockhill from the *complete* text. See also *The Texts and versions of John de Plano Carpini and William de Rubruquis* (as printed for the first time by Hakluyt in 1598, together with some shorter pieces) by C. R. Beazley, London, 1903. The latest ed. of the text of J. of P. C. is that by F. L. Pullé, Florence, 1913.

In 1247, Innocent IV. sent a second mission to the Tartars or Mongols. It was " addressed especially to the Mongol General, Baitu [2] (Baiju) " in Armenia, and was placed in charge of the Dominican, Ascelin (or Anselm). Simon of St. Quentin, a friar who went with him, told Vincent of Beauvais about the expedition, and he inserted portions of the narrative in his *Speculum Historiale*, Lib. xxxi, c. 40–52. Another Dominican, Andrew of Longumeau, seems to have also accompanied Ascelin for at least part of his journey. It does not appear to be generally known that Matthew Paris has preserved a part of his account of his journey in his

---

[1] He was met by Salimbene, *Chron.*, p. 206.

[2] *Cf.* Matrod, *Notes sur le voyage de Fr. Jean de Plan-Carpin*, p. 5, Paris, 1912. For the various edd. of all these early missionaries, see R. Streit, *Bibliotheca Missionum*, Münster-i-W., 1916.

Additamenta, vol. vi, pp. 113–15, *R. S.* The narrative really closes with the word " Hungariæ ".

The next mission to Central Asia was sent by St. Louis IX. At its head went the Frenchman, William of Rubruquis, " the meanest of the Minorite Order " as he calls himself. In 1253, he set out for the court of the Mongol leader, Sartach, whose conversion to Christianity had been often reported. W. of R. probably met John of P. C. before he left France in the company of Louis IX., in 1248.

His narrative, like that of John, is of the very highest importance.[1] For the original text, see Michel and Wright in *Recueil des Voyages*, vol. iv, Paris, 1839, and Beazley (see above). For English translations see also Beazley, and W. W. Rockhill, *The Journey of William of Rubruck to the Eastern Parts* (1253–5), translated for the Hakluyt Society, London, 1900. L. de Backer, *Guillaume de Rubrouck*, Paris, 1877, has given us a poor French translation of it.[2]

Hayton (Hethum or Aiton) I., King of Lesser Armenia († 1271) visited the Mongols after Rubruquis. He set out seemingly in 1254. We know of this journey both by the narrative of Kirakos, one of the King's suite, and by the history written by the King's nephew, Hayton, Prince of Gorigos, who subsequently became a Premonstratensian monk in Cyprus. Pope Clement V. gave him an abbey at Poitiers where, in 1307, he dictated his history in French to Nicholas Faulcon. In sixty chapters, it gives a geography of Asia, the history of the Mongol Khans, etc. Hayton's

[1] *Cf.* Matrod, *Le voyage de Fr. Guillaume de Rubrouck* (1253–5), Paris, 1909, and E. R. Beazley, whose work, *The Dawn of Modern Geography*, we have used freely. Louis had previously (Feb., 1249) sent the above-mentioned Andrew and others to Ilchikadai (Eteltay, Eldegay, or Achatay), the lieutenant of Baitu. *Cf.* Mat. Par., *Adit.*, vol. vi, pp. 163–5 ; Joinville, pp. 142–9, and the letter of John P. Sarrasin, pp. 254–5, both ed. F. Michel, Paris, 1881.

[2] Colonel Yule, *Marco Polo*, i, 102, regards William's *Itinerary* as having " few superiors in the whole library of travel ". W. of R. (p. 282 ed. Rockhill), gives his opinion on the inadvisability of sending poor Friars to the Mongols. They needed to be impressed by show. " It seems to me inexpedient to send another friar to the Tartars as I went, or as the preaching friars go ; but if the lord Pope, who is the head of Christians, wishes to send with proper state a bishop and to reply to the foolishness they have already written . . . once to Pope Innocent IV. of blessed memory . . . he would be able to tell them whatever he pleased . . . They listen to whatever an ambassador has to say . . . but he must have several interpreters, abundant travelling funds, etc."

French narrative is given by De Backer, *L'Extrême Orient au Moyen-Age*, p. 125 ff., Paris, 1877. Omont has given, from another MS., the first three books of Hayton's work which bore the name "*Fleur des histoires de la terre d'Orient*", Paris, 1902. Bretschneider, *Medieval Researches from Eastern Asiatic Sources*, i, p. 164 ff., London, 1888, has given an English translation of the account of his master's voyage by Kirakos.[1]

The best known and greatest of all these thirteenth century Christian travellers to the East is the Venetian merchant, Marco Polo (1254–1324). The best edition of his travels is that in the *Recueil de Voyages*, vol. i, Paris, 1824. The best English version is that of Colonel Yule, ed. Cordier, London, 1903.[2] Polo's narrative, originally written in French in 1298, has been translated into most of the modern European languages.

About 1286, after having obtained a commission from Pope Honorius IV. to preach to the Orientals, the Dominican Ricold of Monte Croce near Florence († 1320, about eighty years old) sailed for the Levant. Thence he travelled through Asia Minor, Mesopotamia, and India. He was, perhaps, the most learned of all the travellers of his time. In his *Itinerary* and *Letters* he has left us a most valuable account of his travels, labours, and studies. The former may be read in Laurent, *Peregrinationes Quatuor*, Leipzig, 1893. De Bracker has published an old French version (1351) by John the Long of Ypres.[3] His letters may be read in the *Archives de l'Orient Latin*, II, ii.

The last of the great thirteenth century travellers to whom I shall here call attention is the Franciscan Odoric of Pordenone, near Friuli (b., *c.* 1286, † 1331). His travels began about 1317, and closed about the beginning of 1330. His *Description of the East*, says Beazley (iii, p. 253), contains "the fullest, most graphic, and the most amusing picture of Asia left by any religious traveller of this age." One of the best editions of the original Latin text is to be found in Yule's *Cathay and the way thither*, vol. ii, London, 1866. An English version will be found in the same work. L. de Backer, *l.c.*, has published the French version of Odoric made by the same John,[4] who made the version of Ricold.

---

[1] The original Armenian narrative, as first written down by King Hayton's follower, Kirakos Gandsaketsi, is extant.

[2] We often use the ed. of H. Murray, London, 1844.

[3] "Et fu ce livre translatés de latin en françoys en l'an de grace mil. ccc. li. Fait et compilé par frère Jehan le Long d'Ippre, moine de l'évesque de Tarvenne." *L'Extrême Orient.*, p. 256.

[4] *L.c.*, p. 90. H. Cordier tells us all about Odoric and his books in his *Les voyages en Asie du b. frère Odoric*, Paris, 1891.

Modern Works.—E. S. Holden, *The Mogul Emperors of Hindu-stan*, Westminster, 1895 ; C. R. Beazley, *The Dawn of Modern Geography*, 3 vols., London, 1897 ff. ; Sir H. H. Howorth, *Hist. of the Mongols*, London, 1876. *The History of Genghizean the Great*, by Petis de la Croix, Eng. trans., London, 1722 ; R. K. Douglas, *The Life of Jenghiz Khan*, 1877 ; J. L. Mostheim, *Hist. Tartarorum Ecclesiastica*, Helmstadt, 1731. This last work can only be used with caution.

In the preceding pages mention has not unfrequently been made of the Tartars or Mongols,[1] and of their influence on European affairs. A little more at least must now be said about them.

The Empire of the Mongols or Tartars.

In the year 1162 there was born on the banks of the Onon one who was to be the greatest conqueror the world has ever seen, the one who was afterwards to be known as Chingiz or (Ghengiz) Khan, the Inflexible. His father was the chief of a small Mongolian tribe that wandered between the Rivers Orkhon and Selenga to the south of Lake Baikal. His mother was of the Huyri (Iugures, Uigurs), a Turkish tribe of Nestorian Christians, a fact which may account both for Chingiz Khan's being wrongly supposed by some to be a Christian,[2] and for his not being unfavourable to Christians. His remarkable career of conquest soon brought him into collision (1188) with the Naimani (Yaman in Rubruquis) and the Keraits. They were Turkish tribes and Nestorian Christians who had for some time been ruled by Nestorian

---

[1] The Tartars (or Tatta nomads) were a Mongolian tribe who after-wards gave their name to all the Mongols. *Cf.* Howorth, i, p. 700 ff.

[2] Hence in the anonymous *Relatio de Davide rege Tartarorum christiano* of the year 1221 ap. Eccard, *Corpus hist.*, ii, pp. 1451–4, we see the deeds of Chingiz assigned to one David of the Nestorian Prester John dynasty. The recital begins thus : " Hæc est materia totius processus Regis David, filii Regis Israël, filii regis Johannis credentis in Christo Jesu." Written no doubt wholly from hearsay, the short account closes with a petition to all Christians to pray for the success of King David, " quia obediens est Deo et sanctæ ecclesiæ . . . qui est rex regum, qui destruxit Legem Sarracenorum . . . qui est rex Orientis." *Cf.* Yule, *Cathay*, i, p. 175.

Christian chiefs, one or more of whom had borne the name of, or had been known as *Prester John*.[1] Of this personage, says William of Rubruquis, the Nestorians report " ten times more of him than was true. For so the Nestorians which come out of those parts use to doe. For they blaze abroad great rumours and reports upon just nothing. Whereupon they gave out concerning Sartach, that he was become a Christian, and the like also they reported concerning Mangu Can (Khan), and Ken Can ; namely, because these Tartars make more account of Christians than they doe of other people, and yet in very deede themselves are no Christians ".[2] The Naimani and the Keraits with their King Unk (or Wang) Khan, were soon subdued by Temudjin, as Chingiz was first called, and there were not wanting those who attributed the downfall of Unk Khan to his having forsaken " the faith of Christ " for a Chinese wife.[3]

Proclaimed " Lord of Lords " about the year 1205,[4] the terrible Chingiz Khan in person or through his sons and generals carried his conquests East and West, quenching all opposition in blood ; so that when this terrible man, said to have been born with a clot of blood in his tiny hand, closed his marvellous career of victory in death (in 1227), he held sway from the Chinese Sea to the banks of the Dnieper. The wonderful story of

[1] The Prester John with whom Alexander III. corresponded (*supra*, vol. x, p. 228 ff.) was the Kerait Togroul, the Unc Can of whom W. of R. speaks in the passage cited in the text. He was also the Prester John who was defeated by Chingiz Khan. With him the dynasty, such as it was, came to an end. Jacques de Vitry, *Hist. Hierosol.*, c. 76, p. 1092 ap. *Gesta Dei per Francos* expressly calls Prester John an Asiatic Nestorian.

[2] C. 19 of the old English version of W. of R. ap. Beazley's *Carpini*, p. 214. *Cf.* p. 168, *ib.*, for the original.

[3] Bar-Hebræus, ap. Howorth, *Hist. of the Mongols*, i, p. 543.

[4] *Cf.* the important letter of Ivo of Narbonne regarding the Tartars who besieged Neustadt whilst he was there. Ap. Mat. Par., iv, 272, an. 1243.

" the horrible devastation of infinite countries " [1] by
Chingiz ere long reached Europe. It would seem that,
whilst yet he was far off, an account of his conquests
was " first described to Christendom by ' the people of
Count Raymond ' (III. of Tripoli, † c. 1200) on their
return to Tripoli from various trading journeys in the
uplands, and especially by some merchants whose trade
lay in spices and precious stones ".[2] But the rumours
that reached the west of the rapid and bloody overthrow
of Kingdoms by the Tartars caused the wildest stories
about them to be circulated among the people. It was
popularly believed among the Greeks that they were
monsters with heads of dogs who fed on human flesh.[3]

But the West was not to depend for long on vague
rumours concerning the Tartars. They were themselves
soon at the heels of the reports concerning them. Over-
running with incredible speed the countries on the great
central plain of Asia, they appeared in Europe. For
it was their belief, as it had been that of their conquering
predecessors, the Huns of Attila, that they had been
called " by oracle or vision to challenge dominion over the
whole earth " [4] "—wherever ears could hear or wherever

The Tartars invade Europe, 1224.

---

[1] According to European chroniclers, " many " assign the year 1202
as the date of the beginning of the kingdom or empire of the Tartars,
" who killed their lord, the King of India, by name David, the son of
Prester John " and then set out to conquer " depopulacionem aliarum
terrarum." *Ann. Pegavienses*, ap. *M. G. SS.*, xvi, p. 268; and Vincent
of Beauvais, *Spec. Hist.*, xxix, c. 69–70. See also Joinville, pt. iii,
c. 6, for the subjugation of Prester John (seemingly Unk Khan) by
Chingiz.

[2] Beazley, *Dawn*, ii, p. 445.

[3] *Cf.* George Pachymeres († 1310), *De Michaele Palaeol.*, ii, c. 25,
p. 134 ed. Bonn. Describing themselves, the Tartars in their usual
boastful style, proclaimed : " Our horses are of the quickest, our
arrows piercing, our swords like lightning, our hearts are as hard as
the hills, and the number of our soldiers is like to sands of the sea."
See the letter of Houlagou Khan to the Sultan of Egypt, ap. Makrizi,
Hist. des Sultans Mamlouks, i, p. 101 ed. Quatremère, Paris, 1837.

[4] The letter of Ivo. *Cf.* the *Chronicle of Novgorod*, p. 65, Eng. trans.,

horses could travel." In 1224 the people of Russia heard the terrible cry: " Lo the Tartars come, the Tartars come " ! [1] and the Tartars,[2] hitherto to them an unknown race, burst upon them. Russia, i.e., the Russian states which were then to be found upon both banks of the Dnieper, was rapidly overrun.

Not much is said in the Chronicles of Europe about this invasion, as the invaders retired quickly ; but the Russian Chronicle of Novgorod speaks of it " for the sake of the memory of the Russian Knyazes (Princes) and of the misfortune which came to them from them. For we have heard that they have captured many countries ". After inflicting a severe defeat on the Russians by the River Kalka, where " a countless number of people perished (May, 1224), . . . the Tartars turned back from the River Dnieper, and we know not whence they came, nor where they hid themselves again ".[3]

Second Tartar invasion, 1236 and following years.

Perhaps because the victory on the Kalka was but pyrrhic, the wave of Tartar invasion recoiled, but only to gather itself together for a second dash against the eastern frontiers of Europe. The death of Chingiz († 1227) delayed the formation of the second wave, but after his son Ogodai [4] had been elected Great Khan, the Tartars again swept westwards. Georgia, invaded by them in 1236, raised the cry of alarm, and its Queen

and the evidence of the Russian archbishop Peter, ap. Mat. Par., iv, 388. From Carpini and the other travellers of his age we find that the Tartars were as much given to sorcery and divination then as they were centuries afterwards in the days of the Abbé Huc.

[1] Will. of R., c. 19.

[2] Even in 1238 the Austrian Annals (*Contin. Garst.*, ap. *M. G. SS.*, ix, p. 597, speak of them as the " ignota gens Tartarorum ". The *Chron. of Novgorod*, p. 64, under the year 1224 says: " The same year for our sins, unknown tribes came, whom no one exactly knows who they are, nor whence they came out, nor what their language is . . . nor what their faith is. But they call them Tartars."

[3] *Ib.*   [4] Also written Occoday, Okkodai, Oktai.

Rusudan in vain implored help from Gregory IX.[1] Harassed by Frederick II., he could do nothing. Georgia was overrun, and rumours of the terrible doings of the Tartars began now to fill Europe with alarm. In " the same year the godless Tartars having come, they captured the Bolgar Land (Great Bulgaria on the Volga, the present Kazan, etc.), and took their great city, and they slew all, both wives and children ".[2] In 1237 word reached Europe that they had slain no less than forty-two bishops in Greater Armenia, and it was reported that it was their intention to invade Hungary. To see what truth there was in this story four Friars Preachers travelled for a hundred days through Russia, and returned to say that the Tartars had already conquered Great Hungary.[3] The terrible horsemen were soon in Russia once more ; and are said to have written to the emperor Frederick, summoning him to acknowledge himself the vassal of the Great Khan, and to ask him what office he would like to hold in his court (1238). To which bombastic offer Frederick was credited with the sarcastic reply that he knew something about birds and would be his falconer.[4]

[1] Cf. supra, vol. xii, p. 79.

[2] Chron. of Novgorod, an. 1236. Eng. trans., p. 81.

[3] Albert, Trium Fontium, Chron., ap. M. G. SS., xxiii, p. 942. A narrative of their journey—the work of Bro. Richard (Julian) has come down to us, ap. Endlicher, Rerum Hungar. Mon. Arpadiana, p. 248 ff., or ap. Theiner, Mon. Hungar., i, p. 151. This brief story appears to be unknown to Beazley. The most remarkable thing which the Friar relates is the feeling which he found both among Saracens and pagans that they must become Christians and subject to the Church of Rome. The Saracens of Ueda : " tam princeps quam populus illius regionis publice dicunt, quod cito fieri debeant Christiani et ecclesie Romane subesse." Endlicher, p. 251. Cf. ib., p. 252, for similar assertions of the pagan inhabitants of " Great Bulgaria " and p. 254 of the pagan Mordvins. These latter are Finns, and are still to be found " in the Russian provinces west of the Middle Volga ". Bretschneider, ii, 70 n.

[4] " Quod satis scit de avibus et bene erit falconarius." Albert, ib., p. 943. Old or Great Hungary was the district East of the Middle Volga.

Whatever truth there may be in this story, there is no doubt that meanwhile the Tartars were swarming through Russia " like locusts ", killing " men, women and children, monks, nuns, and priests, some by fire, some by the sword, and violating nuns, priests' wives, good women, and girls in the presence of their mothers and sisters " (1238).[1]

From this date for many years onwards the Chronicles of the West are full of the doings of the Tartars. Popes, Emperors,[2] and Kings busy themselves about them, and are constantly engaged in asking for help or endeavouring to furnish help against them. Even the Saracens wrote to the West for help against the common foe.

The battle of Lignitz, 1241.

After the defeat of the Poles at Lignitz (1241) the Tartars overran Silesia, Poland, Bohemia, and Hungary,[3] and struck fear into all the West. Recourse was at once had to the Pope. The Hungarians sent to implore the intervention of Gregory IX. (May 18).[4] Sending consolatory letters to King Bela IV., Gregory (who was followed in this by Innocent IV.) ordered a crusade

---

[1] *Chron. of Nov.*, p. 82. *Cf. ib.*, 83–4. *Cf.* also on the devastation of Russia, the letter of Peter, a Russian archbishop, ap. Mat. Par., iv, 386.

[2] In his letter of July 3, 1241, to Henry III., about the Tartars, even Frederick II. does not know whence they have sprung. Ap. Mat. Par., iv, 112. He records the capture of Kiev (1240), the ruin of Russia, and the invasion of Hungary, Poland, and Bohemia, in which last country he records a check to the Tartars. He asked for Henry's help against the common foe, and with the Westerns generally, he speaks of them as being well called Tartars, for they are like demons from Tartarus. According to Paris, *ib.*, 119 f., many suspected Frederick himself of intriguing with these Tartars. *Cf.* iv, 635. Reports from Hungary about the Tartars will be found *ib.*, vi, p. 75 ff.

[3] See various *Annals* in *M. G. SS.*, xix.

[4] Mat. Par., iv, 114 and 547, and especially the *Miserabile Carmen super destructione Hungariæ* (c. 32, ap. *M. G. SS.*, xxix, p. 560) of the chaplain Roger who had suffered at the hands of the Tartars. See the letter which Stephen, bp. of Waitzen, took to Gregory IX. ap. Theiner, *Vet. Mon. Hungar.*, i, p. 182.

to be preached against the Tartars,[1] and assured the Hungarian monarch that he would be able to do very much more for him if only Frederick " styled Emperor " would but make peace with the Church.[2] The Crusade was not altogether a failure, though Bela afterwards blamed Gregory for not helping him, and Alexander IV. had to point out to him that the suddenness of the Tartar inroad, and Frederick's oppression of the Church prevented Gregory from accomplishing very much.[3] For when, after devastating practically the whole of Hungary, the Tartars retired (1242), Bela re-entered his country with a number of Crusaders and restored general confidence.[4] The Tartars had withdrawn because their Great Khan Ogodai had died († 1241 or –2),[5] and his ch'ef generals (among them his nephew Batu in command of the Western armies) had to return to Karakorum, their capital, to elect his successor.

But the Tartars did not withdraw from Russia, and Russia turns to Rome, 1244.

[1] Epp. of June 16, 21, *ib.*, p. 183 ff. *Cf. Chron. min. Erphord.*, ap. *M. G. SS.*, xxiv, p. 199, and *Gesta Trev., Contin. IV.*, p. 403 f. Innocent IV. was hardly elected when he proclaimed a Crusade against the Tartars, and took other steps regarding them. *Cf.* epp. of July 21 and 22, 1243, ap. Theiner, *Mon. Hungar.*, i, p. 187 f.

[2] Ep. of July 1, 1241, ap. Theiner, *l.c.*, p. 185.

[3] Ep. of Oct. 14, 1259, ap. Theiner, *Mon. Hungar.*, i, p. 239 ff. " Mundus certe universus agnovit . . . quod ea tempestate qua ecclesiasticæ subventionis implorasti suffragium, Fridericus . . . acerrima in Sedem Apostolicam tyrannide sæviebat . . . intendens, ut oppressa illa et filiis ejus . . . subjugatis, ipse singulariter velut immane desolationis idolum præ cæteris coleretur."

[4] The *Carmen*, c. 40, p. 567. " Nunquam tamen noster tutus fuit descensus, donec rex Bela maritimis de partibus, per cruciferos de insula Rodin, et dominos de Frangapanibus multis agminibus militum adjutus . . . in Hungariam venit." *Cf.* Thomas of Spalato, *Hist. Salonitana*, c. 38. According to the *Annals of Austria, Contin. Sancruc.*, ap. *M. G. SS.*, ix, p. 640, Frederick interfered with the preaching of this Crusade : " Sed d. imperator hoc fieri prohibuit, eo quod rex Ungariæ ab eo vocatus venire contempsit."

[5] Carpini, c. 28, says he was poisoned, " which is the cause while they have for a short space absteined from warre." *Cf. ib.*, c. 30.

so the Russians too turned to the West and to the Pope. Regarding Frederick and the Tartars as the two great dangers that threatened the Church,[1] Innocent decided that both of them should be carefully considered at the council of Lyons.   First-hand information on the Mongol danger was given to the Fathers of that assembly by a certain Peter, a Russian archbishop,[2] if not by others.

The Council of Lyons and the Tartar question.

Acting on the information put before it, the Council laid it down that the peoples on the frontiers should instantly fortify them in every way, and should send immediate notice of the coming of the Tartars to the Apostolic See, so that help might be sent at once. Innocent himself agreed to contribute " magnificently " to the cost of such military works, and to cause the nations to contribute their share to expenses which were for the common good.[3]

Dispatch of diplomatic missionaries, 1245.

But with general measures Innocent was not content. He hoped by using the zeal of the Franciscans and Dominicans to strike at the root of the evil, and to stop the cruelties of the Tartars by making them Christians, and fearful of offending God. Accordingly, before the Council met, he organized two missions to them.   The first he placed in the hands of the Franciscan, John of Plano Carpini, his penitentiary,[4] and furnished him with a letter to the King and people of the Tartars to the following effect : " Since not only men but irrational animals and even the mechanical mundane elements are united by some kind of natural bond, after the example of the heavenly spirits whose hosts God, the

---

[1] " Valde namque tristamur quod tot fidelium sanguinem Tartaricus vel potius Tartareus mucro eis parcere nescius devoravit." Ep. of Sept. 24, 1249, ap. Mat. Par., vi, 172.

[2] Mat. Par., iv, 386 ff., and *Annal. de Burton*, i, p. 272 ff.   Innocent named the Tartar question as the first of the five great troubles which afflicted the Church. Mat. Par., iv, p. 434.

[3] Can. 16, ap. Hefele, *Conciles*, v, p. 1653 f., new French ed.

[4] *Cf.* Carbio, c. 17.

Author of the Universe, has in a perpetual and peaceful order, we are compelled to wonder, not without reason, how you, as we have heard, have entered many lands of Christians and of others, have wasted them with horrible desolation, and still, with continued fury, cease not to extend further your destroying hands, dissolving every natural tie, and sparing neither age nor sex, but direct against all indifferently the fury of the sword. We, therefore, after the example of the Prince of Peace, desiring all mankind should live in peaceful unity and in the fear of God, warn, exhort, and beseech you earnestly to desist henceforth wholly from such outrages; and especially from the persecution of Christians. And since by so many and such great offences you have doubtless greviously provoked the wrath of the Divine Majesty, we urge you to make satisfaction to God by suitable penance. Moreover, be not so daring as to carry your rage further, because the omnipotent God has hitherto permitted the nations to be laid prostrate before your face by the power of your ravening sword; for He sometimes in this world does not punish the proud for a season to the end, that after they have failed to humble themselves, He may at length punish them in this life, and even still more in the world to come. And behold we send you our beloved brother John (of Plano Carpini) and his companions bearers of these presents, men conspicuous for religion and honourable conduct, and endowed with a knowledge of the Sacred Scripture, whom we hope you will kindly receive with divine reverence, and honourably treat as if they were ourselves, placing confidence in what they say from us, and specially treat with them on what relates to peace. Moreover we would wish you to tell us through these brothers what has moved you to this extermination of other nations, and what are your further intentions; and we beg you to give them a safe conduct in going and returning, and to furnish them with all necessaries so that they may safely return to us. We have chosen to send you the said friars as men trained by the long observance of rule, and as fully instructed in the Sacred Scriptures, and because we believed that, as men following the humility of Our Saviour, they would be more useful to you. But if we had thought ecclesiastical prelates or powerful nobles would have been of great profit or more acceptable to you, we would have sent them. Given at Lyons on the third of the Ides of March in the second year of our Pontificate (March 13, 1245)." [1]

The other mission, which was also entrusted to a Franciscan, Lorenzo of Portugal,[2] was to take a more southerly route, and to reach the Tartar headquarters by way of Asia Minor and Armenia. It is conjectured that this second mission, " of which we hear nothing more . . . was merged in or superseded by the new embassy of 1247." [3] This embassy was entrusted to the Dominican Ascelin, and " was addressed specially to the Mongol General Baitu ". It is supposed to have been accompanied by the Dominican, Andrew of Longumeau, who would seem to have been the author of the fragmentary account of the voyage which has reached us under the name of brother Andrew.[4]

---

[1] Ap. Theiner, *Mon. Hungar.*, i, p. 195. We have used to some extent Murray's translation in his *Marco Polo*, p. 49 f.

[2] The letter (March 5, 1245) recommending Lorenzo and his companions to the Tartars was rather more doctrinal in character, explaining the mission of Our Lord and His constitution of a vicar on earth of whom Innocent was now the representative. Ap. *ib.*, p. 194 f.

[3] Beazley, *Dawn*, ii, p. 277.

[4] Ap. Mat. Par., vi, 113. Luard appears to assign this fragment to the year 1245, but it probably belongs to the year 1248, as it seems to me, and is the work of A. of L., who was afterwards sent on another Tartar mission by King Louis in Feb., 1249. Vincent of Beauvais, *Spec. Hist.*, 1. 32, c. 2, has left us a notice of the mission of Ascelin; ed. Beazley, *Carpini*, pp. 74 and 107. According to Beazley, *ib.*, p. 269, Ascelin irritated Baitu by implying that the Pope was superior even to the Great Khan; and in response to the exhortation of the friar that he

As the journey of John of Plano Carpini to the far
East was the first of which a full account has reached
us, we will here give a brief notice of it, as it will serve
to show what was the general character of these papal
embassies to the Tartars. After urging the Christian
Princes to help the Friars in their great endeavour,[1]
Innocent sent forth John and his companions " to the
Tartars and to the other nations of the East ".[2] They
decided to go to the Tartars first, as they feared " that
through them dangers might come to the Church of
God in the immediate future ".[3] And although they
feared they might be killed by the Tartars, or be
imprisoned by them, and though they feared that on
their journey they would have much to suffer from
hardships of every kind, still " we did not spare ourselves so that we might carry out the will of the lord
Pope, and be of some use to Christian men ", if it were
only by discovering the exact intentions of the Tartars.[4]

The travellers were helped on their way by Wenceslas
III., King of Bohemia, who advised them to proceed
through Poland, as they had kinsfolk there who would
help them to pass into Russia. When, in following
his advice, they reached the duchy of Lenczy, they met
the Russian Vasilko, or Basil, Prince of Vladimir.
Learning from him that they must go provided with

The Friars
are helped
on their
mission by
Christian
Princes.

---

should become a Christian, he broke out : " What, become dogs like
you and your Pope." After Ascelin and his companions had been very
badly treated for a while, they were dismissed (July 25, 1247) with
the General's reply dated " the region of Sitiens " (said to be between
Gokcha Lake and the Araxes) July 20. Innocent was commanded to
come in person and submit to the master of all the earth. Ascelin had
made the mistake in appearing before the Tartar in his poor friar's
clothes.

[1] *Cf*. Innocent's letter to Coloman (Kaliman), King of Bulgaria ;
ep. of March 21, 1245, ap. Theiner, *l.c.*, p. 197 btm.

[2] Carpini, p. 43.   [3] *Ib*.

[4] *Ib*., " Mandatum etiam a supremo pontifice habebamus, ut cuncta
perscrutaremur et videremus omnia diligenter."

gifts for the Tartar princes, they bought "certaine
skinnes of bevers and other beastes",[1] "as they did
not wish that the affairs of the lord Pope should be
obstructed on this account."[2] Vasilko then conducted
them into his own territory (S.W. Russia). "And
when being requested by us, he had caused his bishops
to resort unto him, we reade before them the Pope's
letters, admonishing them to return to the unitie of the
Church. To the same purpose also we ourselves
admonished them. . . . Howbeit because Duke Daniel
(Danil),[3] the brother of Vasilko aforesaid . . . was absent
they could not at that time make a finall answere."[4] On
the way to Kiev, John fell dangerously ill, but he had
himself conveyed in a cart through the snow "so as not
to interfere with the affairs of Christendom".[5] At
Kiev they met a Tartar chief, who after receiving presents,
allowed them to procure hardy Tartar horses and a
guide, by whose aid they reached Kanev on the Dnieper,
a town "immediately subject to the Tartars" (Feb. 4,
1246). Soon after this they were "horribly set upon"
by a company of armed Tartars who wanted to know
why they had come to them. They explained that they
were the legates of the lord Pope "who is the father and
lord of the Christians", and that he had sent them to
promote peace between the Tartars and the Christians,
to exhort them to become Christians, and to blame them
for their merciless treatment of the Hungarians, Poles,
and others.[6] Following up some confused deductions
from what they had heard of the secular antiquity of
the line of the Sovereign Pontiffs, the Tartars also wanted
to know : "concerning the great Pope, whether he was
of so lasting an age as they had heard ? For there had

---

[1] *Ib.*, p. 127. Latin original, p. 92.   [2] Rockhill's version, p. 2 f.
[3] Prince of Galicia (Galich), 1205–64.
[4] Carpini, *ib*.   [5] Rockhill's version, c. 4, p. 4.
[6] Carp., c. 20, p. 128. Text, p. 93.

gone a report among them that he was five hundred
yeeres olde." [1]

After further bestowals of presents as they were The
Franciscans
before Baitu.
passed on from one Tartar chief to another,[2] the envoys
were conducted to Baitu (Bathy) who " is the mightiest
prince among them except the Emperor ". His *Ordu*
or court " in the land of Comania " by the Black Sea was
reached on April 5, and, when introduced into the tent
of the great chieftain, they were warned not to tread
upon the threshold. They delivered the papal letters
to him on their knees, and with the aid of interpreters
translated them into " the Russian, Tartaran and Saracen
languages ". When he had understood the object of
their journey, Baitu, whom Carpini regarded as cruel
but experienced in war, and kind to his men but feared
by them, bade them go forward to the emperor Kuyuk.

Half starved with cold and hunger, the unfortunate
friars, who left Baitu on April 8, journeyed on for weeks
over plains where they saw the proofs of the Tartar
ravages, " many skulles and bones of dead men lying
upon the earth as it were upon a dunghill," and " innumer-
able cities with castles ruined, and many towns left
desolate ".[3]

At length the travellers left the plain and, after passing John reaches
the Ordu or
Court of
Kuyuk,
July, 1246.
through the mountainous country of the Naymani,
" entered wee into the lande of the Mongals whome wee
call Tartars." [4] Then they rode forward at even
increased speed, " because our Tartarian guides were

[1] This question was really put to William of Rubruquis. See his
narrative, c. 24. *Cf. supra*, vol. iii, p. 321, for the Saracen idea of
" the old dotard Peter, Petrulus senex ".

[2] " Because we wished to live, and to carry out satisfactorily the
order of the lord Pope." Rockhill's version, c. 7, p. 7.

[3] Carpini, cc. 23 and 24. *Cf.* Joinville, pt. iii, c. 6, and the letter of
the Constable of Armenia, ap. *Les Grandes Chroniques*, iv, p. 296 ed.
P. Paris.

[4] *Ib.*, c. 25, " Deinde terram Mongalorum intravimus quos Tartaros
appellamus." P. 98.

straightly commanded to bring us unto the court Imperiall with all speede, which court hath beene these many yeeres ordained for the election of the Emperor." By dint of such hard riding that they had often no time to eat, the envoys reached the court of Cuyuc (Kuyuk) the Emperor elect, on July 22, 1246.[1]

Arrived at the court, " hee caused (after the Tartars' manner) a Tent and all expenses necessarie to bee provided for us. And his people entreated us with more regarde and courtesie, then they did anie other Ambassadours. Howbeeit wee were not called before his presence because hee was not as yet elected." [2]   At the court (Syra Orda) of the Khan the friars found a great crowd of ambassadors from subject states, among them being the Russian Duke, Yaroslav of Sazhdal, the two sons of the King of Georgia, a Sultan to represent the Caliph of Bagdad, and some other ten Saracen Sultans.[3]

The enthrone- ment of Kuyuk, 1246.

Kuyuk, however, was not proclaimed Great Khan at Syra Orda (perhaps near Lake Gueuca) but at the golden Orda (court, tent, residence), " in a goodly plaine, by a river's side [4] between certain mountaines," Aug. 24, 1246. One fact which Carpini tells us about him is enough to account for the persistence in the West of the belief in Prester John, and in the Christianity of the Tartars or of their chief. " Certain Christians of his familie earnestly and strongly affirmed unto us that he himselfe was about to become a Christian. A token and argument thereof was, that he retained diver's Cleargie men of the Christians. Hee had likewise at all times a Chapell of Christians neere unto his great Tent."

---

[1] *Ib.*   [2] *Ib.*, c. 26.

[3] *Ib.*, c. 26. Carpini was told there were some 4,000 ambassadors, " partly of such as paide tributes and such as presented gifts, and other Soldans and Dukes which came to yeeld themselves, and such as the Tartars had sent for, and such as were governors of lands."

[4] The Orkhon.

" But," continued the practical Italian, " be it known unto all men, that, whilest we remained at the Emperor's court . . . the said Cuyuc (Kuyuk) . . . erected a flag of defiance against the Church of God and the Romane empire . . . unless peradventure (which God forbid) . . . they will become obedient unto him." [1] Hence did he engrave on his seal " God in heaven, and Cuyuc Can on earth".

After keeping the papal envoys waiting for over a month after his proclamation as Great Khan, Kuyuk bade them appear before him and state their business in writing. He then asked if there were any " with our lord the Pope who understood the Russian, the Saracen, or the Tartarian language? Thereupon Carpini, now clothed as became a papal messenger,[2] replied that there were not, though there were some Saracens in the land, but that they lived at a distance from the Pope. They therefore suggested that it would be best if the Tartars put down what they had to say in their own language, and then interpreted it to them. They would then translate the letter into Latin and deliver it and the translation to the Pope.

This suggestion was acted on, and when the letter had been written and interpreted to the friars, and they had put it into Latin, the Tartars "caused us to interpret unto them eche sentence, to wit (wishing to know) if we had erred in any word. . . . For they said unto us: Take heed that ye understand all things thoroughly, for if you should not . . . it might breed some inconvenience." [3]

Carpini before Kuyuk.

---

[1] *Ib.*, c. 28. *Cf.* c. 31.

[2] William of Rubruquis when some years later he stood in the presence of Baitu felt his disadvantage in being in the coarse habit of his Order. " There we stoode in our habite, bare-footed, and bare-headed, and were a great and strange spectacle in their eyes. For, indeed, Frier John de Plano Carpini had byn there before my coming : howbeit, because he was the Pope's messenger, he changed his habit that he might not be contemned." W. of R., c. 21.

[3] Carpini, c. 31.

When the envoys were ready to return to the Pope
with the Emperor's letter, it was hinted to them that
Kuyuk would be ready to send ambassadors with them.
But the wary friars, reflecting that these men would
really be spies, and would observe the weakness of the
Christians through their dissensions, said that they would
rather that no ambassadors were sent, as they would not
like to be responsible for their safety among "the
arrogant and proud nations " of the West.[1]

Carpini
returns to
Europe,
1246-7.

Accordingly, in the month of November (1246) the
intrepid friars set out on their long and dangerous return
journey, and reached Kiev on June 8, 1247 : " The
citizens of Kiow on having intelligence of our approch,
came foorth all of them to meete us with great joy.
For they rejoiced over us, as over men that had been
risen from death to life. So likewise they did unto us
throughout all Russia, Poland, and Bohemia. Daniel
and his brother Wasilico made us a royall feast ; and
enterteined us with them against our willes for the
space of eight dayes.

The
Russians,
etc., profess
subjection to
Rome.

" In the meane time, they with their Bishops and other
men of account being in consultation together about
those matters which we had propounded unto them
in our journey towards the Tartars, answered us with
common consent saying : that they would holde the
Pope for their special Lord and Father, and the Church
of Rome for their Lady and Mistress. . . . And for the same
purpose they sent their Ambassadours and letters by us
also unto our Lord the Pope." [2]

A year or two later William of Rubruquis found other
peoples in the Near or Far East who also professed their
wish to submit to Innocent. Certain Nestorians, wrote
William, " confessed that the Roman Church was the

[1] *Ib.*, c. 32.
[2] C. 33.

head of all Churches, and that they should receive their patriarch from the Pope if the roads were open." [1]

After a sojourn among the Tartars of over a year and four months, and after a total absence of over two years, the friars handed the letter of Kuyuk Khan to Innocent, who was still at Lyons (1247).[2]

This high-sounding document read as follows : " The strength of God, Kuyuk Khan, the ruler of all men to the great Pope. You and all the Christian people who dwell in the West have sent by your messengers sure and certain letters for the purpose of making peace with us. This we have heard from them, and it is contained in your letter. Therefore, if you desire to have peace with us, you Pope, Emperors, all Kings, all men powerful in cities, by no means delay to come to us for the purpose of concluding peace, and you will hear our answer and our will. The series of your letters contained that we ought to be baptized and to become Christians ; we briefly reply that we do not understand why we ought to do so. As to what is mentioned in your letters that you wonder at the slaughter of men, and chiefly of Christians, especially

Kuyuk's letter to Innocent.

---

[1] W. of R., p. 213 ed. Rockhill, who notes that when in Rome in 1288 the Nestorian envoy of Arghun, Rabban Sauma, was allowed by Pope Nicholas IV. to say Mass, and was given communion by him on Palm Sunday. Beazley, *Dawn*, ii, p. 352, adds that to the Nestorian patriarch, Mar Jabalaba III., who had sent Rabban, valuable papal presents were sent at this same time. From Fortescue, *The Lesser Eastern Churches*, p. 98 f., it appears that Rabban's religious position was not grasped in Rome. *Cf. infra* under Nicholas IV.

[2] *Cf.* Benedict the Pole, c. 9, ap. Rockhill, p. 39. Salimbene met Carpini on his return at Villefranche on the Rhone as he was making his way to Lyons, and among other things heard from him that he had told the Khan that the two great authorities in the West were the Pope and the Emperor, that all the others got their power from these two, and that the greater of them was the Pope. Salimbene, p. 203, gives a copy of Kuyuk's letter, and his editor, p, 207, another. Benedict has also given us a copy of Kuyuk's letter. His narrative has been edited by d'Avezac, in vol. iv of his *Recueil de voyages et de mémoires*, Paris, 1839. The letter may be read on p. 594.

Hungarians, Poles, and Moravians, we answer shortly
that this, too, we do not understand. Nevertheless, lest
we should seem to pass it over in silence, we think proper
to reply as follows. It is because they have not obeyed
the precept of God and of Gengis (Chingiz) Khan, and,
holding bad counsel, have slain our messengers,[1] wherefore
God had ordered them to be destroyed, and delivered
them into our hands. But if God had not done it, what
could man have done to man! But you, inhabitants of
the West, believe that you only are Christians, and despise
others; but how do you know upon whom He may chose
to bestow his favour. We adore God, and, in His strength
will overwhelm the whole earth from the East to the
West. But if we men were not strengthened by God
what could we do?"[2]

The result of
Carpini's
voyage.

If the Pope was perhaps inclined to be awed by the
high tone of this letter, his judgment was steadied by
the advice given by the Friar as to how the Tartars
were to be resisted.[3] And as time went on, and other
ambassadors had visited the Tartars, he learned to
appreciate still better the strength and weakness of the
dreaded foe. Rubruquis, for instance, writing in 1253,
declared[4] that "if the Tartars should but once knowe
that the great Priest, that is to say the Pope, did cause the
ensigne of the crosse to bee displaied against them, they
would flee all into their desert, and solitarie places". And
of the Tartars themselves who were the backbone, as it
were, of the Mongol tribes, he wrote[5] that, "through

---

[1] This refers to the murdering of the Tartar ambassadors before the
battle of Kalka. *Cf. The Chronicle of Novgorod*, p. 65.

[2] Translation by Murray, *Marco Polo*, p. 59. Yet Bar. Hebræus,
Chron. Syriacum, i, p. 525, would have us believe that K. "was a
true Christian!"

[3] Carpini, c. 18, p. 90.

[4] C. 13, pp. 205–6.

[5] C. 19, p. 215.

continuall warres, they are nowe all of them in a maner, consumed and brought to nought."

Innocent also now clearly understood, through the labours of Carpini, whom he highly praised and rewarded,[1] that whatever bits of Christianity had been accepted by a few of the Tartars, they were the irreconcilable foes of Christendom.[2]

One result of the dispatch of envoys to the Tartars by Innocent was that they in turn sent ambassadors to him. Matthew Paris relates under the year 1248[3] that " in the summer of this year two Tartar messengers came from their Prince to the lord Pope ; but the particulars of their message were kept so secret from the *personel* of the papal curia that they were not clearly known to the clerics, notaries, or others of the court, nor even to the friends of the Pope. The letter which they brought to the Pope had been translated into three more known languages when its bearers approached the western countries ". After this definite statement of ignorance, what Paris goes on to say is clearly of but little value. " From some indications, however, it was suspected that the Tartars had offered to make immediate war on

Tartar envoys to the Pope, 1248.

---

[1] Salimbene, *Chron.*, p. 210 f.

[3] With the journey of Ascelin, accompanied or followed by Andrew of Longumeau, in 1247, there is no need for us to occupy ourselves at great length. The mission was not very successful ; it did not reach the great Khan, and has only been recorded in a fragmentary manner in Vincent of Beauvais, and possibly in Matthew Paris (see note below). The envoys by their want of tact only drew down abuse upon themselves and upon the Pope who sent them. In fact, it was only the intercession of Baiju's (or Baitu's) chief wife that saved their lives. The curious reader will find a satisfactory account of this mission in Murray's *Marco Polo*, pp. 60–4, or ap. Mortier, *Hist. des Maitres Gén. des FF. Précheurs*, i, p. 383 ff.

[3] v, p. 37. It is certain that Tartar envoys did reach the Pope this year. See his letter to " Bayonoy (Baiju) regi illustri, et . . . baronibus exercitus Tartarorum ". Ep. of Nov. 22, 1248, ap. *Reg.*, n. 4682, ii, p. 113. " Nuntios vestros . . . benigne recepimus."

Vatatzes, Frederick's son-in-law, a Greek schismatic, who had been disobedient to the Roman curia. It was believed that this offer was not unacceptable to the Pope, for he gave the envoys some very costly garments and furs of various kinds. Moreover, he had frequent friendly conversations with them by means of interpreters, and in secret made them valuable gifts in gold and silver." These data furnished by Paris himself appear to be supported to some extent by notes which he gives in his *Additamenta* from a " brother Andrew, a Dominican who lately came to Lyons, and who two years before had been sent by the Pope to the King of the Tartars ".[1]

The mission to the Tartars of Andrew of Longumeau.

" Pope Innocent," we are told, " having bidden the Provincial of France send some of his brethren to preach among the Cuman Tartars, in hopes that abundant fruits might be reaped among them, on the announcement of this decree in the Provincial Chapter, so many and such distinguished Friars offered themselves for the task that it came to be known as the *Chapter of Tears*. Nor was it without good cause, for some wanted to be sent, and begged the favour with tears, while others grieved over the departure of brethren, whom they loved

---

[1] " Frater Andreas et alius Prædicator nuper venerunt Lugdunum ; quorum unus missus fuit elapso biennio a d. Papa ad regem Tartarorum." VI, p. 113. I presume the " unus " to refer to Andrew of Longumeau who is known to have been sent to the East. In Luard's ed. of M. P., the *Addit.*, No. 61 (vi, pp. 112–17), is assigned to the year 1245. But this *additamentum* is obviously made up of a collection of notes that have no logical or chronological connexion with each other. The few paragraphs which concern "frater Andreas" certainly do not belong to the year 1245, for it was in that year that the first embassy was sent by Innocent to the Tartars, and these paragraphs tell of the *result* of an embassy to them. They therefore, as it seems to me, must be assigned to the year 1248. In 1253 Will. of Rubruquis speaks of " Ken Can (Kuyuk Khan, 1246–8), at whose court Frier Andrew was ". *Cf.* pp. 214 and 322, *Carpini*, ed. Beazley. Even if Andrew did not on this occasion reach the court of Kuyuk himself, he certainly reached that of his great general, Baiju (Baitu) or Baiothonoy.

well, to such incredible hardships and martyrdom ; here one group wept for joy on getting the coveted permission, there another bewailed their misfortune in being refused." [1] Among those chosen at this Chapter were Ascelin, Simon of St. Quentin, and others, of whose unsuccessful mission we have already spoken in a note.

From the same Order about the same time Innocent also chose Andrew of Longumeau (Longjumeau) and another to go to certain Jacobite and other Eastern patriarchs who had expressed a desire for union with Rome. [2] He also commissioned them, as we have just seen, " to the King of the Tartars." [3] Journeying for forty-five days from Acre by Antioch, Aleppo, and Niniveh, they reached the camp of Baiju, on the borders of Armenia and Persia. In this camp, in which were some thirty thousand Tartar horsemen, Friar Andrew found a monk (whom he calls a Catholic [4]) who had obtained great influence with Kuyuk Khan. He had seemingly been commissioned to watch over the interests of Christians, and to see that, if they were willing to accept the dominion of the Tartars, they were not to be molested in their faith. [5] The said monk sent to Innocent by Andrew an ebony sceptre or staff (baculus), an envoy, and also letters directed to Frederick and to the Pope, in which they were blamed for quarrelling when there was soon coming to

---

[1] *Vit. Frat.*, p. 151 ed. Reichert ; Eng. trans., p. 124.

[2] Raynaldus, *Annal.*, an. 1237, n. 87 ff., and 1247, nn. 32–43. *Cf.* Mortier, *l.c.*, i, p. 381 f., and *infra*.

[3] *Cf.* Innocent's letter (*Reg.*, 4682) of Nov. 22, 1248, just cited to Baiju, in which he declared to him : " Olim . . . nuntios nostros ad vos destinavimus." It would seem probable that Andrew's mission to Baiju was only secondary, his chief one being to the Oriental patriarchs.

[4] " Quidam actu et habitu et fide religiosus et catholicus." Mat. P., vi, 113.

[5] *Ib.*, p. 114.

crush them that King whom all Christendom could not resist.[1]

The envoy of " the monk " was no doubt one of those Tartars dispatched to the Pope by Baiju, of whom we have already made mention. Innocent sent them back to their master with a letter " to the illustrious King Bayonoy (Baiju), and to all the noble princes and barons of the army of the Tartars " (Nov. 22, 1248). After saying that he had received their envoys graciously, and listened to what they had to say, he told them that holding, however unworthily, the place of God on earth, it was his duty to see that every rational creature attained to the knowledge of his Maker, and that therefore he had for that sent his messengers to them. He is now more anxious than ever about them, seeing that the truth has now been laid before them. Nor should they boast because, by the permission of God, they have overcome so many nations, but rather fear that He will punish their wrongdoings.[2]

This frequent interchange of letters and presents between the Pope and the Tartars, or, perhaps more likely, constant and deliberate lying on the part of the wily Tartars, who were anxious to secure Christian co-operation for the crushing of the Saracens, caused fresh reports to be circulated about the conversion of the Great Khan to Christianity (1249). King Louis received definite offers of assistance from the " Catholic " Tartar sovereign,[3] and he also sent Franciscans to them—

---

[1] Such seemingly is Paris' summary of the letter of the monk Simeon ; for the monk of whom Paris here speaks would seem to have been Simeon, known to the Tartars as " the monk father, rabbanata " (rabban in Syriac denoting monk, and ata in Turkish father), of whom we shall speak presently. He was a Nestorian, so that Andrew must have meant that he was a " Catholic " in spirit or in sympathy. The Latin transcription of his title is Raban Ara.

[2] *Reg.*, n. 4682, ii, p. 113 f.

[3] Mat. Par., an. 1249 ; v, p. 87. According to Thomas of Cantimprè (*De apibus*, ii, 54, n. 14) St. Louis heard at Damietta that the King of the Tartars had a Christian mother, and that, though himself a pagan,

among others the experienced Andrew of Longumeau
(Feb., 1245), and some years later William of Rubruquis
(1253).

Louis also informed Innocent that his envoys had
reported conversions of the Tartars, and had asked that
the Pope would authorize the consecration of some of
the Friars as bishops, and permit certain relaxations
for the new converts, which, if forbidden by ecclesiastical
discipline, were not opposed to the law of God. Innocent
accordingly instructed Cardinal Eudes (or Odo) of
Châteauroux, his legate with Louis, to act as his fuller
knowledge should dictate.[1]

Right up to his death the Tartar question was kept
before Innocent. A few months before he died an
" Armenian cleric, an envoy of the King of the Tartars ",[2]
whom the Pope calls " the priest John, your chaplain ",[3]
appeared before him and complained that when he had
landed in Apulia, he had been robbed by King Conrad,
and kept by him in durance until such times as death
put Conrad himself " in the hands of the Prince of
Darkness ".[2] After that, he continued, he had with
difficulty contrived to escape alone, without his escort,
and without the letters of the Tartar King asking for
complete instruction in the Christian faith and ritual.
Influenced by a miracle, his master Sartach, son of
Baitu, had already received baptism. When illness had
reduced his son to the brink of death, he had summoned

Further Tartar envoys reach Innocent, 1254.

he loved Christians. His father had killed " the Christian King of
India " (i.e., Prester John ?), and had taken his daughter to wife.
Hence the King of France sent four friars to the great Khan with a
" tent-chapel " and other gifts. Thomas, who had conversed with
men who had spoken to the missionaries, tells of the conversion " of
many thousands of Tartars ".

[1] Ep. of Feb. 20, 1253, ap. Hauréau.

[2] Carbio, c. 39, p. 114.

[3] Ep. of Aug. 29, 1254, to Sartach, ap. Raynaldus, *Annal.*, 1254,
n. 2.

a number of Christians, and told them that they should all lose their heads unless his son recovered by their prayers, but that if his son recovered he would embrace their faith. The Christians fasted and prayed, and the s'ck man got better. True to his word, the Khan was baptized and over fifty thousand Tartars with him.

After being duly honoured by the Pope, the Armenian returned to the East with letters to his master.[1] The letter which has come down to us, simply congratulated Sartach on his conversion, and urged him openly to profess what he believed.[2]

Was Sartach a Christian ?

It is very hard to say how much truth there is in the reported conversion of Sartach, and whether John was really his accredited agent.[3] William of Rubruquis informs us that much that he heard on his outward journey about Sartach, he " found nothing so ".[4] And when he left that potentate, Coiat, a Nestorian of great authority in Sartach's court, bade him : " doe not make report that our lord is a Christian, but a Moul (Mongol). Because," continues William, " the name of Christian seemeth unto them to be the name of some nation. So great is their pride, that albeit they believe perhaps some things concerning Christ, yet will they not bee called Christians, being desirous that their own name, that is to say Moul (Mongol) should be exalted above all other names." [5]

---

[1] *Ib.*, p. 115.

[2] *L.c.* He excused (n. 4) the delay in John's return by telling of his capture. According to Bar-Hebræus, *Chron. Syriacum*, i, p. 509 ed. Bruns and Kersch, Leipzig, 1789, Sartach was not only baptized but was made a deacon ! The same author gives many details about the Tartars.

[3] Will of R. lets us know that there were pretended envoys who made it their business to impose upon both the Tartars and the Pope ; for he tells us of one who was seized by the emperor Vatatzes, and who was engaged in trying to deceive both Mangu Khan and the Pope. *Cf. W. of R.*, ed. Rockhill, p. 181. *Cf.* p. 282.

[4] C. 1, ed. Beazley, p. 186.

[5] *Ib.*, c. 18, p. 213.

Then, giving his own opinion about the Christianity of Sartach, he added : " Now whether he believes in Christ or no, I knowe not. . . . This I am sure of, that he will not be called a Christian. Yea rather he seemeth unto mee to deride and skoffe at Christians. He lieth in the way of the Christians, as namely of the Russians, the Valachians, the Bulgarians of Bulgaria the lesser, etc. . . . who all of theme passe by him as they are going to the Court of his father Baitu to carie giftes ; whereupon he is more in league with them. Howbeit if the Saracens come and bring greater giftes than they, they are dispatched sooner." [1]

However, whether Sartach and other Tartar Princes really became Christians of any kind or not, or whether, to work their own ends, some at least of them merely pretended to be such, Innocent does not deserve the less credit for his efforts to save Europe from their ravages by trying to lessen the dissensions of those in more immediate touch with them [2] ; by stirring up resistance to them [3] ; and by endeavouring to convert them to the faith of Christ ; and for this purpose having boys who knew Arabic or other Oriental languages trained in the University of Paris. [4]

RUSSIA.

We have already seen how some of the seventy-two Dukes or Princes who at this period were the ruling

Russian princes seek reunion with Rome.

[1] *Ib.*, c. 20, p. 215. Hayton, however, says he was a Christian, and so also, notes Bretschnider (i, p. 167), " Bar-Hebræus informs us that he (S.) loved the Christian religion, that he was baptized, learned to read, and became a deacon."

[2] *Cf.* his efforts to stop wars between the Hungarians and Bohemians. Carbio, c. 37, p. 113 ; and to heal the differences between the Latins and Greeks in the Isle of Cyprus. *Cf.* Hauréau, p. 63 ff.

[3] *Cf.* ep. of May 15, 1253, n. 88, p. 78 ap. Turgeneff, *Hist. Rus. Mon.*, and ep. of May 19, 1254, n. 90, *ib.*

[4] *Cf.* Denifle, *Chart. Univ. Par.*, i, pp. 212–13.

authorities in Russia turned to the Pope for help against
the Tartars, and how Carpini reconciled some of them to
the Church of Rome. Innocent's *Register* shows the share
that he himself took in this work of reunion. His principal
correspondent was Daniel or Danil Romanovich, Prince
of Galicia, one of those with whom Carpini came in
contact. Finding that his relations with the Russian
Princes were increasing, Innocent named as his legate
in Russia, Albert, archbishop of Prussia, Livonia, and
Esthonia.[1] Albert or Alberic Suerber, or Suebeer, was a
Dominican, and had been archbishop of Armagh (1240–6).
As such he had come into frequent collision with the King
of England, who complained that the archbishop had
obtained permission from the Pope to sue the King's
subjects outside the realm for lands and advowsons,
without mentioning to him the King's privileges.[2] These
troubles with the King were probably the cause why
he resigned his dignity to Innocent after the Council of
Lyons. The Pope then sent him to Prussia,[3] and
ultimately (1253) fixed his see at Riga in Livonia.
Innocent next took Daniel under his special protection,[4]
granted his request to keep certain Dominicans at his
court,[5] and urged him to receive the legate with favour,
to listen to what he had to say, and to assist him in his
efforts against the Tartars.[6] The Pope had reason to hope,

---

[1] Ep. Jan. 10, 1246, ap. *Reg.*, n. 1726, and epp. of May 3, 1246, *ib.*,
nn. 1817–19, or ap. Turgeneff, n. 61.

[2] *Cal. of docs., Ireland*, i, n. 2717, *R. S. Cf.* J. Stuart, *Hist. memorials
of Armagh*, p. 93 ed. Coleman.

[3] *Annals of Ulster*, vol. ii, p. 307, *R. S.*, and *Annales Stadenses*,
ap. *M. G. SS.*, xvi, p. 360 f. He died *c.* 1273.

[4] Turg., n. 64. *Cf.* n. 74. At the same time, he assured the Duke that
he was quite justified in endeavouring to recover such of his territories
as were in the hands of enemies. Ep. n. 67 of Aug. 27, 1247.

[5] *Ib.*, n. 63. He gave them the same powers " as those who had been
sent to the Tartars ". *Cf.* n. 64.

[6] *Ib.*, n. 65, addressed by mistake in Turgeneff to " John " instead
of to Daniel.

so he wrote, that Daniel would do this, because he had heard that he was wishful to renounce the rites and customs of the Greeks who had receded from ecclesiastical unity, and (realizing that a body must have a head and only one head) to obey the Pope as the successor of Peter, to whom were committed the keys of the Kingdom of Heaven.[1] In connexion, however, with the Greek rites, it may be noted that he permitted the Russian Church to use fermented bread in the sacrifice of the Mass.[2] Besides this concession to Daniel's religious feelings, he granted another to his political ones. To lessen any fears he might have that crusaders from foreign countries coming to help him might take advantage of his difficulties, Innocent complied with his request by deciding that no crusaders or clergy could acquire lands in the Duke's territories without his consent.[3] Ultimately, too, he complied with Daniel's request by sending the lord Abbot of Maçano (Mezano ?) to crown him *king* of Galicia.[4] Meanwhile, convinced of the Pope's claims, or, at any rate, of his goodwill, Daniel sent special messengers and letters to Innocent, begging him to receive back into ecclesiastical unity "and devotion to the Roman Church", "himself and his whole people".[5] This the Pope instructed his legate to do.[6]

Innocent also entered into negotiations concerning reunion with the famous Alexander Nevski, Duke (Knyaz) of Vladimir-Suzdhal,[7] but seemingly with no success. However, he made it plain both to Daniel

---

[1] *Ib.*, p. 59.　　　[2] *Ib.*, n. 68.　　　[3] *Ib.*, n. 69.

[4] Carbio, c. 17. *Cf.* the *Rocznik (Annals) Krasińskich*, an. 1253, "Daniel dux Russie in regem coronatur." Ap. *Mon. Polon. Hist.*, iii, 132. Hence he is no doubt "our very dear son in Christ, the illustrious King of Russia", to whom Innocent alludes in a letter to the Poles on May 14, 1253, ap. Theiner, *Mon. Polon.*, i, 107.

[5] T., *ib.*, n. 72, Sept. 9, 1247.　　　[6] *Ib.*

[7] *Ib.*, n. 78, Jan. 23, 1248. His father, Jaroslav II. had been received into the Church by Carpini. *Cf. ib.*

and Alexander that their safety was a matter of concern to him, as he asked them as soon as they heard of any hostile movements of the Tartars to inform the Teutonic Knights who would in turn inform him, so that measures might be taken against them.[1] Unfortunately, even for their political well-being, the Russians did not adhere to Rome, and as a consequence had for two centuries and a half to endure the Tartar yoke.[2] Some of the Princes, Daniel, for instance,[3] seem to have fallen back into schism almost immediately; but others are said to have still been in communion with Rome in the days of Gregory X.[4]

Russia's union and disunion with Rome.

In connexion with Russia's union with Rome, it will, for clearness sake, be well to add another word or two. Theiner, who has written much and well on this question, has noted [5] that the Russian Church of Kiev remained united to Rome after the days when the Patriarch of Constantinople (Michael Cerularius) consummated the Greek schism, right down to the thirteenth century. This,

[1] *Ib.*, and n. 77, Jan. 22, 1248. *Cf.* also *Reg.*, nn. 4089–90. *Cf.* R. du Caillaud, *Essai sur l'Église russe*, p. 88 ff.

[2] J. B. Ostrowski, in his *The hist. of Poland* (London, 1841), points out how union with Rome and the West kept Poland civilized and European, and union with Constantinople and Greece caused Russia to become degraded and Asiatic. Pp. 69, 259–60.

[3] *Cf.* ep. of Alexander IV. to him (Feb. 13, 1257, ap. Raynaldus, *Ann.*, 1257, nn. 27–8) reproaching him with his apostasy, especially after the favours bestowed upon him by the Church : " Personam tuam ad regalis dignitatis apicem sublemavit, faciendo te inungi sacri chrismatis oleo, tuoque imponi capiti regium diadema." Daniel carried his ephemeral kingdom with him to the grave. *Cf.* Ostrowski, *l.c.*, p. 370.

[4] At any rate, Stephen V., King of Hungary, names in 1272 as his relations and friends : " Leonem generum nostrum Ruthenorum Ducem, Mitizlaum fratrem ejusdem, et Wazulem (Vasili) filium Wazule Duces Rutenorum." Ap. Theiner, *Mon. Hungar.*, i, p. 303. *Cf. Vicissitudes de l'Église Catholique en Russe*, p. 26, Paris, 1845.

[5] See his *L'Eglise schismatique Russe* (from the Italian), p. 9 ff., Paris, 1846. *Cf.* his *Vicissitudes de l'Eglise Cath. des deux rites en Pologne et en Russie*, Paris, 1845.

he says, is clear from the fact that the old Russian liturgical books were all Catholic,[1] and that from the ninth to the thirteenth century there is no trace of schismatical opinions in the writings of the Russian prelates. In view of more recent research this latter point is untenable.

At the end of the thirteenth century (1299) under the metropolitan Maximus, the chief see was transferred from Kiev to Wladimir,[2] and then, in 1325, to Moscow, which, naturally enough, brought about various difficulties. Accordingly, about 1415, two separate metropolitans were constituted. One, as patriarch of Kiev, ruled the southern Russian provinces; the other, as patriarch of Moscow, ruled the northern provinces. The influence of Moscow was in favour of the schism, while that of Kiev, less under the control of the more distant Muscovite princes, kept its subjects longer in union with Rome.[3] But, in the sixteenth century, the patriarch of Moscow became the sole metropolitan, and since then schism has become the order of the day.

With the progress of the Russian Church in schism went its subjection to the State. Its slavery began at the time of the consummation of the Greek schism in the eleventh century. When Cerularius threw off subjection to Rome, Jaroslav I. (1019–54) at once rejected the authority of the patriarch of Constantinople, and encroached on the rights of his own metropolitan.

Despite some reaction, the subjection of the Russian Church to the State increased till the invasion of the Tartars, when the Church recovered its freedom ; for, in 1313, Usbeck Khan in his famous *jarlik* confirmed its rights. But, after the defeat of the Tartars in the last

---

[1] Cf. *supra*, vol. iii, p. 219.

[2] See Karamsin, *Histoire de Russie*, iv, p. 205, Paris, 1819.

[3] So, in 1418 Gregory Semiulac, metropolitan of Kiev, submitted to Martin V at the Council of Constance. *Cf.* Finke, *Acta Conc. Constanciensis*, ii, pp. 164–7, Münster-i-W., 1923.

quarter of the fifteenth century, Ivan III. and Ivan IV. the Terrible, completed the subjection of the Russian Church. This last adulterous tyrant, like a similar one nearer home, declared himself " supreme head of the Russian Church ".[1]

Since 1460 union with the Greek Church had merely been nominal [2] ; and, on Jan. 23, 1589, Godownow, the ruler of the Czar, Theodore I., the son of Ivan the Terrible, with the bought approval of Jeremiah II., patriarch of Constantinople, made his favourite Job, " patriarch of all the Russians." He thus cut off all communication with Constantinople, and proclaimed Moscow the third Rome, and its ruler the third among the patriarchs.[3] The final step in the subjection of the Russian Church to the State was taken by Peter the Great, who even again with the approval of another Jeremiah of Constantinople, placed the Russian Church under the Holy Governing Synod, Feb. 24, 1721.[4]

The Lithuanians.

Intimately connected with the Russians from the first time they appear in history to the present day are the people now known as Lithuanians. Allied in race with the old Prussians, they are first met with as a number of loosely connected tribes, in the country to the south-east of the Baltic. In the thirteenth century one of their chiefs, Ryngold, is credited with having begun to weld many of these tribes together by force. His work was continued by his son Mendog or Mindowe, whose successes aroused the jealousies or fears of the Teutonic Knights and other military religious orders in those parts. The better to resist them, Mindowe, his wife, and a large number of his people embraced Christianity, and were

[1] Theiner, L'Eglise schismat., p. 20.

[2] Ib., p. 23.

[3] Ib., pp. 29–30.

[4] Note that after the participation of Isidore, patriarch of Kiev, in the Council of Florence, Kiev and eight bishoprics of the southern provinces remained in union with Rome till 1520.

baptized. Then, by special envoys, he submitted himself
and his kingdom to the jurisdiction and protection of the
Apostolic See. Accordingly, by letter dated Milan, July 17,
1251, Innocent duly received the Kingdom of
" Luthawia ", as he called it, and all the lands which its
King had taken or might take from the infidels, under
the rule and sway (" in jus et proprietatem ") of Blessed
Peter.[1] At the same time, he ordered the neighbouring
bishops to see to it that the new Christian kingdom was
not molested,[2] and he commissioned Henry, bishop of
Chelm, solemnly to crown the Lithuanian chief. He was
also, with the assistance of two or three other bishops,
to consecrate a bishop for Lithuania, and in behalf of the
Pope, to receive from him the oath of fidelity to the Holy
See. Finally, the bishop was instructed, in the matter
of exacting tithes from the new converts, so to act that
the new converts would realize that the yoke of Jesus
Christ was sweet and His burden light.[3] For some reason
or other, Innocent's orders as to the consecration of a
bishop do not appear to have been at once carried out.
At any rate, some two years later (June 24, 1253), he
wrote to Albert, archbishop of Livonia and Prussia (or
of Riga), pointing out that the King of " Luthavia "
was prepared to build and endow a cathedral, and so the
archbishop must find a suitable candidate, and one, too,
who was acceptable to the King ; and, by virtue of the
authority of the Apostolic See, consecrate him.[4] In
consequence of this mandate, one Christian was consecrated, and, despite the wishes of Albert, made directly
dependent on the Holy See.

But as Mindowe had become a Catholic mainly for
political reasons, he at length ceased to practise his religion
for the same reasons, and, on his murder, his country
relapsed into civil disorder and into paganism. The

---

[1] *Reg.*, n. 5437.   [2] *Ib.*, n. 5438.
[3] *Ib.*, n. 5439.   [4] *Ib.*, n. 6680.

political power of the land was, however, revived by Gedymin, who became the ruler of at least a great portion of the Lithuanian people in 1316; and Christianity became fixed in their country when its lord, Jagello (or Jagiello), became a Catholic (1386) to marry Hedwig of Poland. By their marriage Lithuania was united to Poland.

Poland.

Like his predecessors for centuries, Innocent was in close touch with Russia's unhappy neighbour, Poland, and his name frequently figures in the annals and diplomatic collections of that country. These show him calling on the Poles to help the Empire of Constantinople,[1] and to oppose the Tartars, bidding them not wait till they hear the sound of their trumpets.[2] He even, as Matthew Paris would have loved to record, stripped Poland of money for the help of the Eastern Empire and the other enterprises to which he lent financial assistance.[3] But, at the same time, seeing that, as the Poles themselves in their difficulties with the Germans reminded him, they are and always have been directly subject to the Apostolic See, "and in sign of that subjection have paid the tax (census), which is commonly called Peter's Pence," he bade his legate Opizo, Abbot of Mezano, protect them against any encroachments on their territories by William of Holland, King of the Romans, or by any others.[4]

The Kingdom of Thessalonica

In their efforts to support the Latin Empire of Constantinople, the Popes naturally supported the Kingdom of Thessalonica. Of the Latin nobles who took

---

[1] *Codex diplom. Maj. Poloniæ*, i, pp. 207–11.

[2] *Ib.*, pp. 278–9. He sent as his legate to rouse them, the abbot of Mezano, "an upright and learned man, and by his worth dear to the Pope and his brethren." Cf. *Zdarzenia Godne Pamięci*, ap. *Mon. Pol.*, iii, pp. 306–7.

[3] "Frater Hugo cardinalis et legatus Teuthoniæ, Provincie, Francie, Poloniam spoliat pecunia." *Recznik Kras., l.c.*

[4] Ep. May 17, 1253, ap. Rod., iii, pp. 167–8, or *Cod. Dip., l.c.*, p. 280.

part in the siege and capture of Constantinople (1204), one of the most powerful was the commander-in-chief, Boniface, Marquis of Montferrat. Disappointed at not being elected emperor of Constantinople,[1] he aimed at making his feudatory Kingdom of Thessalonica as extensive and as independent as possible. But his death in 1207 caused the kingdom to fall into the feeble hands of his baby son, Demetrius. Taking advantage of this state of things, the kingdom was attacked by Theodore Angelus,[2] despot of Epirus, one of the fragments of the Byzantine Empire, which after the capture of Constantinople fell into Greek hands. The fragment from Dyrrachium to Naupactus, known as the Despotat of Epirus, fell at first into the hands of Michael, the uncle of the Emperors Isaac II. and Alexius III. On his death (1214), the reins of government were assumed by his brother Theodore Angelus, who at length took Thessalonica itself (1223), and conquered the kingdom. On account of the importance of this country as a bulwark of Constantinople, Honorius III. supported the efforts of Demetrius to recover his kingdom. The efforts, however, failed ; and, after the early death of Demetrius, various nobles assumed the title of King of Thessalonica. The cause of one of these, William dalle Carcere, Lord of Negropont, who had married Helen, the niece of Demetrius, was taken up by Innocent IV.[3] But, despite both papal and imperial support, the power of Theodore could not be shaken ; and, though, through the gift of the exiled Baldwin II.,[4] in 1266, first one member and then another of the House of Burgundy assumed the empty title of King of Thessalonica, the kingdom remained in

---

[1] *Cf. supra*, vol. xi, p. 259.

[2] His full name was T. A. Comnenus Ducas.

[3] *Cf*. ep. Apr. 23, 1244, ap. *Reg.*, i, n. 637.

[4] For the golden bull of Baldwin II. in behalf of William and Helen see Raynaldus, *Ann.*, 1243, n. 45.

the hands of the Greeks. The title became extinct in 1320, after the reigning duke of Burgundy had sold his claims to Philip of Tarentum, the titular King of Romania.[1]

Theodore Angelus and Rome.

Theodore Angelus, the conqueror of the Latin Kingdom of Thessalonica, and the founder of the Greek Empire of the same name, was a typical Greek ruler. While his power was unassured, he entered into communications with Rome and submitted to the Pope (1218).[2] But as conscience had nothing to do with his political actions, he threw off all allegiance as soon as he could to any spiritual or temporal authority outside his own dominions. As soon as he felt powerful enough to resist external foes, he declined to submit to Rome, and put pressure upon his bishops to refuse to acknowledge the jurisdiction of the patriarch of the Greek Empire of Nicæa, who claimed the powers of the Greek patriarch of Constantinople. He threatened again to acknowledge the supremacy of the Pope. Accordingly, with that servility towards the secular power which has ever marred the character of the Greek clergy, one of his principal clergy, Bishop John of Naupactus, wrote in the name of the Western Greek Empire to the patriarch Manuel or his successor, Germanus, pointing out " that it was against the will of their Emperor that bishops should be sent from the East to fill up sees in the West ", and begging that autonomy might be granted to the Greek Church of Thessalonica, within three months, as it was feared that Theodore would submit to Rome.[3]

---

[1] Cf. Finlay, *Mediaeval Greece and Trebizond*, chaps. v and vi, p. 135 ff. and Miss Gardener, *The Lascarids of Nicæa*, p. 116 ff.

[2] Cf. *Reg. Honor. III.*, nn. 1023–4 ; 1029–31 ed. Pressutti, and *supra*, vol. xiii, p. 156.

[3] Miss Gardner, *The Lascarids of Nicæa*, p. 125 f., quoting " *Epérotica sæculi XIII* ", n. 26, by Vasilievsky in *Byzantina Chronica*, vol. iii, 1896, Academy of St. Petersburg. As the ecclesiastical disputes between Thessalonica and Nicæa do not concern us, we must refer the

JACOBITES AND OTHER EASTERN CHRISTIANS.

The desire of the Russians to return to union with Rome was, as we have already noted, shared by various Eastern Christians at this period.[1] Already, in 1237, Gregory IX. had received the following very important letter on the subject :—

Submission of Eastern Christians to Rome.

" To the most holy father and lord Gregory, by the grace of God, sovereign Pontiff, Brother Philip the unworthy prior of the Friar's Preachers in the Holy Land, due and devoted obedience in all things.

" Blessed be God, the Father of Our Lord Jesus Christ, who under your pontificate, Holy Father, has deigned to bring back to the shepherd sheep who have for a long time been wandering astray . . . Whole nations, estranged from the Church, have returned to unity, and submit to your authority and that of the Church. The Patriarch of the Eastern Jacobites,[2] a man venerable by his learning, character, and age, came this year, with a large company of archbishops, bishops, and monks of his nation, to adore God in Jerusalem. To him we expounded the dogmas of the Catholic faith, and the grace of God so acted upon him that on Palm Sunday during the solemn procession, which on that day comes down the mount of Olives, he promised and swore to obey the Roman Church, and formally renounced his heresy. He has handed over to us his profession of faith, written in Chaldaic and Arabic, as a lasting testimony of his sincerity, and, in leaving Jerusalem, he took the habit of our Order.

reader to p. 127 ff. of *The Lascarids* of Miss Gardner, who is certainly justified in her remark (p. 23) : " Paradoxical as it may sound, the superiority of the rival see (Rome) was the only guarantee of independence to the Byzantine clergy and monks."

[1] *Cf. supra*, p. 192.

[2] Ignatius II. See a letter of Greg. IX., July 28, 1237, congratulating him on his return to unity. Potthast, vol. i, n. 10421

" This patriarch has jurisdiction over Chaldeans, Medes, Persians, and Armenians, whose territories have been largely ravaged by the Tartars. His power extends even beyond these territories, over seventy provinces inhabited by numerous Christians subject to the Saracens, and, with the exception of the monks who are exempt, all paying tribute to them.

" Two other patriarchs followed this example, one a Jacobite of Egypt, and the other an eastern Nestorian, who have subjects in Syria and Phœnicia. Moreover, in accordance with the wish of the King and the barons, we have hastened to send four of the brethren into Armenia to learn the language.

" We have heard, too, about another patriarch called Jakelicus, the Catholic who rules over all the Nestorians throughout Greater India, the Kingdom of Prester John, and other remote eastern countries. He has promised brother William of Montferrat . . . that he will return to the bosom of ecclesiastical unity. We have also sent brothers into Egypt to the Patriarch of the Egyptian Jacobites who go further in their errors than the Orientals, adding, after the manner of the Saracens, circumcision, to their other errors. Of him, too, we have also heard that he wishes to return to ecclesiastical unity. . . . Hence seeing so great a gate open for the spreading of the truth of the Gospel, we have devoted ourselves to the study of the languages of these peoples.[1] . . . It is for you, then, Holy Father, to provide for the gathering together and for the peace of those returning to the Church." [2]

Andrew of Longumeau and Lorenzo of Portugal.

The work of reconciling these Easterns to the Church,

[1] Especially Arabic, which, says Philip, is the language most used.

[2] Ep. ap. Mat. Par., iii, 396 ff. ; also ap. Raynaldus, *Annal.*, 1237, n. 87, and in French ap. Mortier, *l.c.*, p. 381 f. This submission of the patriarch of the Jacobites made quite a sensation in Europe, and is noted in several chronicles. *Cf.* also *Chron. reg. Colon. Contin.*, iv, p. 270.

begun in this way by the Friars and Gregory IX.,[1] was carried on by them and Innocent IV. Among others sent to the East by the Pope was Andrew of Longumeau (1245), of whose success speak various letters from the East, and the Franciscan, Lorenzo of Portugal, one of the papal penitentiaries. A most ample commission was given to Lorenzo. He was granted jurisdiction in " Armenia, Iconium, Turkey, Greece, and the Kingdom of Babylon, and over the Greeks in the (Latin) patriarchates of Antioch and Jerusalem and the Kingdom of Cyprus, as well as over the Jacobites, Maronites, and Nestorians ". He was also, as Innocent expressed it, sent as an " Angel of peace " to protect the Greeks, who were not unfrequently ill-treated by the Latins.[2] To facilitate the work of the peacemaker, Innocent had already written to the Greek and Maronite Patriarchs and to the *Catholicus* of the Armenians to ask them to receive Lorenzo favourably.[3]

Lorenzo took up his work, especially what appears to have been his principal work—that of defending the Greeks under Latin domination—with such vigour that they turned insolent, and the Pope had to warn his legate not to put himself into opposition to the patriarch of Jerusalem.[4] However, his protection of the Greeks seems to have so warmed towards him the Greek patriarch of Antioch, that Lorenzo evidently imagined there was hope of his submission to the Pope. Of this, he informed

[1] *Cf.* Gregory's letter of congratulation to the Jacobite Patriarch on his decision "humbly to obey the holy Roman Church in all things". Ep. July 28, 1237, ap. Raynaldus, *l.c.*, nn. 88–9.

[2] Ep. of June 5, 1246. " Mandamus quatenus Græcos . . . auctoritate apostolica protegens, turbari eos violentiis . . . non permittas." Ap. Raynaldus, *Annal.*, 1247, n. 30 ; *Reg.*, n. 3047. *Cf.* epp. of Aug., 1247, ap. *Reg.*, nn. 4051–3.

[3] Aug. 6, 1246, *Reg.*, n. 3046.

[4] Ep. June 4, 1247, *Reg.*, 2745. A fuller analysis of this letter is given in Eubel, *Bullar. Francis.*, n. 454. *Cf.* n. 7 for the date of the first letter in note x.

Innocent who bade him admonish the patriarch either
to come to him himself or to send a representative to
him, and he instructed Lorenzo if necessary to advance
the sums necessary for the journey from the papal
treasury.[1]

No progress
towards
reunion
among the
Greeks.

But progress towards reunion among the Eastern Greeks
was not to be made at this time. Indeed, it has made but
little advance among any of the Greeks even to this day.
One ever hates whom one has wronged, and seemingly
the heavier balance of wrongdoing between the Greeks
and the Latins must be awarded to the Greeks. Hence,
in the letter of brother Philip, which we have just quoted,[2]
we find the assertion that while other nations have
submitted to Rome, " the Greeks alone persist in their
wickedness, and everywhere secretly or openly oppose the
Roman Church; they revile all our sacraments, and every
sect foreign to their own they call wicked and heretical."
The experience of the Dominican Philip was also that of
the observant Dominican traveller, brother Felix Faber,
nearly two hundred and fifty years later. He also notes
how they rebelled against " the authority of the Church
of Rome. Several times convicted by reason, they have
returned to the bosom of the Church, but have relapsed
twelve times ; and now, obstinate in their errors, they
. . . pitilessly persecute the Latins in every way they
can. Never would the Turks and Saracens have grown
so powerful had not these Greeks been traitors. The other
Eastern Christians would long ago have been brought
back to the unity of the Church, and might easily be
brought back at this day, if these proud and faithless
Greeks did not prevent them, and lead away again those
who have been brought back".[3]

---

[1] Ep. Aug. 7, 1247, *Reg.*, 4051, and Raynaldus, *ib.*, n. 3. " Tu ipsis
expensas necessarias de bonis nostræ cameræ largiaris."

[2] From Mat. Par., iii, 396.

[3] Ap. *Palestine Pilg. Text Soc.*, vol. viii, p. 434, or vol. i, pt. ii, of

At this time the natives of Syria and Mesopotamia were to a very considerable extent Monophysites, known from Jacob Baradæus, one of the most important propagators of the sect, as Jacobites (sixth century). At their head was the Patriarch Ignatius II. or David (1222–52), and to him Friar Andrew proclaimed the position of the Pope in the Church, and the need that all Christians should be in communion with him. His zealous words were listened to with readiness by the reigning patriarch, who acknowledged the supremacy of the Pope.[1] He entrusted to Andrew a letter for Innocent along with two professions of faith. The Pope was offered " sincere adoration in spirit and flesh " by " the Pastor of Syria and of the Eastern Jacobites, and he is hailed as the Father of Fathers, the most holy Innocent, who holds the See of Blessed Peter ". He had placed, he said, upon his head the papal letter which he had received from brother Andrew, a man adorned with every virtue, and he had been blessed by it as by a likeness of Jesus Christ.[2] Then having set forth his profession of faith, he concluded it by saying : " We receive all who follow the faith of the Prince of the Apostles, and who walk in the way of

Brother Andrew with the Jacobites and Nestorians, 1247.

Felix F., a Dominican who got a licence to go to the Holy Land from Sixtus IV.

[1] Etheridge, *The Syrian Churches*, p. 149, correctly states that " some of the Jacobite patriarchs have at various times entered into communion with the See of Rome ", but he is wrong in stating that " the first who did this was Ignatius, in 1552, who sent his profession to Pope Julius III." All the Jacobite patriarchs take the name of Ignatius. Better informed, Neale, *A hist. of the Holy Eastern Church*, i, 153, writes : " There have been many attempted reconciliations between the Syrian Jacobites and Rome, of which the most celebrated was that in 1247, between P. Innocent IV. and the Patriarch Ignatius," and the Maphrian (the next in rank to the patriarch) Bar Maadu. On the Jacobites and Nestorians see Jacques de Vitry († 1240), *Hist. Hierosol.*, i, cc. 75–6, translated into English in the *Pal. P.T.S.*, vol. ix.

[2] " Et benedictionem recepimus ab ipsa, sicut a similitudine imaginis Jesu Christi." Ep. ap. Raynaldus, *Annal.*, 1247, n. 36. *Cf.* for these letters, *Reg.*, nn. 3036 and 3038, but in full ap. R.

Blessed Peter, and we damn and excommunicate everyone who deviates from the faith of Blessed Peter, and of the Council of Nice, and who corrupts the integrity (rectitudinem) of the Christian faith, from the time of Simon Magus to the present day." This faith he declared to be that of the Egyptians, Armenians, Libyans, and Ethiopians.

At the same time he asked the Pope that the election of their Patriarchs should take place according to their own customs, and that they should not be subject to the Latin patriarchs, but like them should simply be immediately dependent on the Pope himself.[1]

The Nestorians submit to Rome.

At this period the most widely spread and influential Christian sect in Asia was that of Nestorius. The envoys of Innocent and those of King Louis found them everywhere, and, as we have seen, Rubruquis found some of them who acknowledged the primacy of the Roman Church. The words of the traveller are supported by documents which have been transcribed into Innocent's Register.

If Andrew did not meet the Nestorian patriarch himself (mar Sabarjesu V.), who resided at Bagdad, he met his envoy, the monk Simeon, the *rabban ata* (monkfather) of the Mongols, and the *raban ara* of the Latins, of whom we have spoken before. The "Vicar of the East" as Simeon styled himself, addressed the Pope as the "Father of Fathers . . . the sun of justice whose light shines over the four quarters of the world . . . and who holds the place of Blessed Peter, his lord the most holy Pope of Rome, and, before God, of all the quarters of the world". He asks the Pope to pardon his sins, as in his hands is " the power of binding and of loosing and

---

[1] " Et iterum sicut recipiunt (Latini episcopi) sententias et judicia vestra ita et nos." R., n. 38. Quite similar to this is the second profession of Ignatius, and also that John, Bar-Maardani, *Maphrian* or Primate of the Jacobites, ap. *Reg.*, n. 3039, and R., nn. 41–2.

of all mysteries ". He pleads, however, with Innocent
to forgive Frederick on account of the needs of the Holy
Land, and he concludes by telling him that he had put
into the hands of Andrew and his companions, " men who
deserve to be honoured by everyone," a profession of faith
(libellus de fide) which he had brought " from the bosom
of the East, to wit from the land of China ", and another
one from the archbishop of Nisibis, subscribed by five
other bishops.[1]

While the first document is lost, that of Enstaib [2] *The arch-
has come down to us.[3] The profession of the archbishop bishop of Nisibis
contains a clear full repudiation of Nestorianism, and sums condemns
up with the words : " Christ then is one, one Son, a being Nestorianism 1247.
of two natures, one divine and the other human, one
individual, one person."

Whilst heretics in Asia were thus returning to the *Armenia
obedience of the successors of St. Peter, others who had from 1216–1243.
already returned to it continued in that obedience
despite considerable difficulties. Conspicuous among
these others were the ever unfortunate Armenians, who
had submitted to Innocent III.,[4] under the *Catholicus*
John VII., the Magnificent (1202–20). This union was
maintained, at least during the pontificates of
Honorius III., Gregory IX., and Innocent IV., by John's
successor, Constantine I. (1220-67).

[1] *Reg.*, n. 3035, but in full ap. Raynald., 1247, nn. 32–4.

[2] Or Ensoaib for Isouyahb or Jesujab, son of Malc, bishop of Nisibis
since 1233.

[3] *Reg.*, 3037, or in full ap. R., *ib.*, n. 43.

[4] *Supra*, vol. xii, pp. 58 ff. The misery of his countrymen, a prey to
Tartar and to Saracen, at this period is set forth by the patriarch
Constantine himself. " Nam regio nostra in qua peccatum abundabat,
et nequitia, sanguine et lacrymis perfundi visa est, habitatores ense
necati, vel a bestiarum dentibus laniati, eorumque cadavera, et ossa
in aggerem congesta ; qui que cædem effugerunt, miserabiliter
venumdati, atque in dissitas orbis plagas captivi abducti sunt." *Cf.*
his *Canonica epist.*, 1243, ap. Balgy, *Hist. doct. Cath. inter Armenos*,
p. 294.

Hence we find Honorius III. giving his blessing to the marriage between the son of Andrew, King of Hungary, and the daughter of Leo II., King of Armenia,[1] and protecting the last-named country from the designs of John of Brienne.[2] Gregory IX. also had the most cordial relations both with the King and with the bishops of Armenia. Besides granting various privileges to its King Hetoun (or Haiton, etc.),[3] he took the politic step of confirming all the religious customs of the Armenian Church which " had been in use since the days of Gregory the Illuminator and St. Sylvester, and which were not in disagreement with the rules laid down by the Fathers and the Holy Canons." [4] At one time, indeed, it seemed as though he were going to listen to the claims put forward by the Latin Patriarch of Antioch, and to subject the *Catholicus* of the Armenians to his jurisdiction.[5] Finally, however, he disallowed his pretensions and confirmed the jurisdiction of Constantine " who is called the Catholicos ", over the Church of St. James in Jerusalem, and over such other churches as he had ever held in Syria.[6] Moreover, as marking Constantine's direct dependence upon himself, and not upon the patriarch of Antioch, he sent him, in response to his petition, a new pallium, as the former one was worn out, and, in addition, as a pledge of the apostoli love, a mitre, stole, and ring.[7]

---

[1] Ep. March 4, 1219, ap. *Reg.*, n. 1912.

[2] Ep. Aug. 11, 1220, ap. *Reg.*, n. 2610. Honorius had indeed, not unnaturally, some trouble with Armenia. *Cf. Reg.*, n. 5222, Dec. 17, 1224, and n. 6027.

[3] On him see Issavdens, *Armenia and the Armenians*, p. 313 ff., Venice, 1878. For the privileges granted him, see Gregory's *Reg.*, 4732–4–5.

[4] *Reg.*, vol. ii, n. 4733, March 1, 1239.

[5] Ep. June 26, 1238, ap. Raynaldus, 1238, n. 34.

[6] Ep. March 8, 1239, *Reg.*, n. 4739.

[7] Ep. March 10, 1239, *ib.*, n. 4740, or ap. Raynald., 1239, n. 83.

Acting under the influence of Innocent IV., Constantine assembled his suffragans at a Council at Cis (1243), and there issued several canons for the reform of discipline in the Armenian Church.[1] And, again, in 1251, he summoned the fifth Council of Cis. Of the work of this synod, a brief notice has been left us by the learned contemporary Armenian historian and theologian, Vartan.[2] " In the year 1700 of the Armenian era," he wrote, " the great Pope Innocent by letter bade all peoples who professed the Christian name, to profess that the Holy Ghost is God, proceeding from the Father and from the Son.[3] The Syrians, Greeks, and Georgians [4] did not acquiesce, but the Armenians did." The historian goes on to tell us that they searched the Fathers and found that the doctrine of the Pope was in accordance with the teaching of antiquity, and particularly of their great patron, St. Gregory the Illuminator.[5]

Armenia during the pontificate of Innocent IV.

Under stress of endless wars, and the consequent increasing difficulty of communicating with the Popes, the greater part of the Armenians fell away from communion with Rome. When then they were visited by the traveller Johann Scheltberger († after 1437) in the fourteenth century, they were set down, with some exaggeration,[6] as altogether out of union with the Catholic Church. " They are now," wrote Johann,[7] " separated from the Church of Rome. Their priests make the

After Innocent's time the majority of the Armenians fall away from Rome.

---

[1] Cf. the letter in the preceding note.

[2] Known as " the Great " († 1271). His history has been published in Armenian at Moscow and at Venice.

[3] Cf. ep. May 28, 1249, to the Greeks, ap. *Reg.*, ii, n. 4750.

[4] As far as the Georgians are concerned, this statement of Vartan does not appear to be certain.

[5] Vartan, quoted by Balgy, *l.c.*, p. 67, and by Tournebize, *Hist. de l'Arménie*, p. 290. Cf. Somal, *Quadro della storia lett. di Armenia*, p. 107.

[6] Cf. *supra*, vol. xii, p. 58 ff.

[7] Ap. Hakluyt, *Voyages*, No. 53, pp. 91–3. It was during this period of their union with Rome (an. 1250) that several Armenians came to England. Mat. Par., v, pp. 116 and 340.

Sacrament with unleavened bread. . . . They place much confidence in our religion (the *Catholic*). . . . They say that between their religion and ours there is only a hair's breadth, but that there is a great division between the Greek and their religion."

Unfortunately, but very ephemeral results followed from these reunions, whether in Russia or in Asia. Some of them have been ascribed to fear of the Tartars ; and it is quite possible that their inroads did direct attention towards Rome. On the one hand we are told that " the name of the Supreme Pontiff was famous among the Tartars ",[1] and on the other it was a general belief in the East that the Pope was as powerful a temporal as a spiritual potentate. " The kings who were subject to his sway " were spoken of,[2] and the Crusaders were thought to be the Pope's own soldiers.[3] While, therefore, there was fear of the Pope among the Tartars, there was among the Christians of the East an exaggerated notion of his temporal power. These false impressions, then, might easily induce some to attach themselves spiritually to Rome in the hope of securing thereby temporal protection. But no doubt the real reason of these returns to Rome was on the one side the intrepidity and the extraordinary virtue and zeal of the Friars,[4] and on the other the energy of the Pope in organizing missions of the Friars in every direction—to Morocco even and to Tunis,[5]

---

[1] Vincent of Beauvais, *Spec. hist.*, l. xxxi, c. 93.

[2] See the letter of Simeon recently quoted ap. Ray., 1247, n. 34.

[3] *Cf. supra*, vol. xi, p. 275, n.

[4] Even Matthew Paris who did not love the Friars tells us that their preaching was heard even to the ends of the earth. *Chron.*, iv, p. 346.

[5] *Cf.* epp. of Innocent of Oct. 18, 23, 25, 31 ; Dec. 19, 1246, etc., ap. Eubel, *Bullar. Francis.*, pp. 41–2. Several of these letters are given in full by Mas Latrie, in his *Les relat. des Chrétiens avec les Arabes*, Documents, p. 12 ff. At this time, the last remnant of the great African Church once in communion with Rome was the Church of Morocco : " Marrochitana ecclesia sola et unica in partibus ipsis filia Romanæ ecclesiæ." Ep. of Oct. 31, 1246, to the Christians of Morocco.

as well as to the other places we have spoken about in
detail.

However this may be, the real or reported return to
the Roman obedience of so many peoples made a great
impression upon thinking men in the West. Adam Marsh,
the learned Franciscan friend of our great bishop
Grosseteste, in the course of an address which he presented
to Innocent on the occasion of the assumption of the
Cross by Henry III. (March, 1250), thus apostrophized
him : " O best of priests in that the merciful God, who
ever with temptation maketh issue that we may bear it,
and whose place you hold on earth, consoling us in the
midst of our tribulation, is seen, in the divine events which
He hath wrought in these our days, to be animating the
whole world . . . to offer most fitting devotion to your
supreme dignity (præsulatus vestri)."

Impression in the West of the Romeward movement of the East.

For, continued the writer, when you were well nigh
overwhelmed by raging Tartars, oncoming Saracens,
dissentient Greeks, hostile Latins, and erring subjects,
then, lo ! there came great wonders, unexpected miracles,
direct from the Father of Light—the conversion of
the Tartars, the consternation of the Saracens, the
supplication of the Greeks, the repression of the Latins,
and the correction of your subjects.[1]

Of most of these matters which Adam Marsh imagined
ought to have brought joy to the heart of Innocent IV.,
we have already written. It remains to say something of
the " Græcorum obsecratio ", of the overtures for
reunion made by the independent Greeks of the Empire of
Nicæa. If any Pope deserved to succeed in winning the
Greeks back to ecclesiastical unity, that Pope was
Innocent, the Magnificent. Towards the Greeks who were

Negotiations for reunion with the Greeks of Nicæa.

---

[1] Ep. c. 5, of Adam M., ap. *Mon. Francisc.*, p. 426 ff., *R. S.* The
" Latinorum repressio " has no doubt reference to the death of
Frederick II., and the " correctio subditorum " to the taking of the
last strongholds of the Albigensians.

in subjection to the Latins whether in Asia Minor or in
Cyprus,[1] he showed himself a true father, doing all that
he could to protect them from oppression by their
Frankish rulers. He also displayed a most conciliatory
spirit to the Greeks who owed allegiance to the wily
Vatatzes, and, but for his death in the midst of
negotiations with them, it is perhaps possible that he might
have gained them. It was his principle with regard to
such Greeks as had professed their allegiance to the
Apostolic See " to tolerate their rites and customs as far
as he could before God in order to retain them in their
obedience ".[2]   Unfortunately, however, his enlightened
policy was not always followed.[3]   If it had been, the
relations of the Greek Church to that of Rome would
to-day have been probably very different to what
they are.

John
Vatatzes.

In his consideration of the world and its rulers,
Innocent must constantly have been thinking of John III.

---

[1] *Cf.* his instructions to his penitentiary, the legate Lorenzo already
referred to. " Wherefore," said Innocent to him, " we bid you protect
the Greeks in those parts, of whatsoever denomination, by our apostolic
authority, and not permit them to be outraged or disturbed in any way.
You must cause full compensation to be made to them for any
molestations or injuries inflicted on them by the Latins, and insist
on the Latins in those parts wholly abstaining from any such acts for
the future." Ep. of June 5, 1247, ap. Raynaldus, *Ann.*, 1247, n. 30.
Cf. the privileges which he granted to the Greeks of Cyprus, Albania,
and other provinces who were returning to the unity of the Roman
Church. Epp. of July 21, and Aug. 8, 1250, ap. *ib.*, 1250, nn. 41-7.
Cf. also with regard to the Greeks in Cyprus who were devoted to the
Roman Church, epp. of Feb. 17 and 25, and March 6, 1254, ap. *Reg.*,
vol. iii, nn. 7331–2 and 7338. The last cited letter also *in part*, ap.
Raynald., 1254, n. 7 ; Potthast, 15265.

[2] *Cf.* his letter just quoted of March 6, 1254, ap. Mansi, *Concil.*,
xxiii, p. 578.

[3] Not even completely by his successor Alexander IV. *Cf.* his constitution regarding the relations of the Greek and Latin hierarchies
in Cyprus of July 3, 1260, ap. Mansi, *Conc.*, xxiii, p. 1038 ff. It is given,
but not in full, ap. Raynaldus, *Ann.*, 1260, nn. 37–50.

Vatatzes, emperor of Nicæa (1222–55), and his thoughts about him must have been more anxious than encouraging. Able and crafty, an adept in the Byzantine political art of playing off one enemy against another, Vatatzes was the never sleeping foe of the miserable Latin Empire of Constantinople which the Popes felt themselves bound to support. Then, too, especially after he had taken for his second wife Anna-Constantia, a bastard daughter of Frederick II., had he become the close ally of the emperor of Germany.[1] He was evidently a man to be watched and cultivated. However, he, too, had his difficulties, which would prevent him from altogether opposing the Pope, and which might even drive him to seek his friendship. He was in fear of the Tartars, and, with all his ecclesiastical high-handedness,[2] he had to take account of the moderate party, small, perhaps, though it was, in the Greek Church, which was easily disposed to listen to proposals for unity.

The first in Innocent's time to make an attempt to induce Vatatzes to submit to Rome was his sister-in-law, Maria, who had married Bela IV., King of Hungary, and who had herself recognized the supremacy of the Pope. We have a letter of Innocent to her (Jan. 30, 1247) in which he thanks her for the efforts she has already made to cause " the return of Vatatzes and his people to the bosom of mother Church ", and he begs her to send " discreet men " to him to work for the same end.[3]

Efforts to bring Vatatzes into the Church, 1246.

---

[1] Carbio, c. 27 ; Mat. Par., iv, 299, 357. On *Constance de Hohenstaufen*, cf. Diehl, *Figures Byzantines*, p. 207 ff. Paris, 1908.

[2] After the death of the Patriarch Methodius (1240), he kept the see vacant for four years. It was not till 1244 that Manuel was appointed. For, as the historian George Acropolita observes (*Annal*, c. 42, p. 77 ed. Bonn), he could not easily find a worthy man, " or rather one who was acceptable to himself." Princes, he continues, are wont to advance to such offices men who will do their pleasure in order that their will may not be opposed.

[3] Ap. Theiner, *Mon. Hung.*, n. 377, i, p. 203.

Whether these " discreet men " were sent or not,
Innocent for a time, at least, seems to have supported
Baldwin II., the Latin Emperor of Constantinople, and
Vatatzes to have given aid to Frederick.[1] However, after
the defeat of Frederick at Parma (1248), Vatatzes,
convinced that to support him any longer would be to
waste his resources, and mindful, too, that Baldwin was
still in Europe seeking help against him,[2] turned to the
Pope, and made him fresh proposals of reunion. The
worthy Salimbene met his envoy at Vienne on his way to
Lyons, to ask Innocent to send a legate to his master
(1249).[3] When the Greek envoy appeared before the Pope
at Lyons, the legate for whom he asked was the General of
the Franciscans, John of Parma, a man distinguished
not only for his amiability, but also for his spirituality
and learning.[4] Hence was he beloved by Innocent " as
his own soul ", and would have been made a cardinal
by him had not death intervened.[5] The emperor
Vatatzes also had heard of his sanctity, and begged the
Pope to send him to him, " because he hoped that through
him the Greeks would return to the obedience of the
Roman Church."[6] Receiving John with a kiss, the Pope
told him that the Greeks wished to be reunited to the
Roman Church. " Take, therefore, to them," said
Innocent, " a goodly company of your brethren,

---

[1] Mat. Par., an. 1247, iv, 626 ; v, 38.

[2] Cf. ep. of Innocent, May 28, 1249. Potthast, n. 13, 384, relative
to help for the Latin Empire. Cf. ep. of June 11, ib., n. 13400.

[3] Chron., p. 321.

[4] " Literatus et spiritualis homo," says Peregrinus of Bologna,
Chron., p. 143 ed. Little, as an appendix to his Eccleston, De adventu
fratrum. Cf. Sal., p. 324, and Catal. gen. minist. O.F.M., ap. M. G. SS.,
xxxii, p. 662.

[5] Salimbene, p. 304.

[6] Ib. The envoy of Vatatzes, bore the same name as our gossip
(Salimbene), was half Greek and half Latin, and spoke both Greek and
Latin very well. Ib., p. 321.

and it may be that through you God will work some good." [1]

Selecting a number of suitable brethren,[2] John set out for the East. He was well received by the Emperor (1249), and soon made such an impression on Vatatzes and many of the Greeks that they regarded him not merely as a holy, prudent and learned man, but " as one of the ancient Fathers or Doctors, or as one of Christ's own disciples ".[3] It was in vain that Frederick protested, calling on his brother to think of what he was doing, and bidding him " reflect if he ought to act thus with a friend . . . and since he had traversed the path of error far enough, no longer to proceed along it ".[4]

The mission of that " angel of peace ", the mystic, John of Parma, prospered.[5] Vatatzes became deeply attached to the lowly friar, and would have given him numberless presents. However, he was greatly edified when John gently declined them. But, determined to honour him, Vatatzes begged him whenever he rode forth with his companions to carry in his hands " a certain *scuriata* (a kind of whip) ". Thinking it was nothing

---

[1] *Sal.*, ib., p. 321. *Cf.* Potthast, nn. 13385–6, May 28, 1249, or at length ap. *Reg.*, nn. 4749–50, vol. ii, p. 129 f. In his formal letter to John (n. 4749), Innocent declares that in all his troubles his one aim was to protect the Catholic faith and gain souls to God, " nil aliud in hoc certamine intendimus, nisi ut fidem tueamur Catholicam, et Deo animas . . . lucremur."

[2] *Sal.*, p. 322, and Carbio, c. 17, p. 91.

[3] Angelo Clareno, *Hist. trib.*, iii, ap. S., *ib.*, n. 5.

[4] Ep. ap. H.-B., vi, pt. ii, p. 921 f. This letter is not dated, and H.-B. refers it to the mission of bro. Lorenzo. But as we have seen his mission was to the Greeks of Antioch and other places where the Greeks were under Latin sway. It therefore may safely be connected with this mission of John.

[5] Innocent, writing (Aug. 8, 1250) to the Greek envoys who were about to come to him, expresses his joy : " Audito quod prudens Græcia, novo superni sideris irradiata fulgore, gratanter accepit humilem pacis angelum, dilectum filium Johannem." Ep. in full ap. Eubel, *Mon. Francis.*, p. 250.

more than what it seemed, John made no difficulty in agreeing. It was, however, says Salimbene, who tells us this story, an imperial emblem, and, when the Greeks saw it, all genuflected before brother John, " as do the Latins when the Body of the Lord is elevated and shown to the people in the Mass." [1]

Envoys from Vatatzes sent to the Pope, 1250. It was at length decided to send to the Pope an embassy from the Greek Emperor and the Greek Church with definite proposals for reunion. Innocent was, of course, delighted, and Frederick furious. Writing to his venerable brethren the archbishops and bishops, and to his beloved sons the lay members of the embassy, Innocent expressed his joy that " prudent Greece ", newly illuminated from on high, had received his beloved son John, and, moved by him, had taken steps to heal the pest of schism " which damnably rent the unity of the universal Church ". . . . " Oh ! if in our time such a grace were sent from heaven that, in the midst of the waves which toss the unsinkable barque of Blessed Peter, the old rent of schism which threatens such danger to the Christian faith, might be firmly closed, then might the Lord dismiss in peace the servant of His servants." He concluded by assuring the envoys that he was anxiously awaiting their presence, and would procure for them a safe-conduct through such territories as were devoted to the Church across which they might pass. [2]

About the same time,[3] Frederick wrote a very different letter to his son-in-law. He expressed his surprise that Vatatzes had made special mention to him of the embassy of Friars Minors and Preachers which " that Pope " (iste Papa) had sent to confer with the prelates of his

---

[1] *Sal.*, pp. 304–5.

[2] Ep. Aug. 8, 1250, ap. Eubel, *l.c.* in full. This letter was found only recently by Paul Sabatier at Assisi.

[3] H.-B., who gives this letter, vi, pt. ii, p. 771 ff., dates it " May or June ", 1250.

Church. How could " that man (iste) who is called the
Prince of Priests, and who is wont publicly to excommunicate the Greeks, venture to send an embassy to his
majesty ? Did not " that man " upbraid me for giving
you my daughter in marriage ? Behold " these our
bishops " taking up arms instead of their crosiers! They
are not pontiffs of Christ's Church, but ravening wolves.
He who in his corner at Lyons is thinking great thoughts
is despised by all as the father of lies. The envoys whom
you are entertaining are full of guile. They have not
gone to you on account of the faith, but to sow discord
between father and son. As a father he must blame him
for wishing to send envoys to the Pope without consulting
him. However, he will send ships to bring the envoys
from Durazzo ; but he will first fetch over the imperial
ambassadors.

But the imperial spleen availed nothing. On this
occasion the Greek bishops appear to have been in earnest,
and when they landed at Brindisi seemingly would not
allow themselves to be cajoled by Frederick. Accordingly
the imperial embassy was not allowed to leave Apulia,
but was detained there till after Frederick's death
(Dec., 1250).[1]

At length, however, the envoys were allowed to proceed, The Greek
and met the Pope at Perugia, where he had arrived from envoys
meet the
Lyons in November, 1251. They were naturally received Pope, and
by Innocent with great honour, and, after the return
1251-2.
preliminaries of the proposed union had been discussed,
the Greeks returned to Vatatzes for final instructions.[2]

A year or two later, the ambassadors, in magnificent The Greeks
style, returned with a number of definite proposals come back
again, 1254.

---

[1] In c. 30, p. 107, Carbio says they were detained for a year and a half.

[2] Carbio, *ib. Cf. Catal. Gen. Minist. O.F.M.*, c. 6, p. 662, ap. *M.G.SS.*,
xxxii. From Carbio, c. 17, p. 93, it would appear that the Franciscans
were not detained so long as the Greeks but were allowed to proceed
to see Innocent before he left Lyons.

(1254). But the same fate awaited them, when they landed in Apulia, as they had experienced before under Frederick. They were prevented from proceeding on their journey for several months.[1] However, on the death of Conrad (May, 1254), they made their way to Rome, joined the Pope at Assisi, and went with him to Anagni.[2] Among other documents which they brought with them was a letter from the patriarch of Nicæa, Manuel II., addressed " to the President of the highest apostolic Thrones ".[3] He praises Innocent for his zealous efforts for reunion, and briefly enumerates the points for discussion. These latter are, however, given at length by Alexander IV. in a letter to his legate, the bishop of Orvieto, when he attempted to reopen the negotiations for reunion in 1256. The Greeks offered in the first place to recognize the supreme principality of the Roman See, and its Pontiff in reference to the rest of the Patriarchal Sees ; (2) Canonical obedience was to be paid to Innocent and to his lawful successors ; (3) Appeal to the Roman Church by Greek ecclesiastics was to be allowed ; (4) Free recourse to it was also to be allowed in connexion with any questions which might arise in the Greek Church ; (5) Obedience was to be paid to sentences issued by the Roman Pontiff which were not opposed to the canons ; (6) In councils the first seat was to be given to him, and when signatures were required he was to be the first to affix his ; (7) In questions of faith, which might arise therein, he was to give his pronouncement (sententia)

---

[1] Carbio, c. 36. Most of what Matthew Paris has to say on this embassy (v, 456) is only an additional example of his untrustworthiness when telling of foreign affairs. *Cf.* also the author of an *Anonymous Chronicle*, of no great importance, ap. Sathas, *Bibliotheca Med. Aevi*, vol. vii, p. 511, Paris, 1894.

[2] *Ib.*, c. 38.

[3] A copy of this letter in the original Greek exists in the Bodleian library, Cȯd. Baroccianus, No. 131, fol. 360 f. Norden, *Der Papsttum und Byzaz*, gives it for the most part in German, p. 756 off.

before the others, and to proclaim his decision which, if not opposed to the Gospels or the canons, was to be accepted by the rest [1]; (8) In causes connected with ecclesiastical persons and other matters which might be treated of in Councils, the rest were to acquiesce in the decisions which the authority of the Roman Pontiff might dictate, provided that they were not opposed to the decrees of the sacred Councils.

Over and above this, the envoys asked that Constantinople should be restored to Vatatzes,[2] and that the Latins should be removed from the Greek patriarchal sees.

To these proposals and professions, continued Alexander IV., "whilst I was still in a subordinate position," Innocent, with the consent of his brethren gave a general approval in the hope that the Church which made them would, after its return to the bosom of the Church, readily enlarge their bounds.[3]

However, in the course of discussion on these points, it appeared that, in connexion with the seventh, there was likely to be some trouble over the question of the Procession of the Holy Ghost, "in which the Greek Church seemed to differ somewhat from the Roman." Innocent pointed out that it was irrational that the Greeks should allow to the Pope the power of defining in other articles of faith but not in that one.[4] Still, not

[1] No. 7. " In quæstionibus fidei, si quæ ibidem (in councils) fortassis emerserint, præ aliis dare sententiam, suæque voluntatis proferre judicium, quod dummodo Evangelicis et canonicis non obviet institutis, obedienter cæteri suscipient et sequenter." Ap. Raynaldus, *Ann.*, 1256, n. 48.

[2] Hence George Pachymeres (1243–1310), *De Michaele Palæologo*, l. v, p. 366, states that the Greeks were prepared to enter into communion (λειτουργεῖν) with the Latins, and enrol the name of the Pope on their diptychs if he would abandon the Latins in Constantinople. *Cf. ib.*, p. 374 ed. Bonn.

[3] *Ib.*, n. 49.

[4] *Ib.*, n. 50. "Non enim videbatur rationabilis causa, qua Græca

to impede the work of reunion, Innocent agreed that the form of the Creed should not be changed in the Council which was to be held forthwith, except by mutual consent, but that the Greek Church might retain it in the form in which it was left by the said Council, provided that the Greek Church thought the same as the Roman Church with regard to the Blessed Trinity.[1]

The question of possession of Constantinople. As for the restoration of Constantinople to the Greek Emperor, Innocent declared that he could not decide anything without considering the claims of the Latin Emperor; but he agreed to push the claim of Vatatzes in every way. With regard to the patriarchates, Innocent thought it was only fair that those who actually held them should keep them till death, unless the forthcoming Council came to some decision in the matter. But, as to the Patriarch of Constantinople, Innocent was willing that Manuel should forthwith be acknowledged as the rightful patriarch of Constantinople, and should enjoy his rights when once the city of Constantinople fell into the hands of Vatatzes.[2]

Deaths cause the failure of the attempt. Unfortunately this fair prospect of reunion between the two Churches was destroyed by the death about the same time of Innocent, of Vatatzes, and of the patriarch Manuel (1255).[3] When the endless negotiations were reopened by Alexander IV., the Greeks, especially the

ecclesia movebatur, ut diffiniendi potestatem, quam Romanum pontificem habere non negat in cæteris fidei articulis, velit eum in hoc uno articulo non habere."

[1] " Dummodo de sanctæ Trinitatis fide Græca Ecclesia in omnibus catholice sentiat cum Romana." *Ib.*, n. 51.

[2] This letter, along with the other letters of Alex. IV. on the Greek question, is also given by F. Schillmann at the end of his article : " Zur byzantinischen Politik Alexanders IV." Ap. *Römische Quartalschrift*, 1908, 2, 3, 4, p. 114. In the eds. both of Raynald. and Schillmann the bishops of the Greek embassy are given as " *Quisicensem* et Sardensem ". From Pachymeres, *l.c.*, p. 367, it is clear that they were Andronicus of Sardis, and George of *Cyzicus*.

[3] *Cf.* Peregrinus, *l.c.*, p. 144.

epileptic despot, Theodore II., Lascaris, were in a different mood, and at the despot's bidding his *Prætor*, the historian George Acropolita, sent home from Berrœa (in Macedonia) the papal envoys who had come to continue the work for reunion begun by Innocent (1257).[1]

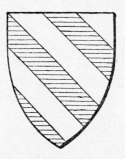

ARMS OF INNOCENT IV.

Bendy argent and azure.

---

[1] *Annales*, c. 67, p. 149. On Theodore II., Lascaris, see J. B. Pappadopoulos, *Théodore II.*, Paris, 1908, who at times follows the mistakes of Muralt, and Miss Gardiner's very pleasing book, *The Lascarids of Nicæa*, p. 197 ff. Innocent also made a vain attempt to bring back the Bulgarians to the unity of the faith, offering to all a council of Greek and Bulgarian prelates. *Cf.* Potthast, nn. 11606 and 11613, March, 1245.

CHAPTER VI.

THE BRITISH ISLES.

Works.—In treating of Innocent's relations with England, it will be necessary to discuss his taxation of the English Church. For the convenience of the student, therefore, it may be well to give here a list of books which throw light on the question of papal taxation, even though some of them have already been quoted,[1] and though some of them deal rather with taxation of the fourteenth century than with that of the thirteenth. E. Jordan, *Le saint-siège et les banquiers Italiens*, Brussels, 1895 ; " La faillitè des Buonsignori," ap. *Mélanges Paul Fabre*, Paris, 1902 ; and *De mercatoribus cameræ apostolicæ*, Rennes, 1909 (very valuable) ; Em. Re, *La compagnia dei Ricardi in Inghilterra, e il suo fallimentò alla fine del sec. XIII.*, ap. *Archivio della soc. Rom.*, vol. xxxvii, 1914 ; G. Arras, *La chiesa e la storia economica del Medio Evo*, ap. *ib.*, vol. xxviii (1905), p. 300 ff., and xxix (1906), p. 145 ff. ; S. K. Mitchell, *Studies in Taxation under John and Henry III.*, New Haven, Yale University Press, 1914, full but not too clear ; C. Samaran and G. Mollat, *La fiscalité pontificale en France au XIVe siècle*, Paris, 1905. This work has been pronounced by a competent authority (W. E. Lunt), " the best general survey of the papal financial system which has yet appeared," W. E. Lunt, *The financial system of the Mediæval Papacy*, ap. *Quarterly Journal of Economics*, vol. xxiii, p. 251 ff., Boston, 1909, a very good paper, of which I have freely availed myself, and by the same author, *The account of a papal collector in England in* 1304, ap. *Eng. Hist. Rev.*, vol. xxviii (1915), and ap. *ib.*, p. 398 ff., *Papal taxation in the reign of Edward I.*, and ap. *ib.*, vol. xxix, 1916,*Collectors' accounts for the clerical tenth levied in England by order of Nicholas IV.*, and " Early assessments for papal taxation", ap. L. Delisle, *Mémoire sur les opérations financières des Templiers*, Paris, 1889 ; C. Daux, *Le cens pontifical dans l'Église de France*, ap. *Rev. des. Quest. Histor.*, vol. lxxv (1904), p. 1 ff. ; A. Clergeac, *La Curie et les Bénéficiers consistoriaux* (étude sur les communs et menus services), Paris, 1911 ;

---

[1] *Cf.* vol. ix, p. lvii.

U. Berlière, *Inventaire des libri obligationum et solutionum des Archives Vaticanes*, Rome, 1904 ; and C. Lux, *Constitutionum Apostolicarum de generali beneficiorum reservatione . . . collectio et interpretatio*, Wratislaviæ (Breslau), 1904 ; J. F. Willard, " The English Church and the lay taxes of the fourteenth century," ap. *The University of Colorado Studies*, Boulder, Colorado, 1907 ; and the same authors " Side-lights on the assessment and collection of the mediæval subsidies," ap. *Transactions of the English Hist. Soc.*, 1913.

THE relations of Innocent with England which have left the deepest mark on its history were financial. For this reason, and incidentally because the financial operations of the Popes were of the greatest importance in the advancement of commercial prosperity, it will be well to say something about them, in order that the action of Innocent in the domain of finance may be more correctly appreciated. During his pontificate and that of his successors in the thirteenth century, that papal system of taxation was fostered which was to reach its highest development in the fourteenth century, and which, under the attacks especially of the French clergy and Kings, was to collapse at the beginning of the fifteenth.[1] Of the impression produced on England by the money transactions of Innocent, it is hoped that the subsequent narrative may give a sufficiently adequate account. But, of the effect of papal financial methods on European commerce, it must be enough here if we accept in proof the authoritative conclusions of an expert. " The Papacy," says Mr. Lunt, " not only organized one of the earliest and best of the mediaeval financial systems, but, by means of its operations, influenced profoundly the general economic development of Europe. . . . The changing of the sums received for taxes from money of local circulation into that of universal acceptance, the deposit and transfer of those sums, and the loans demanded of the clergy who were responsible for them

Innocent's financial relations with England.

[1] Samaran, *La fiscalité*, p. ii.

stimulated the commercial and financial enterprise of the Italian banking houses, if indeed, their business as papal fiscal agents was not the initial cause of transalpine activities."

When Innocent became Pope he found the Holy See overwhelmed with debt.[1] The emperor Frederick had, in his efforts to enslave the Church, very considerably reduced its revenues by seizing and ravaging its territories, and by plundering those who were bringing money to it. Gregory IX. had accordingly been compelled to borrow money which the continuance of the struggle against the Empire had prevented him from paying off. This legacy of debt Innocent had to face with revenues still further diminished by his flight from Italy, and under conditions of greater strain on these lessened resources brought about by the ever-growing business which the papal court had to transact for the whole of Christendom.[2] The steady growth of centralization in the government of the Church (involving a great increase in the number of its officials), and the development of Feudalism, certainly increased the prestige of the Popes of this period, both in the spiritual and temporal order. But

---

[1] *Cf. supra*, p. 22. As Daux, *Le cens pont.*, p. 71, observes, the treasury, against which much is often said, was, from its regular habit of subsidizing great undertakings, such as the Crusades, nearly always empty. We have seen how Innocent IV. was dunned for money. Urban IV. makes the same complaint: " Nobis fatigatis quotidie gravibus et importunis clamoribus creditorum et maxime Romanorum, quibus in magna summa pecuniae Ecclesia ipsa noscitur obligata." And he also gives as the reason of the pecuniary difficulties of the Holy See the expenses it has incurred " for the defence of the liberty of the Church, and the Sicilian affair ". Ep. of Jan. 23, 1262, ap. *Reg. Urb. IV.*, i, p. 33 ed. Guiraud. *Cf.* Mat. Par., *Chron.*, v, p. 511, for a similar state of things under Alexander IV.

[2] It was by Rome that, as St. Louis IX. stated, " the arduous and intricate matters of Christendom were usually settled." Ap. Mat. Par., *Chron. maj.*, iv, 647 ; and Innocent himself declared, ep. May 22, 1253, ap. Rymer, i, 471, " Habet ecclesia Romana humeros communibus oneribus assuetos."

it threw a financial responsibility upon them with which their ordinary income was inadequate to cope, and which neither the ecclesiastical nor the civil powers of Christendom made any effort to meet.

It therefore behoved Innocent to consider well from what sources he was to draw money. The days had long gone by when the income from the estates or *patrimonies* of the Church had enabled the Popes not only to meet the needs of the local Roman Church, but to be the almoner of the Catholic world. The *Patrimonies* had been lost during the disorders of the tenth century, and the revenues of the papal states, which had been more or less thoroughly organized by Innocent III. were, to a very considerable extent, in the hands of the great adversary of the Church, the emperor Frederick II. Moreover, as King of Germany, the two Sicilies and Jerusalem, that same adversary was also able very largely to prevent pecuniary aid of any sort from reaching the Pope from any portion of the Empire.

Sources of income not available to Innocent.

Then there were the tributes from the vassal kingdoms of the Holy See. But the revenue from this source was uncertain. The actual rulers of these states were generally unwilling and, at times, unable to pay their tribute-money. It was often wholly withheld, as was that of Sicily by Frederick ; and even when ultimately forthcoming, it was very frequently in arrears.[1] Then, for Peter's Pence, Frederick would no doubt often be able to stop some of it, as for instance that of Poland, from reaching the Pope, and the greater part of it that was raised in some

---

[1] In 1220 we find Henry telling Pope Honorius III. that he is afraid that his non-payment of the tax may cause him to lose his favour. *Patent Rolls*, Henry III., vol. i, p. 267. In the year 1248 we find Innocent reminding Henry that the annual tribute of 1,000 marks was due, and asking him to pay it to the Knights Templars at Lyons, " from whom he had borrowed the sum in anticipation." Gasquet, p. 276, quoting *Pub. Record Off.*, Papal Bulls, bundle 53, n. 3. *Cf.* Rymer, i, 442, Oct. 6, 1246.

countries, in England, for example, never reached Rome
at all.[1] The great shortage of money arising from the
serious decrease in these important sources of papal
revenue could not, of course, be made up by the income
derived from the taxes (census) due from such churches,
monasteries, or estates as were under special papal
protection or were exempt from the jurisdiction of the
ordinary. The revenue got from this source was also
very often in arrears.[2] Besides, it had never been really
large; and it was rightly not deemed advisable to increase
the number of exemptions.[3] What has been said of the
exemption taxes can be also said of those of the chancery.
The taxes charged on the documents that were issued
from the papal Chancery, or that were entered in its

---

[1] *Cf. supra*, vol. viii, 90, 202 ; vii, 329 n., 332, and especially ii,
321 n. A letter of Pietro Griffi, a collector of Peter's Pence in England in
the days of Julius II., informs us that Gregory V. (X. ?) had agreed that
the bishops of England should collect the Rome-Scot in their own way,
but should transmit annually to Rome a definite sum from each
diocese. The highest amount was paid by the diocese of Lincoln (£42),
and the lowest by that of Ely, viz. £5, or " centum solidi ", according to
ep. 272 of Gilbert Foliot (ap. *Materials for the hist. of Thos. Becket*,
v, p. 211, *R. S.*). Ep. 172 (ap. *ib.*, p. 210) shows that Exeter paid
£9 5s., and that the whole sum paid was practically £200. This comparatively small sum appears to have been the amount paid to the
Holy See for centuries. *Cf.* D. Tesoroni ap. *The Archæological Rev.*,
iv (1890), p. 45 ; and O. Jensen, " The Denarius S. Petri in England,"
ap. *Transac. of the Roy. Hist. Soc.*, 1905, p. 219 ff. ; but especially P.
Griffi's own work : *De officio collectoris in Anglia* in the Vatican library.
MS. Ottoboni Lat., n. 2948.

[2] *Cf.* Berlière, *Inventaire*, p. vi f., quoting Fabre, *La perception du
cens apostolique dans l'Italie centrale en* 1291, ap. *Mélanges d'archéol. et
d'hist.*, x, p. 369 ff., and—*en France en* 1291, ap. *ib.*, xvii, 231, and—
en Allemagne en 1291, ap. *Rev. Numismatique*, 1899, p. 532 ff.

[3] It is indeed said that " by the close of the thirteenth century the
creation of new ones (exempt churches or monasteries) had almost
ceased ". Lunt, *Financial system*, p. 276. How comparatively small
the income from exempt religious institutions really was may be argued
from the fact that in the British Isles a total of twenty-three exempt
churches paid a sum of only £10 6s. 4d. *Cf. Lib. Cens.*, i, 224–6, and
230–4 ed. Fabre. The calculation is that of Mr. Lunt.

registers at the request of private persons [1] could not
have left a large margin for the papal treasury when the
expenses of the Chancery itself had all been met. If then
the deficit in the Pope's income arising from the failure
of his more important sources of revenue could not be
made up by the exemption and the chancery taxes, it
is not to be supposed that such chance additions to his
income as legacies, and free offerings could as a rule
make that deficit good.

There still remained the taxes to be drawn from the *Income on*
personal incomes of the clergy of Christendom,[2] for we *which*
Innocent
have seen that it was held that, in theory at least, all *could rely.*
benefices belonged to the Pope as Head of the Church.[3]
There was, moreover, the analogy of the taxation of the
laity in England at least, to appeal to; for, from the
days of Henry II., the custom of the taxation of personal
property had become established. Innocent found that
this important source of revenue had been exploited by
his predecessors, not, it is true, in a manner that was
always desirable, but, unfortunately, in a manner that
he did not see his way to alter. He admitted, as we have
noted, that great grievances resulted from the methods

---

[1] *Cf.* Delisle, *Mém. sur les actes d'Innocent III.*, p. 11. In the days of
Innocent's successor, Alexander IV., the tax-book of the Chancery,
says Mr. Lunt, specified the fees for eight classes of letters.

[2] *Cf. supra*, vol. xiii, p. 86 ff., on papal revenues. The " spiritualities
and temporalities, the movable and immovable goods " of the clergy
were laid under contribution. *Cf. Annal. de Burton*, p. 364, *R. S.*

[3] *Cf. supra*, vol. xiii, 304 ff., on papal taxation, where certain
quotations of Bishop Grosseteste on the Pope's rights in the matter of
Church property are given. That the disposition of all benefices in
the Church belongs to the Popes was set forth in a decree (" Licet
ecclesiarum ") of Clement IV., Aug. 27, 1265, which was embodied in
his *Sexti Decretal.* by Boniface VIII. " Licet ecclesiarum, personatuum,
dignitatum, aliorumque beneficiorum ecclesiasticorum plenaria
dispositio ad Romanum noscatur Pontificem pertinere, etc." Lib.
iii, tit. iv, c. 2, ap. *Corpus. J. C.*, ii, p. 1021 ed. Freidberg. *Cf. Reg.
Clem.*, iv, n. 212 ed. Jordan.

in vogue of taxing the clergy, and he made efforts to
remedy some of them. His necessities, however, were
allowed to override what was in accordance with strict
justice, and it may even be said that Innocent extended
the various unsatisfactory means of taxing the clergy
which had been practised by his immediate predecessors.
He continued from time to time to demand tithes or
different proportions of their income,[1] i.e. he taxed
both their *spiritualities* or income derived from tithes,
offerings, and suchlike spiritual sources, and their
temporalities or lands and rents which they held in the
same way as the laity.[2] He continued also to employ
the system of Provisions, and to develop that of the
Servitia, or the payment by prelates for their appointment
or for the confirmation of that appointment.

The
Servitia.

Originally the *servitia* appear to have been presents
made voluntarily to the Pope by prelates on the occasion
of the papal confirmation of their appointment. But, as
time went on, these gifts came to be expected, and at
length, seemingly in this thirteenth century, the payments which had been free became fixed *servitia, communia*,
or *minuta*. The former payment, the *common services*,
which was the principal amount exacted, was divided
between the treasury (camera) of the Pope and that of
the cardinals,[3] the latter, the *petty services*, was divided

[1] This taxing of the revenues of the clergy originated with the
imposition of the *Crusade* tax at the beginning of the thirteenth century.
The tithe was levied on the valuation (taxatio) of the benefice which
had been officially made, i.e. after it had been " taxatus ad decimam ",
or simply " taxatus ", i.e. the tax was not levied on the gross revenue
of the incumbent, but on what was reckoned to remain after the
necessary charges on it had been deducted.

[2] Rostand, a papal collector of tithes in 1255, wrote : " Inter-
pretatione sedis Apostolicæ nomine proventuum ecclesiasticorum
intelligantur obventiones provenientes de baroniis ac maneriis, ecclesiis
et personis ecclesiasticis deputatis." *Annal. de Burton*, ap. *Annal.
Monast.*, i, p. 354, *R. S.*

[3] On July 18, 1289, Nicholas IV. decreed that the cardinals were to

among the officials of the Pope and the college of cardinals.[1] The payments became more systematized and more important as the appointment or confirmation of bishops and abbots fell, with the advance of the thirteenth century, more and more into the hands of the Pope.[2] Finally Urban V. decreed that all bishops and abbots with an annual income respectively of two hundred and one hundred florins should pay *servitia*, which in the thirteenth century amounted generally to a third of the annual income.[3]

Innocent, then, for his revenues had to rely mostly on the income tax of one-tenth or one-twentieth or some other proportion of their revenues which he levied on the clergy, on Provisions, and on *Servitia*. In connexion with these taxes it cannot be said that any of them were unjust in themselves, and if they had been managed with moderation might never have been objected to. But the calls on the incomes of the clergy were made too frequently and Provisions, useful as they were to reward merit, or to

How far Innocent's taxation was just.

share the revenues of the states of the Church, in addition, no doubt, to the *Servita*, with the Pope. Ep. 468 ap. Theiner, *Cod. diplom.*, i, 304.

[1] The first mention of the *petty services* is said to be in a letter of Urban IV., of Oct. 4, 1263, in which he says that Werner, Archbishop of Maintz, promised Alexander IV., among other things, 50 marks, " pro familia Papæ." *Cf.* Clergeac, p. 157, and Rodenberg, Epp. *Rom. Pont.*, iii, p. 476, n. 8.

[2] It is believed that the appointment or confirmation of all archbishops and of most of the bishops was in the hands of the Pope by the close of the thirteenth century.

[3] Lunt, *F.S.*, p. 285. The same author notes that the amount of the *petty services* was determined in each case by the number of cardinals sharing the *common services*. They got half the *common services* (see *Calendar of Pap. Registers*, i, 376, for an example), and the share of a single cardinal was the sum to be paid for the *petty services*. *Cf.* also Father Coleman's *Introduction* to *De Annatis Hiberniæ*, Dundalk, 1909. It was not till the following century under Clement V., and not under John XXII. as Coleman supposes (*cf.* Samaran, *Fiscalité*, p. 23) that the tax known as *Annates* was levied in behalf of the Pope.

secure incumbents faithful to the Roman Church,[1] or to check the undue interference of Kings in episcopal elections or in spiritual concerns generally,[2] were so abused either through the importunities of suitors [3] or through nepotism on the part of Popes or temporal rulers that they were abolished by the Council of Trent.

The Popes were, indeed, fully conscious that the financial calls which they were making on the ultramontane Churches were excessive. They could only fall back upon the fact that it was the loss of the States of the Church, and of the revenue of the Kingdom of the two Sicilies that forced them to tax the universal church.[4]

[1] This was very important during turbulent times in regard to the greater sees. Hence John XXII., in reserving to himself the appointment of the sees of the province of Ravenna for two years, says he did so : " ut per providentiam Sedis Apostolicæ de pastoribus et prælatis in partibus disponeretur prædictis, qui Nobis et Ecclesiæ Romanæ devoti et fideles existerent, et aliis scirent et possent præesse utiliter et prodesse." Ep. of March 27, 1325, ap. *Reg. Vat.*, t. 113, f. 174 to, n. 1031 ; Cod. B., 69–70, quoted in full by Lux, *Constit. App.*, p. 63. *Cf.* a general reservation of benefices in Lombardy ordered by Clement IV. to secure the appointment of persons " devoted to the Roman Church ". *Reg.*, n. 631, May 28, 1268, ed. Jordan.

[2] Hence they were very useful in Ireland as they furnished the Popes with a weapon to combat the Black Statute of Kilkenny, which forbade the granting to an Irishman of a benefice in the English parts of the country. *Cf.* ep. of Honorius III., Apr. 26, 1224, ap. *Royal Letters of Henry III.*, i, p. 541, *R. S.*

[3] This importunity is brought out by Benedict XII. in abolishing the provisions, reservations, etc., granted by his predecessors. " Experimento didicimus quod per *importunam instanciam* multi hactenus a nonnullis . . . Rom. pontificibus in multis . . . ecclesiis . . . super collacionibus, provisionibus, reservacionibus (etc.) . . . multas . . . apostolicas literas impetrarunt, ex quorum impetrancium multitudine eedem ecclesie sunt plurimum pregravate." Ep. of Dec. 18, 1335, Cod. B., ff. 94–7, given in full ap. Lux, *l.c.*, p. 71.

[4] Urban IV. ep. May 3, 1264, ap. Rodenberg, iii, n. 594, p. 588, wrote that if the Roman Church recovered these revenues : " Nec oporteret eandem Rom. ecclesiam sic frequenter ad Ultramontanas ecclesias pro ejus necessitatibus habere recursum ipsasque totiens aggravare. Sufficerent enim si suum patrimonum et regni census ejusdem, etc."

All these various taxes due to the Holy See were The Collectors of the Taxes.
sometimes collected by one of the permanent resident
authorities in a country, as for instance, by one of its
bishops. Thus, about the year 1220, Guttorm, archbishop
of Norway, transmitted to St. Victor's in Paris taxes "due
to the Roman Church" from Norway,[1] while Pandulf
was instructed to send the various taxes due from
England to the Templars and Hospitallers in the same
city.[2] Sometimes too, those who had been appointed
to collect the moneys that were raised for the Crusades
were also commissioned to collect the sums due to the
Pope. Generally, however, special collectors were
appointed [3] who were supplied with lists of the taxes
due to the Holy See, and of the names of those from whom
the taxes were due.[4] Not unfrequently these special
collectors were Italian merchant bankers (mercatores,
campsores) who were used by the Popes not merely to
transmit to Rome the sums collected for them, but also
to collect those sums.[5]

These collectors had to take an oath to do their duty
faithfully, carefully abstaining from every kind of
injustice or oppression.[6] In due course the head collector
—the collector general—had to give an account of his
stewardship to the cardinal chamberlain (camerarius)

[1] Ep. of Honorius III., Jan. 12, 1221, ap. Potthast, n. 6480.

[2] Ep. of Aug. 18; 1220, ap. *ib.*, n. 6331.

[3] On one of these, a certain John Anglicus (English), who was Provincial in Saxony in 1231, and in England in 1256, see A. P., *Collectanea
Anglo-Minoritica*, p. 65 ff., London, 1726.

[4] *Cf.* the lists of taxes due from Spain, etc., supplied to Master
Synitius " a cleric of our treasury " (camera) from " the registers of the
Roman Church ". Ep. of March 21, 1264, ap. *Reg. Caméral* of Urban IV.,
ap. *Reg.*, i, p. 131 ff. ed. Guiraud. *Cf.* Daux, *Le Cens*, p. 69.

[5] Clement IV. often used them to collect his dues. *Cf.* Jordan,
Le St.-Siége, p. 8.

[6] Cadier, *Le registre de Jean XXI.*, n. 105, Feb. 13, 1277.

assisted by notaries as chancellors and by bankers (mercatores) as accountants (rationarii).[1]

When the various sums had been collected they were at times conveyed to Rome by the collectors themselves. Owing, however, to the great risk which they ran of being robbed, they generally paid over the moneys to some Italian merchant bankers, especially to those who had been appointed bankers to the Holy See,[2] or put them in the hands of the Templars. The sacred character of these latter and their martial prowess made them very suitable depositaries of sums of money, as they could easily dispatch them safely by their knights who were constantly on the road from one of their houses to another, or from one country to another as they passed backwards and forwards on their way to or from the Holy Land.[3]

But from the time of Alexander IV. the Popes almost always employed the merchant bankers, especially those of Siena, to transmit the moneys due to them.[4] It was

---

[1] Re, *La comp. dei Riccardi*, p. 91, and he cites in proof *Collettoria*, 213, c. 4, Archiv. Vaticano. " A.D. 1281, pontificatus d. Martini P. IV anno primo, mensis Augusti die 26 coram venerabili viro d. Berardo d. Pape Camerario, presentibus magistro Bernardo notario . . . mag. Paulo . . . notario camere, Hicto et Ribellato de Florentia ac Thura de Senis mercatoribus camere per rationem redditam per . . . d. Berardum de Podio . . . superintendentem ad colligendum decimam Terre Sancte, etc."

[2] They are spoken of as " Cameræ sedis apostolicæ mercatores ". *Cf.* e.g. *Reg. Nich., IV.*, nn. 96–100. Potthast, 18, 201. These Italian merchant companies came to England in the first instance to purchase wool. *Cf.* W. E. Rhodes, " The Italian Bankers in England and their loans to Edward I. and Edward II.," ap. *Historical Essays*, ed. Tout, Manchester, 1907.

[3] Occasionally the knights used their own discretion as to the way in which the sums entrusted to them were to be used, and we find Honorius III. blaming Aymar, the treasurer of the Knights Templars at Paris, for transgressing his orders and sending money to the Holy Land, whereas the Pope had exhausted his treasury in sending competent supplies himself. Ep. of Aug. 6, 1220, ap. Potthast, n. 6321.

[4] Ep. of Alex. IV., Oct. 12, 1255, ap. Rymer, i, p. 568 f. *Cf.* e.g. *Regist. Urb. IV.*, nn. 10, 48, 51, 52, vol. i, p. 4 ff. ed. Guiraud.

natural, therefore, that the Popes should favour the bankers (especially as they kept representatives in the papal household), and should strive to obtain for them the repayment of their loans.[1] And so we find Innocent IV. threatening the archbishop of Cashel with ecclesiastical penalties, if repayment of borrowed money was not made to Boniface Bonsignori, Aldebrand Ildebrandi, and their partners, merchants of Siena.[2] This firm was employed by Innocent himself, and one of its members, Boniface Bonsignori, with his brother Orlando, was one of the Pope's friends,[3] and as such was often used by the Sienese to forward the business which they had with his patron.[4]

From many points of view, perhaps indeed in the main, these *mercatores* were very useful to the country, and their protection by the Popes did much to improve and to simplify what may be called international financial relations. They relieved the financial difficulties of our Kings, and developed the trade of the land not only by the example of their business methods, but by the money which they circulated.[5] But not all the firms were honest ones, nor were the honest ones always honest.[6] They at times cheated even the Popes themselves,[7] and threatened

Mercatores Caursini.

---

[1] *Cf.* Bliss, *Calendar*, i, pp. 124 and 309.

[2] *Ib.*, p. 305. Ep. of Sept. 9, 1254. *Cf.* a similar threat to Margaret, countess of Flanders. Ep. May 8, 1254, ap. Rod., iii, 254.

[3] *Cf.* epp. Feb. 25 and July 18, 1253, nn. 190 and 222 ed. Rodenberg, vol. iii.

[4] *Cf.* Jordan, *De Mercatoribus*, pp. 10–11.

[5] E. A. Bond, " The Italian Moneylenders," ap. *Archæologia*, vol. xxviii (1840), p. 207.

[6] Hence we find our King Henry III. ordering the mayor and sheriffs of London to seize some of the goods of Dentesalve, a Florentine banker, for not transmitting to Rome money which had been given him to send there. *Close Rolls*, Henry III., i, p. 528.

[7] Jordan, *l.c.*, p. 15.

to seize the possessions of their very churches,[1] and at times
made such immoderate demands that they had to be
checked by them.[2]   Especially as moneylenders were they
often hated with justice, and their usuries were often without justice referred to the Popes, who employed and protected them.   Under the name of Caursini or Caorsini,[3]
they are frequently much abused. Matthew Paris accuses
some of them of clipping the coin, and of being worse
than the Jews in their usuries,[4] and even a man like
Grosseteste could say stinging things about them.   On
one occasion we are told that the chamberlain (treasurer)
of the Pope demanded from the Bishop a fee of a thousand
pounds when he was visiting the curia, and told him that
he could borrow the money from the merchants.   Grosseteste, however, replied that he would not give them an
occasion of committing mortal sins by their usuries, but
that if he reached England in safety, he would deposit
the sum in the Temple at London.[5]

[1] *Cf.* ep. Feb. 5, 1256, of Alexander IV. urging the bishop of Hereford
to collect the tenth and to pay the merchant bankers the money they
had advanced to Henry for the Sicilian expedition, as they were very
importunate with him, and were ready to lay their avaricious hands
on the possessions of the churches of the city. Rymer, i, 581.

[2] Jordan, p. 9, n.

[3] Supposed to be derived from Cahors, whose citizens according to
Dante, *Inf.*, xi, ll. 45–50, were usurers.   Matthew Paris, iii, 188 f.,
gives 1229 as the date of the arrival of the C. in England, and *ib.*.
p. 328 ff., gives a form of the document used by the Caursini to bind
their debtors.   Interest was charged " as a recompense for losses ".
In fact Innocent IV. himself declared that at times " when pre-
occupied with much business or overcome by the importunities of
creditors " he had given a sort of sanction to " losses, expenses, and
interest ".   " Dirigimus scripta nostra in quibus interdum variis solici-
tudinibus occupati, nonnunquam vero improba victi creditorum ipsorum
instantia, de dampuis, expensis et interesse fecimus mentionem."
Then, denouncing " the pernicious vice of usury ", he would appear
to grant that there were cases in which interest could lawfully be
charged. *Cf. Reg.*, i, n. 42, p. 11.

[4] *Chron.*, v, 16, 245, 362, 404 ff.

[5] Eccleston, *De Adventu*, p. 115 ed. Little.

It was to no purpose that both Kings and Popes denounced those who practised usury. The Caursini were too useful to be crushed, and their oppressions continued, for they knew how to take advantage of that principle in Canon Law that a company (societas) could not be guilty of usury, but only individuals.[1]

This much may, perhaps, suffice to make the subject of the papal taxation in the thirteenth century more readily intelligible. More will have to be said on the matter when we come to the Avignon Popes, as they not only greatly extended the system of taxation which they found in vogue, but also devised new taxes altogether.

Turning now to the financial dealings of Innocent with England, we need not be surprised to find, after what has just been said, that they began early in his reign. Crushed by a debt which was said to amount to about three hundred thousand pounds,[2] and constantly robbed by Frederick's agents who were guarding the roads and seizing moneys that were being sent to him,[3] Innocent soon experienced the pinch of poverty. He accordingly sent (Jan., 1244) as nuncio to England one of the clerks of his treasury or *camera*, one Master Martin, in order to collect all arrears of moneys due to Rome, and to try to raise a further supply of money for his needs, or " rather for those of the whole Church which was attacked by so powerful an enemy ".[4]

Master Martin sent to England for money, 1244.

---

[1] R. J. Whitwell, " Italian Bankers and the English Crown," p. 209, ap. *Transacs. of the English Hist. Soc.*, 1903, quoting A. Pelagius († June, 1352), *De planctu Eccles.* ii, 46 R. (1474), Ulm.

[2] Mat. Par., *Chron.*, iv, p. 429 f.

[3] *Ib.*, iv, 278, an. 1243. *Cf.* M. P., *Hist. Anglorum*, ii, p. 478, where he says that Frederick strove to injure the Pope to the detriment of the whole Church : " Frethericus . . . variis (Innocentium) lascessivit injuriis, et multimodis insidiis, in ecclesiæ universalis dedecus et nocumentum, circumvenire nitebatur."

[4] *Ib.*, *H. A.*, ii, 478-9. In this instance, as in so many others, Paris in this work modifies the passionate language of his *Greater Chronicle*.

The nuncio was the bearer of letters to the bishops and abbots of England in which Innocent said that their previous loyalty to the Apostolic See made him hope that they would help him now in his need. The sums hitherto collected under the authority of his predecessor had not been sufficient to free the Church from the debts which it had contracted for the defence of the Catholic faith, the liberty of the Church, and its Patrimony. Urged by necessity, he appealed to them to help him to meet the heavy debts which were pressing on the Church by supplying him with that sum for which Master Martin would ask them in his name. Should they comply with his request, he would be able to praise their devotion and " not be compelled to proceed in this matter in any other way. Given at the Lateran on January 7, in the first year of our Pontificate ".[1]

Armed with these letters, and with the King's permission, Master Martin proceeded to ask or, according to Matthew Paris, to demand pecuniary assistance for the Pope. He soon, however, rendered himself very unpopular by the methods which he employed in raising money. Exacting excessive procurations for himself, he refused to accept gifts of less value than thirty marks (twenty pounds), enforced his demands by the use of excommunication and other spiritual penalties, and, laying hands on rich prebends, gave one of them to one of the Pope's nephews, who was a mere boy.[2] At times

Cf. *Ann. de Dunstap.*, ap. *Annal. Monast.*, iii, 166, *R. S.*, and *Annals of Tewkesbury*, i, 132, *ib*.

[1] Ap. Mat. Par., iv, 369 f. *Cf*. Innocent's letter to the archbishop of Athens, etc., July 13, 1243, in which he says that the Apostolic See : "ipsius non solum in mobilibus bonis suis pene penitus sit exausta, sed et maximis quoque debitis obligata." Ap. *Reg.*, i, p. 6.

[2] Mat. Par., *Chron.*, iv, 284, 368, 379, 416. We have here an illustration of one of the methods by which Matthew Paris produces exaggerated impressions where he may be telling the exact truth. In no less than four different places, separated by considerable intervals, does he

the nuncio's arbitrary measures were opposed by deeds just as lawless, and on one occasion in the diocese of Lincoln, his agents were ill-treated. Martin at once applied for advice on the matter to the diocesan, Grosseteste, who was helping him to raise the money required by the Pope.[1] The Bishop, believing that the nuncio's overbearing conduct was largely responsible for the outrage, replied indeed with great courtesy and justice, but at the same time not without giving him a warning as to his future conduct. Being anxious, he said, for the honour of the Pope and for that of his nuncio, and knowing the holiness of the Pope, and believing in that of his nuncio, he was convinced that even the mere appearance of wrong should be absent from all that they did. Hence, while saying that the perpetrators of the outrage ought to be punished, he advised Martin always to produce his authority for his acts, to use tact in the interpretation of his mandates, and lastly to employ argument before the application of force.[2]

We have seen that, in the letters which Innocent addressed to the clergy of England, he had called upon them to supply the sum for which Martin should

Martin's formal demand.

tell the same story of the coming of Master Martin, and of the means he used to raise money. How far, however, he was telling the exact truth is hard to tell. In one place he says (p. 369) that Martin did not get any encouragement from the King (" nullam de regis adjutorio spem reportans," p. 369), and in another that the King favoured him (" Rex quoque parti suæ favit . . . forte propter remunerationem," p. 416).

[1] Ep. 119, p. 340, *R. S.*, to King Henry, who had expressed his astonishment that " tallagium de viris religiosis et clericis . . . colligere ad opus d. Papæ proponimus . . . secundum formam a magistro Martino d. Papæ nuncio . . . traditam." He tells the King that, if he did not help the Pope in his present dire needs, he would not be honouring his father, and assures him that such as advise him to oppose the raising of money for the Pope have no care for the royal honour.

[2] Ep. 106, p. 315 ff.

ask them. The nuncio accordingly appealed for ten thousand marks.[1]

Unfortunately for Master Martin, his demand immediately followed one from the King. For weeks Henry had been trying to induce the clerical and lay magnates to grant him pecuniary assistance, and at length on February 22, 1244, had only succeeded in inducing them to grant him a scutage of twenty shillings towards a dower for his eldest daughter.[2] When the nuncio, who had arrived in England just about that time,[3] heard that a grant had been made to the King, he summoned the clergy together immediately, and laid before them the Pope's demand for ten thousand marks. Addressing them as well-beloved sons of the Roman Church, he urged them, as they had helped their King, to help their spiritual father who was struggling against the rebels of the universal Church.[4] The clergy, however, who felt that they were between the hammer of the King and the anvil of the Pope,[5] at first put off giving a definite reply to the nuncio's demands on the ground that the King was ill, and that some of the bishops were absent.[6] The nuncio accordingly bade them meet again in Lent.

Meanwhile the clergy were still further moved to resistance by the King's forbidding such of the prelates as held baronies direct from him, to pledge their lay fees to the Roman Church, as he would then lose his dues (servitium debitum) from them.[7] Moreover, Walter de Ocra, an envoy from the emperor Frederick, appeared in London, and in his master's name urged the English

---

[1] Mat. Par., iv, p. 369. The mark was worth 13s. 4d. or two-thirds of a pound.

[2] Mat. Par., iv, 368, 372.

[3] The *Annals of Dunstable*, p. 166, *R. S.*, say that he came about Easter (Apr. 3). But a letter of Innocent (March 3, 1244) which concerns Martin would seem to imply that he was in England then. *Calendar*, i, p. 207.

[4] M. P., iv, 374.   [5] *Ib.*, p. 371.   [6] *Ib.*, p. 375.   [7] *Ib.*

people not to give pecuniary help to the Pope, haughtily declaring that any moneys sent to the Pope would be added to the imperial treasury, and that if the Emperor's request was disregarded, he would severely punish any of the English whom he could find in his dominions.[1]

When then a number of the prelates met the nuncio for the second time, they again refused to grant the subsidy that was asked. The country, they declared, was impoverished by war, and if, after having complied with the request for aid made by the agent of Gregory IX., they were to grant that made by Innocent's nuncio, a precedent would be created. Besides, it was said that the Pope was about to call a General Council, and the prelates of the realm would be put to great expense to attend it. And, " if our holy mother the Roman Church is burdened with debt it is right . . . that aid should be given to her by all her children assembled in the great Council." [2] *It is referred to the coming General Council.*

Unable, therefore, to get the ten thousand marks, Martin proceeded so to exercise the right of Provisions as to enrage the lay patrons of the livings. Accordingly a number of the nobles took upon themselves to order the seaports to be watched to prevent the introduction into the Kingdom of papal letters dealing with money. In consequence of this, an envoy from the Pope was seized at Dover. His letters were confiscated, and he himself lodged in the Castle. However, on the protest of Master Martin to the King, the latter ordered the envoy to be released at once, and the letters to be handed to the nuncio.[3] *The nobles order the ports to be watched, 1245.*

Despite this support given by Henry to the nuncio, there is no doubt that he frequently opposed him himself. This is clear from a letter of Innocent addressed to him *The King opposes Martin.*

---

[1] *Ib.*, p. 372, and also p. 313.

[2] *Ib.*, p. 376. "Et quod principaliter tangit ab omnibus comprobetur, ut sic melius ecclesia relevetur, et singuli minus præ. graventur."

[3] *Ib.*, p. 417.

(Apr. 10, 1245). The Pope declared that, as he was anxious to preserve the King's rights, it was only proper that the King should show himself a true son of the Roman Church, and have a care for her interests. But, he continued, he had heard that, at the suggestion of the nobles, the King had forbidden the nuncio Martin to make certain provisions by papal authority until he had received definite instructions from Rome regarding them. Though anxious to oblige the King, the Pope insisted that he must reward those who had helped him in his difficulties, and so begged the King not to hinder him from recompensing them with benefices. He concluded, however, in the hope of pacifying the nobility, by assuring the King that he had no intention of presenting to benefices of which laymen were the patrons.[1]

An inquiry is made as to the total of the revenues held by foreign clerks.

The opposition of the magnates of the realm was not, however, to be easily quelled, and they soon further roused that of the fickle King by impressing upon him that enormous ecclesiastical revenues were held by Italians, and that a great deal of money therefore found its way out of the country. To verify the truth of this assertion, Henry caused an inquiry to be made as to the exact amount of the revenue drawn from ecclesiastical sources that was held by Italians in England. On the first occasion of his informing us of this fact, Matthew Paris avers that it was found that foreign clerics drew annually from the country "sixty thousand marks, a sum more than equal to the annual revenue of the whole of England ".[2] Unfortunately but little reliance can be placed on the figures of Matthew Paris in this matter. For if it is not strictly true that the revenue of the

[1] Ep. ap. Rymer, i, 256, Rec.

[2] " Ad quam summam non attingit reditus annus totius regni Angliæ," iv, p. 418. One MS. has 40,000 marks. Cf. iv, 443. According to Mitchell, Studies in taxation, the revenue in King John's time was barely 40,000 marks (p. 16), but in 1242 it was 67,500 marks. Ib., p. 238.

country was at this period less than sixty thousand marks, it is still less true that if the foreigners drew sixty thousand marks, they drew " more than seventy thousand ", and that the last-named sum was more than three times the revenue of the King.[1]

However, as it was more than once stated to the Pope more or less officially that the revenues held by Italians in England amounted to 60,000 [2] or over 50,000 marks,[3] there is no doubt that there was just ground for complaint. Accordingly, a letter of protest was drawn up to be presented to the Pope during the session of the Council,

Master Martin leaves England, 1245.

[1] " Reditus regis merus non ad ejus (70,000 marks) partem tertiam computatur." *Chron.*, v, 355, ad an. 1252. If, however, we cannot rely on all the figures of Matthew Paris, can we accept his statement about the 60,000 marks (iv, p. 418) as it is repeated in the letter of the English to the Pope at the Council of Lyons ? *Ib.*, iv, 443. If we do accept the calculation, it would mean that we must suppose that the foreign churchmen held a very large proportion indeed of all the ecclesiastical revenues of England. It is a despairing task to try to work out mediaeval figures to uniform results, but we may make some rough deductions from the numbers, round and otherwise, given us by Matthew Paris and others. Paris, for instance, tells us (v, 282) that the tithes of the revenues of the clergy and people of England amounted to 600,000 marks in three years, or 200,000 in one year. From the fact that the clergy were supposed to contribute a third of the general tithe, we may form some idea of what their tenth amounted to, and so what was their total revenue, if we bear in mind that the taxes were levied on something under the full revenues, and that incomes below a certain sum were not taxed at all. Hence in very round numbers we may say that the tithe of the clergy was 60,000 marks (£40,000), and their income 600,000 marks (£400,000). With their 60,000 marks then, the foreign ecclesiastics would draw a tenth of the whole church revenue of England. But according to Stubbs, *Constitutional Hist. of England*, ii, p. 549, the total revenue of the clergy in 1291 was £200,000. If that is the case, then the foreign ecclesiastics would have drawn a fifth of the whole ecclesiastical revenue. It is hard, however, to believe that they drew a tenth, still less a fifth, of our ecclesiastical revenues. Matthew Paris is assuredly not to be trusted on money matters.

[2] M. P., iv, 418.

[3] Rymer, i, 471 f., ep. Inn. IV., May 22, 1253, wrongly assigned in the first ed. of Rymer to 1252.

which he had summoned for the year 1245. At the same
time, Master Martin was brusquely informed (June 30)
by an agent of a number of the barons that, if he did
not leave the kingdom within three days, he would be
cut to pieces. The nuncio, who was staying in " the
new temple ", in which, under the care of the Knights
Templars, he was storing the moneys he had received,
was struck with terror, and hurried to the King. From
that weakling, however, who was willing enough to use
a papal envoy when it suited him, he got no help. Henry
assured him that the barons were so irritated with his
interference with their rights that he had had great
difficulty in restraining them from tearing him limb from
limb. Martin next asked the King to give him a safe-
conduct out of the Kingdom, and was greeted with the
testy reply : " May the devil take you to hell." [1]

Setting this dialogue down as so much idle gossip,
retailed by Matthew Paris, we may accept his statement
that Master Martin left England in a hurry, that some
of the Italians holding livings in the country were in
great alarm for their safety, and that some usurious
Caursins or bankers also left the country.

A protest is
sent to the
Council of
Lyons, 1245.</div> Difficulties did not end with the departure of the nuncio,
and he left behind him one, Master Philip, to continue
his work of raising money.[2] A deputation, with the letter
of protest just mentioned,[3] was therefore dispatched to
lay the grievances of the English before the Council of
Lyons.[4] Before this assembly the envoys professed their

---

[1] Mat. Par., iv, 421.

[2] *Ib.* The same author, resting as so often on gossip, says that
Innocent broke out into a furious rage when Martin told him how he had
been treated. *Ib.*, iv, pp. 422–3.

[3] It was addressed : " Reverendo in Christo patri Innocentio, Dei
gratia summo pontifici, magnates et universitas regni Angliæ recom-
mendationem cum pedum osculo beatorum." *Ib.*, p. 441.

[4] Henry reminded the English, Irish, and Gascon prelates who were
going to the Council to be careful not to do anything at it which would
compromise his kingly rights. Rymer, i, 434.

devotion to their mother the Roman Church but begged that the rights of the patrons of livings should not be interfered with by the abuse of Provisions, that Italians who did not fulfil the duties attached to the livings, but carried the revenues out of the country, should not be granted them, and that the English might in future be spared such pecuniary inflictions as had been practised on the country by Master Martin, without, they were sure, the knowledge of the Pope. The envoys also protested against the payment of the tribute promised by King John, and against the abuse of the clause " Notwith-standing ", so often introduced into the papal letters.[1]

Though the envoys pressed for an immediate answer to their protest, the Pope declared that the questions raised by it were too important for that, but he promised to send a reply as soon as possible.[2] No reply, however, was forthcoming during the course of the Council, as Innocent had too many other important matters to attend to. The English envoys, therefore, left Lyons in great anger, declaring that they would not suffer King John's tribute to be paid, nor themselves to be deprived of their rights of patronage.[3] Innocent, however, on his side insisted that the bishops should affix their seals to the " tribute charter " of King John in order that its binding force might be reaffirmed.[4]

Though no definite answer was given to the English protest by the Council or by the Pope during its session,

Effect of the English protest.

---

[1] *Ib.*, p. 440–5.

[2] *Ib.*, p. 445. he *Annals of Cesena*, ap. *R. I. SS.*, xiv, p. 1100, say that the English envoys appealed " to a future Pope " on this matter. But our native historians say nothing of this extreme measure. The belief of our countrymen as to the position in the Church of the " one supreme pontiff who by divine institution presides over all the nations of the earth " is at this period well stated by Adam Marsh, ap. *Mon. Francisc.*, i, 414 ff.

[3] So at least says Mat. Par., iv, pp. 478–9. If the nobles ever made these declarations they did not act up to them.

[4] *Ib.*

it is thought that some of the decrees of the Council
show its influence on them. It was proclaimed for
instance that legates had no power, in virtue of their office,
to confer benefices, and that excommunications were not
to be fulminated without due consideration and without
the fulfilment of various formalities.[1]

Moreover, soon after the closing of the Council,
Innocent addressed a resolution to the Prelates of England
as well as to the clerical and lay patrons of livings. It
annulled the suspensions of the patrons' rights of
presentation issued by Master Martin, except in special
cases which were not to be more than twelve in number,
and it restored to the patrons of the livings their powers
of collation to them (August 3, 1245).[2] This Innocent
did, as he declared, because he was unwilling that the
English should be injured by himself or by his agents,
inasmuch as they were inflamed with "a fervent
devotion" towards the Apostolic See.[3] Further, he
appears to have reduced the subsidy of ten thousand
marks asked for in his behalf by Master Martin to six
thousand.[4]

Renewed
protest from
England
against
Provisions,
1246.

Unfortunately these decrees remained inoperative,
either on account of the issue of fresh grants by the
Pope containing the clause: "Notwithstanding"

[1] Mat. Par., iv, 462, 467. Cf. Gasquet, Henry III., c. 13.

[2] M. P., iv, 518 and 520, or Rymer, i, 262, R. In the following year,
June 10, 1247, Innocent put an end also to another abuse in connexion
with Provisions. It sometimes happened that those to whom "provisions" had been granted took livings of much higher value than
those which they had been granted. If, for instance, a living of fifty
marks had been granted, and one of a hundred became vacant, it was
taken. Innocent declared that, if a living worth more than five marks
in excess of what had been granted was taken, the whole grant became
void. Ep. ap. M. P., vi, p. 133.

[3] "Fervens Anglorum meretur devotio, ut eos Apostolica sedes,
tamquam speciales filios . . . favore ipsos muniat oportuno." Ib.,
p. 521.

[4] Cf. supra, p. 247 f., and infra, p. 256.

previous concessions, or because they were set aside by
the papal agents. Accordingly, on the summons of the
King, the clerical and lay magnates of the realm met
" at a general parliament in London " (March 18, 1246) to
consider the papal taxation grievances.[1] Especial indigna-
tion was expressed that in several places one Italian
succeeded another who were ignorant of the language of
the country, and had no concern about improving their
parishes.[2] After the questions of extraordinary tithes,
Provisions, and the rest had been discussed, it was
decided to make a further effort to get a final settlement
of the grievances of the nation by fresh letters and fresh
envoys. A number of letters from the King,[3] from the
bishops,[4] the abbots,[5] and from the nobles[6] were
dispatched to the Pope or to the cardinals. All the letters
express the great love of the English people for their
mother " the holy Roman Church ", and all earnestly
implore the Pope to put an end to taxation practices
which are injuring the country and alienating the
affections of the people from the Holy See.[7] On the
day after Easter (April 9) the prior of Wenlock and a
number of others set out to present these letters to the

---

[1] M. P., iv, 518, 526, *Ann. de Dunstap.*, p. 169, *Ann. de Burton*,
p. 278 ff.

[2] " Qui (the Italians) idioma nescientes, nec prædicant, nec eleemo-
synas faciunt, libros et vestimenta nec inveniunt, nec ecclesiis, sicut
deceret, deserviunt." *A. de. D., ib. Cf.* M. P., iv, 527 ff.

[3] Epp. of March 28, 1246, ap. Mat. P., iv, 534–5.

[4] *Ib.*, p. 529.

[5] *Ib.*, p. 531.

[6] *Ib.*, p. 533. See also Rymer, i, 265, R.

[7] The King said : "Novit Ille qui nihil ignorat quod matrem nostram
Romanam ecclesiam semper habemus in visceribus dilectionis sinceræ."
The bishops say that " idem regnum (England) sacrosanctæ Romanæ
ecclesiæ specialiter extiterit devotum". The abbots and priors speak
of the English Church " quæ scarosanctæ Romanæ ecclesiæ membrum
speciale". And the barons salute the Pope as " the chariot of Israel
and the driver thereof ". 2 Kings ii, 12.

Pope,[1] and it was meanwhile forbidden to pay him any tallage until their return.[2]

England is called upon to pay the Holy Land tax, etc.

Before the royal envoys could reach Lyons, there arrived in England a papal letter dated March 24, calling on the English clergy to pay the subsidy of six thousand marks which they had agreed to at the Council of Lyons in place of the ten thousand asked for by Master Martin.[3] Innocent also decreed about this time that the property of all clerics who died intestate should be confiscated for the use of the Pope.[4] The English clergy were moreover expected to pay the one-twentieth for the Holy Land which had been imposed by the last General Council, but to which the English deputies had objected on the grounds that the tax was to be collected by the Pope's nominees, and that the people suspected that moneys which they had subscribed for the Holy Land had been diverted by the Roman curia to other purposes.[5]

Henry forbids the payment of these levies *ad interim*.

Pending, however, Innocent's reply to the protest of the King and Parliament of London, Henry forbade the introduction into the country of papal bulls dealing in any way with the raising of money,[6] and, as we have already stated, he also forbade the collecting of any of the moneys already ordered or the sending out of the Kingdom of any which had been previously collected.[7]

The Pope offers a compromise.

Meanwhile the English envoys were putting the national protest before the Pope, and they at length succeeded in making an impression upon him. Accordingly on

[1] M. P., iv, 551.

[2] *Ib.*, iv, 554.

[3] Ep. of March 24, 1246, ap. M. P., iv, 555.

[4] *Ib.*, p. 552. The opposition made to this enactment caused its withdrawal soon after (1247). *Cf. Ib.*, p. 604.

[5] *Ib.*, pp. 473 and 521 f.

[6] *Ib.*, p. 510.

[7] *Ib.*, pp. 554 and 557. Unfortunately Matthew Paris is our fullest authority for this period, but his assertions or facts are arranged in such a disorderly manner that it is exeedingly difficult to put them in logical order.

June 12, Innocent addressed a letter to Henry in which he says that he cannot agree to the remission of the twentieth as that tax for the Holy Land was imposed upon all Christendom by the General Council. With regard, however, to the question of Provisions, although he cannot avoid their use, as he must reward those who are standing by him in his adversity, he promises so to moderate their use in England as to content the King.[1]

When the English envoys laid this letter before an assembly of the King and nobles at Winchester (July 7, 1246), it was deemed unsatisfactory,[2] and by proclamation in the different towns the King forbade the giving of any money to the Pope. But Henry was now going too far. Many in England, including the King's brother Richard, duke of Cornwall, were interested in the Crusade. Consequently when more severe letters came from the Pope, Henry gave way,[3] and not only were moneys collected for the Crusade,[4] and for the Empire of Constantinople,[5] but even the subsidy of six thousand marks was raised for the needs of the Pope.[6] Moreover in the following year the clergy at Oxford agreed to give the Pope a further sum of eleven thousand marks.[7]

Henry at last gives way, 1246.

---

[1] Rymer, i, 441 f. *Cf.* Mat. Par., iv, 550 and 598.

[2] M. P., iv, 560. Paris even assures us that the Pope had said to the English envoys : " The King of the English, who is now kicking like Frederick, has his own ideas. I too have mine, and I will follow them."

[3] *Ib.* Paris goes on to say (p. 578) that, when Innocent heard of this opposition of the King, he talked of putting England under an interdict, but was persuaded not to do so by the English Cistercian cardinal John Tolet, who begged him not to bring on the Church the hatred of England.

[4] For Grosseteste's co-operation in the raising of this tax see his ep. of Aug. 1, 1247, ap. M. P., vi, p. 134 ff., and v, p. 146.

[5] *Ib.*, iv, 564 f.

[6] M. P., iv, p. 577. Innocent at once sent the money to the Landgrave Henry.

[7] M. P., iv, 622–3, Apr. 7, 1247.

s

Almost enough has now been said to enable the reader
to realize what were the pecuniary relations between
England and Rome during the whole of Innocent's reign.
It only remains to add that these relations continued to
be much the same as those we have already described.
Innocent continued to make demands on the clergy for
tithes,[1] and to send fresh agents to collect money for him[2]
and the clergy continued to make protests at home,[3] and to
send them by letters to him,[4] while the King at times
opposed the levying of the taxes,[5] and at times later on,
in order that he might get money himself for his proposed
Crusade[6] or for his designs on the Kingdom of Sicily, he
supported the demands of the sovereign Pontiff.[7] The
Pope's excuse, which was no doubt in the main a just one,

---

[1] M. P., iv, 580, for a graduated tax, ad an. 1246. *Cf. Ann. de Burton*,
p. 277 f. and 280 f. Despite protests, *ib.*, pp. 590, 594–7, the prelates,
at length give way, and a sum of 11,000 was paid. *Ib.*, pp. 622–3.

[2] Two Franciscans are sent in 1247. *Ib.*, iv, 599. *Cf.* pp. 612 and 61 ff.
I have already remarked on the difficulty of putting the facts of Mat.
Paris in order. Even the author himself tells us that his *order* is "pre-
posterous "; but he excuses himself by a proverb to the effect that
the finger flies to where there is pain, i.e., as money was ever his trouble,
his pen perpetually touched on it. "Ordo quidem præposterus, sed
necessario commutatus, ubi enimdolor, ibi et digitus." P. 618. Marinus,
a papal chaplain, was sent in 1247, *ib.*, p. 601 ; and Master John Rosso
to Ireland, p. 602. The same year, though Paris speaks of it in 1250,
Berard de Nimpha collected money for the Crusade. *Ib.*, v, 146. *Cf.*
vi, 134 ; and in 1252 Master Albert collected money, etc., for himself
when he came to arrange about the Sicilian affair. *Ib.*, v, p. 347 f.

[3] The clergy declared that they believed that the Pope did not really
understand the state of the country, or else he would not make his
demands for money. M. P., iv, 581 ff. *Cf.* p. 594.

[4] M. P., iv, 595–6, ad an. 1247. Again " the English Church " professes its adherence to " the holy Roman Church our mother ".

[5] M. P., iv, 581.

[6] M. P., v, 282, 325. Even in 1247 Paris asserts that there was
connivance between the Pope and the King in the matter of getting
taxes out of the people. iv, 623.

[7] " Interim igitur tam Papæ quam regi in sua tirannide mutua,
favorem et fomentum præbenti, ira suscitatur." M. P., v, 334, ad
an. 1252.

was always the same—the Emperor's persecution of the Church, and the fact that he was contending for the general interests " of the Churches and churchmen ".[1]

The Pope's necessities, then, were the cause of the continuance of the pecuniary abuses of which the English clergy complained. Stirred up by the increasing evils caused by their continuance, bishop Grosseteste of Lincoln at length resolved that he would himself strongly put the grievances of the English Church before the Pope in person.[2] Utterly unlike Matthew Paris, the bishop had no obsession on the subject of money or of taxation. He had shown in his writings and in his conduct that he understood the needs of the Pope, and was willing to do what he could to meet those needs.[3] But he did not think that those needs should continue to be met by methods which experience showed led to the grossest abuses.

Accordingly, in 1250, he journeyed to Lyons, taking with him a carefully prepared written protest. He may perhaps have chosen that year because he thought that after Frederick's defeat at Parma, and his subsequent retreat to his Sicilian dominions, Innocent would not so much as before be embarrassed with difficulties of every kind. At any rate on May 13, with archdeacon Robert Marsh by his side, he stood before Innocent and his

The intervention of Grosseteste, 1250.

Grosseteste goes to the Pope, 1250.

---

[1] M. P., iv, 617–18.

[2] A little later he stoutly opposed unjust taxation attempted by the King. Mat. Par., v, 325.

[3] Stevenson in his excellent biography of Grosseteste says : " There is no reason for thinking that either then (1247) or at any other time, Grosseteste opposed a well-considered and *bona fide* demand by the Pope for his own necessities." P. 260. He also quotes Prothero as seeing this clearly. *Simon de Montfort*, p. 142. Hence he ascribes to " some tenth-rate hearsay evidence " (p. 283) the following expression which Paris puts into the bishop's mouth : " Money, money, how much power you have, especially in the Roman Curia." v, 98.

cardinals. While the Pope himself and two of the cardinals were furnished with copies of the memorandum (sermo), the cardinal deacon John of St. Nicholas "in carcere Tulliano", read it aloud from a fourth copy.

Grosseteste's
sermo to the
Pope.
The "sermon" began with a brief sketch of the foundation of the Church, and of its first saintly rulers. Among these rulers, continued the memorandum, "the most holy Popes who presided in this See by a special prerogative most specially assumed the place of Christ." [1] With the increase of the Church relaxation set in, and now it is torn by infidelity, schism, and vice. The cause of this is to be sought in the evil lives of the pastors of the Church, and especially, though it is dreadful to say it, in the malpractices of the papal curia,[2] i.e., in its dispensations and provisions. Providing by these means for the temporal lives of a few individuals, it causes the loss of thousands of immortal souls. Let not this be done by him who "most directly and chiefly" holds the place of God on earth. The rights of patrons are violated to satisfy the claims of one's own flesh and blood, to reward service, to please the powerful, or for some other such reason. Nor must it be allowed that the Curia does these things for the common good. The holy Fathers provided for that by long suffering, and not by evil ways, such as these. Woe to such as say let us do evil that good

---

[1] "Tamen speciali prærogativa præsidentes in hac sacratissima sede sanctissimi Papæ, et specialissime gerunt typum personam et vicem Christi." P. 251, ap. Brown, *Fasciculus Rerum*, ii, London, 1690. This *sermon* is on the lines of the letter which he addressed to his Dean and Chapter. Ep. 127, p. 357 ff. Here also he puts before them the special position of the Pope. He is the power superior to the bishops (p. 366), from whom they get their power (p. 367). *Cf.* pp. 364, 389, and 390, where he says that the Pope in the Church is like the Judge Samuel over the people of Israel. "Ipse (Samuel) enim erat in populo Israelitico sicut sol populi, quemadmodum et dominus Papa in universali ecclesia."

[2] "Dicere . . . expavesco, silere tamen non andeo . . . Causa et fons et origo hujus est hæc Curia." P. 252.

may come of it. Moreover, it is the special concern of those who preside over the See of Rome to strive to fashion the Church on earth after that in heaven. The God-like properties (the deificatio) bestowed on them have to be by them passed on to others, but they certainly have not to act in any way which would result in harm coming to others. For this most holy See is the Throne of God, and like the sun to the earth. It must then enlighten and vivify or the earth will perish. This See whom all have to obey must beware of commanding anything that is wrong, lest it be the cause of schism.

The memorandum then proceeds to show that the episcopal power in England is bound fast by the secular power, by appeals and by exemptions. Whatever evil may be committed by those who have been exempted from episcopal jurisdiction, cannot be checked by the Bishop.

Everywhere, moreover, is there dissatisfaction with the servants of the Curia, and, if the Curia cannot look after its own household, how will it look after the Church of God. Its constant use too of the clause " non obstante " (notwithstanding all previous concessions) is filling the world with distrust of charters ; its use of the sword makes one fear lest it should perish by the sword, and its acceptance of presents causes dread lest it should pervert justice.

The " sermon " concludes by assuring the Holy Father that these abuses have been brought to his notice, not in a spirit of presumption, but in the hope of securing remedies for them.

From this brief analysis of this famous protest, the reader will assuredly be prepared to accept the criticism regarding it of its author's biographer : " The unflinching courage displayed by Grosseteste in placing the facts before such an assembly is hardly equalled in history, and it must be recognized that Innocent showed no small

degree of toleration and breadth of view in allowing such
a document to be read aloud." [1]

Did
Grosseteste
refuse a
living to a
nephew of
Innocent ?
1253.

There is some reason for believing that Grosseteste
was not content with merely protesting against the
abuse of papal power, but that he emphasized his protest
by strong action. On January 26, 1253, Innocent issued
an order to Hugh Mortimer, " archdeacon of Canterbury,
and to Master Innocent our writer sojourning in England,"
bidding them, " all things to the contrary notwithstanding," to confer a canonry in the diocese of Lincoln on
his nephew, Frederick de Lavagna (puerulus),[2] " a mere
boy." Appended to this letter, as quoted by Matthew Paris,
are notes to the effect that it roused the anger of bishop
Robert.   This anger is said to have led Grosseteste to
pen an indignant letter to the Pope's two commissioners.[3]
In this letter he is supposed to refuse to invest Frederick
with the said canonry. As a matter of fact, however, no
mention whatever is made therein of Frederick or his
claims. The letter, indeed, concludes with a denunciation of " those things which they call provisions ", and
is taken up with a refusal to do certain acts which are
not specified. Grosseteste declares that as a devout son
he obeys the mandates of the Apostolic See, but the
things commanded by the commissioners are opposed
to the mandates of the Apostles. They cannot, therefore,

[1] Stevenson, *Grosseteste*, p. 285. *Cf.* A. L. Smith, *Church and State*,
p. 124 : " The Pope who could allow an indictment like this to be
spoken to him was a strong and wise man. It was characteristic of his
cool business-like good sense that he saw it was better not to burk
the indictment, and that he made it easier for the utterer of it to stay
on six months in Lyons after it, and to carry his affairs to a successful
issue."

[2] Ep. ap. Mat. Par., vi, 229 ff., or ap. *Ann. de Burton*, i, 436 ff. In
the last-named *Annals*, F. de L. is referred to as " cuidam Romano
puero parvulo ".   P. 311.

[3] Mat. Par., v, 389 ff., where it is spoken of as " the very best letter
of Robert, bishop of Lincoln " ; ep. 128 of Grosseteste, p. 432 ff., where
by mistake the letter would seem to be addressed to the Pope. The
full and complete address is given in the *Burton Annals*, p. 311.

have been ordered by the Holy See, and so he will not obey them. This language, which under the circumstances must be set down as too general, has led some authors to regard the letter as a forgery, or at least as a mere literary exercise.[1] It may perhaps with more justice be said to be a letter in which Grosseteste was dealing, not with the particular case of Frederick, but with the whole method of procedure of the papal commissioners. Hence Matthew Paris does not refer it to Frederick's canonry, but to a command that " he should do something which seemed to him to be unjust and unreasonable ".[2] It is indeed certain that " because they were seeking mere temporal profits ", he did refuse to invest certain papal nominees and cardinals' nephews,[3] but whether Frederick de Lavagna was one of them would appear to be uncertain.

Still more uncertain is the language which Innocent is stated by Paris to have used when this letter was brought to his notice. " Who," he asked angrily, " is this raving old man . . . who in his rash audacity judges our conduct ? By Peter and Paul, were it not for my natural generosity, I would render him a by-word to the whole world." It was with difficulty that the Spanish cardinal, Giles de Torres, restrained the angry Pontiff by reminding him that what Grosseteste asserted was true, and that it would never do to take action against him, as he was universally respected for his learning and piety.[4]

Supposed outburst of Innocent against Grosseteste.

[1] *Cf.* Smith, *Church and State*, p. 110 ff. This learned lecturer points out among other things that this letter " was not inserted among Grosseteste's till a much later age ". P. 117. Ch. Jourdain in his *Excursions historiques*, calls in question the authenticity not only of this letter but of the *sermo* of 1250, and also of Grosseteste's death-bed conversations, as reported by Matthew Paris, p. 149 ff.

[2] v, 389.

[3] Eccleston, *De adventu minorum*, p. 64, *R. S.*, ap. *Mon. Francis.*

[4] Mat. Par., v, 393. All this is nothing else but Matthew Paris and contains no more truth than the *Lanercost Chronicle's* statement that Innocent excommunicated the intrepid bishop.

Success of
Grosseteste's
action.

Whatever may be thought of the authenticity of some
of the things which Grosseteste is supposed to have said
or written, there is abundant evidence to show that he
put the abuses of the practice of Provisions before the
Pope, and that his reclamations were not made in vain.
Adam Marsh congratulated him " on the persevering
fight " which he had waged at Lyons [1]; and on its at
least temporary success [2]; and after the bishop's death,
he wrote of "that fearless reply to that dread majesty
you wot of written with such prudence, eloquence, and
strength, and with the help of God, to the profit of all
future ages." [3]

Innocent's
concessions.

The effect then of Grosseteste's endeavours is seen
in two concessions granted by Innocent on the subject
of Provisions. Writing from Perugia (May 23, 1252),
Innocent declared that the great difficulties of the times
and the importunity of individuals had caused him at
times to think more of persons than of Churches. Desiring
to end this, he granted to all whom it concerned full power
to present to those benefices which were in their gift,
notwithstanding all grants to the contrary from the
Apostolic See. [4] This decree was addressed to all the
bishops of the Catholic world, but would appear not to
have gone far enough to meet the situation in England.
There was need for the existing state of things to be
faced. Accordingly, almost exactly a year after the issue
of the last-mentioned decree (May 22, 1253), Innocent
addressed another to the hierarchy of England. Complaints
had been made to him that over 50,000 marks a year went
to aliens. He therefore proposed to reduce the amount

[1] Ep. Adæ, 49, Aug. 15, 1250, ap. *Mon. Francis*, p. 155, and ep. 50,
p. 157.

[2] *Ib.*, p. 158.

[3] Ep. Adæ, 190, p. 325. " Imperterritam illam responsionem . . .
ad formidandam quam nostis majestatem destinando."

[4] Ap. Mat. Par., vi, 210 f.

to 8,000 marks, and to require residence and due ordination from those to whom papal provision was made. He had almost ceased, he said, for some years to give benefices in England, and did not even wish to insist on the sum named. It must be the task of the bishops to execute his concessions in such a way as not to cause complaint.[1]

Some six months later (November 3, 1253), acting, we are expressly assured, under the influence of Grosseteste's representations,[2] Innocent dispatched to the bishops and certain abbots of England some thirty copies of a duly authenticated bull.[3] It was the final strong expression of his remorse on the subject of Provisions which we have quoted before. It definitely removed all impediments to the full exercise of rights of presentation, and gave permission to everyone, acting as his representative, to tear up all documents emanating from him or his legates in a contrary sense.

Moreover, Alexander IV., Innocent's successor, in annulling a number of Provisions granted by him, said that he did so the more readily as he had been given to understand that, had not death prevented him, his predecessor would have recalled them himself.[4]

As far as Innocent IV. was concerned, papal Provisions were dead.[5] Unfortunately, his successors could not or

---

[1] *Calendar*, i, p. 286; Rymer, i, 471.

[2] " Literis d. episcopi Lincolniæ . . . lectis et intellectis " say the *Annals of Burton*, i, p. 314 ff., which cite this papal document. It is also given ap. Mat. Par., vi, 260 ff., and Rymer, i, 494 ff.

[3] Episcopis . . . Angliæ xxx paria literarum vel amplius, bullata, . . . transmisit." *A. de B.*, *ib.*

[4] Ep. Alex. IV., Apr. 5, 1255, ap. Rod., iii, p. 317. " Litteras (Innocentii IV) super . . . beneficiis . . . viribus carere decernimus . . . præsertim cum idem predecessor, sicut accepimus, intentionem habuerit super hoc salubre adhibere remedium et ad revocationem eorum ante suum obitum intendebat."

[5] It would appear that Provisions subsequent to this date were granted in Ireland (*Calendar*, i, pp. 295, 308), in Scotland (*ib.*, pp. 298,

would not consent to be so generous. We shall see the
Statute of Provisors passed under the reign of Edward III.
(1351) to protest against the revived abuse of Provisions,
and not long before that event another great English
bishop, the book-lover, Richard of Bury († 1345), who,
though like Grosseteste, he regarded " the most holy
Roman court " as " the fount of faith ",[1] bore sad witness
that " Papal Provision " was still " importuned " for
worthless subjects by the prayers of cardinals and
powerful friends which could not be rejected.[2]

Taking it then for granted that Innocent financially
oppressed the Church of England,[3] though not to the
extent that a hasty reading of Matthew Paris would lead
one to suppose, we may now pass on to consider his
relations with King Henry and with the English hierarchy,
and with Archbishop Boniface and Grosseteste in
particular.

Innocent and
Henry.
The relations between Innocent and Henry were in
the main cordial. There was mutual love between them,
but there were not wanting men who held that it arose
more from love of what they could both extract from the
purses of the English than from a desire of helping one
another to obtain the kingdom of heaven.[4] The King
was declared by others " to be devoted to the Pope and

303), and even in England (ib., pp. 302, 303). There would appear,
however, to be some special circumstances connected with many of
these Provisions. The Popes it may be noted were not the only ones
to make an evil use of ecclesiastical benefices. Innocent had to forbid
(Jan. 9, 1253, Calendar, i, p. 303) the transference by many prelates in
England of such livings to secular purposes.

[1] Philobiblion, c. 8.

[2] Ib., c. 9.

[3] Cf. Annales Cestrienses, an. 1251, p. 71 ed. R. C. Christie, 1887.

[4] Ann. de Burton, i, p. 323, R. S. " Cum inter d. Innocentium . . .
et d. Henricum . . . esset amor reciprocus, prout populus prædicabat,
magis ob amorem pecuniæ de Anglorum marsupiis . . . exhauriendæ,
etc." Cf. Mat. Par., v, 334.

to the Roman Church ",[1] and he himself bade Innocent rest assured that "he would ever show obedience, fidelity, and devotion to the lord Pope as to our spiritual father, and to the holy Roman Church as to our mother ".[2]   In return for the King's goodwill, Innocent was constantly granting Henry marks of his favour.   He confirmed agreements or treaties which the King made with foreign powers, as with Provence,[3] and Wales: [4] at the request of Henry or his wife, he often granted dispensations for their friends to hold more than one benefice; [5] he confirmed the dower which the King settled on Eleanor,[6] and again "at the humble request of the King" he confirmed his last will and testament "by his apostolic authority ".[7] Moreover, what was a matter of the greatest consideration to the ever impecunious Henry, Innocent not unfrequently used his influence to support his demands for money. In the beginning of the year 1244, Henry, "with his own mouth," asked the clergy and barons for money for his wars.   As he was not likely to get it from them, at least on his own terms, he produced a letter from the Pope to the English clergy in which he urged them to help the King "who, as a devout Catholic prince, has ever sought with filial subjection and a deep sense of duty to show reverence to his mother the Roman Church ".[8]

Again, as soon as Henry began to talk about following King Louis on his crusading expedition (1247), Innocent listened to his request for pecuniary help, and at first

Innocent authorizes the raising of a tithe for Henry's Crusade. 1250.

[1] Mat. Par., v, 511.

[2] Ep. Grosseteste, n. 117, p. 338.

[3] Rymer, i, 423, and *Reg.*, i, n. 638 (1244).

[4] Rymer, i, 425, Apr. 7, 1244.

[5] *Calendar*, i, pp. 212, 218, 225–6, 252.

[6] *Reg.*, i, n. 639. In 1254 Innocent annulled Henry's marriage with Joan of Ponthieu.   Orig. bulls, ap. *Cal. of docs. relating to Scotland*, i, p. 406.

[7] *Reg.*, n. 644, Apr. 30, 1244.   "Testamentum . . . confirmamus et presentis scripti patrocinio communimus."

[8] Ep. of July 29, 1244, ap. Mat. Par., iv, 364 f.

instructed his agents in England to do what they could
to divert to the King legacies left for the Holy Land, and
moneys paid for the redemption of vows made to take
the Cross.[1] But whether Henry was really anxious to fight
the Saracen or not, he was keenly anxious for money to
enable him to pay off the debts which his follies and
extravagances were daily increasing. He was not content
with a share of legacies and redemption money. Louis IX.
had been granted a tenth of the revenues of the Church
of France, so Henry petitioned for a similar grant. In
his reply, Innocent told the King that he had not
authorized Louis to collect the tenth until the consent
of the French clergy had first been obtained. However,
as the English prelates have given a similar consent,[2]
" we have thought proper to grant your Highness a tenth
of all the ecclesiastical revenues of your kingdom and
of all the other territories subject to your jurisdiction
for a term of three years to help you to succour the Holy
Land." The collection of the tithe was, however, not to
begin until all arrangements for the starting of the expedition had been finally concluded. But at the moment,
he said, he did not think it advisable that the King should
set out, seeing that the other great defender of the Church,
St. Louis, was away, and that the Church was still in
danger from Frederick.[3]

Other letters followed to the bishops and to the superiors
of the Dominicans and Franciscans, calling on them to

[1] Epp. of Aug. 30, 1247, ap. *Reg.*, i, p. 615. Henry's devotion to the
Roman Church is again set forth.

[2] Rymer, i, 452 f., ep. Apr. 11, 1250. " Prælati nobis suis litteris
supplicarunt, quod tibi curaremus abunde . . . . ad tantum negotium
de ipsius regni Angliæ proventibus ecclesiasticis providere." *Cf.* ep.
to various bishops of England of Apr. 30, *ib.*, p. 456. The grant was
made " de vestro et aliorum Regni ejusdem assensu ".

[3] *Cf.* Mat. Par., v, 102 f., 134 f., and his usual exaggerations in
connexion with this action of the Pope in advising Henry to delay his
expedition to the Holy Land and *ib.*, pp. 282, 324 ff. *Cf. Chron. monast.
de Abingdon*, an. 1251, p. 43 ed. Halliwell.

rouse " the great English fighters (strenui Angliæ pugiles) "
to save the Holy Land, and to urge the people by promises
of indulgences to contribute to the expenses of the
Crusade.[1]

Opposition was at once raised to this tax, because it
was not clear when Henry proposed to set out for the
Holy Land. Accordingly, soon after Easter in the year
1252, the King swore that he would start on June 24,
1256,[2] and wanted to begin the raising of the tithe at
once. This was, however, firmly refused by the clergy,[3]
on the ground that he was not authorized so to do by
the papal grant. The consequence was that, despite the
anger of the King, the collection of the tax did not
begin till after Easter, 1254.[4]

The tax was levied both on spiritualities (the benefices, The Norwich
i.e., the *rectoria*, *vicaria*, tithes and offerings) and on valuation.
temporalities (rents, income from lands) [5]; and to ensure
its yielding as much as possible, the old assessment made
in 1219 was set aside, and a new one was ordered to be
made, which came to be known as the " Norwich taxation " [6] for a reason which the following quotation will
make clear. " In obedience to the Pope's mandate," say
the *Burton Annals*,[7] "Walter, bishop of Norwich, although

[1] Rymer, i, p. 45 ff., Apr. 26, and p. 456, Apr. 30, 1250. There was
opposition to the levying of this tithe because Henry wanted to raise
it under conditions which were not those laid down originally by the
Pope (*cf*. ep. ap. Rymer, i, 452, to Henry with Mat. Par., v, 324 ff.),
but which he had induced the Pope to modify in his behalf in a letter
of Feb. 14, 1251. *Calendar*, i, 267 ; *cf*. p. 279.

[2] Rymer, i, 473, ep. of June 6, 1252.

[3] Mat. Par., v, 324–33 ; *Royal Letters*, ii, 95.

[4] *Roy. Let.*, ii, 101.

[5] *Cf*. Mitchell, *Studies*, p. 269 ff. " Taxatio generalis tam de temporalibus quam de spiritualibus facta fuit per Angliam exceptis baroniis."
Ann. de Wigornia, an. 1254, iv, 443, *R. S. Cf. Ann. de Dunstap.*, iii, 196.

[6] Thos. Wykes speaks (*Chron.*, iv, 225, an. 1269) of the " antiqua
beneficiorum taxatio " (that of 1219) and of " Walteri Norwicensis ep.
taxatio".

[7] i, p. 325.

against his will," caused a new assessment of ecclesiastical
property to be made throughout the whole kingdom.
Calling himself " the executor of the business of the
Cross deputed by the Apostolic See", he bids all deans
and others, " in virtue of the obedience by which they
were bound to the Apostolic See," " faithfully to ascertain
the real value of all ecclesiastical benefices." [1]

Innocent
urges Henry
to go to the
assistance of
Louis, 1250. It was certainly not the Pope's idea that Henry should
get such considerable financial aid from the clergy for
his own personal needs, and he accordingly pressed him
to fulfil his vow of succouring the Holy Land. We have
seen above that, for a brief period, Innocent dissuaded
our King from following Louis. But as the year (1250)
wore on, and it became more clear that Frederick's power
was broken, the Pope urged Henry to set out as soon as
possible.[2] The " Fœdera " contains a large number of
bulls issued by Innocent to facilitate the King's departure

---

[1] Walter orders the deans " justas æstimationes omnium ecclesiasticorum beneficiorum fideliter inquireretis; vobis in virtute obedientiæ
qua sedi apostolicæ tenemini . . . injungimus quatenus . . . plenius
inquiratis veritatem, etc." *Ib.* This " Norwich assessment " remained
in force till it was superseded by the assessment made in 1291 by order
of Nicholas IV. which was the last " valor ecclesiasticus " made in
England till the days of Henry VIII. Portions of the Norwich valuation are still extant. In her paper, " The Finance of Malton Priory,
1244–57," ap. *Transactions of the R. Hist. Soc.*, vol. xviii (1904), p. 131 ff.,
Miss R. Graham shows that though the total income of the house was
in 1254 over £500, the Nor. A. of its spiritualities and temporalities
was £281 3s. 4d., and its tenth therefore £28 2s. 4d. The *Ecclesie de
Bernwelle Liber Memorandum*, ed. J. W. Clark, Cambridge, 1907, has
preserved a list of the spiritualities of the diocese of Ely with their
values and the sum to be paid by each, according to " Taxacio facta
per bone memorie d. Walterum ". P. 191 f. The author of the *Liber*
(written *c.* 1295) says that the valuation of Walter was tolerable, but
that the effect of these taxations was that the poor were robbed, the
wealthy enriched, money for alms was taken away, and beggars died
of hunger. Finally, the *Norfolk Archæology*, xvii, 1910, gives the
fragment which pertains to the diocese of Norwich.

[2] Pub. Rec. Office, *Papal Bulls*, Bundle xix, n. 21, quoted by Gasquet,
p. 286.

—taking his kingdom under his protection, granting privileges to the intending Crusaders, etc.[1] This line of action continued till towards the close of the year 1253, when Innocent offered the throne of Sicily to Henry's son Edmund. His interest then all turned to the affairs of that kingdom.

Nevertheless he declared that the tithe which he had authorized Henry to collect for three years for the Crusade, and which in May, 1254, he extended to five years, was " for the same undertaking ".[2] However, he very readily listened to the request of the King's envoys to commute his vow, and allow him to undertake the Sicilian instead of the Palestine expedition. He did so, because, as he said, he judged that the possession of Sicily would make it all the easier to help the Holy Land, and that the recent death of Conrad would facilitate the conquest of Sicily.[3] *Henry's vow to go to the Holy Land is commuted, 1254.*

Though then, Innocent's inclinations and policy led him to comply with many of Henry's wishes, he by no means complied with them all. He refused, for instance, the King's request to grant him a bull prohibiting the coronation of Alexander III., the young King of Scotland, without his previous permission, as he was anxious to increase his hold on Scotland. He could not, wrote Innocent, do a thing which would redound to the prejudice of a King's dignity.[4] *Innocent opposes Henry.*

Nor would he hearken to Henry's wishes regarding his alleged rights in Provence. In 1245 had died Raymond Berenger IV., count of that district, and the father-in-law of St. Louis IX., and his brother Charles of Anjou and of Henry III., and his brother Richard, Duke of Cornwall. At once to the detriment of his rights as Henry

[1] Rymer, i, pp. 480, 481, 483–6, 493.

[2] *Ib.*, i, p. 516, ep. of May 23, 1254. *Cf.* confirmations by Alexander IV. of March 28, and Apr. 22, 1255, ap. *Cal.*, i, 314; Mat. Par., v, 452.

[3] Rymer, i, p. 517 f., May 31, 1254.

[4] Rymer, i, p. 463, Apr. 6, 1251.

declared, Charles took possession of Provence. Thereupon our King wrote to Innocent to beg him to interfere in his behalf. He asked for three things, to wit : that the Pope would protect his rights and those of his brother in Provence, that he would send a legate to forbid Charles to occupy any more of its towns or fortified places, and lastly that the will of Raymond should not be proved before a certain fixed date. To this the Pope replied that he could not directly interfere, but that he would urge Charles and Louis to have due regard for the rights of Henry and Richard.[1]

Henry's treatment of the English Church causes trouble with the Pope.

With all Henry's mildness in some directions, his general weakness of character and his perpetual want of money rendered him not frequently very arbitrary in his dealings both with his barons and with the Church. His wilful dealings with the former caused the Barons' Wars, and with the latter brought him at times into opposition with Innocent. Matthew Paris is continually complaining of his tyrannical treatment of the Church, —of his constant interference with the freedom of ecclesiastical elections, his seizure of vacant ecclesiastical revenues, and the extortions which he practised on the Church generally.[2]

The case of Richard of Wyche.

The election, for instance, of the saintly Richard of Wyche to the see of Chichester brought him into collision with the Pope. The royal candidate (Robert Passelew) for the vacant see had been rejected by archbishop Boniface on the grounds of ignorance and unfitness of character, and Richard was forthwith elected in his stead without any waiting for Henry's consent.[3] The King was furious, and his agents followed the bishop-elect to Lyons to protest against the second election. But

[1] Ep. March 1, 1246, ap. *Reg.*, i, n. 1967.

[2] iv, 259, and the whole affair of William de Raleigh, bishop of Winchester, 423 ; v, 3, 51, 54, 240, 329, 466, etc.

[3] *Ib.*, iv, 401, 412.

Innocent himself consecrated Richard for Chichester, and Roger de Weseham for Lincoln, both against the will of the King. Henry was, moreover, given to understand that the asking for his assent to an episcopal election was a privilege and not a right, and that he had rendered himself unworthy of it by his constant abuse of it.[1] In revenge, Henry refused to allow Richard the temporalities of his see, and it was only after being threatened with excommunication that he handed them over to the Saint in a ruinous condition.[2]

As he was, moreover, anxious that the great see of Winchester should be in the hands of a friend, Henry begged Innocent, as he had already begged his predecessor, not to allow William de Raleigh, bishop of Norwich, to be transferred to Winchester. He assured the Pope that the translation had been opposed by Otho, cardinal of S. Nicholas in Carcere, and that the prior of Winchester with a number of others had elected Boniface of Savoy to the vacant see with the approval of the legate. The King further begged the Pope not to allow the Church of Winchester to be burdened with debts through the action of Benedict de Burgh, a monk of Winchester, and his party who, adversaries of the King, are going to Rome against the will of their prior. The Pope is adjured not to sanction their raising loans.[3] Henry also wrote to the merchant bankers, especially to those of Florence, Siena, and Rome, urging them not to advance the monks any money.[4]

That of William de Rayleigh, 1243–4.

Nevertheless, Innocent confirmed the translation of William. Henry at once vigorously protested (Dec. 1,

---

[1] *Ib.*, iv, 426. *Cf.* Sister M. R. Capes, *Richard of Wyche*, p. 92 ff., London, 1913, and Flanagan, *A. hist. of the Ch. in England*, i, p. 498 ff.

[2] *Cf.* the Dominican, Ralph Bocking, Richard's biographer, writing about 1270, Ap. *Acta SS. Bolland.*, April 3, i, p. 282 ff.

[3] *Cf. Calend. of Pat. Rolls*, Henry III. (1232–47), p. 400.

[4] *Ib.*, p. 401.

1243), declaring that the Pope had acted in ignorance of his appeal to Gregory IX., and of the fact that he looked upon William as an enemy, and not as a friend as the Pope had been given to believe.[1] At last, however, Henry gave way, and confirmed William in the see of Winchester (1244).[2] Fuller ideas of the relations between Innocent and Henry will no doubt be formed after their mutual relations with the English episcopate have been further considered.

Boniface of Savoy, archbishop of Canterbury.

Probably the most famous family in Europe at this time was that of Thomas I., count of Savoy († 1233). An admirer of it assures us that it was because they were " handsome and strong, brave and chivalrous " that his sons, William and Thomas, Peter, Boniface, and Philip, played their great parts in the world, and that their ambitions were greatly helped by the charm, beauty, and intelligence of their sisters, Margaret and Beatrice, and of the Queens who were the latter's daughters.[3] We have already seen something of the assistance which this family afforded Innocent in the days of his flight from Italy and during his stay at Lyons. Had it not been for the friendliness of the sons of Thomas, who held sway in Piedmont and Savoy, he could not have crossed the Alps, and it was due especially to the protection of Philip of Savoy, bishop-elect of Valence, and afterwards archbishop of Lyons, that he felt safe during his long residence in that city.[4] To this family, then, Innocent was bound by ties of gratitude, and Henry III. by ties of blood, for he had married Eleanor of Provence, daughter of Beatrice of Savoy (1236). One result of this marriage was that

---

[1] *Ib.*, p. 410.

[2] *Ib.*, pp. 433 and 435.

[3] F. Mugnier, *Les Savoyards en Angleterre au XIIIe Siècle*, p. 3, Paris, 1891. Beatrice married Raymond Berenger IV., and had the four daughters spoken of above. *Cf.* Mat. Par., vi, 442.

[4] Mat. Par., iv, 426. *Cf.* v, 236, 248.

England was overrun by Provencals and Savoyards, as Henry always showed a predilection for foreigners. Chief of these Savoyards was Boniface, bishop-elect of Belley. Uncle of the Queen, he was known for his handsome person in the chronicles of Savoy as " Absalom ",[1] and was in that country afterwards hailed as " blessed ".

Through the influence of Henry he was elected to the see of Winchester (1240), and on the death of St. Edmund, the same influence insured his election to the see of Canterbury (Apr., 1241).[2] To secure the confirmation of Pope Gregory IX., Henry caused a statement to be drawn up, and signed with the royal seal, as well as with the seals of several bishops and abbots, in which the virtues of Boniface were strongly stated. The Pope, however, died soon after the arrival of the bearers of this document in Rome, as they had been seized at sea, maltreated, and then imprisoned by the Genoese allies of Frederick, and hence delayed on their journey. Owing, therefore,

---

[1] Cf. Mat. Par., iv, 104. In this country the character of Boniface of Savoy is usually judged from the prejudiced utterances of Matthew Paris. Unfortunately even Gasquet only quotes that author in dealing with him. To judge fairly of him, however, the reader should consult the old French Chronicle of Savoy, ap. Mon. Hist. Pat. SS., ii, 146–8, and especially Thos. Wykes, probably an Augustinian canon of Osney, who is regarded as the best of the annalists of his age (pp. 235–6 ed. Luard), and Adam Marsh (ap. Mon. Francisc., i, p. 163), who tells us that the canons of St. Bartholomew's, Smithfield, spread abroad outrageous calumnies against him. It is from these stories that Paris has drawn his pictures of Boniface, pictures which he himself later on obliterated. The French Chron., which dates from about the end of the fourteenth century, says that he ruled his diocese well, and " moult fust agreable a tout le peuple, et lappelloyent le segond saint arccuesque apres saint Thomas ". P. 147. See also Birchington, Hist. de archiepp. Cantuar. (597–1369), ap. Wharton, Anglia Sacra, i. Cf. Vita de' beati Umberto e Bonifacio di Savoia, Torino, 1839, and particularly G. Strickland, " Richerche storiche sopra il B. Bonifacio," ap. Miscellanea di Storia Italiana, i, p. 349 ff., Torino, 1895, and a paper by Rev. H. Thurston, " Bl. Boniface," ap. The Tablet, Oct. 18, 1913.

[2] Mat. Par., iv, 104 f.

to the brief pontificate of Celestine IV., and the long vacancy of the Papacy which followed, it was not till Sept. 17, 1243, that Innocent IV. confirmed Boniface's election, giving him full administration in "both spirituals and temporals".[1]   And on April 2, 1244, he sent him the pallium by the hands of Hugh, the Provincial of the Dominicans in France, and of Hugh, sub-prior of Canterbury.   At the same time, Peter d'Aigueblanche, bishop of Hereford, was commissioned to invest him with it and to receive from him the oath of fealty to Rome.[2]   Boniface, however, was not consecrated till January 15, 1245, when he received consecration at Lyons from the hands of Innocent himself.[3]

Boniface is empowered by the Pope to receive first-friuts.

Whilst with the Pope, Boniface put before him the great liabilities of the arch-diocese, and so to free it from its overwhelming burden, obtained from him power to raise ten thousand marks by taxing the whole province of Canterbury.   Papal letters addressed to its prelates set forth that by divine providence inferiors were at one time called upon to help their superiors, and at others superiors had to assist those beneath them.   From various causes, wrote Innocent to Grosseteste, and especially from its having been plundered by friend and foe alike during the long vacancies, the archiepiscopal see was in danger of being crushed beneath the weight of accumulating interest. But, as the see of Canterbury is specially beloved by the

---

[1] Cal., i, p. 200.   The letter is printed in full in Gervase Gesta reg. contin., ii, 198 ff.   On Henry's exertions at Rome to secure the election of his uncle, Boniface, see Calendar of Patent Rolls, Henry III., 1232–47, p. 400, R. S.   On the affairs of the see of Winchester, and Rome, cf. ib., pp. 400–1, 410, 433, 435.

[2] Cal., i, p. 208.

[3] Mat. Par., iv, 425. Innocent also consecrated about the same time Richarde de Wyche and Robert de Weseham as bishops of Chichester and Chester respectively.   Our King's proctor objected on the ground that his consent to their promotion had not been given.   He was, however, told that his master's abuse of the favours granted him rendered him unworthy of them.   Ib., p. 426.

Roman Church, and as its present archbishop is a particularly devoted and noble member of that Church, and is distinguished by the purity of his life and the nobility of his birth, we have decided by the advice of our brethren, to assent to his petition, and to allow him for seven years to collect the firstfruits of all the benefices of the province of Canterbury which shall become vacant, till a sum of ten thousand marks is reached.[1]

This privilege naturally caused a great deal of discontent ; but by papal authority excommunication was threatened to all, with the exception of the royal family, who should offer any resistance to the decree.[2] Opposition was therefore put down for the moment ; but when Boniface obtained the Pope's consent to raise 2,000 more marks,[3] and proceeded to cause money to be raised irrespective, so it was said, of the total amount which had been granted to him, opposition sprang up again. Innocent had to appoint a cardinal to look into the matter ; and at last decided that Boniface must be content with the 12,000 marks, and must restore any money that he had collected over and above that sum.[4] At any rate, the money raised was faithfully applied by the archbishop to clear off the debts of his see (22,000 marks), and he used to say that he was really responsible for the grand works inaugurated by his predecessors as he had paid for them.[5]

[1] Ep. of Aug. 27, 1246, ap. Mat. Par., iv, 506 ff. *Cf. ib.*, v, 36, and similar letters, ap. *Reg.*, i, nn. 1935-6. On Aug. 26, 1245, a similar privilege for the same reason had been granted to the bishop-elect of Verdun. *Reg.*, i, nn. 1451-4, and in 1252 was to be granted to Lawrence of St. Martin, bp. of Rochester. Mat. P., v, 273.

[2] Ep. Inn., June 5, 1247, *Reg.*, i, 2814. *Cf. ib.*, nn. 3369, 3371, 3396-7.

[3] Ep., Nov. 9, 1247, n. 3410.

[4] Ep., Aug. 1, 1251, *Reg.*, iii, 5447. By mistake Gasquet, p. 298, speaks of another 12,000 marks. But reference is here made to the original 10,000 marks plus the subsequent 2,000 marks.

[5] *Contin. of Gervase*, ii, 251. *Cf.* Wharton, *Anglia Sacra*, I, ii.

If then Boniface incurred unpopularity with the
clergy of his province by taxing them, he was praised
by those directly interested in the see of Canterbury
for clearing it from debt. He was also praised by these
latter for securing the right of visitation throughout
the province, despite the resistance of all his suffragans
and their chapters.[1] He had not been long in England
before, in imitation of the action of Grosseteste regarding
his chapter, he claimed the right " to visit ", i.e., to be
received by, " the heads and members," whether secular
or regular, of the different dioceses of his province,
and then to make canonical inquiries concerning them
and their work.[2] When he began to put his claims
into action (c. May, 1250), strenuous opposition was
aroused, and the affair was laid by both parties before
the Pope.[3] Boniface relied upon a decretal of Innocent
himself in which that Pontiff authorized archbishops
" to visit " cathedral and other churches, and monasteries,
and to examine both the bishops and clergy and even the
laity. They were to be allowed moderate procurations,
but were forbidden to receive fees or presents (1250).[4]
Before the close of the month of May, Boniface himself,
and the proctors of the bishops who had collected funds
for the appeal,[5] appeared before the Pope.

Despite the Savoy influences which Matthew Paris
avers the Pope himself felt to be excessive,[6] Boniface

---

[1] Gerv., ib., p. 250.

[2] " Libertates sibi et successoribus suis cum magno labore et expensis
magnis adquisivit (Boniface) videlicet omnem visitationem per totam
suam provinciam tam in capitibus quam in membris, visitationem diei
per d. papam taxata quatuor marcis sterlingorum ; omnibus suffraganti-
bus suis sibi resistentibus cum capitulis suis." Ib. Cf. Chron. mon. de
Abingdon, p. 44 ed. Halliwell.

[3] Mat. Par., v, 119 ff. All " curiam papalem adierunt super his
omnibus querelam coram sum. Pontifice reposituri." Cf. ib., pp. 126,
138, and vi, 190 f.

[4] Ib., vi, p. 188 ff.   [5] Ib., v, p. 186.   [6] Chron., v, 225–6.

at first lost on various side issues. It was decided that
he had exceeded his powers in excommunicating and
censuring those who had objected to his visitations.[1]
The archbishop, however, continued to press the main
question, and Henry supported his efforts by writing
to Innocent in his behalf.[2] After a struggle of two years
Boniface to some extent gained his point. Innocent
decreed that he had the right to visit the cathedral
chapters and the religious houses of his province, but not
the ordinary secular parochial churches unless at the
special request of the ordinary (1252).[3]

Boniface had hardly returned to England (Nov., 1252), Aylmer, bishop of Winchester.
when he was drawn into a dispute with Aylmer, bishop
of Winchester.

Aylmer (Aymer or Æthelmar) de Lusignan or de
Valence, was our King's half-brother, as he was the son
of Isabella, John's widow, who afterwards married
Hugh X., count of la Marche. For this brother, even
when of immature age,[4] and of an unbridled temper,
Henry was anxious to secure a bishopric. In 1249 he
tried to get him that of Durham ; but the monks of that
city told him plainly that Aylmer was neither old enough
nor learned enough to be a bishop.[5]

---

[1] *Reg.*, ii, nn. 4864–5, Sept. 27, 1250, or ap. Mat. Par., vi, 197 ff. ;
also *Reg.*, ii, nn. 4887–8, Oct. 11 ; n. 4910, Nov. 8. The letter of Oct. 11
is in full ap. Rymer, i, 458 f. *Cf.* Mat. Par., v, 212. Later on too, in a
dispute with the chapter of Lincoln into which Boniface entered after
Grosseteste's death, he lost his cause, and was rebuked by the Pope
in addition : " archipræsulis redarguens austeritatem." Unfortunately
we have only again the authority of Paris to offer. v, 413.

[2] Mat. Par., v, 205, 218.

[3] *Reg.*, iii, n. 5670–2, Apr. 22, 1252 ; or *Cal.*, i, p. 276. *Cf.*
Mat. Par., v, 302, 346 ; vi, 228. Innocent said that there was no need
for the archbp. to visit the parishes because the province of Canterbury
had always been blessed with bishops who did their duty. See also
Chron. monast. de Abingdon, p. 45 ed. J. O. Halliwell.

[4] He was not 30 in 1255. *Cf. Reg. Alex. IV.*, i, n. 686.

[5] Mat. Par., v, 55.

He is elected
to the See of
Winchester,
1250.

Next year (1250) on the death of William de Raleigh, bishop of Winchester, Henry made a successful attempt to get Aylmer elected to that important see. We can easily imagine in what form his licence to choose a successor to William was given to the Chapter of Winchester. The *Patent Rolls* show us that, if he had no particular interest in an election, he simply told the dean and chapter to elect a good man, and one who would be useful and loyal to him and to his realm.[1] But, if he was more concerned about the election, he gave the electors to understand that, if they hearkened to his wishes, he would in the future listen to theirs.[2] And when, as in this case of Aylmer, he was most interested in the matter, he did not content himself with giving leave for the election of an upright and loyal man, but, adding threats to promises, put every kind of pressure on the electors.[3] The chapter, accordingly, elected Aylmer, because, if they should resist the King, they despaired of any assistance from the Pope, inasmuch as he was, they argued, " in a critical position, and, through fear, avoided giving offence to princes,"[4] and so would not grant them the assistance he was wont to give to the oppressed.[5] In the customary form,[6]

---

[1] *De licencia eligendi episcopum concessa.* " Virum honestum, nobis et regno nostro utilem et fidelem eligatis." July 24, 1217, regarding the see of Chichester. *Patent Rolls*, i, p. 83, *R. S.*

[2] *Ib.*, p. 163, regarding the see of Worcester.

[3] Mat. Par., v, 179 ff.

[4] The Pope " in arcto positus, principes offendere vitat ". *Ib.*, p. 182.

[5] " Videntes dies malos, nec ad sinum patris nostri Papæ qui solet ad eum confugientibus suffragari, patere refugium." *Ib.*, p. 183.

[6] " Noverit sanctitas vestra nos, quantum ad nos pertinet, assessum præbuisse canonice electioni facte de N . . . in episcopum N., unde vestram sanctam paternitatem rogamus attencius, quatenus eidem electioni assensum vestrum prebere, ipsamque misericorditer confirmare velitis." *Patent R.*, *ib.*, p. 160. Innocent at times confirmed an election, despite the want of Henry's confirmation. *Cf. Reg.*, i, 3669, Feb. 20, 1248.

Henry confirmed the election of his half-brother and asked the Pope to give his assent to it.[1] The papal confirmation arrived in due course, and, according to Paris, was accompanied by a demand that, as a sort of return, the boy Robert, the son of the count of Burgundy, should be provided with a living worth two hundred marks.[2]

As we have said already, Boniface had hardly returned to England (1252), when he was involved in a violent dispute with Aylmer. The bishop had filled up the vacant mastership of the hospital of St. Thomas, Southwark, which was situated indeed in the diocese of Winchester, but was in the gift of an official of the archbishop. Instead of invoking law, first the official and then bishop used violence. Boniface being then appealed to, excommunicated the bishop's men, who had certainly conducted themselves very outrageously ; and, as the bishop's men set the excommunication at naught, the archbishop appealed to the Pope. Meanwhile the King's Poitevin friends sided with Aylmer, while the Provençal party of the Queen supported Boniface. Innocent, however, settled the matter by a compromise. Aylmer was to appoint to the mastership, but was to pay three shillings annually in acknowledgment of the right of patronage.[3]

Although many other circumstances brought Boniface into relation with Innocent, we may now leave him, and turn once more to his friend, Robert Grosseteste, bishop

Aylmer versus Boniface.

Grosseteste and the Roman Church.

----

[1] Mat. Par., v, 184. According to Paris, the King's messengers were to coax or bribe the Pope to give his assent. As Boniface kept a firm hand on the monks, it is idle to expect fair play for him or his from Paris.

[2] v, 224, 227, 240. *Cf. Hist. Angl.*, iii, 107, n., and the actual letter of Innocent to the archbishop of Canterbury concerning " the pro-vision ". Ap. M. P., vi, p. 148. In his wonted manner, Mat. P. says 500 where the original says 200.

[3] Mat. P., v, 348–53.

of Lincoln, for Innocent is perhaps best known to Englishmen from his intercourse with that great bishop. Already
have we had occasion to bring the two names together
on the subject of Provisions. We may now associate
them in connexion with Grosseteste's efforts at reform.
But, before proceeding to do so, it may be as well to see
what were Grosseteste's views on the Papacy, as it is
often supposed that he was in some way anti-papalist.
There is no doubt that he was prepared to oppose King [1]
or Pope, if either of them moved out of the sphere of
his legitimate authority. But the fact that he opposed
Innocent on the question of Provisions did not prevent
him from acknowledging him as the bishop of bishops,
as the representative of Christ on earth, and from
emphasizing " that special obedience with which he
was bound to obey the constitutions of the Apostolic
See ".[2] He laid it down as an axiom that both swords,
the material as well as the spiritual, belong to Peter ;
but the spiritual sword is wielded by the Princes of the
Church who hold the place of Peter, but they use the
temporal sword by the hands of secular princes who
ought to employ it under the direction of the Princes
of the Church.[3] He compares the Pope in the Church

---

[1] *Cf.* ep. 72,* p. 205 ff., for a strong letter on Henry's violations of the
liberties of the Church. *Cf.* ep. 102, p. 308. " Regia namque potestas,
cum rex a recto dicatur regimine, non potest nisi rectum præcipere."
Cf. ep. 124, p. 348 ff., and ep. 36 of Adam Marsh, ap. *Mon. Francisc.*,
p. 139, where he says that a certain action of Grosseteste has rendered
him " d. regi et etiam Curiæ Romanæ odiosum ".

[2] Ep. 9, p. 47. " Illinc vero obedientia qua teneor obtemperare
constitutionibus sedis apostolicæ." He also declared that, from the
day when he received the higher rank of bishop, he felt himself more
than ever bound to obey " the supreme pontiff and the holy Roman
Church". Ep. 36, p. 127.

[3] Ep. 23, p. 91. Similarly, after quoting Rom. xiii, 4, he adds :
" Utraque pax et utraque lex regimini Petri et obtinentium locum
Petri commissa est." But the reins of temporal peace and of civil
law were held by Peter and his vicars through the ministry of Princes,

(to whom even " the whole human race " owes obedience) [1]
to the sun in the Universe. [2] The supreme Pontiff is to
him the master builder (summus artifex) in the Church
who has to have the final fashioning of everything
in it. [3] He declares, moreover, that nothing shall
ever separate him from the obedience he owes to the
Roman Church, [4] and that he would be glad to go to Rome
to show that obedience by offering his homage to the
Pope in person. [5] Then, turning to the English episcopate
he points out that, during a vacancy of the archiepiscopal
see of Canterbury the bishops of that province are
immediately subject to the Holy See [6] ; for the Pope is
the apex of the episcopal dignity, and other bishops
have what power they possess from him. [7] As the moon
and the planets only shine by light received from the
sun, so the bishops' power comes from the plenitude
of that of the Pope. [8]

Grosseteste first came in touch with Innocent with
reference to the great Benedictine abbey of Bardney,
a few miles from Lincoln. Its abbot had to be summoned

Grosseteste
appeals to
Rome about
Bardney.

---

etc. Mr. A. J. Carlyle is then clearly justified in stating not merely that
Inn. IV. contended that temporal power belonged to the Pope, and
was delegated by him to secular Princes, but that this theory was
held by Hostiensis and other canonists of the later thirteenth century.
Cf. Rev. hist. de droit français, 4th ser., vol. v.

[1] Ep. 35, p. 123.   [2] Ep. 36, p. 126.   [3] Ep. 37, p. 129.

[4] Ep. 49, p. 144. " Ab obedientia S. R. ecclesiæ non timore coacta
sed caritate protensa, ' tribulatio aut angustia aut persecutio ' (Rom.
viii, 35) . . . meam parvitatem . . . ' non separabit '." *Cf.* Epp. 72,
p. 230, and 77, p. 249, where he says the Pope has " summa omnium
animarum solicitudo ". Speaking in ep. 86, pp. 271-2, of our own
country in particular, he shows the special reasons Henry has to show
fidelity to the Pope, and that it is the especial business of the archbishop of Canterbury to give effect to the will of the Pope " facta d.
Papæ, ut debitum sortiantur effectum, confovere ".

[5] Ep. 105, p. 313. *Cf.* ep. 106, p. 315, for his anxiety to keep the
honour of the Pope untarnished.

[6] Ep. 110, p. 324 f.   [7] *Ib.*, p. 326.

[8] Ep. 127, p. 364 ; *cf.* epp. 116, 117, 119.

by Grosseteste to appear before him regarding a debt
he was alleged to owe a certain cleric.   The abbot refused
to obey the citation, and was at length excommunicated
by the bishop, and declared to be deposed.   The abbot
then appealed to the monks of Christ Church, Canterbury,
on the supposition that *sede vacante*, they had the
archiepiscopal right of receiving appeals.   Grosseteste,
of course, took no notice of this appeal, nor of the
excommunication which the monks proceeded solemnly
to pronounce against him.   Both sides turned to Rome,
and on August 23, 1243, Innocent issued a peremptory
order to the monks to withdraw the excommunication,
" without prejudice to either side " on other matters
in dispute between the two parties.[1]   This was not
enough for Grosseteste, and he wrote to Cardinal Otho
to protest that the fact that, during the vacancy of the
see of Canterbury, elected suffragans were confirmed
by the Pope proved that the jurisdiction of the monks
was not admitted.   He, therefore, begged the cardinal
to urge Innocent to prevent further recurrence of such
humiliation of the episcopate.[2]   We find, indeed, that on
April 27, 1244, the Pope granted an " indult to the bishop
of Lincoln that no one shall issue against him sentence
of suspension or excommunication . . . without special
licence from the Pope ".[3]   But whether he took any
further steps in the matter does not appear.[4]

Grosseteste's
dispute with
his canons.
We know, however, that he took stronger action in
supporting Grosseteste against his chapter.   The bishop

---

[1] Mat. Par., iv, 245–8, 257–8.   Grosseteste had to complain that
King Henry supported the recalcitrant monks. Epp., p. 308.

[2] Ep. 110, p. 324 ff.

[3] *Cal.*, i, p. 209.

[4] In 1248 he granted a privilege to the monastery (*Reg.*, i, n. 3774),
which may have had some connexion with this dispute.   In any legal
affair dealing with matters in the diocese of Lincoln, the Bardney monks
were not to be summoned to places more than two days' journey from
their monastery.

found that, with all his zeal for reform, he could effect very little improvement if he were denied the exercise of his right of canonical visitation.[1] As something " new and unaccustomed ", considerable opposition was aroused by Grosseteste's thorough method of carrying out his visitations. The head and front of the opposition came from the chapter of Lincoln, and it took Grosseteste six years (1239–45) to obtain a full recognition of his rights. On January 23, 1239, Gregory IX. issued a licence to the bishop " to exercise his office in regard to the visitation of the chapter of Lincoln, which has hitherto not been visited by himself or any other, without paying attention to vexatious appeals ".[2]

The chapter, however, resisted their bishop's attempt canonically to visit them, and an appeal was made by both sides to Rome to appoint arbitrators.[3] After vainly trying to induce the chapter to obey the bishop,[4] Gregory IX. commissioned the selected arbitrators to adjust matters between the parties, and failing that to refer the matter to him within two years.[5] But the arbitration came to nothing as the chapter appealed to the new Pope Innocent against its award.[6] The dispute dragged on. There was a fresh attempt at arbitration, and there was even an attempt on the part of the chapter to invoke the secular power,[7] and to fall back on forgery.[8] The unhappy strife was, however, settled at last when Grosseteste was in France at the time of the Council of Lyons. On August 25, 1245, Innocent,

[1] Epp. Gross., n. 77, p. 248.

[2] Cal., i, 178. Cf. epp. Gross., n. 82.

[3] Epp. G., n. 80, p. 253 ff. Cf. Mat. Par., iii, 528–9, and epp. G., nn. 81–2.

[4] Cal., i, 185–6, Jan. 17, 1240.

[5] Cal., i, p. 189, Apr. 24, 1240.

[6] Ib., pp. 203–4, Dec. 22, 1243. Cf. Ann. de Dunstap., i, p. 149.

[7] Epp. G., nn. 90–8.

[8] Mat. Par., iv, 154–6. Cf. Stevenson, Grosseteste, p. 200.

who had received the bishop most graciously, issued a
bull in which Grosseteste gained all that he contended
for.   The bishop was notified that he was to be admitted
to visit " the dean and chapter, canons, clerks choral,
and ministers . . . the chaplains, and their parishioners.
The canons, however, are not bound to take an oath
of obedience ".[1]

Grosseteste's
failures at
Rome.
Grosseteste was not, however, always successful in
the appeals which he made to the Pope against others,
or which others made against him.[2]   Where, however,
it seemed to him that obedience involved no sin, he
always submitted to the authority of the Pope ; for that
was " an authority which to disobey was like the sin of
idolatry (1 Kings xv, 23) ".[3]   But, if he thought that
an order was given him which he could not fulfil without
violating his conscience, then he was immovable.   Hence,
according to Matthew Paris, he even, in the Lent of 1251,
incurred suspension for refusing to admit to a rich
benefice in his diocese a certain Italian who was ignorant
of English.[4]   This statement of Paris is, however, open
to grave suspicion.   He gives no particulars either as

[1] *Cal.*, i, 219: *Cf. ib.*, Aug. 26, 1245, and Mat. P., iv, 497 f. The
Pope gives as one reason for his settling the dispute his desire to save
expense to the churches. *Cf.* ep. Inn., Sept. 25, 1252, ap. Mat. P.,
v, 300, in which Innocent supports Grosseteste's efforts to compel
religious and others properly to endow the vicarages dependent on
them. For Grosseteste's reception by the Pope, *cf.* epp. G., n. 113.
" Prospere venimus ad curiam d. Papæ apud Lugdunum, ibidem ap
ipso d. Papa et cardinalibus sui gratia satis decenter et honorifice
suscepti."

[2] *Cf.* e.g., Mat. Par., v, 96 ff., and vi, 152, regarding an attempt made
by Grosseteste to force various religious houses to surrender property
and *ib.*, v, 109 f., in connexion with a quarrel between Grosseteste and
the sheriff of Rutland. See also v, 279.

[3] Epp. G., 119, p. 341. *Cf. ib.*, n. 130, an. 1250, p. 440.

[4] v, 227. Some authors doubt which Lent is here referred to. But
as the last definite date to which Paris refers is Feb., 1251 (v, 225),
" Quadragesima sequente " is no doubt " the ensuing Lent " of the
same year.

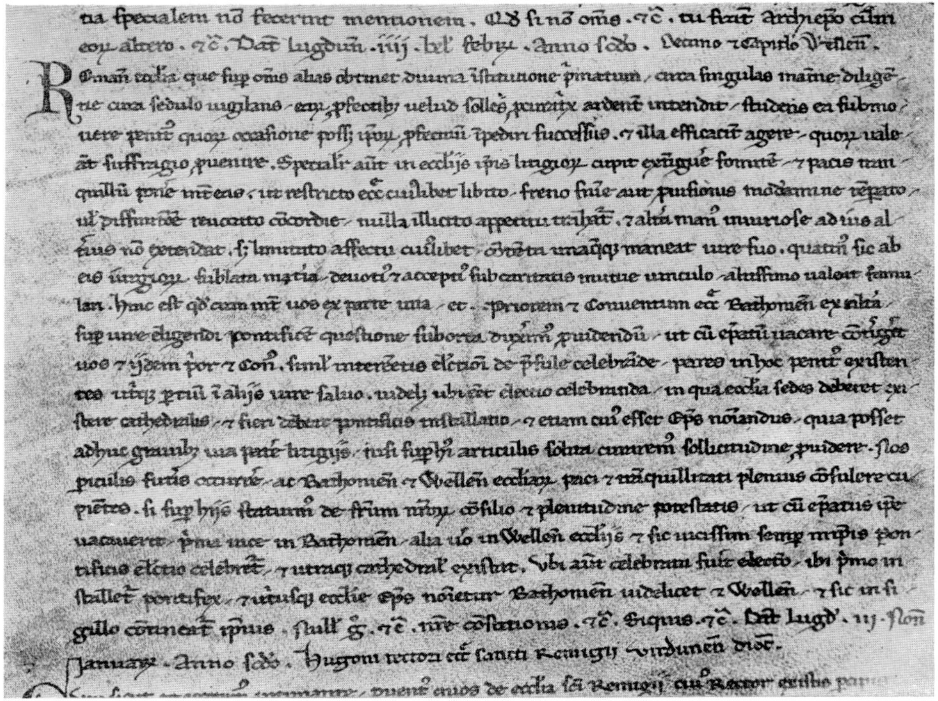

LETTER OF INNOCENT IV. (JAN. 3, 1245) FROM HIS REGISTER.

[face p. 286.

to the name or status of the *certain* Italian, nor does
he say by whom the bishop was suspended. Besides,
no other mention is to be found of this suspension ;
and yet, if a fact, the suspension of such a famous bishop
must have made a great sensation. Further, with regard
to the precisely similar case of Frederick de Lavagna,
Paris himself says that the cardinals impressed upon the
Pope that it would not become them to condemn him,
inasmuch as he was really acting justly, and was believed
to have no equal amongst all prelates.[1] We have no
hesitation, therefore, in expressing our belief that there
is as little truth in this statement of Paris as in the
denunciation of the Pope which he puts into the mouth
of the dying bishop,[2] or as in his story of Grosseteste's
appearing " to the most wretched Pope Sinibald " in
his last illness, and poking him in the side with his
pastoral staff.[3]

Before turning to Ireland we may add two more York and
the Isle of
items of interest concerning England. In 1244 (Feb. 19), Man, 1244.
Innocent definitely empowered Gray, archbishop of
York, to confirm and consecrate the bishops of the Isle
of Man. Up to that date they had been, as subject to
the Church of Norway, consecrated either at York or at
Nidaros (Trondjem). But the latter city was so distant,
and so difficult to reach by reason of " the most dangerous
sea " which had to be traversed that, said Innocent,
few dared to cross it. Accordingly he finally subjected
the interesting little island to York.[4]

Into his struggle for independence David, Prince of Innocent
and Wales,
Wales, who was Henry's nephew, tried to inveigle the 1244.
Pope. He assured Innocent that Wales was a fief of
the Holy See, and that therefore Rome was wronged

[1] v, 393.   [2] v, 403 ff.   [3] v, 429 f.
[4] Ep. ap. *Hists. of the Ch. of York*, vol. iii, p. 157 f., *R. S.*, or ap. P. A.
Munch's notes to his ed. of *The Chronicle of Man*, Cristiania, 1860,
pp. 30, 138, and 156. Innocent's letter is dated Feb. 16, 1244.

when he was compelled to hold it of the King of England. Somewhat impressed by the Prince's contention, Innocent wrote to the abbot of Ber-Conway for further information. Enlightened by him, the Pope pursued an absolutely non-committal policy with the Prince.[1]

IRELAND AND SCOTLAND.

Nothing very remarkable between Rome and Ireland or Scotland.

The Papal Registers and the Chronicles of these two countries show that there was nothing exceptional in the relations between them and Rome during the reign of Innocent IV. With regard to the former country, Ireland, however, attention may be called to the efforts made by the Pope to keep even the balance of justice between the English and Irish. Pope Honorius III. had condemned " an iniquitous decree made by some Englishmen that no clerk of Ireland, however good and learned he might be, should be promoted to any ecclesiastical dignity ".[2] But when in 1250 the Irish bishops, by way of retaliation, decided not to admit an Englishman to any of their canonries, Innocent condemned their conduct also, and forbade such exclusive regulations.[3] On the other hand, he issued a " constitution whereby in the province of Cashel, the evil custom of giving credence to an Englishman on his oath touching a theft if supported by six Englishmen, while an Irishman, whose innocence is attested by thirty witnesses, has to make restitution, was abolished, and equal justice was ordered to be done between English and Irish ".[4]

[1] " A quo (the abbot) plenius instructus, sub dissimulatione transivit." " Justitia ad Walliam," ap. *Memorials of St. Edmunds*, vol. iii, p. 752, *R. S.*

[2] *Cal.*, i, 97, Apr. 26, 1224.

[3] *Cf.* S. Malone, *A church hist. of Ireland*, quoting the *Liber Munerum publicorum Hiberniæ*, pt. iv, 55–6, ed. R. Lascelles, 2 vols., London, 1852. The *Liber* contains an abstract of the statutes at large published in Ireland, letters patent and close, etc.

[4] *Cal.*, i, 283, July 20, 1253.

Finally as illustrating the fact that Italians were given livings in Ireland as in all other countries at this time, a passage may be quoted from the *Annals of the Kings of Ireland* [1] : " Raighned (really Reiner), archbishop of Armagh, came from Rome, bringing with him a pallium in which he said Mass at Armagh on the feast of SS. Peter and Paul." Unfortunately, however, the *Annals* do not tell us whether any progress was made under this Italian archbishop in the settlement of the dispute regarding the primacy of Armagh which, under his predecessor, Albert Suerbeer, was attacked by the archbishops of Cashel, Tuam, and Dublin, and into which Innocent had caused inquiries to be made.[2]

With regard to Scotland, we have already seen that Innocent protected the independence of Scotland against Henry.[3] Some years before that, on the occasion of the proposed marriage of the son of Alexander II., King of Scotland, with the eldest daughter of Henry III., various treaties were drawn up between the two kings. To ensure their observance they were sent to Innocent for confirmation by the Scotch King and his nobles " who subjected themselves to his jurisdiction in order that by ecclesiastical censures he might coerce them and their heirs, if ever they should act against the said treaties ".[4]

At the request of the King and bishops of Scotland, Innocent agreed that ecclesiastical cases arising within that country should not be tried by his Legates outside the Kingdom ; and that, should the Roman see for some lawful reason, wish some cases to be heard out of

Privilege for the Church of Scotland.

[1] Vol. i, p. 331, ed. O'Donovan. The *Annals of Loch Cé*, i, p. 371, *R. S.*, and *Cal.*, i, 251, show Innocent exercising his ordinary jurisdiction over bishops and monks.

[2] *Cal.*, i, 204, Feb. 13, 1244.

[3] *Supra*, p. 271.

[4] *Cf.* their letter to Innocent, ap. Mat. Par., iv, 383 f.

Scotland, they were to be tried not in the diocese of York but in that of Carlisle or Durham as nearer.[1]

Although, on the ground that the King of Scotland was the liegeman of the King of England, Innocent would not grant that he could be crowned without Henry's consent, he would not, as opposed to the dignity of the Scottish King, grant tithes of ecclesiastical benefices in Scotland to Henry.[2] He moreover decreed that, notwithstanding any papal decree in behalf of England, all offerings, etc., made in Scotland for the Crusade should be assigned to Scotch Crusaders.[3]

We may add two more facts pertaining to Scotland just as items of curiosity. The first is that Innocent gave the monks of Dumfermline permission to " wear caps suited to their order, seeing that they live in a very cold country, due reverence being observed at the elevation (in the Mass) and the gospel, and at other times in the divine office ".[4] The second, illustrating the suppression of the Culdees [5] that was now going on, is that he confirmed to the prior and chapter of St. Andrew's the prebends of the Culdees which had been adjudged to them by cardinal John Tolet.[6]

---

[1] Cf. Cal. of docs. relating to Scotland, i, p. 307 ; or Rymer, i, 263, Sept. 11, 1245.

[2] Cal., i, 333, or R., i, 277, Apr. 6, 1251.

[3] Cal., i, 336, Sept. 4, 1251.

[4] Cal., i, 215, Apr. 24, 1245.

[5] On them see supra, ix, p. 214 f.

[6] Cal., i, p. 271. Cf. the Chronicle of Melrose, an. 1253, for the journey of the prior of St. Andrew's to Rome in that year, concerning a disputed election to that see.

CHAPTER VII.

JEWS (THE TALMUD), HERETICS, ETC.

WE have already had occasion frequently to record that the Popes, for the most part, protected the Jews, especially from personal violence. Innocent was no exception to this rule,[1] though, in accordance with the policy of Louis IX. and Pope Gregory IX., he did decree that they should not be allowed to have Christian servants, and that their Talmud should be burnt.[2]

In the Gospels we find it stated that our Lord rebuked the Jews for setting the " tradition of their ancients " above the " commandments of God ", and for " teaching the doctrines and commandments of men ".[3] These " doctrines of men ", which were gradually added to the law of Moses, were written down and published about the year 220, or at any rate during the third century, by the Rabbi Jehuda. To this collection of Jewish religious and legal customs, known as the *Mishnah* (repetition or Second Law), were afterwards added commentaries upon it. Two great collections of these commentaries, known as *Gemaras* (completions), at length came into existence. The first of these, written for the Western Jews, the Jews of Palestine, was called the Jerusalem *Gemara*, the second written for the Eastern Jews, was published in Babylon in the fifth century, and was hence known as the Babylonian *Gemara*. The combination of the Mishna with one or other of the

---

[1] " Innocent lui-même se montra, en général, fort bien-veillant pour ses sujets de race juive." E. Rodocanachi, *Le Saint-Siège et les Juifs*, p. 132.

[2] Ep. of May 9, 1244, ap. Raynaldus, *Annal.*, an. 1244, n. 40 ff.

[3] *Cf.* St. Mat., c. xv, St. Mark, vii, 7 ff.

Gemaras is known as the *Talmud* (study).[1] Among the great mass of material which went to make up the Talmud, there were inserted a number of vilely insulting statements concerning our Lord, similar statements to those which caused Tertullian to declare that no other peoples except the Jews could have made them.[2]

It is ordered to be burnt.

Attention to the anti-Christian and even anti-Mosaic portions of the Talmud was directed by a converted French Jew called Nicholas Donin (1238).[3] Gregory IX. at once ordered the copies of the Talmud to be seized, and handed over to the Dominicans or Franciscans in order that they might be examined (June 9, 1239).[4] They were found to be full of errors, and were ordered first by Gregory IX. (1242), and then by Innocent IV. to be publicly burnt (May 9, 1244).[5] The condemnation

---

[1] The combination with the Jerusalem Gemara is known as the Jerusalem Talmud, and that with the Babylonian Gemara as the Babylonian Talmud. According to Butler, *Horæ Biblicæ*, p. 9 f. Christians prefer the former as being less disfigured by fables and trifles, but Jews the latter, as descending more into minutiæ. It is *The* Talmud.

[2] *Ad nationes*, i, 14. Abrahams, *Jewish Life in the Middle Ages*, p. 416, allows that there are a " few violent polemics against Christianity " in the Talmud. See also Graetz, *Hist. of the Jews*, ii, p. 640, London, 1891.

[3] *Cf.* especially N. Valois, *Guillaume d'Auvergne*, ch. viii, Paris, 1880. Valois found the thirty-five articles which Nicholas laid before the Pope as embodying the teaching of the Talmud. See also M. L. Rodkinson, who has translated the Talmud, *The Hist. of the Talmud* (2 vols., New York, 1913), i, 66, and Graetz, *l.c.*, iii, pp. 591 and 596. Some critics say that Rodkinson's " rendering is incomplete ".

[4] *Cf.* Potthast, 10759–60. *Cf.* the bull of Innocent IV. of May 8, 1244, ap. *ib.*, 11376.

[5] The letter is given in full, ap. Denifle, *Chartular. Univer. Paris*, i, p. 173. Innocent thus describes the Talmud : " Magnus liber est apud eos (the Jews) excedens textum biblie in immensum in quo sunt blasphemie in Deum et Christum ejus ac beatam Virginem manifeste, intricabiles fabule, abusiones eronee, ac stultitie inaudite." According to Thomas of Cantimpré, *Bonum universale de apibus*, i, c. 3, n. 6, ed. Douay, 1627 (written about 1260), the Talmud was burnt by order of St. Louis IX., and that even " the Oriental Jews regard as excom-

passed on the Talmud by the Popes was in accordance with that passed upon it by a large number of the Jews themselves. " Observe," cries out the famous preacher, Thomas of Cantimpré,[1] " that all the Eastern Jews regard those Jews as heretics and excommunicate who, against the law of Moses and the Prophets, accept the book known as the Talmud."

The execution of Innocent's decree was, however, delayed in France by an appeal which a number of French Jews made to him. They declared that, without their Talmud, they could nôt interpret the Bible and their law in accordance with their faith. To this the Pope replied that, by the command of God, he was bound to tolerate them ; and that, as he was unwilling to deprive them of their law, he was unwilling to deprive them of their books. He accordingly directed his legate Otho (Eudes of Châteauroux), cardinal-bishop of Tusculum, to re-examine their books, and to tolerate all that could be tolerated without injury to the Christian faith.[2] Otho, however, wrote back to Innocent to say that the contention of the Rabbis was absurd, as the book was full of fables, and that " it would be a great scandal, and a lasting disgrace to the Apostolic See, if by its decree books were tolerated after copies of them had been solemnly and justly burnt before the University, clergy, and people of Paris ".[3]

---

municated heretics all those who accept the Talmud". He goes on to denounce an archbishop who, " corrupted by money," persuaded the King not to continue to burn the Talmud. But he assures us that the archbishop died the very day that some copies of it were returned to the Jews. Later on, we find Nicholas IV. ordering it to be opposed in England by sermons, etc. Cal. of Papal Reg., i, p. 491.

[1] L.c., p. 18. From the eighth century there had been among a number of the Jews a teaching (Karaism) which denied the authority of the Talmud.

[2] Cf. ep. Aug. 12, 1247, ed. Denifle, l.c., p. 201.

[3] See his letter, ib., p. 204, and his renewed condemnation of the Talmud, ib., p. 209, May 15, 1248. Many copies (cartloads it is said),

Innocent
saves the
Jews from
unjust
persecution,
1247.
A little later the Jews were again at the feet of
Innocent. They complained that, on the charge of
eating the heart of a murdered boy by way of communion
at their Paschal ceremonies, their people were plundered,
maltreated, and even slain. Hearkening to their prayers,
Innocent wrote strong letters to the bishops of France
and Germany. He reminded them that Christianity
had sprung out of Judaism,[1] that the charge of ritual
murder brought against them was false, and that so far
from being ordered by their law, it was directly against
it. To treat them unjustly was to violate the privileges
of the Apostolic See which had been granted them,
and was to act against God and justice. He bade the
bishops be kind to those whose conversion the Lord
was awaiting, and not to allow them to be ill-treated
on these or any similar charges.

His words
are appealed
to in the
twentieth
century.
Innocent spoke, and his voice has resounded through
the ages to our own days. The charge of ritual murder
has constantly in all ages and in all countries been
brought against the unhappy Jews. Only some few years
ago it was revived in Russia, and the well-known Jew,

---

of the Talmud and other books of the Jews had in fact been burnt in
Sept., 1242, by order of St. Louis. *Annales Erphord.*, an. 1242. *Cf.*
Valois, p. 132. When Clement IV., July 15, 1267, caused the Talmud
and all the books of the Jews in Aragon to be seized, he decreed that
all of them which contained the text of the Bible, and, in general, all
which did not contain blasphemies or errors should be restored to them.
The others were to be kept under lock and key. Potthast, 20081–2.
We find that even under Philip le Bel the burning of the Talmud went
on. *Cf.* Douais, *L'Inquisition*, p. 213, and his ed. of Bernard Guidonis,
Practica inquisitionis, pp. 67–71, Paris, 1886. Bernard gives several
forms connected with the seizure of copies of the Talmud. *Cf.* form 53,
e.g.: " In libris Juadæorum, maxime in Talmutis, et glosis et exposi-
tionibus eorumdem, plurimi continentur errores, pariter et horrores
ac blasfemie nominis D. J. Christi ejusque . . . Genitricis."

[1] " Non considerato prudenter quod quasi ex archivio eorum Chris-
tianæ fidei testimonia prodierunt, etc." Ep. of July 5, 1247, ap.
Raynaldus, *Annal.*, an. 1247, n. 83 f., or ap. *Reg.*, i, n. 3077, p. 463,
or Potthast, 12596.

Baron Rothschild, wrote to cardinal Merry del Val. the Secretary of State of Pope Pius X., to ask if the letter of Innocent IV. exonerating the Jews from ritual murder was not authentic. As the letter is to be found in Innocent's Register, the answer the Baron received was of course in the affirmative.[1] If the Popes did not always show themselves indulgent towards the Jews, they ever protected them from injustice affecting their lives and property.

For brevity's sake we will merely allude to Innocent's efforts to effect reforms in the Benedictine Order,[2] and to the great work which he accomplished in organizing the Church in Prussia,[3] and we will conclude his biography with a few words on his treatment of heretics.

Though Innocent was severe with regard to obstinate heretics, he would not suffer men to be oppressed by means of accusations of heresy. Hence he revoked a sentence against Raymond VII. of Toulouse, and ordered him to be absolved.[4] And if he sent legates and took proceedings against the *Albigensian* heretics of Languedoc,[5] Croatia, and Dalmatia[6] and Bosnia,[7] and against one

Innocent's harsh treatment of heretics.

---

[1] *Cf. The Tablet* newspaper, Nov. 1, 1913, p. 690 ff. On July 7, 1274, Gregory X. renewed the bull of Innocent on this subject (Potthast, 20861), and it has been frequently renewed since.

[2] Mat. Par., v, 81, 380 ; vi, *Additamenta*, nn. 119–21, p. 234 ff. *Cf.* Gasquet, p. 332 ff.

[3] *Cf. Reg.*, i, nn. 4, 5, 23, 24, 70, 115, 711.

[4] *Reg.*, i, n. 697, and Rod., vol. i, nn. 45 and 69.

[5] *Reg., ib.*, n. 31.

[6] *Ib.*, n. 29 ; Potthast, 11095. In connexion with these countries, we have already told how Innocent allowed their inhabitants to use the Sclavonic tongue in their liturgy (see vol. iii, p. 245 f.). The liturgy of S. Methodius, still used in parts of Dalmatia, owes any suppression to Venice, and not to the Popes. Here we may add an observation from brother Felix Fabri, who visited Jerusalem in 1484. Speaking of the different peoples who live there, he names the *Glagolæ* who say Mass " in their own mother tongue . . . receive their holy orders at Rome, and are not heretics ". *Palestine Pilgrims Text Society*, vol. viii, p. 433.

[7] Potthast, 12, 407.

of their antipopes in Bohemia,[1] still he would not have
them unduly harassed, but insisted that time should
be granted them in which they might abjure their heresy.[2]
But Innocent certainly bore heavily upon the confirmed
heretic.   Already, acting in conjunction with the secular
power, Gregory IX. had tolerated the imposition of the
death penalty on obstinate heretics.[3]   It was held that
heresy was more truly high treason against God than
rebellion was high treason against an earthly ruler.
Further, if death alone was adequate punishment for
the latter offence, it was still more the proper expiation
of the former.   On similar grounds, Innocent IV. unhappily sanctioned the use of torture in the examination
of supposed heretics.   If the civil law was justified in
using torture to discover those who had stolen the goods
of this world, it could surely be employed in searching
out heretics who were thieves of immortal souls.   Innocent,
accordingly, bade the civil authorities " force all captured
heretics to confess, and to accuse their accomplices by
such torture as would not imperil life or injure limb,
just as thieves and robbers are forced to accuse their
accomplices and to confess their crimes.   These heretics
are true thieves, murderers of souls, and robbers of the
sacraments of God ".[4]

[1] *Ib.*, nn. 11450 and 11818.   [2] *Reg.*, i, n. 317.

[3] *Cf. supra*, vol. xiii, p. 430 ff.

[4] *Cf.* Innocent's bull of May 15, 1252.   Potthast, 14592.   It begins
" Ad extirpanda de ".   The translation of Vacandard, *The Inquisition*,
p. 150 f. is here used.   Innocent's decree was confirmed by Alexander IV.
(Potthast, 17714, Nov. 30, 1259) and other Popes.   *Cf.* Douais, *L'Inquisition*, p. 173.   A great many of Innocent's letters are concerned with
instructing the Dominicans as to the procedure to be followed in
dealing with heretics.   *Cf.* Potthast, e.g., nn. 11073, 11089, 11092,
11094, 11193, 11631, 12830.   I have not come across any writer of this
age who objected on principle to the use of torture.   Brunetto Latini
would limit its use to the case of those against whom there are strong
suspicions, and in the case of great crimes.   " En ce point om le puet
bien metre en gehine (to the torture) pour faire li regehir sa colpe, et
autrement non."   *Li Tresors*, l. iii, pt. ii, c. 19.

Unfortunately, in this particular of the treatment of heretics, Innocent was a man of his age, and was unable to rise above it. In other matters he could soar beyond it, and be justly regarded by men as " The Magnificent ". But, in this respect, he was no better and no worse than the men of his time, and the tendency which had set in to treat public heretics with severity was considerably increased during his pontificate.

It is by dwelling on one aspect of Innocent's policy, to wit, that with regard to the treatment of heretics ; it is by giving a one-sided view of the taxation of the Church to which he was compelled to resort [1] ; it is by setting forth the unfounded opinion that, in his struggle with Frederick II., he was fighting only for temporal power ; it is by gratuitously imputing to him the turning of " everything spiritual, everything religious " into " one political end " [2] ; it is by strangely misusing authorities [3] ; and, above all, it is by blindly placing

A caricature of Innocent IV.

[1] " *Taxation*, law-making, judicature, were not so much ' usurped ' by Innocent III. and Gregory IX. (and there is no reason, we may subjoin, for not adding Innocent IV.), as thrust upon them." Smith, *Church and State*, p. 56.

[2] *Ib.*, p. 228.

[3] On this head we will give one striking example. Mr. Smith says that the degradation of the German Church (which he assures us was effected by Innocent IV.) and "its ruthless conversion into an agency of temporal warfare, produced a deep resentment not only among German laity, but among the finer minds of the clergy". P. 228. Now, what is the proof offered for these assertions ? For the feeling among the German laity, the only proof proffered is an " interesting poem of the minnesinger Freidank", who we are not told was an " enthusiastic imperialist ". *Cf.* Scherer, *A History of German Literature*, i, p. 216. " The clerical feeling " we are told "comes out in four documents". They are : (1) " the Peacock, a bitter satirical poem on the Council of Lyons " (we are not told that its author was probably not canon Jordan of Osnabruck, but one of the Goliardi, and that he wrote in a frankly Ghibelline spirit) ; (2) and (4) " a strange mystical appeal from a Dominican friar one Arnold," and " an academic demonstration . . . that Innocencius Papa " was Antichrist ;—we are not told that of this Arnold nothing on earth is known, except that he was very likely the author of the " academic demonstration " and that these tracts

unbounded trust in Matthew Paris, that that caricature of Innocent IV. has been produced which is usually presented in our country as his true portrait.

Elements
from which
a true
portrait of
Innocent can
be made. But a very different picture of Innocent will be formed if due consideration be given to the fact that the heretics whom he had chiefly in view were men whose teachings were subversive of morality and civil life ; if consideration be given to his financial rights and needs, and to the duty of his subjects to support him as set forth by such a man as bishop Grosseteste, one of the most esteemed prelates of the age ; if consideration be given on the one hand to Frederick's delinquencies in the moral, ecclesiastical, and political orders, and on the other hand to the fact that Innocent was the recognized guardian of the moral order, and the acknowledged head of that Church whose liberties were assailed by the Emperor,[2] and that Frederick was false to all his feudal obligations [3] ; and, finally, if due consideration be given

show him an out and out imperialist—(3) in a call to all princes to reform the Church and recover the temporal sword. I do not know to what document this refers, and Mr. Smith does not tell us. In any case it is only a reflexion of Frederick's language. One surely need not pause to point out that, especially when feeling is running high, anything can be proved by quoting the satirical poets and the party pamphlets of unknown or anonymous partisans. What value is attached I will not say by Englishmen, but by impartial Americans to the declaration of " the 93 witnesses " that Germany was not the cause of this war (1916), though the 93 bear the best known names in Germany ! On friar Arnold, see above, p. 105.

[1] *Supra*, vol. xii, p. 218 ff.

[2] Hence even imperialistic annals note that, like his predecessors, Innocent had to contend with Frederick " pro libertate tocius ecclesie et ablatis possessionibus Romane ecclesie". *Ann. Scheftlar.*, ap. *M. G. SS.*, xvii, p. 342.

[3] As King of Sicily, he committed the unforgivable feudal crime of injuring the interests of his liege lord. *Cf.* Carlyle, *A Hist. of Mediæval Political Theory*, ch. i. " Personal loyalty." He broke his feudal oath to defend the liberty of the Church. *Cf. ib.*, pp. 34, 39, and 40, and in general ch. ii, " Justice and Law." Lastly it must be borne in mind that, according to feudal law, a vassal (Frederick II.) had to lose his fief (Sicily) if he failed to fulfil his obligations (*ib.*, pp. 59–60), and

to the fact that other contemporary authors put before us a very different Innocent IV. to the one presented to us by Matthew Paris, who was a rabid partisan, bitterly opposed to anyone who would impose any tax on his beloved monastery, or who favoured the " upstart " democratic friars against the long-established aristocratic Orders of the Church.

Innocent IV. was indeed pre-eminently clear-headed and practical. He saw that Frederick was the great enemy of the Church and of the liberties of Europe,[1] and he, therefore, subordinated many things, at times perhaps too many things, to the all-necessary end of preventing the universal domination of the head of the Holy Roman Empire of the German nation.[2] He was possessed with the idea of greatness. He would have all that he touched great. He would have the Church great. She should include the Greeks and take into her fold the ancient heretics, and the countless heathen of Asia. He would have learning great, as the Universities of Paris, Toulouse, Valencia, Piacenza, and Narbonne realized with gratitude.[3] He would even have his family great, and the cities of Lombardy also. To no little extent, too, did he succeed in his grand conceptions ;

Innocent the Magnificent.

that it was the duty of the people to prevent a sovereign from breaking his oaths. *Ib.*, pp. 52, 74, and 125. The whole of this splendid work of Carlyle should be carefully read by all who wish to form a just idea of the great politico-religious struggles of the Middle Ages.

[1] " Ses cuers (that of Frederic) ne baoit à autre cose fors que à estre sires et souverains de tout le monde . . . Il cuidoit bien par lui et par ses filz sous prendre tot l'empire et la terre toute, en tel maniere que ele n'issist jamais de leur subjection." Brunetto Latini, *Li Tresors*, l. i, pt. ii, c. 95.

[2] " Innocentius p," writes his successor, Alexander IV. '' . . . nimia duri temporis tunc eum importunitate cogente, plura, quamquam forte invitus, fecisse dinoscitur, que ipsemet proponebat succedente opportunitate utiliter immutare." Ep. Aug. 18, 1255, ap. Rod., iii, n. 408.

[3] On Innocent's connexion with the Universities of Paris, etc., see above, p. 19 f. On Narbonne, see *Reg.*, i, pp. 405, n. 2717. Hence too did he grant privileges to men of science, e.g., for Pelagius " physicali scientia erudito ". *Reg.*, i, n. 195.

for, even whilst he lived, men acclaimed him Innocent the Magnificent.[1]

The picture of Innocent IV. usually produced in our country, when not made up of material, often wholly worthless, drawn from Matthew Paris, is fashioned by means of ready-made traits elaborated by Gregorovius [2] or other Germans. To readers then who prefer to accept an already formed appreciation of a great character rather than make one for themselves, we offer the following extracted from a distinguished French author : " The strife between the hierarchy and the empire continued more formidably as the rival powers found more illustrious champions—on the one side Frederick I. and Frederick II., as great in the field as in the council chamber ; on the other side, Popes Alexander III., Innocent III., and Innocent IV., consummate politicians and heroic priests. After two centuries of warfare, the vanquished Empire renounced its usurpations on the spiritual order. The Popes, in aiming at aggrandizing the Church, had achieved her freedom ; the two powers separated—force returned to its own province, and the rights of conscience were saved." [3]

[1] *Mon. Pat. Chron.*, *ap*, *R. I. SS.*, viii, 689,   Cf. *Chron. Estense*, *ib.*, xv, pt. iii, new ed., p. 24, which reproduces the sentiments of the monk of Padua,

[2] *Rome*, v, pt, i, p. 306.

[3] F. Ozanam, *Hist. of Civilization in the Fifth Century*, i, 38 f. Eng. Trans., London, 1868. *Cf.* the important judgment of E. Berger, the editor of Innocent's *Register*. He tells us, ii, p. ii, that Innocent had to struggle " pour sauver l'Église d'un désastre irrémédiable ", and p. ccxc, " Le Saint Siège était sorti d'une des crises les plus redoutables qu'il eût jamais traversées, grâce au sang-froid, à la décision, à l'incomparable ténacité de ce grand pontife.   Les qualités de premier ordre aux-quelles Innocent IV. a dû sa victoire, etc." If excuse be needed for making these quotations, one can only say that one must adopt occasionally an apologetic style in writing for " persons born with minds made up against her (the Mediæval Church) which might almost be said to be the case with English persons ". Smith, *Church and State*, pp. 58–9.

INDEX

301

Printed in Great Britain by Stephen Austin & Sons, Ltd., Hertford.